Engines of Diplomacy

Engines of Diplomacy

Indian Trading Factories and the Negotiation of American Empire

David Andrew Nichols

The University of North Carolina Press *Chapel Hill*

For Drew McCoy

who set me on my path

David Nichols

Set in Alegreya Sans by Westchester Publishing Services
Manufactured in the United States of America

Portions of the text were previously published, in substantially different form, in
" 'The Main Mean of Their Political Management': George Washington and the Practice
of Indian Trade in the Early Republic," in *George Washington in and as Culture*, edited by
Kevin Cope (New York: AMS Press, 2001), and in "A Commercial Embassy in the Old
Northwest: The U.S. Indian Trading Factory at Fort Wayne, 1803–1812," *Ohio Valley
History* 8, no. 4 (Winter 2008): 1–16, reproduced here with permission.

The paper in this book meets the guidelines for permanence and durability
of the Committee on Production Guidelines for Book Longevity of the
Council on Library Resources.
The University of North Carolina Press has been a member of the
Green Press Initiative since 2003.

Library of Congress Cataloging-in-Publication Data
Nichols, David Andrew, 1970–
Engines of diplomacy: Indian trading factories and the negotiation
of American empire / David Andrew Nichols.
pages cm
Includes bibliographical references and index.
ISBN 978-1-4696-2889-9 (cloth: alk. paper)
ISBN 978-1-4696-2689-5 (pbk: alk. paper)
ISBN 978-1-4696-2690-1 (ebook)
1. Trading posts—United States—History. 2. Indians of North America—
Government relations—1789–1869. I. Title.
E93.N5 6 2016
323.1197—dc23
2015032056

To Corinna Nichols
Soror et Scholastica

Contents

Illustrations, Maps, and Tables

Illustrations

Maps

Tables

Acknowledgments

Books like this one could not exist without the dedication, skill, and professionalism of librarians and archivists. For the present volume I am deeply indebted to the staff of the National Archives in Washington, D.C., which holds the Records of the Office of Indian Trade. I am also grateful to the employees of Cunningham Library at Indiana State University; the Filson Historical Society in Louisville; the Historical Society of Pennsylvania; the Library Company of Philadelphia; the Missouri Historical Society Library and Research Center; the Ohio Historical Society; and Young Library at the University of Kentucky.

I have presented parts of this book to colleagues at the annual meetings of the Indiana Association of Historians, the Missouri Valley History Conference, and the American Society for Ethnohistory, as well as a Social Science Research Colloquium at Indiana State University. I gratefully acknowledge the thoughtful questions and comments provided by Stan Buchanan, Brian DeLay, Nicole Etchison, Chris Fischer, Richard Lotspeich, Dennis Smith, Russell Stafford, Kylei Tumey, Bassam Yousif, and Keri Yousif. Indiana State University provided travel funds to help me attend the first and third of these conferences. My colleagues in ISU's Department of History have been supportive of this project since its inception and have helped make Indiana State a welcome professional home.

Don Hickey, the dean of War of 1812 scholarship, kindly read and commented on an earlier version of Chapter 6, which is much stronger for his input and insight. Two anonymous readers gave the entire manuscript an equally thorough and incisive critique. The book would be a much poorer one without them. At the University of North Carolina Press, Mark Simpson-Vos has proved a master of the academic editor's art, and has been generous with his time and support since we first discussed this project a decade ago. Thanks are equally due to Lucas Church, Stephanie Wenzel, Jad Adkins, and Susan Garrett for their diligent editorial and marketing work, and to Christy Hosler and Westchester Publishing Services for their copyediting expertise.

Portions of Chapters 1, 2, 5, 6, and 8 of this book have appeared in print before, as "A Commercial Embassy in the Old Northwest: The U.S. Indian Trading Factory at Fort Wayne, 1803–1812," *Ohio Valley History* 8, no. 4 (Winter 2008), and "'The Main Mean of Their Political Management': George Washington and the Practice of Indian Trade in the Early Republic," in *George Washington in and as Culture,* edited by Kevin Cope (New York: AMS Studies in the Eighteenth Century, 2001). I thank AMS Press and the editors of *Ohio Valley History* for permission to reprint these materials.

This project first germinated in a graduate research seminar led by Michael Green at the University of Kentucky, and his enthusiasm for my study of the U.S. trading factories ensured that I would see the project through to completion. Mike took the time to read the first draft of the manuscript cover to cover, and he helped me make it a leaner and clearer book. I am glad he had the chance to see my work before his untimely death in 2013. Theda Perdue and several of her and Mike's brilliant students, notably Cary Miller and Christina Snyder, were all professional role models for me. My partner, Susan Livington, my brother Patrick, and my sister Corinna have provided years of support and encouragement. My sister, in particular, has listened too often to my weary descriptions of copying old invoices, remarking on one occasion that "I'm sure someone's been doing the same sort of thing since the Sumerians." To her, appropriately, I offer this book's dedication.

Engines of Diplomacy

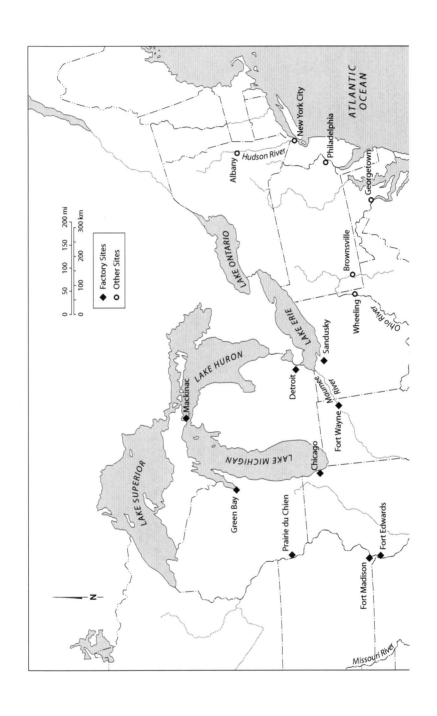

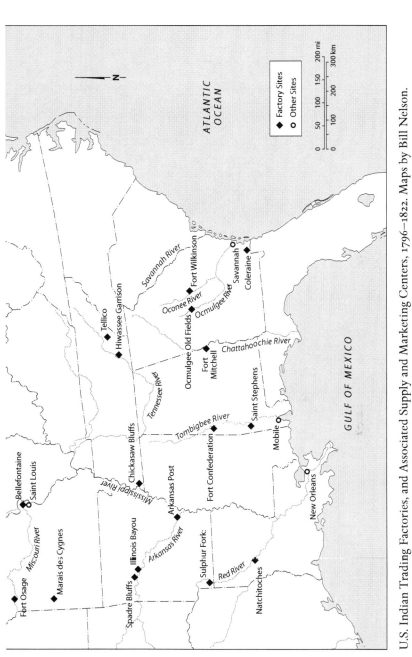

U.S. Indian Trading Factories, and Associated Supply and Marketing Centers, 1796–1822. Maps by Bill Nelson.

Introduction

Small and shaky as it was in the 1790s, the early American national government did not lack audacity. In 1795 it began an ambitious experiment in public enterprise: a system of federally funded trading posts that grew over the next dozen years into a far-flung network, extending from Fort Wilkinson in Georgia to Mackinac Island in the northern Great Lakes to Fort Osage on the Missouri River. The posts, known as factories, purchased Native Americans' animal pelts and other wares at prevailing local prices, and sold them goods at lower prices than those charged by private traders. The founders of the factory system, in particular President George Washington, hoped that the factories would tie Indian nations to the United States with cords of economic interest, and at the same time drive unscrupulous private peddlers and scheming British traders out of business. Thanks to Congressional support, the system survived the embargo of 1807–9 and the War of 1812—though British soldiers and Indian warriors destroyed several factories during the war—and the last trading houses remained open until 1822, when Congress voted to shutter them.[1]

The vote to close the factories came after a vitriolic speech by Senator Thomas Hart Benton of Missouri, an advocate for private traders in Saint Louis and a bitter foe of the factories. Benton laid it on thick, accusing the public agents, or *factors*, who ran the individual factories of "abuse" and "misconduct," characterizing their merchandise as "the rubbish of Georgetown retail stores," arguing that the system had achieved none of its goals, and branding it "worse than useless." While other senators came to the defense of the factors and their superintendent Thomas McKenney, most found the American federal government ill-suited to administer an extensive business like the fur trade. In the end, the Senate voted 17-11 for immediate closure of the trading houses and liquidation of their stock. Three decades later, Benton's hostility toward the factories still smoldered. In his memoirs, the former senator asserted that the history of the factory system conclusively demonstrated "the unfitness of the federal government to carry on any system of trade," and "the liability of the benevolent designs of the government to be abused."[2]

Benton's negative assessment of the factory system became the touchstone for future scholarship. Progressive Era historians like Frederick Jackson Turner, Katherine Coman, and Royal Way followed Benton's lead by attempting to deduce—chiefly from congressional records and reports of the Office of Indian Trade—the reasons why the factories failed in their mission. While dismissing Benton's charges of fraud, these scholars agreed that the factors had simply labored under too large a regulatory burden, too high an operating expense (high transport costs, in particular), and too great a competitive disadvantage. Most importantly, the factories failed because of the superior enterprise of private fur traders. The members of the latter group sold their Indian trading partners liquor, gave them gifts, offered them credit, and even married into their families, all of which gave them an insurmountable advantage. Even one of the factories' scholarly defenders, Milo Quaife, agreed that the factories had failed because the factors "could not stoop to the practices" which gave private traders the upper hand.[3]

In the mid-twentieth century, several authors, notably Aloysius Plaisance, Ora Brooks Peake (in the only book-length study of the factories), and Russell Magnaghi, turned their attention to the functional mechanics of the factory system. In their studies, these scholars described the trading houses' construction and furnishings, listed the goods the factors sold, reported the value of the furs they purchased, and discussed the vicissitudes of factory life—disease, fire, and spoiled goods. In general these works followed a narrative format, and their authors did not spend much time analyzing the factories' significance. Peake did devote a chapter of her book to clearing up some of the misconceptions held by earlier historians, observing that the factors followed many of the same practices as their private competitors—like offering credit and gifts to their Indian customers—that their goods were comparable in quality to those sold by private traders, and that other historians had overstated their transportation problems. She then offered her own explanation of why the trading houses had failed: the fur trade was a complex business requiring ample capital and a skilled workforce, resources that the undercapitalized and amateurishly managed factories lacked.[4]

Peake constructed a more sophisticated argument than those of the factory system's nineteenth-century opponents, but she followed the same laissez-faire economic logic. More importantly, neither Peake nor her contemporaries answered the question that the factories' supposed failure suggests: given the disadvantages under which the factors labored, given the supposed "unfitness of the federal government to carry on any system of trade," why did the factory system last so long? Thomas Benton had a simple answer to that question: congressional equivocation and inertia, combined with the "invocation" of George Washington's name by the factories' supporters. However, this explanation ignores the dynamic, turbulent state of American politics during the factory system's heyday. Congress and the presidency experienced wrenching political changes in 1800, when Democratic-Republicans ousted the Federalists from control of the federal government, and between 1812 and 1815 (during the American war with Great Britain). After both events, federal officials and legislators reassessed their government's priorities and concluded that maintaining Indian trading houses should remain among them.[5]

Moreover, the men who voted to support the factories on these occasions neither blindly worshiped the sainted Washington nor advocated (in Milo Quaife's words) "state socialism." They were, instead, Jeffersonian Republicans, who celebrated George Washington's virtues but opposed many of his policies, who favored limited government and light taxes, and who viewed government forays into private enterprise as corrupt and unconstitutional. One might have expected them, on principle, to have terminated the factory system in 1801. Instead, the Democratic-Republicans dramatically expanded the factories' scope, staff, and capital, and after the War of 1812 they agreed to rebuild some of the old trading posts and open new ones. Either the members of the party repeatedly betrayed their principles, or they considered the Indian trade something other than a purely economic enterprise.[6]

There is good reason to assume the latter. The trading factories grew from an Indian policy that one historian has called "expansion with honor"—more cynically, conquest on the cheap. When Americans of the Revolutionary era considered the 100,000–150,000 Native Americans who lived between the Appalachian Mountains and the Mississippi River, they saw not peoples but a problem. Whites coveted those Indians' lands, and they wanted the inhabitants subjected to American laws or expelled from the country. However, insurmountable obstacles blocked the most direct path to that goal, military conquest. The Indians valued their independence and their lands, and were prepared to fight for them; their warriors, numbering at least 20,000, were skilled fighters, and traders from British Canada and Spanish Florida kept them well-armed. History had demonstrated that Native Americans could raise the cost of conquest well above the price that the financially strapped state and federal governments could pay. During the Revolutionary War, American militia and soldiers burned numerous Cherokee, Iroquois, and Shawnee towns and killed thousands of Native people, and yet the survivors refused to surrender or accept the status of "conquered peoples." Ten years later, when the new U.S. government made war on the Great Lakes Indian confederation (1790–94), it expended over $2.5 million and 1,200 casualties. American officials had to find a cheaper way to subjugate their Indian adversaries.[7]

Fortunately for American expansionists, their colonial predecessors had developed nonviolent means of turning Indians into clients and procuring their lands. One was diplomacy, the use of hospitality and treaties to resolve interethnic disputes and buy land. Another was trade: when Indians exchanged furs and other commodities for European goods that they could not manufacture for themselves, they became dependent on and indebted to their trading partners. Both processes were slow and complicated, but they cost less than warfare.[8]

Trade and diplomacy were not, however, separate policy options. Native Americans considered them two sides of the same coin: "The trade and the peace we take to be one thing," as an eighteenth-century Iroquois diplomat put it. For Indians, as for most indigenous cultures throughout the world, commerce was not merely a way for societies to pursue material advantages. It also created a bond of mutual obligation between peoples who would otherwise remain strangers and enemies. While Native North Americans were not above "higgling and haggling" to obtain the highest prices for furs and skins and the lowest ones for European cloth and guns, they viewed trade primarily as a social and political act, a demonstration of reciprocity and good intentions, rather than a purely economic exchange. Thus, for example, Native Americans commonly began trade missions with the customary ceremonies of interethnic diplomacy: pipe smoking, feasting, oratory, and gift exchanges. Conversely, Indian leaders commonly insisted that diplomatic agreements and treaties must include provisions for regular trade.[9]

The Indians who visited the U.S. government's trading houses brought this view of trade and diplomacy with them, and turned the factories from mere business establishments into de facto embassies. Accompanying and following the factories' Native American customers came hundreds of Indian travelers and chiefs, who visited the trading houses to avail themselves of the factors' hospitality and to discuss political events in their towns or incidents of frontier violence. Factors who wanted to avoid offending their clients allowed them to use the posts as taverns and sleeping quarters, and by the second decade of the nineteenth century one longtime Indian agent, Return Jonathan Meigs, could observe that "the Indians consider the public trading-houses as their fathers' houses . . . [and] rallying points where the Indians feel at home." Soon Indian agents were using them as sites for diplomatic conferences, taking advantage of the factories' intermediate locations, their ready supply of trade goods, and their reputation among the Indians for hospitality. Between 1796 and 1816, federal commissioners signed nine formal treaties at or near U.S. trading houses.[10]

American policy-makers, Indian agents, and factors did not have to venture outside of their own cultural universe to understand Native Americans' close association of trade with diplomacy. While eighteenth-century European-Americans, who came from more internally differentiated societies than did Indians, did not regard mercantile and diplomatic activities as identical to one another, they did believe that trade and diplomacy complemented one another. Enlightenment essayists in Britain, France, and Germany had developed a commercial ideology that held that free and unfettered trade between nations would refine people's manners, diminish their prejudices, and lessen the probability of war. Charles Secondat, Baron de Montesquieu, observed that "commerce is a cure for the most destructive prejudices"; Joseph Addison praised merchants for "knit[ting] mankind together in a mutual intercourse of good offices"; and Joseph Priestley argued that "no person can taste the sweets of commerce . . . but must grow fond of peace, in which alone the advantages he enjoyed can be had."[11]

Early American political leaders agreed with these sentiments. One of the most prominent, George Washington, wished "that the manly employment of agriculture and the humanizing benefits of commerce, would supersede the waste of war and the rage of conquest." During the early national era, Washington and other American leaders promoted foreign, interstate, and Indian trade in order to foster peace and prosperity. Indeed, one of the central accomplishments of their statecraft, the U.S. Constitution of 1787, grew in part from legislators' efforts to encourage and regulate trade between the American states and with foreign nations.[12]

Somewhat more quietly, American leaders acknowledged, as European leaders were beginning to do, that trade was also an imperial enterprise, and that economic influence often preceded political domination. The British East India Company dramatically demonstrated this dynamic during the second half of the eighteenth century, but French and British officials in North America had already learned the principle in their dealings with Native Americans. Traders fostered Indian reliance on goods that Indians could neither repair nor replace without European assistance. White officials could then use "gifts" of cloth, gunpowder, or liquor to procure the good offices of chiefs, ransom captives, recruit warriors, or purchase land. The French expertly adapted the peltry trade to their struggle for mastery in America. From the 1690s through the 1750s, New France used a network of Native American alliances, sustained by a heavily subsidized peltry trade and ample gifts, to maintain tenuous suzerainty over the Mississippi Valley and the Great Lakes. After France's defeat in the Seven Years' War, both the British and Spanish imperial governments learned that Indians could check American settlers' expansionism, and that traders and treaties most cheaply guaranteed alliances with Indians.[13]

This was a lesson that Americans, too, learned early, and applied to the creation of their trading factories. In the 1780s, American officials observed that British traders threatened their jurisdiction, insofar as they preserved Indians' economic independence from the United States and made it difficult to negotiate with them. Commerce, observed one Army officer, served as "a political engine" giving Britain and Spain considerable "influence . . . over the savages." An outright ban on foreign trade with the Indians, however, was not a viable option: Native American hunters could simply take their furs to Canada or Spanish Florida, and Jay's Treaty allowed British traders to continue operating within the United States. Private American traders still lacked the capital and expertise to compete effectively with their European counterparts, and American officials worried that their unscrupulous practices might alienate potential Indian allies.[14]

The factories offered a solution to these problems: freed from the need to make a profit, the federal government could purchase Indians' peltry at market rates and sell them manufactured goods at cost (that is, cheaply), thereby driving foreign competitors out of business and making the United States the Indians' chief trading partner. This was certainly a possibility: thanks to high transport costs and uncertain markets, profit margins in the fur trade were thin enough that even a few trading posts with cut-price wares could threaten private traders. William Panton and

John Leslie, the principal partners of a Scottish firm based in Florida, predicted that federal trading houses in the Southeast would rob them of $400,000 worth of business, while some British traders in the Great Lakes region decided to close up shop after they learned of the opening of the Detroit and Fort Wayne factories. Thus the factories served not merely as embassies but as outposts of an American commercial empire.[15]

One should not assume, however, that Europeans and white Americans were the only people building empires in the North American interior. American officials may have regarded the factories as flags in the continental map, but they actually stood within contested zones of intercultural encounter, zones that historians once called frontiers and now describe as borderlands. The United States government wanted to enlarge its influence in these borderlands, but so too did Native American nations, communities, and leaders. For them, the trading houses functioned as political theaters and sources of power and prestige—or, to apply another metaphor, as national banners pinned to the same conceptual "map" the Americans used.[16]

Thus, Indian chiefs often stipulated the places where factories would be built, or called their locations inconvenient to press the U.S. government to move them. They treated individual houses like personal storehouses, from which they bought large quantities of merchandise on credit for redistribution to their kinsmen, and on which they subsequently delayed repayment for years, as though receiving tribute from the Americans. Men and women expected hospitality from the factors, in the form of meals and gifts, which they sometimes received with such aristocratic hauteur that their hosts described them as "their red majesties" or "princesses and ladies of rank." Conversely, Native Americans expected the factors freely to receive (and credit them for) their own hospitable gifts, in the form of foodstuffs like wild rice and maple sugar, which the factors found hard to market; this suggests that Indians saw the Americans both as hosts in their trading houses and guests in Native homelands.[17]

Hunters also weighed down the factories with tons of deerskins, a product the Office of Indian Trade found hard to sell but which diplomatic factors felt they could not refuse. When factors did refuse to buy particular Indian wares, like the horses the Comanches offered to sell to the Sulphur Fork factory—thereby integrating that factory into their own commercial network—Native Americans found other traders who would accept them. And while Indian customers sometimes tolerated poor-quality merchandise from the factors, they just as often indicated that they had high standards and refined tastes, demanding patterned jewelry and point blankets, ice skates and queensware. The message that the Creeks and Caddos, Sauks and Osages, Miamis and Ho-Chunks and other Native Americans had for the factors and their masters was simple enough: the trading houses stood not in borderlands but on Native ground, and Indians made the rules and occupied the superior position. Officials in Philadelphia and Washington assumed the factories were outstations of the American empire; factors on the ground might well wonder whose empire really owned them.[18]

Policy-makers in the capital did understand that Native Americans guarded well their political and cultural autonomy, but they believed that the factories could undermine this by promoting a kind of cultural imperialism: the "Indian civilization" policy of the early U.S. government. First proposed by Congress in 1787, this program encouraged Indians to adopt commercial agriculture, textile manufacturing, and English literacy, thereby remaking them in the image of European-Americans and preparing them for assimilation into the mainstream American population. While the factories necessarily encouraged Native American men to continue their profession of hunting, individual factors and agents believed the trading houses could also nudge Indian men and women toward more "civilized" pursuits. This conformed to the commercial ideology that had helped produce the factories, whose exponents believed that trade not only led to peaceful international relations but also to increased industry, property ownership, and refinement. Principal Southern Indian agent Benjamin Hawkins urged the factors at Fort Wilkinson to pay Creek women premium prices for homespun cloth, thereby encouraging them to spin and weave. The Creek and Choctaw factories sold their Native American customers cowbells, cotton cards, and carpentry tools, helping some southeastern Indians trade the products of hunting for the implements of European agriculture. Later, Superintendent of Indian Trade Thomas McKenney encouraged the factors to establish model farms at their trading houses, thereby demonstrating agricultural techniques to their Indian customers. "Our object," he wrote, "is not to keep these Indians hunters eternally. We want to make citizens out of them, and they must first be anchored to the soil."[19]

McKenney sought to make an explicit connection between the factories and the civilization program. In 1816 he proposed that Congress expand the factory system, run the houses at a profit, and use the proceeds to fund schools for Indian children. McKenney's proposal garnered the support of Protestant missionaries (probable recipients of educational funds), who proclaimed the superintendent's plan doubly benevolent, since the factories would protect Indians from the corrupting influence of private traders while mission schools transformed them into Christian farmers. However, it sat poorly with American fur traders, who by the 1810s had acquired ample influence, and with the western officials who shared traders' interests.[20]

McKenney inadvertently gave these traders and their representatives an important rhetorical weapon when he proposed that Christian missionaries—men and women whose deportment and objectives differed markedly from those of fur traders—administer his proposed Indian schools. Congress sharpened this weapon when in 1819 it enacted only part of McKenney's plan, appropriating $10,000 per annum for Indian schooling but taking the money from the Treasury rather than from factory profits. Benton and other opponents of the factories could then argue that there was neither an operational nor a conceptual link between the factories and Indian civilization, because one was the province of grubby shopkeepers and the other the domain of evangelists. When Congress solicited depositions on the factories' shortcomings prior to its debate on closing them, one of its deponents, Ramsey Crooks—a lieutenant of fur-trading magnate John Astor—ridiculed the idea that the factors could serve the civilization program. "I should imagine," Crooks wrote, "they were selected more for their trafficking than apostolic abilities," and were poorly suited "to teach repentance and remission of sins to the children of the wilderness."[21]

That the factory system drew the ire and ridicule of private traders should not surprise anyone. Instead, their opposition raises one final salient point about the trading factories: they were highly sensitive to local pressures, and controlled as much by local actors as by the national government. Native Americans were, as we have noted, the most influential of these actors, but many white Americans also influenced the factors' actions. Army soldiers frequently provided the factors with labor and sometimes bought provisions and merchandise from them. On other occasions, soldiers and officers quarreled with factors and threatened them with violence. Private traders also profoundly affected the factories' operations. They established prevailing local prices for peltry, which the trading houses copied; they sometimes discouraged Indians from trading with the factors; and at other times licensed traders bought goods from the factories for resale to their own Indian trading partners.[22]

One other group of local actors with a stake in the factories' success was white settlers. While frontier farmers usually regarded the federal trading posts as little more than stores where they could buy merchandise, some federal officials hoped to use the factories to acquire Native American land, by luring their more prominent Indian customers into debt. The U.S. government would "be glad to see" this happening, wrote Thomas Jefferson in 1803, "because we observe that when these debts get beyond what individuals can pay, they become willing to lop them off by a cession of lands." Some initial experiments with debt-for-land swaps yielded promising results: in 1802 Creek leaders ceded over three million acres to Georgia in return for cancellation of $10,000 in debt, while in 1805–6 federal commissioners used factory debts to leverage two land purchases from the Cherokees. Thereafter, though, Native American resistance to further land cessions and the northern Indians' comparative reluctance to buy goods on long-term credit prevented the government from executing further debt/land exchanges. After the War of 1812, the United States could bully and bribe demoralized Indian leaders into surrendering land, no longer needing the factories to grease the wheels of negotiation. Frontier settlers thus had no reason to want the factories kept open, and most stayed silent during the final battle between merchants, missionaries, Congress, and the War Department over their closure.[23]

In sum, the U.S. Indian factories served as both imperial and local institutions, representing points of intersection between the political ambitions of policy-makers in Washington City and the interests of white farmers, fur traders, and Native American chiefs and commoners. In the short term, Congress's faith in the political usefulness of the factories ensured that they would remain open, to the benefit of some local actors and the consternation of others. In the long term, the structure of the American "empire," with the eventual statehood and representation it guaranteed western whites, ensured that the factories' frontier opponents would have a large say in their ultimate disposition.[24]

It is tempting to say that western interests, specifically fur traders and the officials who supported them, destroyed the factory system. Yet to the extent one can attribute the factories' demise to "enemy action" rather than simple retrenchment and the weakness or silence of the houses' supporters, the enemy who brought them down was not a westerner but an easterner. John Astor of New York saw the federal trading houses as the main obstacle to his attempt to monopolize the western fur trade. After the War of 1812, Astor—who by this time had over $400,000 invested in his American Fur Company and had also become one of the U.S. government's leading creditors—personally lobbied Congress to abolish the factory system, even pressuring President James Monroe not to interfere with his interests. In 1821–22, Astor's former attorney, Thomas Benton, initiated the hearings that would bring down the Office of Indian Trade, and Astor's lieutenant, Ramsey Crooks, provided Benton with many of his talking points.[25]

Perhaps the most striking lesson one can learn from the demise of the factories is that American leaders did not so much localize as privatize their continental imperium in the nineteenth century. Wealthy private interests triumphed, in the end, over both local actors and national leaders, and borderlands became places where a few prominent white men made the rules.[26]

1

A Trade upon Public Ground

In reminiscing about the Indian factories, Thomas Hart Benton laid the blame for the unlamented institution on George Washington and on the government officials who exploited his memory. Benton might have gone back a bit further, however, for originality did not rank high among Washington's intellectual gifts. The president had most likely borrowed the idea of government-run trading houses from several colonies that maintained them, notably Massachusetts, Pennsylvania, and Washington's own Virginia. More importantly, Washington had received instruction in the importance of Indian trade, and the tight connection between it and peaceful interethnic relations, from a persuasive source: a Native American leader alarmed at the lack of trade between his people and Washington's.[1]

Washington's lesson came in October 1770, during a trip to the Ohio Valley. Stopping in Pittsburgh, then a small village populated by soldiers and Indian traders, the Virginian received an invitation to meet the Ohio Seneca chief White Mingo and six other Iroquois at the home of master trader George Croghan. White Mingo gave Washington a wampum string and a message for Virginia's governor: in the aftermath of the bloody Seven Years' War, the region's Indians wanted "to live in peace and harmony with the white people," but feared that "we did not look upon them with so friendly an eye as they could want," because "their brothers of Virginia did not come among them and trade as the inhabitants of the other provinces did."[2]

For the Iroquois, and for the Great Lakes Indians against whom Washington levied war during his presidency, and indeed for all Native peoples in North America, trade was no mere economic activity. It prefigured, symbolized, and secured peace and friendship. American Indians recognized that trade brought them material benefits, but they valued still more the bond of reciprocity and trust that the exchange of goods sealed, and to which exotic goods like wampum or silver jewelry or calico cloth gave ongoing testimony. Trade was diplomacy, and Native Americans generally accompanied it with the other rites that renewed international amity: feasting, smoking, and the exchange of speeches and kinship metaphors. The absence of trade corresponded to a suspension of friendly relations, one step removed from war. No wonder White Mingo and his companions worried about Virginia's intentions.[3]

Washington promised to pass the message to his governor, and he hoped that Virginians and Indians would in future have "stricter connexions." He understood, and the Iroquois emissaries almost certainly recognized, that Virginia should care as much about Native Americans' intentions as vice versa. Though they had in the previous century lost much of their population and become reliant on European goods, Indians were not people with whom the colonists, or their independent American successors, could afford to trifle. French-allied warriors had ravaged Virginia's backcountry counties during the Seven Years' War, and British-allied warriors would harry rebel troops and settlements a few years later during the Revolutionary War. Conversely, peaceful relations with Native Americans brought many advantages: the profits of the peltry trade, access to Indian scouts and guides who could facilitate long-range travel, intelligence about other Europeans' activities, and, perhaps, the ability to persuade Indians to part with their lands. Most of these were public goods, and if one could best secure them through trade, it followed that governments should exercise more control over that trade than private individuals.[4]

This principle underlay the U.S. government's Indian factories, which Washington first proposed at the end of the Revolutionary War and persuaded Congress to create ten years later. Eighteenth-century writers like Archibald Kennedy and Benjamin Franklin had observed that the British and French colonies' survival and development depended on their influence over Native Americans. Washington and his contemporaries believed it no less essential to the ambitious new United States. However, trade implied reciprocity, and within both the colonial Indian trade and the post-Revolutionary factory system, both parties would influence one another. Commerce might give Native Americans a better impression of the United States and increase their reliance on white Americans, but only if American traders made their own sacrifices. American factors would have to behave according to Indians' expected norms, show them deference and hospitality, freely purchase the pelts and other products they generously provided, sell them goods at predictably low prices, offer credit to those who needed or expected it, and maintain their stores in locations convenient to their Indian customers, even if this proved expensive or generated conflict with foreign traders.

For Native Americans, trade did not burden, but it could endanger. It made them reliant on imported goods and exposed them to alcohol and disease. They could not avoid it, however, unless they wanted to live in constant suspicion of their Indian and white neighbors, and most did not. Moreover, trade conveyed power: it supplied chiefs with exotic goods that displayed their foreign connections, and it obliged Europeans to conform to Indians' own norms. Like Europeans and white Americans, Native Americans valued commerce too greatly ever to abandon it. They had, after all, never done without it.

WHEN THE UNITED STATES GOVERNMENT commissioned the first federal Indian factories in 1795, it entered into a business that had existed for centuries, that extended throughout the continent, and that had long shaped North America's interethnic and international relationships. Native North Americans had been trading with one another since the earliest migrations from Asia, traveling hundreds of miles on foot or by water to exchange scarce and useful commodities. Some of these commodities, like copper, mica, or obsidian, were materials whose color, structure, or distant provenance gave them spiritual power and prestige value, affirming the status of the elites who displayed or gifted them. Others, like maize and pemmican, served more utilitarian purposes. Animal hides and furs fell into the latter category and constituted a significant part of inter-Indian trade by the time of the first European voyages to America.[5]

The European fur trade also had a long pedigree, dating to the Roman imperial era. Scandinavian hunters sold furs to southern European merchants throughout the Middle Ages, and fishermen plying the Grand Banks in the sixteenth century opened an informal trade with the Micmacs and Beothuks who visited their fish-curing camps on the Canadian coast. The fishermen bartered knives and copper kettles for animal skins, demonstrating to merchants back home the riches they might derive from the North American trade.[6]

In the early seventeenth century, chartered companies of gentleman-adventurers opened fur-trading posts on the Atlantic seaboard of North America. The French established Quebec on the Saint Lawrence River, the Dutch built Fort Orange on the Hudson, and the English erected Jamestown and Plymouth. All stood near Indian communities or athwart rivers that gave ready access to them. The companies professed other motives for colonization, like blocking Spanish expansion or spreading the Gospel, but all wanted pelts and profits.[7]

Later in the century, traders pursuing new markets extended the European trading network deep into the continent. The French built posts on the Great Lakes from which licensed traders and independent *coureurs de bois* (woods-runners) fanned out into the Canadian interior, reaching the Great Plains by 1688. England conquered the Dutch fur-trading colony of New Netherland, and English merchants established two additional bases of expansion, Rupert's House on Hudson Bay and Charles Town on the southern Atlantic coast. Hudson's Bay Company *factories*, as the company (in emulation of medieval merchants) called its trading stations, attracted Cree and Assiniboine hunters from throughout the massive Hudson Bay drainage basin. By the mid-eighteenth century the HBC annually purchased up to 60,000 pelts of beavers, whose under-fur European hatters prized. Meanwhile Carolina traders led pack trains to Indian communities throughout the Southeast, and by the mid-1700s South Carolina annually exported 160,000 deerskins, which English clothiers converted into fine leather breeches, gloves, and shoes.[8]

The Indians who first participated in the Atlantic fur trade integrated new trade goods into their pre-Columbian material culture. Glass beads and brass kettles resembled the crystals and copper that Native Americans had been trading with one another for centuries. New metal tools allowed Indian craftsmen to increase or perfect their manufacture of traditional commodities: steel drills allowed Algonquians to mass-produce wampum; iron axes and chisels let the Hurons perfect their bone-carving and pipe-making; and metal scissors and awls made it easier for Indian women to fabricate clothing.[9]

Moreover, Native Americans integrated Europeans into their own social patterns and obliged them to adhere to their commercial protocols, which drew close associations between trade, gift-giving, and the creation of kinship ties between strangers. White traders who wanted a long-term relationship with Indians learned to follow their rules. They opened each trading season with feasting and gift-giving; extended credit—a form of temporary generosity—to prominent chiefs and war captains; and cemented commercial alliances by living in Native American towns and marrying into Indian families. Indians thereby turned traders into kinsmen and allies as well as business partners, and they made it clear that their rules governed the colonial trading game.[10]

Within a few decades of its inception, however, the Atlantic fur trade began to disrupt the lives of its Indian participants. Reliance on European consumer goods was one ill effect. Peoples as diverse as the

Blackfeet, Cherokees, and Montagnais came to prefer many European goods to their own manufactures, beginning to substitute iron for stone tools, metal cookware for pottery, and woven cloth for buckskin. Native American men and women began to specialize in killing animals and dressing and transporting pelts, neglecting their craft skills in the process. This heightened their reliance on Europeans for the necessities of life.[11]

Dependence begat the problems commonly experienced by workers in a global economy: price fluctuations, overproduction, and resource depletion. When the prices of furs fell in Europe, white traders in North America increased the number of furs they charged Indian hunters for goods. Indians considered these increases breaches of hospitality and good faith. In the 1640s, Roger Williams reported that "the Natives are very impatient when for English commodities they pay so much more . . . not understanding the cause of it . . . many say the English cheat and deceive them." Even when traders lowered their prices, Native Americans' growing demand for European goods forced them to expand their hunting, and animal populations dwindled. By 1675 Algonquian hunters had killed most of the commercially useful fur-bearing animals in southern New England, and one hundred years later the deer and beaver populations of the Great Lakes and the Southeast had also come under severe pressure. White farmers contributed to this decline by felling trees for farmland and allowing their livestock to forage in the woods, crowding native animals out of their habitats.[12]

Moreover, while most of the things European traders brought in their packs were useful or prestigious, some had pernicious effects. Indian men prized alcohol, for instance, because it made them feel powerful and licensed anti-social behavior. Some, like the northern Great Lakes Indians, also viewed liquor as a seal of diplomacy and an emblem of good relations: the Ojibwas called it "milk," the foodstuff that bound parents to children and held families, real or metaphorical, together. Yet liquor also led to accidents, ill health, and violent disputes, and men's demand for it often prevented them from buying necessities. Chiefs enjoined white officials to keep "wicked whiskey sellers" away from their kinsmen, and many colonies restricted the liquor trade but could not enforce their prohibitions. By the 1770s British and French Americans sold as many as 170,000 gallons of rum each year to their Indian neighbors.[13]

Another commodity, firearms, had equally troubling side effects. Indian warriors prized European muskets and rifles for their range, their ability to penetrate the light armor some nations used in combat, and the shock they induced in enemies unfamiliar with gunpowder. The new weapons dramatically increased the lethality of internecine wars, however, and forced Indian nations without guns to find partners willing to supply them, lest they fall prey to better-armed neighbors.[14]

Yet another lethal import, albeit an unintentional one, was the array of pathogens that accompanied traders to Native American communities. American Indians, long isolated from Eurasian disease pools, suffered high mortality rates when exposed to unfamiliar diseases like smallpox. Native Americans' aversion to quarantine and their use of feasts and sweat baths to treat the sick accelerated the spread of these epidemics. Most of the Algonquians of eastern Massachusetts died in an epidemic between 1616 and 1619, as did 50 percent of the Hurons and Iroquois in the 1630s and 40s, half of the Cherokees in the following century, and over 60,000 Plains, Pueblo, and Pacific Northwest Indians in the smallpox pandemic of 1779–82.[15]

The confluence of dependency, firearms, and disease increased the scope and intensity of warfare. Indian warriors had fought ritualized wars for centuries, usually to avenge crimes or acquire captives. With the advent of the fur and gun trade, however, Native Americans also began to fight one another for access to prime hunting territory or to rob rivals of their pelts. Muskets and metal weapons increased the casualties from warfare, which, combined with deaths from imported diseases, gave warriors new incentives to acquire captives and thus to go to war. The Five Nations of Iroquois became caught in this feedback loop of mortality and war from the 1640s to the 1690s, during which time they campaigned against Native American rivals from Illinois to New England, and they suffered devastating invasions of their homeland in return. In the upper Great Lakes region and on the northern Plains, the Blackfoot, Cree, Dakota, and Ojibwa nations fought over beaver grounds for more than a century.[16]

In the Southeast, a different kind of interethnic commerce—namely a thriving trade in slaves—produced some of the most devastating interethnic wars of the eighteenth century. The French, British, and Spanish all employed Indian slaves in North America or on Caribbean sugar plantations, and they hired southern Indians to raid their neighbors for captives. Joint Creek-Carolinian raiding parties killed or captured nearly all the Indians of northern Florida by 1706, and subsequent campaigns decimated the Yamasees and Tuscaroras. The Indian slave trade declined after 1715, but by then as many as 50,000 southeastern Indians had fallen victim to it.[17]

North American Indians did not become passive victims of the fur trade, the slave trade, and the conflicts and dislocations accompanying them. They instead adapted rapidly to change and learned to defend themselves against exploitation. Indian hunters dealt with falling fur prices by patronizing multiple European traders to find the best deals. Chiefs used diplomacy to obtain gifts from European officials and demand protection from dishonest traders. Faced with attacks by Indian rivals or European slavers, Native Americans responded by purchasing guns and forming defensive leagues like the Creek Confederacy. Faced with declining animal populations, Indian men and women began producing other commodities that Europeans wanted, like baskets and pemmican.[18]

In the long run, one might argue, Indian hunters played a losing game. European merchants would ultimately hold the upper hand in the fur trade because their culture let them accumulate capital and invest it in bureaucratized companies. Native Americans' decentralized political cultures prevented them from organizing trading ventures with much more than a large family's resources. Moreover, their societies' emphasis on generosity made it hard to acquire capital. One white observer noted of the Osages, for example, that "to set the heart upon goods and chattels [was] thought to indicate a mean and narrow soul," so an "ambitious" man among them "gives away everything he can get."[19]

In the shorter term, Native Americans would have considered the idea of becoming wealthy merchants laughable, because they viewed trade as a political and diplomatic enterprise not an economic one. Trade played an important role in local Indian politics: the acquisition and display of exotic goods proved Indian leaders' command over distant and powerful forces (such as Europeans), and the redistribution of such goods turned recipients into clients, increasing chiefs' and captains' authority still further. Moreover, commerce, for all its evil side effects, provided tangible evidence of amicable relations between peoples; its sacred transactions converted strangers into kinsmen and bound nations together in amity or alliance. Trade, in short, provided not profit but the infrastructure of power and peace.[20]

European-American officials also recognized that the political advantages of trade with the Indians could outweigh the economic benefits reaped by merchants. Fair trade, conducted according to Native Americans' rules, helped preserve alliances with nations who could provide valuable services, such as scouting and slave catching. Exploitative practices could lead to discontent, the loss of trading partners, and even war, which the fragile English, French, and Dutch colonies could ill afford. If Indians had become reliant on the fur trade by the eighteenth century, their European partners had come to depend on it.[21]

Since commerce was a political enterprise, it made sense to colonial officials to regulate it carefully. In Dutch New Netherland and early Quebec, the proprietors of each colony sought profits more than alliances, and initially they simply restricted trade to their own employees. Thanks to an uncertain European market and competition from unauthorized traders, both companies were losing money by the 1630s, when they turned over Indian commerce to local settlers.[22]

Most of the British American colonies, by contrast, used some form of legal regulation to limit the disruptive effects of the fur trade and restrict it to men of property. The royal governors of English New York vested control of Indian trade in a commission comprised of Albany merchants. South Carolina's House of Commons imposed licensing requirements on the colony's traders in 1707, obliging them to post bond and pay an annual fee, and created an Indian grievance commission to prevent traders from "oppressing the people among whom they live." A later (1731) licensing act restricted Carolina traders to specified Indian towns.[23]

Following the Yamasee War, a conflict officials blamed on exploitative trading practices, the South Carolina legislature and Governor Alexander Spotswood of Virginia created public corporations to control their colonies' fur trade. Spotswood's law restricted Virginia's Indian trade to a single post, Fort Christianna, where a chartered company sold goods to the Saponis and Tuscaroras and ran a school for their children. South Carolina put the trade under the control of public commissioners and limited it to eight public trading houses. Under pressure from merchants, George I vetoed these provinces' Indian legislation and colonial officials closed their trading posts. Despite this royal disapproval, the Pennsylvania assembly in the 1750s opened its own factories for the Delawares, Senecas, and Shawnees, whom Pennsylvanians wanted to detach from the French. The storekeepers at these posts (Shamokin and Pittsburgh) bought Indians' skins, meat, and even their canoes, selling them goods at fixed and low prices. James Kenny, the public trader at Pittsburgh, also received captives whom Indians were returning, bled the sick, and listened to customers' complaints.[24]

Virginia and South Carolina officials unconsciously and Pennsylvania's government intentionally followed the example of another province,

Massachusetts, which created a public fur-trading monopoly to regulate Indian-white contact and counter foreign competition. Massachusetts magistrates had long viewed traders with suspicion, and during King William's War they decided to ban private Indian trade altogether. In 1694 the General Court authorized the construction of fortified trading posts, or *truck-houses*, on the province's northern and eastern frontier. At each a salaried "truck-master" sold goods to the Wabenaki Indians at wholesale and bought their furs at retail prices, to drive unauthorized competitors out of business. The truck-house system grew to a dozen posts by the 1750s, the Massachusetts assembly complaining all the while that the gifts it dispensed and the Indian debts it allowed drained the colony's finances. However, neither the governor nor the Council of Massachusetts intended the posts to make money, and by the 1750s one official reported that they had achieved their primary goals: eliminating private traders and drawing Wabenakis out of the French political orbit.[25]

Of all the European colonial powers, the royal government of New France developed perhaps the most elaborate trading regime, part of an effort to convert its North American borderland into what Amy Bushnell has termed a "strategic frontier." In 1681 France limited the beaver trade to 25 wealthy licensees, required traders to clear their lists of *voyageurs* (salesmen) with the governor, and restricted their destinations and cargoes. On the western Great Lakes and in the Mississippi Valley, the French colonial government established garrisoned posts that served the voyageurs as supply depots. Faced with growing competition from British traders, the Crown also paid French merchants millions of livres in subsidies, which allowed them to sell merchandise to the Indians below cost.[26]

New France's strenuous efforts to control it reflected the Indian trade's indispensability. Unlike those of the more economically diverse English colonies, Canada's exports consisted primarily of furs. In 1752 Phineas Stevens opined that Canadians' "income from thence seems to be the dependence of the whole country," and he suggested that if Britain destroyed the French fur trade, it would wreck the Canadian economy and allow an easy conquest. Stevens made an important but misleading observation: French America depended on the peltry trade not for its economic survival but its political survival. French goods and gifts sustained the friendship of several dozen Indian nations, whose warriors helped French troops harry British frontier settlements in wartime, and who blocked British expansion into the Mississippi Valley. Without the fur trade and the alliances it sustained, New France's *habitants* could not defend themselves against a concerted attack by British colonists, who outnumbered them fifteen to one. With it, a handful of French soldiers and villagers could claim suzerainty over a domain stretching from the Missouri River to the Ohio, though this was a fragile and fictive domain, in which Indian nations controlled the channels of trade and travel.[27]

The French claim of dominion took a blow in the 1740s, when British traders entered the upper Ohio Valley and built trading posts south of Lake Erie. Several thousand Miami and Wyandot Indians welcomed the opportunity to strengthen ties with Britain; access to English trade goods allowed them to chart a political course free of French interference. During King George's War (1744–48), some Ohio Valley Indian warriors offered their services to Pennsylvania, while others attacked French traders and discussed an anti-French alliance. New France's governor, the Marquis de Galissonière, responded to this challenge by ordering a military conquest. French-led raiding parties drove British traders out of the Ohio country, and a French army occupied western Pennsylvania, building forts from Lake Erie to the forks of the Ohio River. France's commercial empire had become, in at least one part of North America, a military one.[28]

The French occupation of the upper Ohio achieved its short-term goals. Local Indians, facing a choice between trading with the French or going hungry, chose the former. Indian warriors helped defend Fort Duquesne and harried frontier settlements in Virginia and Pennsylvania. In the longer run, however, Galissonière's initiative fatally undermined French power. France's belligerence provoked Britain into declaring war in 1756, and the Royal Navy took control of the Atlantic sea-lanes, depriving New France of reinforcements and supplies while allowing British troops to cross the ocean unmolested.[29]

Invading the Ohio Valley also weakened France's alliance with the Indians. An equal relationship based on diplomacy and mutual advantage became one founded on coercion. Native American warriors would now fight for France only as long as the French gave them supplies and kept strong garrisons near their towns. When the goods stopped coming and the soldiers began to starve, France's Indian "subjects" deserted. In 1758, when the beleaguered commandant of Fort Duquesne asked the Delawares for help, they refused, saying that "We have often ventured our lives for him, and had hardly a loaf of bread when we came to him, and now he thinks we should jump to serve him." This proved the epitaph for Fort Duquesne, and the next year British troops also subdued Quebec. By 1760 the French empire in North America had crumbled and Britain claimed mastery of the continent.[30]

British officials and colonial leaders disagreed about the future of Indian-white relations in a greatly enlarged British America. Shortly before the war, several American colonists had argued that a regulated commercial alliance with the Indians was the key to the continent, and that the English colonies needed a central authority to oversee that alliance. Archibald Kennedy and Benjamin Franklin proposed that either the colonies or the Crown create a superintendent of Indian affairs who would issue trading licenses and establish trading houses. Colonial assemblies ignored their advice, but the imperial Board of Trade agreed with the reformers, and in 1756 it commissioned William Johnson and Edmund Atkin as superintendents of Indian Affairs for the Northern and Southern Departments. The new superintendents nominally possessed the power to license traders and appoint agents but found they lacked the resources to exercise much authority. More powerful officials, filled with hubris by Britain's victories, preferred a blunter approach to Indian-white relations.[31]

In the south, Governor Henry Lyttelton of South Carolina provoked a war with the Cherokees (1759–61) by cutting off their gunpowder supply and executing a party of chiefs visiting Charleston. Ultimately, Britain's commander-in-chief, Jeffrey Amherst, had to send an army to burn the Cherokees' towns. Amherst concluded that the Cherokee War demonstrated British supremacy, Native American contemptibility, and the dispensability of gifts. In 1761–62 he imposed these misbegotten beliefs on the Ohio Valley and Great Lakes Indians, ending the distribution of presents, banning or restricting the sale of gunpowder and rum, and demanding the return of white captives.[32]

Amherst's unfriendly policies, coupled with Britain's occupation of France's Great Lakes forts, outraged Indian warriors from Iroquoia to Green Bay. Many began seeking the restoration of a better past, either the former period of French rule and accommodation, or a semi-mythical pre-contact era envisioned by "nativist" prophets, who shared their dreams of a time before Europeans and their artifacts poisoned Indians' lives. The nativists and Francophiles joined forces to drive out the British invaders, and in 1763 they struck their blow, attacking every British-occupied fort in the Lakes country and destroying most of them. Pontiac's War, as historians would call it, failed to drive Anglo Americans out of the western country; smallpox and British reinforcements forced the confederates to abandon their offensive. However, the war did convince Amherst's successors to take more seriously those reformers who had advocated diplomacy and trade.[33]

As Pontiac's War drew to a close, the Board of Trade proposed a new set of imperial regulations for Indian commerce. The "Plan of 1764" restricted trade to specified forts in the Northern Department and Indian towns in the Southern, obliged traders to obtain a license from colonial governors, and empowered superintendents and their agents to resolve interethnic disputes. The Board's proposal never became a formal statute, but Superintendents William Johnson and John Stuart (Atkin's successor) nonetheless treated it as one. Under the new plan's aegis, well-connected British merchants opened or expanded trade with the Indians in British America's borderland. Georgia traders like Lachlan McGillivray enlarged their commerce with the Creeks, increasing the annual volume of deerskins exported through Savannah to 300,000 pounds by 1770. Merchants William Panton and Thomas Forbes moved their headquarters to British-occupied Florida and began trading with the Lower Creeks and Gulf Coast Indians. In the north, the firm of Baynton, Wharton, and Morgan invested £75,000 in the Illinois fur trade.[34]

The licensed traders were, however, swiftly overwhelmed by unlicensed competitors. Independent peddlers and Francophone traders from Detroit and Saint Louis undermined legitimate companies by traveling directly to Native American towns rather than confining themselves to British posts. In the South, hundreds of independent operators plied the southeastern Indians with rum, encouraged Indian men to steal horses, and brought many into debt. Chiefs frequently complained to British officials that independent traders cheated their kinsmen and incited them to violence.[35]

Britain no longer had the power or will to redress such grievances. The expense of regulating the American frontier proved too great for the British government, which faced tax riots at home and in the colonies. In 1768 the Board of Trade abandoned the Plan of 1764, and over the next four years the economizing Secretary of State for America, Lord Hillsborough, closed most of the army's frontier posts. Financial and political considerations drove the change in policy, but in practice it represented a shift from accommodation with Indians to acquiescence in the colonists' exploitation of them.[36]

Colonial legislators and land developers immediately exploited the policy change. By the mid-eighteenth century agricultural staples had replaced furs as the British colonies' most valuable exports, and colonial leaders valued the lands that produced those staples more than the labor of the Indians who owned them. There was no shortage of whites willing to buy real estate from developers, as about ten thousand German and British immigrants came to the colonies every year in the 1760s. Most wanted to farm and would willingly settle in the backcountry if they could buy cheap land there.[37]

Speculators pressured Parliament to approve new colonies west of the Appalachian Mountains, while colonial officials, acting with or without royal approval, negotiated land cessions from the Iroquois, Cherokees, and Creeks. Indian traders played a prominent role in these schemes, for they now believed they could not profit from the fur trade without the protections Britain had withdrawn. Instead, traders like Samuel Wharton began to perceive commerce as a means to the more profitable end of land speculation. More specifically, they proposed that public officials use Indian hunters' debts to pressure chiefs for compensatory land cessions, then pay off the Indians' creditors with the proceeds of land sales. The governor of Georgia used debt to pry a two-million-acre cession from the Creeks, while Virginia's House of Burgesses planned to open a factory at Long Island of Holston and to use debts incurred there to extract land from the Cherokees. (Viewed in light of this project, Washington's assurances to White Mingo assume a more sinister hue.)[38]

By the early 1770s, even the British government had concluded that the value of western lands outweighed the Crown's commitment to protecting and trading with its Indian subjects. In 1772 the Privy Council approved the petition of a prominent land company to establish a new colony, Vandalia, on the Ohio River. Parliament appeared to block plans for settlement of the Ohio Valley when it passed the Quebec Act, a 1774 law that extended the boundaries of Quebec to the Ohio River. However, the act specified that its extension of Quebec's territory would not "affect the boundaries of any other colony," presumably including Vandalia. Moreover, the law coincided with the Coercive Acts, the convening of the Continental Congress, and the buildup to war between Britain and the American colonies, so it proved unenforceable south of the Great Lakes.[39]

The governor of one of the eastern colonies had already begun beating Quebec and the Vandalia Company to the draw by conducting a war of conquest in the Ohio country. In 1774 Lord Dunmore, the governor of Virginia, used the pretext of a backcountry war between white hunters and Shawnees to raise a provincial army, invade the Ohio Valley, defeat the Shawnees, and force them to surrender their land south of the Ohio. Virginia's government had already begun surveying and selling those lands, and the settlement of Kentucky soon began in earnest. In his correspondence the governor blamed the war on cruel and "ungovernable" white frontiersmen, whom he nonetheless quite willingly used as the sharp end of his colonial project.[40]

Dunmore's victory made him a hero with Virginia's gentry, but within six months he became one of the province's villains. Mostly, this resulted from the governor's opposition to the rebellion spreading through eastern North America, but he also engendered hostility by using Indians—specifically, Shawnee prisoners from the 1774 campaign—to defend himself. Genteel Virginians considered this barbarous, but Dunmore was not the first person to recruit Native Americans to fight in the Revolution: the rebel government of Massachusetts had just accepted the services of a company of Stockbridge Mohicans.[41]

For the next seven years, thousands of Indian warriors fought on both sides of the American Revolutionary War. "Civil Indians" from New England enlisted as regulars in the Continental Army; Catawbas and Oneidas joined the rebels as scouts and auxiliaries; and British-allied Seneca and Cherokee warriors raided American settlements. Their participation cost them dearly: raids by American forces left dozens of Indian towns in ashes. Yet the civil war in British North America also brought opportunities to Native Americans: for young men to win glory and plunder, and for opponents of American expansion to join a new alliance against it.[42]

More importantly, the Revolutionary War restored Native Americans to relevance in the eyes of Anglo Americans. On the eve of the conflict, backcountry farmers, ambitious land speculators, and expansionist officials had come to view Indians as nothing more than an impediment to the spread of British settlement. The War for American Independence ended this consensus and caused the British and Continental armies to turn to Native Americans for help. For the duration of the war, Americans and Britons wanted Indian allegiance more than Indian lands. Diplomacy and its concomitants, gift-giving and trade, resumed their former importance.

Indians retained their political relevance—and diplomacy and trade their salience—long after 1783. Eastern North America remained politically divided for decades after the Treaty of Paris, as the British in Canada, the Spanish in Florida, and the American state and federal governments all struggled for control of the continental interior. At the same time, proponents of pan-Indian confederation recruited thousands of warriors into their movement. For more than ten years, the confederates fought American expansion from the Ohio Valley to Georgia. Despite their growing numbers, white frontiersmen lacked the resources to respond effectively, and neither the insolvent states nor the feeble Continental Congress could help them defeat the Indian confederates. Of necessity, Americans would rely on treaties, gifts, and trade to engage with and divide their Indian antagonists—particularly since the Spanish and British used the same tools to support the insurgent Indians' struggle.[43]

WHEN THE AMERICAN rebellion turned into open war, British officials and rebel leaders sought to secure the assistance or neutrality of the Indian nations. In the fall of 1775 the Continental Congress sent commissioners to ask the Iroquois and Ohio Valley Indians to remain neutral. Aware of the vital importance of gifts in Indian diplomacy, the foreign affairs committee directed its agent in France, Silas Deane, to buy £40,000 worth of "articles for the Indian trade." This purchase would both provide Congress with goods for Indian allies and initiate trade with a potential European ally.[44]

Deane's purchase complemented federal efforts to take control of the colonies' Indian trade, which Congress considered a vital intercolonial interest. In January 1776 Congress assigned to its Indian commissioners licensing and regulatory powers comparable to those of Britain's superintendents. Six months later, John Dickinson's draft Articles of Confederation proposed giving Congress exclusive control over all Indian-white relations, so that the federal government could organize "an alliance offensive and defensive" with Indian nations. Some delegates objected to this infringement of local jurisdiction, but George Walton of Georgia and James Wilson of Pennsylvania supported the idea, arguing that Americans had to present a united, benevolent front to the Indians. The final draft of the Articles, completed in 1777, contained a compromise: Congress would have the power to regulate trade and other relations with "Indians, not members of any of the states," presumably those living west of the Appalachians.[45]

Congress's attempt to regulate and engross Indian trade failed, however, for want of resources. Congress depended on grudgingly issued state requisitions and depreciating paper money for revenue, and it could barely supply its own troops, let alone prospective Indian allies. Indeed, in March 1776, Continental Army officers in Montreal seized supplies from two Indian traders—and thus, indirectly, from Native Americans—and gave them to their own hungry soldiers. Even if money were available, goods remained scarce because Britain's Prohibitory Act, backed by the Royal Navy, banned all trade with the rebellious colonies. Late in the war, Marinus Willett declared that if he had the means and authority, "I would not only furnish [the Indians]" but ensure that "they should be the gayest and finest savages in the wilderness." The Army lacked the resources to heed his advice.[46]

Conversely, Britain could supply most of its Indian allies' needs because royal forces controlled the seas and the Great Lakes. Abundant British goods helped persuade warriors from neutral communities to support George III. Seneca adoptee Mary Jemison recalled that royal agents convinced the Iroquois to fight the rebels by promising them "they should never want for money or goods." British agent to the Choctaws Farquhar Bethune considered gift-giving an essential form of diplomatic communication, remarking that "Liberality is alone with Indians true eloquence without which Demosthenes and Cicero ... might harangue in vain." Fine clothes, firearms, and other gifts demonstrated Britain's wealth and power along with its friendship, helping Great Britain recruit more than 10,000 warriors during the Revolutionary War.[47]

Native Americans had a limited impact on the overall conflict. Indian raids on American settlements did screen Canada from American attack, but on the other hand warriors' attacks on white civilians and their torture and execution of some captives gave the rebels valuable propaganda. Moreover, Indians found it difficult to defend themselves and British forces from rebel attacks. They could not prevent Virginia militia from seizing Kaskaskia and Vincennes, a conquest that cleared the way for a surge of white migration into Kentucky and Tennessee. Nor could they always defend their own towns against American troops.[48]

Ineffective Indian resistance during the Revolutionary War contributed to the cockiness of American officials treating with Native Americans after 1783. So did Americans' belief that the United States, by defeating Britain on the battlefield, had obtained by right of conquest Britain's claims to the West. American officials hoped to impose this narrative of conquest on the Indians, so that their governments could seize Native American lands and sell them to white settlers, who would then incorporate the West into an expanding American empire.[49]

With the arrogance of a Jeffrey Amherst, American treaty commissioners informed Indian leaders that they had lost the war, warned them that further resistance would lead to their annihilation, and demanded that they surrender land as an indemnity. Georgia and New York directed the Creeks and Iroquois to sell their border territories for pittances; North Carolina seized and sold Cherokee lands by fiat; Congress took 30 million acres from the Great Lakes and Ohio Indians. Meanwhile, thousands of white families moved into the Ohio and Tennessee Valleys without waiting for any government's leave.[50]

American settlers and officials had, however, overestimated both their own power and Native Americans' demoralization. Warriors who had fought Americans during the war had done so not as subjects of George III but as his allies, and they refused to share Britain's defeat. After 1783 thousands of warriors began reorganizing their confederacy and denouncing the treaties the United States had forced their chiefs to sign. They then resumed their attacks on white travelers and settlers. By 1786 war had returned to the northern borderland.[51]

The thousands of warriors fighting against American settlers did not consider themselves proxies for European powers. Yet British officers and Spanish officials viewed the confederates as surrogate fighters against American expansion and gave them aid. From the Great Lakes forts, which Britain continued to occupy, garrison commanders and Indian agents gave £100,000 worth of gifts to Great Lakes Indians between 1784 and 1788. Spanish officials went further, signing commercial treaties with the southern Indian nations in 1784. Both empires allowed British and Francophone traders to use their posts as bases for operations within American territory.[52]

During the 1780s, firms like the Miamis Company (a partnership of Detroit merchants trading south of the Great Lakes) and Panton & Leslie (Florida-based Scotsmen with a small empire of stores and traders) sent their employees into Indian communities throughout the western United States. Many of these traders realized that if American farms replaced Indian hunting ranges they would lose their livelihoods, so they encouraged warriors to resist the encroachments of white frontiersmen. Some, like a party of French traders based at Muscle Shoals on the Tennessee River, even helped warriors attack American militia. All provided

Native American communities with ammunition and other supplies, thereby serving as material supporters of Indian resistance.[53]

American officials realized that the United States could not control the Trans-Appalachian region unless it pacified the Indian confederacy and secured the allegiance of neutral Indians. Both enterprises required diplomacy, trade, and money—more money than the moribund Continental Congress could provide. Congress's embarrassing relationship with the southern Indians plainly demonstrated these deficiencies. At the Treaty of Hopewell, federal commissioners promised to send traders to the southeastern Indians, and then Congress failed to follow through. In September 1786 Choctaw leader Franchimastabbe warned that he and his captains would have to swear allegiance to Spain unless American traders came to Choctaw country. A year later, Choctaw and Chickasaw chiefs trekked to Philadelphia to beg for supplies, only to return home with empty promises. Congress, barely able to feed the emissaries, passed a resolution barring uninvited Indian visitors from the capital. If trade and gift-giving were the currency of diplomacy, the United States had become, from the Indians' perspective, politically bankrupt.[54]

WHILE THE CONTINENTAL CONGRESS slowly collapsed, a small but influential group of men sought to restructure the national government of the United States. The reformers, who called themselves Federalists, included some who believed that a stronger union would promote interstate trade and manufacturing, thereby fostering "a dynamic, interdependent continental economy." Others believed that Americans needed a centralized "fiscal-military state" to solve problems left over from the Revolution: a crushing public debt, the lack of respect for the United States in Europe, and the vulnerability of U.S. citizens to invasion or piracy.[55]

Indian affairs interested few Federalists, but after state conventions ratified the Constitution, some influential officers of the new government turned their attention to the frontier. The chief architect of the Federalists' Indian policy was Henry Knox, who headed the War Department under the Continental Congress (1785–89) and President George Washington (1789–94). As civilian commander of the United States' small peacetime army on the Ohio River, Knox had followed the escalating war between white settlers and Indian warriors with great concern. In 1787 he advised Congress to adopt a more proactive policy toward the conflict, arguing that the "reciprocal" nature of hostilities and whites' hunger for land made it difficult to blame Indians for starting the war. Instead, the secretary proposed negotiating new treaties with the Trans-Appalachian Indians, paying for previous land cessions, and giving Indian leaders salaries and gifts to ensure their amity. The U.S. government, Knox believed, should thereafter only go to war with Indians who refused to negotiate.[56]

Secretary Knox pitched his policy to Congress and the president by describing it as the government's most honorable and inexpensive option. Between 1789 and 1791, his proposals began to bear fruit in the Treaties of Fort Harmar, New York, and Holston. The first treaty paid the Great Lakes Indians $6,000 for a previous land cession in the Ohio country and guaranteed them their remaining territory. The second confirmed a 1783 Creek cession to Georgia, for which the nation received a $1,500 annuity (and $1,800 in secret salaries for individuals). The third gave the Cherokees a $1,000 annuity for lands in eastern Tennessee.[57]

The "Knoxonian Plan," as one critic derisively called it, promised to pacify the frontier swiftly and cheaply. Instead it merely made the federal government party to an expanding war. The chiefs who signed the Treaty of Fort Harmar repudiated it, and warriors from non-signatory nations soon resumed their attacks on American farms and flatboats. Responsible now for defending both white settlers and the integrity of a federal treaty, Knox and Washington approved punitive expeditions against the Great Lakes Indian confederacy's towns in 1790 and 1791. Both failed disastrously: Native American warriors inflicted nearly 1,200 casualties on the two expeditions. News of these victories inspired Cherokee and Creek warriors to reject recent treaties and begin their own offensive; in 1792–93 their war parties nearly overran Nashville and Knoxville.[58]

Congress authorized a 5,000-man professional army, which General Anthony Wayne began recruiting and training, and the Washington administration renewed its earlier attempt to resolve the conflict with diplomacy and goods. The president sent emissaries to the Great Lakes Indians with promises of large concessions: $50,000 in cash and gifts, $20,000 in "gratuities," a $10,000 annuity, and the return of some previously ceded land. In the South, the War Department offered $13,000 worth of aid, including 5,000 bushels of corn, to the Creeks after the failure of their 1792 harvest; the following year, agent James Seagrove took to Creek country 300 packhorses laden with gifts, as a token of amity. Southwest Territorial Governor William Blount concurrently sought a new treaty with the Cherokees and promised to increase their annuity.[59]

Seagrove made peace with the Creeks, but Cherokee chiefs could not control the dissident Chickamauga faction, which did not agree to a truce until Tennessee militia destroyed several towns in 1794. As for the Northwest Indians, they rejected the United States' peace overtures and demanded the evacuation of all white settlements north of the Ohio, a concession the U.S. government would not grant. In August 1794, Wayne's army routed Great Lakes Indian warriors at Fallen Timbers (near modern Toledo) and destroyed the confederation's towns, compelling the Lakes Indian nations to sign the Treaty of Greenville (1795) and surrender most of modern Ohio.[60]

Thereafter, the American federal government faced the task of securing the fragile peace that force had created. George Washington had been contemplating that task since the end of the Revolutionary War, and he recognized both its difficulty and gravity. He believed that any lasting peace depended first on confining whites to a limited enclave of settlement, and he and Congress tried to do so by creating territorial governments and a statutory boundary between white and Native American territories. As in the 1760s, these controls proved too weak to restrain settlers determined to acquire land or express their hatred of Native Americans. As new immigrants flooded into Kentucky, Tennessee, Ohio, and central Georgia, intrusion and squatting on Indian land became endemic, and a rash of Indian murders in the Northwest Territory went unpunished as all-white juries refused to convict white assailants. The national government could do little to control white frontiersmen.[61]

That government could, however, increase its control over Indians and remove one of their grievances by promoting trade with them. Washington had long considered commerce the most effective way to bind the disparate peoples of the United States together, and he believed that Indians who traded with Americans would find it harder to make war on them. In 1783 he had proposed that Congress build trading posts with which to supply Indians' wants and secure their allegiance. Congress did not do so, but within a few years the U.S. Army found itself running de facto trading posts on the Ohio River. The army's western regiment built a string of forts from western Pennsylvania to Vincennes in the mid-1780s, to keep squatters off public lands. These undermanned strongholds proved an ineffective military barrier, but Seneca and Wyandot hunters visited them to trade furs for food and gunpowder, and garrison commanders allowed the visits in order to maintain good relations with the local Indians.[62]

The Great Lakes Indian War terminated this limited commerce. Early efforts by the Washington administration to open trade with the southern Indians also failed. In 1790 John Doughty tried to establish a garrisoned trading post for the Chickasaws on the Tennessee River, but Cherokee and Shawnee warriors killed several of Doughty's men and forced him to withdraw. Later that year, the U.S. government secretly offered the Creeks many concessions if they agreed to trade exclusively with the United States. However, Spanish officials forced the treaty's chief signatory, the Creek leader Alexander McGillivray, to renounce it, and the Creeks continued to buy most of their goods from Panton & Leslie.[63]

As the wars of the early 1790s drew to an end, Washington renewed his call for federal Indian factories. In a draft of his 1793 message to Congress, the president asked "Would not a trade on *public* ground, with all the bordering tribes of Indians . . . be an effectual mean of attaching them to us by the strongest of all ties, interest?" Like many of his contemporaries, Washington distrusted private traders, viewing them as men of poor character and bad habits, and in December 1793 he asserted that only the federal government could conduct the enterprise "without fraud, without extortion, with constant and plentiful supplies," and "with a ready market for the commodities of the Indians." These became the founding principles of the factory system.[64]

For the previous seven years Congress had sought to promote and regulate American trade with the Indians by licensing private traders, rather than hiring public ones, and it was reluctant to change course. While a committee endorsed Washington's proposal and recommended a $100,000 appropriation, the House of Representatives rejected a trading house bill in 1795, on the technical grounds that its sponsors submitted it too late in the session. When a revised bill came up for debate in the Fourth Congress, several members opposed involving the national government in a business enterprise, which they believed would lose money. Supporters defended trading houses as a benevolent alternative to war with the Indians and as part of a "system" of frontier controls that included trade, forts, and laws. Not until 1796, however, would they make their strongest argument: the U.S. government needed its own fur-trading operation to counter the influence of British trading companies.[65]

Proponents of the trading houses probably hoped to exploit the Anglophobia of the administration's Democratic-Republican opponents, which recent events had intensified. In 1795 the Democratic-Republicans had publicly protested a new treaty with Britain (Jay's Treaty), whose terms they considered unfavorable to the United States; while the Senate approved the treaty, the opposition party hoped to block its implementation by the House. Among other objectionable provisions, Jay's Treaty allowed Canadian traders to continue operating in the United States, thus supplying future Indian insurgencies with arms and advice.[66]

Moreover, the House had just received a lesson in the insidiousness of British merchants. In 1795 a company of Detroit fur traders and American speculators tried to purchase the entire lower peninsula of Michigan—twenty million acres of land—from the United States and the Ottawas. While the fur traders tried to cozen their Indian trading partners into ceding their lands, the company's American partners went to Philadelphia to bribe congressmen into selling them the American preemption right. In December the House of Representatives arrested the company's agents and interrogated them until they admitted that no one had accepted their bribes. The House's questioning ended just as the factory bill came up for renewed discussion, and the issue of British influence was on House members' minds as they debated. John Swanwick, a Democratic-Republican merchant from Philadelphia who supported the trading house bill and opposed Jay's Treaty, used the recent scandal to underscore the need for Indian factories as a counter to British influence.[67]

On 1 February 1796, 58 House members voted in favor of the factory bill, which the Senate approved with minor changes ten days later. The act authorized the president to open factories at "convenient" locations, created a $150,000 capital stock, and directed the factors to preserve but not increase that capital (i.e., keep revenues equal to expenses). "We have hitherto pursued war at a cost of a million and a half of dollars nearly annually," observed Swanwick, "let us now try the fruits of commerce, that beneficent power which cements and civilizes so many nations."[68]

One should not interpret Swanwick's peroration as either empty rhetoric or unalloyed philanthropy. The structure of the congressman's remark indicates that he intended the trading houses to serve the same function as war, if at lower cost. Trade would make Indians dependent on the United States, thus keeping Britain and Spain out of Native American politics. It would also make the Indians more "civilized" and easier to govern, allowing the United States to absorb them and their lands peacefully. The factories would help complete the process of conquest pursued by Americans since 1783.

The factory program would also tie the new U.S. government more firmly to the North American continent's colonial past, bringing it into an enterprise that had changed little in two centuries. French, British, and American traders still sold the same basic goods to Indian hunters, though their customers now consumed more of them than they had done in the seventeenth century. Independent peddlers and small companies still dominated the retail end of the business, despite chiefs' objections to their often abusive practices and the efforts of officials to control or replace them. Native American leaders still regarded trade as the foundation of good relations between peoples, and the exchange of gifts and merchandise remained an essential component of interethnic diplomacy. While some Indian prophets and white frontiersmen criticized intercultural trade and the dependencies it engendered, neither could end a business that their fellow countrymen considered indispensable.

The American Revolution, which replaced a multiethnic empire with a white-dominated settler republic, might have been the death knell of the North American fur trade and Native American autonomy, had not the War for American Independence scrambled the political map of the continent. Several weak successor states and colonial powers now claimed what had been the territory of a unified British empire. All viewed Native Americans as vital chess pieces in their struggle, recognizing that alliances backed by trade would help keep those pieces on their side of the game. Hence Britain's large expenditures on Indian gifts; hence the parsimonious Federalists' acquiescence in Washington's proposal for Indian factories; hence, too, the endorsement of the factory system by the Democratic-Republicans, who disagreed with the Federalists about the future of the republic but not the realities it faced in its borderlands.[69]

Conquest-by-trade, however, necessarily depended on negotiation, on American officials accommodating the needs and expectations of Indian communities. Public trading houses would presumably draw Indian nations into the American economic and political sphere, but at the same time they would pull the U.S. government into Native Americans' interests and conflicts. They also constituted an institutional assertion that trade was a public enterprise, not a private one. American traders and leaders could tolerate this assertion in the short term but not forever.

2

Local Agendas and National Goals

The goals and function of the factory system began to change the moment it became a material reality rather than the inspired idea of one influential president. As actual structures, the trading houses occupied specific points in space, drawing to them customers from particular regions. They could not function without factors, who had their own foibles, nor without goods to sell or gift, nor without transportation to deliver those goods and export Indians' produce. Finally, the factories needed customers, which meant accommodating Indians' desires for convenient locations, for diplomatic gifts and hospitality, and for credit. Since different Native groups often had competing needs or agendas, factors and officials sometimes also had to decide whom to accommodate. All of these material realities imposed choices on the War Department and its factors. Their choices, and those of their Indian trading partners, determined what the factory system would become.

Choices about credit and factory locations benefited particular groups within Indian nations. The Upper Creeks benefited from the relocation of their nation's factory to Fort Wilkinson, much as the opening of the Fort Wayne factory near the Miami towns gave Little Turtle and his people an advantage. Influential Choctaw and Chickasaw leaders profited from the preferential credit they received at their nations' factories. Native Americans' own choices also determined what kind of business individual factories would see and whether or not they could sustain themselves. Great Lakes Indians living near Detroit had little interest in the U.S. factory there, preferring to deal with British and Francophone traders; the Cherokees saw Tellico as a place to visit and shop and smoke, not as a market for their peltries, which they preferred to sell elsewhere. One might say local conditions proved unfavorable for these two factories, but what actually worked against them was the ability of local Indians to take their business across an international boundary. This was an intentional feature of many early factories. American officials tried to locate trading houses in areas that would be convenient for their Indian customers, but they also built them in contested borderlands to undermine foreign traders' influence. Spanish officials responded to the challenge that the Saint Stephens factory posed to their interests by burdening it with expensive tariffs, while British traders responded to the establishment of the Fort Wayne factory by burning it down.

The founder of the factory system had conceived of it as a sort of pacification machine that would take charge of Indians' commerce and manage it well, thereby persuading Indians not to make war on the United States. Other presidents and officials wanted to make the trading houses into imperial engines that would replace British or Spanish influence with American influence, then use credit and goods to persuade Indian leaders to part with their lands. Native Americans, of course, had different uses for the factories, employing them as sources of gifts they could redistribute to potential clients, and as meeting houses for diplomatic conferences. Few had any interest, however, in seeing the United States become their sole supplier or trading partner. Judging by what actually happened at the first factories during the system's first decade, Native American chiefs, hunters, and women most strongly determined what the factories would become, even if American officials liked to think they set the agenda.

BY THE TIME George Washington signed his trading house bill into law, the first Indian factories had opened in Georgia and Tennessee. A year earlier Congress, as a concession to the president, had approved an experimental factory appropriation. Secretary of War Timothy Pickering had begun purchasing merchandise, appointing factors, and selecting sites by the fall of 1795.[1]

Washington and Pickering decided to build the first trading houses in the South—a curious choice, given factory supporters' preoccupation with British Canadian traders. In his first report on the factories, Pickering explained that he had chosen a region where Indian relations with the United States occupied a median position between dependency and autonomy. The Great Lakes region would not have been suitable for the "experiment" because the war with the Lakes Indians had ended too recently, and they remained distrustful of and disengaged from the United States. The secretary also ruled out factories for the Iroquois because they no longer lived in a frontier zone—white settlers now surrounded their towns—and because their peaceful, dependent relationship with the United States made additional federal controls unnecessary. The South, on the other hand, had a large and sophisticated Indian population with a high aggregate demand for European goods, and southern chiefs had wanted federal trading posts for a decade. Moreover, the Washington administration, whose jurisdiction over the southern frontier had always been tenuous, wanted to increase the U.S. government's influence in the region. Factories adjoined by Army garrisons would improve Indian relations, control disorderly whites, and secure the borderland.[2]

In practice, conditions in the borderland exerted a greater influence on the early factories than vice versa. Creeks and Cherokees obliged the factors to meet their expectations and provide them with hospitality and credit. At the same time, southern frontiersmen pressured the national government to acquire Indian land for them, and all three of the first factories became conference centers where U.S. commissioners sought to fulfill frontiersmen's demands and turn a bilateral frontier zone into an exclusive pale of white settlement.

With only $50,000 to spend on the first trading factories, the War Department limited itself to facilities for the Creek and Cherokee nations, the former at Coleraine on the Saint Marys River, the latter at Tellico on the Little Tennessee. Tellico already hosted an Army blockhouse, built in 1794 to protect the Cherokees from hostile whites. The blockhouse stood near the prominent Cherokee town of Chota, and Territorial Governor William Blount had turned it into a diplomatic center, which hosted a "daily and familiar intercourse" between whites and Cherokees. Blount considered the site an ideal one for a trading house. The War Department agreed, and in 1796 the Tellico factory, a 35-by-20-foot wooden store next to the blockhouse's parade ground, opened for business.[3]

Coleraine had no preexisting federal post, but like Tellico it appeared to occupy a border zone between Indian and white settlements. Creek agent James Seagrove recommended the site because of its proximity to the Atlantic Ocean and the towns of the Seminoles and Lower Creeks, the former about 70 miles away, the latter twice that distance but connected to Coleraine by well-used paths. Pickering believed that a factory and garrison on the Saint Marys River could double as a border control station, allowing the federal government to deter Creeks and white settlers from attacking one another. In the fall of 1795, Pickering sent 160 soldiers to Coleraine and appointed Edward Price of Pennsylvania as the factor for the Creek house. He instructed Price to extend every courtesy to visiting hunters and chiefs, to buy their produce at the prices paid by local traders—though "in this matter the views of the Indians must govern"—and to sell goods at cost plus shipping charges (suggesting a

33 percent markup). The secretary made it clear that Price's job was diplomatic, "to satisfy the Indians," not make a profit.[4]

Like many American frontier diplomats, Price devoted ample space in his correspondence to complaints about the unpleasantness of his job, which commenced in January 1796. The Coleraine factory was a ramshackle 28-by-60-foot wooden enclosure situated in a muddy bog surrounded by pine barrens. The goods that Price received from Philadelphia sometimes arrived damaged or unusable. The soldiers at the post slacked off and fought, and their commander interfered with Price's work by opposing his sale of firearms and by proposing that he move the factory to a more elevated site. Indian visitors to Coleraine expected Price to feed and entertain them and their clients.[5]

Price considered his Creek and Seminole trading partners his most taxing charges. Hunters, chiefs, and women "harassed" him for food, liquor, and presents, and they demanded that the post's blacksmith repair their guns and tools at Price's expense. Southern Indian agent Benjamin Hawkins believed the Indians took advantage of the factor, but the Creeks themselves took a different view: they saw Price not as an easy mark but as one of "Washington's men," a representative of their notional father in Philadelphia, whose role obliged him to extend hospitality to his Indian children. In return, they gave the factor not only their business but their amity, to which they testified by visiting the factory in mixed-gender groups. Creek women usually accompanied hunting and trading expeditions, to process carcasses, sell skins and foodstuffs, and most importantly to indicate the party's peaceful intentions, as all-male groups were usually war parties. Price showed little appreciation for this social gesture, complaining to one correspondent that "I have found a great deal of perplexity with their red majesties and their subjects male and female."[6]

All complaints aside, the Creeks and Seminoles proved eager customers. The factory at Coleraine charged lower prices than did traders in Florida, and Native Americans brought in ample skins, along with beef and cotton, to exchange for the factor's wares. In January 1797, Price shipped over $6,000 worth of furs "and other produce" to Philadelphia, and that spring the factory took in another $3,000 worth of peltries. By June, Price had run out of goods and had to give his Indian customers IOUs, which they sold to nearby merchants.[7]

Price's empty shelves reflected a decision by the War Department to move the Coleraine factory's operations to Fort Wilkinson on the Oconee

River. The move originated in boundary negotiations between American officials and Creek leaders in 1796. The commissioners asked the Creeks to help control their border with Georgia by ceding a reservation for a factory and army post. Upper Creek chiefs suggested a site on the west bank of the Oconee, convenient to their own towns, and the president and the secretary of war accepted their proposal. They may have regarded the new site as a more politically legitimate location for a factory, since its selection resulted from negotiation with Creek leaders. Lower Creeks protested the removal of the Coleraine factory but to no avail. In June 1797 Edward Price closed his store and headed to Fort Wilkinson.[8]

For all of the new site's supposed virtues, Fort Wilkinson had serious defects. More remote from the sea than Coleraine, it cost more to supply, since teamsters had to haul freight by wagon to Augusta and then by boat to Savannah. Fort Wilkinson also stood in a more unsettled borderland, one whose white inhabitants despised both the Creeks and the national government. The Oconee River had become the Creeks' boundary with Georgia in 1790, but since that time white settlers had frequently crossed the border to hunt and to graze their cattle. U.S. officials promised to expel the squatters, and in the spring of 1797 soldiers destroyed illegal settlements west of the Oconee and arrested four whites for poaching. State militia surrounded nearby Fort Fidius and demanded the prisoners' release, and while federal officers dispersed the militia and delivered the men to trial, the incident probably made Army officers in the region edgy and ill tempered.[9]

Factor Price himself frequently ran afoul of those officers during his stay at Fort Wilkinson. He angered the garrison's officers by selling food and whiskey to soldiers, believing that this would compensate for the relocated factory's higher operating expenses. In retaliation for Price's interference the officers began punishing enlisted men who frequented the trading house, and in April 1798 several confronted the factor in his home and threatened to kill him. Price fled to Savannah until the commandant guaranteed his safety. However, Price's successors, Edward Wright and Jonathan Halstead, later revived the grocery business, which suggests that the officers didn't really resent Price's trading—they simply hated him.[10]

Army officers were not Price's only adversaries. Georgia officials had little regard for the factory and its employees, representing as they did a federal government with which the state had a vexed relationship. They frequently harassed the factor and jailed him for debts he had contracted while buying goods. "I hardly ever pass the line to Georgia but what I am arrested," he wrote Secretary of War James McHenry. On one occasion in the summer of 1798, officials confined him below the Hancock County jail in a filthy, poorly ventilated "dungeon of a place." Price died four months after describing this confinement, and it is likely such rough treatment contributed to his death.[11]

The Creek factory survived him and remained productive, though the Creeks put it to uses that Washington and Congress had not anticipated. Creek hunters brought in considerable quantities of furs and skins: between 1796 and 1801, the Georgia-based factors shipped over 177,000 pounds of deerskins, two tons of beaver, and 3,500 other furs to Philadelphia and London. Meanwhile, Southern Indian agent Benjamin Hawkins, hoping to promote commercial agriculture, encouraged Creek women to sell cornmeal, eggs, and cotton at Fort Wilkinson. Though Creek hunters grumbled about the better prices the Cherokees got for their skins at Tellico, and observed that they could buy better merchandise in Pensacola, they still sold over $37,000 worth of peltry and other goods to the Creek factory by 1801.[12]

To its customers, Fort Wilkinson sold calico, strouds, sugar, coffee, iron tools, and gunpowder, the last of which Price called "the very primum mobile of the Indian trade." By 1801 the house reported "flourishing trade" and a net worth gain of $15,740. The official report to Congress obscured some shadier facts. Many of the Fort Wilkinson factory's customers were private traders, to whom Price and Wright sold goods for cash so long as they had obtained a license. The factory's assets included nearly $21,000 in personal debts, which suggests that credit sales comprised as much as one-third of merchandise sales. And two of the most valuable commodities sold at the post were whiskey and brandy, which could account for one-third of the factory's daily sales.[13]

To policy-makers in Philadelphia such practices seemed "subversive of the [factories'] main principle," but they reflected the factors' accommodation to local circumstances and Creek expectations. The white traders who patronized the factory had close ties to the Creeks, living in their towns and frequently marrying Indian wives. In supplying these traders with goods, the factors used them to tie the factory to Creek kinship networks. (They also helped overcome one of their private competitors' advantages: their ability to send traders into Indian towns, rather than make customers come to them.) As for liquor and credit, both were long-established elements of the southern peltry trade, and both had official sanction. Benjamin Hawkins had himself approved the practice of extending credit to trustworthy Indians—"trustworthy," in this case, meaning leading men whose goodwill the federal government needed.[14]

The accumulation of Creek debts at the Fort Wilkinson factory resulted from the factors' accommodation of influential Creek customers. These same debts would also allow the federal government to accommodate white Georgians' demand for Creek land, which the United States had agreed to procure for the state in return for Georgia's large western land claims. In May 1802 Hawkins and other commissioners convened a treaty conference at Fort Wilkinson, and there they endeavored to fulfill the administration's promise. The Creeks came to the conference determined not to surrender land, but after much deliberation they did agree to sell two tracts totaling 3.5 million acres. In exchange the nation received a new annuity, along with $10,000 in cash and goods and $10,000 "to satisfy certain debts due from . . . persons of the Creek country to the factory." The Creek chiefs' willingness to sell so much land signified their acknowledgment that neither they nor the Army could keep white intruders out of their border territories indefinitely. However, the opportunity to extinguish half of the debts some Creeks had accumulated at their factory certainly sweetened the deal. Both as a conference site and a trading house, then, Fort Wilkinson proved a powerful resource for the U.S. government in its dealings with the Creek confederacy, and it was an essential element in the three-way negotiations between Union, state, and Indians for land and power.[15]

SHORTLY AFTER OPENING THE FORT WILKINSON factory, Edward Price wrote the factor at Tellico, James Byers, to suggest exchanging advice on factory management. Byers's store had by then been open for more than a year and enjoyed a steady business with the Cherokees, though this would soon decline. In 1796–97 Byers bought and shipped over 35,000 pounds of deerskins, 7,000 pounds of beaver, and over 18,000 other furs to Philadelphia. In 1798, sales fell off somewhat, probably due to Cherokee hunters' realization that they could sell their peltry in Florida for better prices and then pay cash for the cheaper goods at Tellico. Whatever the reason, after a slight upturn in 1799, the Cherokee factory's peltry shipments resumed their decline.[16]

The French émigré Louis-Philippe, visiting Tellico in 1797, noted that the Cherokees sold more than furs and skins: Cherokee men and women

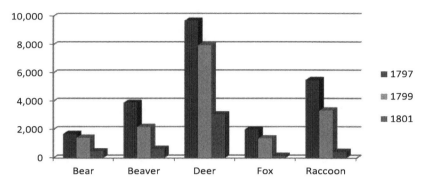

Selected Peltry Shipped from Tellico in 1797, 1799, and 1801. Beaver figures are in pounds. Deerskins represent estimated individual skins, calculated by dividing the total pounds of deerskins shipped by two. Other figures represent individual items. Bearskin shipments for 1797 included 1703 skins and another 1000 pounds of bearskins—probably 50–100 items. Invoices Inward, 1:8, 11–15, 20, 22–25, 31, 36–41, 49–53, 58–60, 64–66 and unpaginated Cherokee factory invoices of 27 Jan., 12 Aug., 14 Oct., and 31 Dec. 1801.

drove cattle to the factory for sale and also sold game, eggs, and fruit to the soldiers who garrisoned the blockhouse. Such sales reflected the Cherokee nation's changing economy: as the profitability of the deerskin trade declined, a growing number of families adopted stock-raising and commercial horticulture to maintain access to the market and the goods on which they had come to rely. They also reflected Benjamin Hawkins's efforts to encourage Native American agriculture by providing the Indians with a market for their produce.[17]

Byers and his successor, John Hooker, shipped the Cherokees' furs and skins to Philadelphia by wagon, a two-month trip, and brought goods to Tellico the same way. Factory invoices and daybooks indicate that local customers preferred to buy textiles, personal ornaments, and farm implements. A July 1797 shipment of new factory goods, presumably ones in which Byers's customers expressed interest, included Irish linen, wooden combs, purple shawls, and several hundred axes, hoes, and cowbells. Additional information on the factory's merchandise comes from archaeological excavations conducted by the University of Tennessee in 1972–73. Researchers on the factory site discovered several dozen French-style gun flints, 107 beads, three silver brooches, four silver earrings, and 177 brass pins. One cannot tell if the Cherokees bought these items in quantity, but the factors clearly kept a supply of each on their shelves.[18]

Tellico did some business with white peddlers, but the low prices Byers charged his Indian customers made the factory unpopular with most private traders. One complained "that Congress was scratching after every bit of a raccoon skin . . . big enough to cover a squaw's ____." The blockhouse also became a lightning rod for Tennesseans who disapproved of the Federalists' conciliatory Indian policy. When interethnic fighting broke out in eastern Tennessee in 1797, some frontiersmen threatened to show their displeasure by attacking the factory.[19]

If some viewed Tellico as a hateful symbol of an unsympathetic national government, the Cherokees continued to see it as a center of diplomacy and negotiation. Cherokee men smoked, gambled, and took their ease at the blockhouse, and the factors extended hospitality to Cherokee chiefs and Chickasaw visitors. The factory also served as a replacement center for damaged annuity goods promised to the Cherokees by treaties.[20]

Federal commissioners viewed the blockhouse as a natural site for conferences, and two were held there in 1797 and 1798. At the former meeting, the Cherokees agreed to help mark the boundary line stipulated in their 1791 land-cession treaty, affirming their consent thereto. At the latter, commissioners purchased from Cherokee chiefs nearly one million acres of land between the Clinch and Holston Rivers. Like Fort Wilkinson, the Tellico factory, which symbolized a frontier of cooperation and trade, now helped accelerate the transformation of that borderland into a zone of white settlement.[21]

USEFUL THOUGH THE Tellico factory had proven to Tennessee settlers, it remained unpopular with frugal legislators. In 1798 Governor John Sevier urged Tennessee's congressmen to oppose renewal of the trading house law, and in early 1800 William Claiborne formed a special committee to investigate the factories. It reported that the factors had kept "irregular" accounts and had probably allowed their capital to diminish. The committee drafted a bill mandating an audit. The Senate delayed consideration of this bill until the next session of Congress.[22]

The House resumed consideration of the trading houses in December. In February 1801 Claiborne's committee reported that while the factories protected Indians from abuse by "private traders," their other uses seemed limited, and Congress ought not to expand them. Other House members were preoccupied with the Electoral College tie between

Thomas Jefferson and Aaron Burr, and it remained for the next Congress to act on Claiborne's report.[23]

The new Congress, and the president who helped set its agenda, took office following a political revolution that appeared to bode ill for the trading houses. The winners of the 1800 elections, the Democratic-Republicans, built their victory on nationwide disgust with the Federalists' expansion of government power, and on the understanding that if elected they would reduce the size of the national government. In 1801–2 the Democratic-Republican–controlled Congress and President Jefferson made good on that promise, reducing federal taxes, cutting back on construction within the new federal capital (Washington), and downsizing the army and navy.[24]

The Indian factories, however, proved an exception to this economizing sweep. In December 1801 Secretary of War Henry Dearborn submitted to Congress a favorable account of the factories' expenditures accompanied by his own approving remarks. The Tellico and Creek trading houses had proven popular with their Indian customers, Dearborn wrote, and had practiced good economy, increasing their capital stock by 3–4 percent while using less than half of their appropriation. The time had come, Dearborn concluded, to make "a much more extensive distribution of the fund" and build factories for other nations whose loyalties (and lands) the United States wanted to secure.[25]

Jefferson and Congress agreed with Dearborn, and in April 1802 Congress reauthorized the trading houses, while Dearborn gained presidential approval to establish four new factories. During Jefferson's presidency the War Department would ultimately open twelve factories, extending the system into the Deep South, the Great Lakes, and the Trans-Mississippi West. Meanwhile, in 1806 Congressional Democratic-Republicans enlarged the factories' capital to $260,000 and appointed a Superintendent of Indian Trade to oversee them. While the Federalists had started the factories, Jefferson and his supporters enlarged the program into a national system.[26]

The Democratic-Republicans expanded the factory program because, while they believed in a limited federal government, they also favored the expansion of American settlements and thought that trading houses could help effect this goal cheaply and peacefully. In 1801 Jefferson told Congress that he looked forward to American farmers settling "the extensive country still remaining vacant within our limits." Title to most of that country, however, belonged to the Indians, and the United States government could not resettle the land without diplomacy, signed treaties, and payment to Native American leaders. (Armed conquest required a larger army than the Jeffersonians wanted to fund.)[27]

Federal trading houses could grease the wheels of land negotiations. Providing chiefs and hunters with inexpensive goods would make American officials "objects of affection to them," while the accumulation of Indian debts at the factories would give chiefs an incentive to sell lands, for "debt[s] . . . when too heavy to be paid they are always willing to lop off by a cession of land." Such had been officials' experience at the Fort Wilkinson conference, and such would presumably be the case for any other Indian nation served by a factory.[28]

The Democratic-Republicans' new factories would serve national goals, but once built they would, like their predecessors in Tennessee and Georgia, serve largely at the pleasure of local actors—hunters, chiefs, traders, officials. The differing fates of Dearborn's first four trading houses demonstrate this point. One factory would close due to its unexpectedly unsuitable location. One became part of a territorial governor's quest for Indian land. Indian leaders would use the other two to improve their own fortunes, in the process glutting the houses with unsalable skins and uncollectable debts. Like many experiments, the second set of Indian factories yielded different results than the experimenters desired.

DETROIT SEEMED an obvious location for an Indian trading post. Situated on the river connecting the upper Great Lakes with the lower, the town had been a center of Indian trade since its founding. Britain had occupied the settlement in 1760, and after the American Revolution British traders turned it into a supply center for the warriors of the Great Lakes Indian confederation. Britain surrendered Detroit to the United States in 1796, but merchants associated with the powerful Northwest Company continued to operate there until the turn of the century, exporting thousands of packs of furs. Shortly before the American flag first flew over the town, local merchants concocted the land speculation and bribery scheme that induced Congress to approve the first Indian factories. It seemed that if the United States government wanted to govern the region's Native American peoples, it would have to control Detroit and its commerce.[29]

Despite its importance, the town probably did not impress factor Robert Munro upon his arrival there in 1802. Though more than a century old, Detroit was still a small, cramped frontier settlement, its streets muddy and labyrinthine, its 500 civilian inhabitants mostly Francophone traders, craftsmen, and farmers. Beyond its borders farms stretched for twenty miles down the Detroit River, while slightly further out stood more than two dozen Ojibwa, Potawatomi, and Wyandot communities. To the south, on the Canadian side of the Detroit River, stood Malden and Fort Amherstburg, where Detroit's British garrison and many of its civilians had moved after the Americans occupied Detroit.[30]

Munro and his assistant, Antoine Peltier, witnessed anemic fur sales at their trading house, a large stone and brick building on the corner of Lernoult and St. James Streets. Between December 1802, when the factory opened for business, and September 1803, when the factor loaded his first shipment of furs onto the brig *Adams*, Indian hunters sold the Detroit house 3,730 muskrat and raccoon pelts, 583 deerskins, and 573 other furs. This was an average of 575 skins per month, an unimpressive figure compared to other factories' returns—Tellico, for instance, took in a monthly average of 1,500 deerskins in 1804. Environmental changes help explain these disappointing fur sales. The game animal population of Michigan had declined in the 1780s, and Ojibwa and Potawatomi hunters now ranged into the upper Mississippi Valley and the country northwest of Lake Superior. Much of what they caught they sold to the voyageurs who followed them, or to British and Francophone traders based at Green Bay and Malden.[31]

Despite a lackluster peltry business, the Detroit house's sales of goods increased from month to month, from $137 worth of merchandise in January 1803 to $790 worth in June 1804. Munro sold his goods cheaply, as the War Department had advised him to add only a 45 percent markup to their Philadelphia prices, while Canadian traders marked up goods as high as 100 percent over Montreal prices. More importantly, the factor readily accepted cash for the merchandise he stocked. Increasingly, his white and Indian customers used the factory as a general store, a source of the imported goods that early nineteenth-century Detroiters craved.[32]

Still, the Detroit factory had not fulfilled its primary purpose: to monopolize the regional fur trade and turn local Indians into American dependents. Only a trading house on the upper Great Lakes could achieve that goal, and in 1805 Dearborn decided to close the Detroit house and open a replacement factory in Chicago. The secretary dismissed Munro that April and ordered the new factor, Ebenezer Belknap, to pick up the Detroit factory's merchandise and records on his way to Lake Michigan. On 11 June, however, the trading house burned in a massive fire that destroyed most of the town. Munro saved most of the factory's wares and records, but both as a physical structure and an institution, the Detroit Indian factory had ceased to exist.[33]

Closing the factory had much to do with its inability to compete with the British, but politics also worked against it. During the factory's period of operation, Michigan came under the jurisdiction of Indiana Territory, to whose officials Detroit mattered little. Detroit residents repeatedly petitioned Congress to create a separate government for Michigan, but they did not achieve their goal until June 1805. They also protested the closure of the factory, but as they lacked connections in Washington they could not change Dearborn's mind.[34]

Conversely, territorial politics help explain why the Fort Wayne factory lasted three times as long as its sister establishment in Detroit. The two trading houses otherwise had much in common. Like Detroit, Fort Wayne occupied a strategic chokepoint: the portage between the Maumee and Wabash Rivers (and thus between Lake Erie and the Ohio River). It stood near the site of an old European trading center and a complex of Miami towns, Kekionga. Anthony Wayne had built the eponymous fort there in 1794, and the War Department made it a distribution center for the Great Lakes Indians' annuities.[35]

Fort Wayne did enjoy one early advantage over the Detroit factory: an important Native American leader helped choose the site. During a visit to Washington in the winter of 1801–2, the Miami captain Little Turtle recommended Fort Wayne as an optimal location for a trading house. The fort stood near several Great Lakes Indian towns, including Little Turtle's own, and would provide them with an alternative to British traders, "who ask very dear for their goods." Secretary Dearborn approved, and he ordered the Indian agent at Fort Wayne, William Wells, to construct a factory building and factor's residence. By the end of 1802 the new factor, John Johnston of Pennsylvania, had ascended the Maumee with the first load of goods for his customers.[36]

Despite Little Turtle's recommendation of the Fort Wayne site, the new factory witnessed lackluster trade during its first years of operation. After a brief flurry of sales in the inaugural month (May 1803), purchases of peltry fell off and remained low until 1806. In 1803 the factory bought a monthly average of 575 skins and furs—just like Detroit—and that average dropped to 135 per month by 1805. Moreover, the factory suffered a big loss shortly before it opened. On 14 April 1803, an Indian set fire to Johnston's house and store, destroying $2,000 worth of goods and furniture. The arsonist confessed that a British trader had put him up to it, and the garrison commander arrested both men, but after the Indian prisoner's kinsmen requested his release, Territorial Governor William Henry Harrison pardoned him and the trader. Harrison believed that the diplomatic benefits of pardoning the men outweighed the damage done to the factory. The young governor avidly promoted white settlement and the purchase of Native American land, and for this purpose he needed good relations with Indian leaders. The Fort Wayne factory he found useful to the extent it improved those relations.[37]

Harrison's land program required frequent treaty councils and annuity payments, which the Fort Wayne trading house facilitated. Between 1803 and 1805, the governor negotiated eight treaties with leaders of southern Great Lakes Indian nations and procured from them half of the future state of Illinois and much of southern Indiana. In return, the signatories received several thousand dollars' worth of annuities, paid primarily in goods—for which Johnston's factory served as a convenient repository. Fort Wayne also hosted Harrison's first treaty council with the Delawares, Potawatomis, and Shawnees, at which Factor Johnston served as an official witness.[38]

Johnston further ingratiated himself with Harrison by serving as the governor's confidant during a dispute with the Miamis and their agent, William Wells. In 1805 chiefs from several towns in northern Indiana denounced as illegitimate land cessions that Delawares had made the previous year. Johnston identified Little Turtle and Little Turtle's son-in-law, Agent Wells, as the principal opponents of the cession, insinuating that both men objected because they had not shared in the proceeds. Harrison did sign another treaty with the objecting nations, paying them $4,000 to quiet their claims, but he also accepted Johnston's interpretation of the causes of the dispute. Thereafter Johnston served as Harrison's eyes and ears at Fort Wayne. He and his factory gained the patronage and protection of a powerful, well-connected official.[39]

While promoting Governor Harrison's land negotiations, the Fort Wayne trading house also served as a bulwark against British influence. Jay's Treaty allowed British traders to operate on U.S. soil, and five of them were in business at Fort Wayne when Johnston arrived there. All took pains to denigrate the factory and draw Indians' attention to their own competitive advantages, like their better quality goods and their knowledge of Native languages. At least one decided to treat the factory as an enemy outpost in his territory, hiring an Indian to torch it. Factor

Johnston and his superiors gladly accepted the traders' summons to commercial combat. Harrison and Dearborn had not done so in the case of Detroit because that town still stood within Britain's economic and political sphere. To put it another way, the Fort Wayne factory stood as an advanced outpost of American influence, while Detroit factory had been an unsuccessful foray into enemy territory.[40]

Secretary Dearborn thus defended the Fort Wayne trading house when principal factory agent William Davy suggested shuttering it and moving its assets to Mackinac. The secretary found the proposal "[in]expedient," as Mackinac was too remote and the closures would oblige the Miamis and Potawatomis to rely on foreign traders. "All circumstances considered," he wrote, "I think we ought to make a further experiment at Fort Wayne." Dearborn left unspoken his assumption that the Fort Wayne factory could compete with the British, where Detroit could not.[41]

Meanwhile, Johnston monitored the mounting woes of British traders, including the Northwest Company. In 1800 the company had nearly 200 traders working in the United States, but their fortunes suffered a blow when Britain and France returned to war in 1803. Skyrocketing shipping costs and the collapse of the luxury trade in Europe dropped the bottom out of the Montreal fur market. By 1806 Johnston could report that his competitors were on the ropes: Canadian traders had gone deeply into debt, private competition forced them to lower their merchandise prices, and the depression of British markets kept them from paying their bills. "Many of them are on the eve of bankruptcy and will be unable to prosecute the trade much longer," the factor predicted.[42]

As his rivals dropped out, Johnston observed an increase in peltry sales to his factory. Fur sales averaged 487 per month during the second half of 1806; in 1807 Johnston bought a record 1,400 deerskins; and between March and May of 1808, the factory shipped over $11,000 worth of peltry, including a staggering 26,839 raccoon skins. (Raccoons thrived in the southern Great Lakes region, and the dark, thick pelts of those in Indiana were particularly valuable.) The Fort Wayne house had become, as Andrew Cayton put it, "the most successful American Indian factory in the Old Northwest." The transformation could not have occurred, however, without the patience and patronage of policy-makers.[43]

DOMINATING THE FUR TRADE of the Great Lakes had been a long-standing goal of the U.S. government. Participating in the deerskin trade with the Choctaws and Chickasaws had been one of its long-standing promises. Congress had agreed to open trading houses for the two nations in 1786, but aside from an abortive attempt to build a post for the Chickasaws, the government failed to honor its pledge for nearly twenty years. The nations lived far from American settlements and the federal government tended to ignore its remoter subjects, who lived outside of its zone of political control.[44]

The United States' attitude began to change after 1795, when Pinckney's Treaty gave Americans access to the Mississippi River and the U.S. government a strip of territory comprising parts of future Mississippi and Alabama. American troops occupied the old Spanish posts at Chickasaw Bluffs and Natchez, and Congress and President John Adams created a government for Mississippi Territory. The administration now needed the goodwill of the Chickasaws and Choctaws, both to protect white settlements that had come under federal jurisdiction and to obtain Native permission for a road from Nashville to Natchez. This gave the War Department incentives to make new treaties with the two nations and to build factories for them.[45]

Chickasaw Bluffs was a logical site for one factory, as the bluffs had hosted a European trading post for several years. In 1795 Spanish troops occupied the site and erected Fort San Fernando de Las Barrancas, part of an effort to assert Spanish control over the upper Mississippi River. Panton & Leslie opened a trading post nearby, which remained open until 1799. Building an American factory at Chickasaw Bluffs would help convert a former Spanish zone of influence into an American one.[46]

In 1802 Secretary Dearborn appointed Thomas Peterkin the factor at Chickasaw Bluffs and sent him there with several thousand dollars' worth of goods. Records are sparse for the next few years, but apparently the Chickasaw factory enjoyed a high volume of business from the start. Between January and March 1804, Peterkin shipped peltry valued at $6,500, which included more than 20,000 pounds of deerskins, most likely from the Chickasaws' hunting range in Arkansas. Business grew apace, and by 1807 the factor and his assistant were shipping about $8,000 worth of peltry per annum, including 35,000 pounds of deer.[47]

Indians trading at Chickasaw Bluffs took some of their pay in cash, but most swapped their furs for goods, particularly ammunition, tableware, and textiles. Factor Peterkin kept his prices relatively low. At Peterkin's factory in 1806, one dollar would buy one pound of gunpowder, two yards of calico or muslin, four broaches, or two large tin cups. Indian hunters could make that dollar by selling four pounds of deerskins, one pound of beaver, or four raccoon skins. This was approximately 2–4 percent of a skilled hunter's seasonal catch, meaning he and the female relatives who assisted him earned $25–50 per season.[48]

Since returns for hunters' labor remained low, the Chickasaws' demand for goods outstripped their ability to pay, and they began to buy on credit. The Chickasaws were no strangers to debt: in the 1780s and 90s they had accumulated over $11,000 in debts to Panton & Leslie, and in the following decade they ran up a collective tab of $5,000 at the Chickasaw Bluffs factory.[49]

Peterkin's superiors might have broached the subject of selling land to pay factory debts, but the Chickasaws had just sold a swath of territory to pay a much larger private debt, and the U.S. government derived little advantage from the deal. Between 1803 and 1805 the United States had bought up the $200,000 in debt that the southeastern Indians owed John Forbes & Company (Panton & Leslie's successors), and then pressed those nations to pay their debts with land. In the Chickasaws' case, commissioners asked for a large cession on the Mississippi River, but Chickasaw leaders only agreed to cede a 345,000-acre tract on the Cumberland and Tennessee Rivers. In return the Chickasaws received $20,000, most of which went to pay the nation's "heavy debts . . . to their merchants and traders." Another $1,000 went to a Chickasaw leader whom the commissioners had tried to co-opt: George Colbert.[50]

George Colbert and his brothers belonged to a Chickasaw family that favored closer ties with the United States and that was becoming one of the region's greatest beneficiaries of federal Indian policy. Federal officials hoped to turn the Colberts into American clients, but ultimately the family profited more from the relationship than did the government. In October 1801 George and his brother William helped conclude the Treaty of Chickasaw Bluffs, which opened the Natchez Trace through Chickasaw country but reserved to the Chickasaws the right to build inns and ferries on the route. The Colbert brothers then used this right to open two profitable inns and a ferry on the trail. George later agreed to serve as the United States' point man in the 1805 treaty negotiations, but he wound up securing for the Americans less land than they wanted at a higher price than they usually paid—and snagging a large gratuity in the bargain.[51]

In the meantime, the Colberts used the Chickasaw Bluffs factory to dispose of pelts and obtain cheap goods on credit. By 1807, members of the Colbert family accounted for one-third of all debts owed the trading house. The Colberts in turn almost certainly resold or gifted much of the merchandise they bought, thereby increasing their wealth and influence. The redistribution of goods had long been a means of accumulating or maintaining prestige in Native American communities; generosity established a bond of solidarity between leaders and followers, while affirming the unequal status of the two. The merchandise that the Colberts did not gift they probably resold on credit, creating a bond of dependence that lasted until the debtor chose to liquidate it.[52]

The War Department wanted the Chickasaw trading house to serve, like its sister factories, as an outpost of empire and a source of American influence. Five years after its founding, the factory had bought thousands of deerskins and extended ample credit but had not increased the U.S. government's sway over the Chickasaws or the region. Its primary consequence had been to increase the influence of one family, rather than that of their "father" in Washington.

OF THE FOUR FACTORIES authorized by Henry Dearborn in 1802, the Choctaw trading house at Fort Saint Stephens enjoyed the highest volume of business and the most support from its Indian clients. The Choctaws had desired a factory for years, and in 1801 Mingo Hoomastubbe and Edmond Folsom proposed that the U.S. government build one on the Tombigbee River, near several newly established Choctaw towns. After further discussion Dearborn and Mississippi Territorial Governor William Claiborne selected as the factory site the old Spanish fort at Saint Stephens, on a bluff the Choctaws called Hoebuckintoopa. The Choctaws' first factor, Joseph Chambers, arrived at Saint Stephens in April 1803 and opened his store for business one month later.[53]

Within a few years Saint Stephens's trading volume rivaled Fort Wilkinson's. In early 1807 George Gaines, Chambers's successor as factor, shipped 27,000 pounds of deerskins and 1,300 other furs, collectively worth $6,650 and comprising most of the factory's purchases for the previous year, to Philadelphia. The Choctaw factory concurrently imported a huge quantity of goods for its trading partners: over $38,000 worth between 1803 and 1805. These included the usual staples of the southern Indian trade as well as sewing supplies, hoes, and cowbells, which reflected the Choctaws' shift from a subsistence economy to one based on stock-raising and home manufacturing.[54]

Commercial hunting still represented an important part of the nation's livelihood, and the Saint Stephens factory helped a few seasoned hunters and captains concentrate economic power in their own hands. Daybooks from October 1807 indicate that a handful of men, like Tisko Hollata and William Jones, dominated the sale of skins to and the purchase of goods from the trading house. In particular, Mingo Hoomastubbe, a prominent Choctaw captain, sold $733 worth of pelts, including nearly 3,600 pounds of deerskins, and purchased $1,463 in merchandise, including more than half a ton of lead and powder. Hoomastubbe, clearly, acted as a middleman for his family and followers.[55]

The record of debts due the factory helps explain why ordinary Choctaws allowed their captains to bargain and buy for them: Chambers and Gaines regarded some Indians as more credit-worthy than others. Five men, including the three mentioned above, accounted for 87 percent of the credit the factors extended. In this respect, the factors followed the same rule as traders in Arkansas, where the Choctaws did much of their hunting: give credit to "honest and active person[s]" who would outfit hunting parties and sell their catch.[56]

While the Saint Stephens factory enriched some Choctaw leaders, it proved less useful to the federal government, at least during its first years in operation. The Jefferson administration's goal in dealing with the Choctaws was to acquire the nation's old hunting ranges, particularly the lands fronting the Mississippi River. To this end, federal commissioners held four treaties with the Choctaws in as many years (1801–5), purchasing from them several million acres of land. The factory facilitated these negotiations indirectly, providing commissioners with a nearby store of gifts and a friendly setting for one treaty council (the 1803 Treaty of Hoebuckintoopa). However, the factory's growing pool of Choctaw debts played no part in the commissioners' bargaining, because federal officials decided instead to use the Choctaws' private debts as leverage.[57]

By the 1805 Treaty of Mount Dexter, Choctaw leaders had ceded to the United States four million acres of land, receiving in exchange a $3,000 annuity and payment of their nation's $46,000 debt to John Forbes & Company. The treaty proved disappointing to the administration, which had wanted the Choctaws' Mississippi Valley lands. President Jefferson did not submit the expensive accord to the Senate for two years, and the War Department did not seek additional Choctaw land for another decade, during which time the Choctaw factory continued to accumulate unrecoverable debts and unmarketable deerskins.[58]

There was one other respect in which the Saint Stephens factory could facilitate American expansion: the trading post and garrison created a federal presence in the fertile Tombigbee-Alabama Valley. Much of this river system lay within the boundaries of the United States, but Spain controlled the port of Mobile and through it the rivers' outflow to the Gulf of Mexico. In 1802 William Claiborne and James Wilkinson began petitioning Spanish officials for duty-free access to Mobile, arguing that Spanish tolls imposed an unfair burden on Saint Stephens. Lifting the duties, Claiborne insisted, would benefit Spain, for the factory increased American "influence . . . in the Choctaw councils" and helped the U.S. government promote peaceful relations between the Choctaws and Spanish.[59]

Intendant Juan Morales and West Florida Governor Vicente Folch did not accept this argument. They believed that unobstructed American access to Mobile would draw a swarm of American farmers to the Tombigbee Valley, and that the U.S. government could not prevent these settlers from invading Florida. The officials insisted that Americans shipping pelts and supplies to and from Saint Stephens stop in Mobile and pay a 12 percent duty. Neither Chambers nor any other American official had an effective response to this demand. In 1805–6 President Jefferson attempted to cozen the Spanish government into selling Mobile to the United States, but the negotiations fell through and the Democratic-Republicans decided not to risk war with Spain. For the foreseeable future, customs duties would comprise a significant expense for the Choctaw factory, a cost of the government's expansion into a contested borderland.[60]

ADAPTABILITY IS OFTEN the key to an institution's survival, particularly a public institution that must serve many different groups and agendas. The U.S. Indian factories experienced their share of difficulties during their first decade: deteriorating sales at Tellico, minimal business at Detroit, punitively high customs duties at Saint Stephens, civil-military disputes at Fort Wilkinson, arson at Fort Wayne. The system survived these trials, however, and even prospered, insofar as both the number and funding of the factories grew dramatically.

To a great extent, the trading houses owed their survival to factors' and officials' ability to accommodate local interests, particularly those of local Indians. Factors ingratiated themselves with Native American communities by keeping merchandise prices low, extending hospitality to visitors, and moving some factories to more convenient locations. They also helped advance the agendas of particularly favored local groups: southern Indian chiefs, to whom they extended most of their credit; American traders, whom some factors supplied with merchandise; and expansionist state and territorial officials, on whose behalf they helped host treaty conferences that resulted in Indian land cessions.

The factories were not merely local institutions, of course. Their personnel and funding came from the American national government, and unless the trading houses served that government's changing agendas their doors would close. The factories passed this test of survival after the "Revolution of 1800," when a new president and Congress with new priorities took office. Under Washington and the Federalists, the first trading houses had been minor adjuncts to Indian diplomacy and supplemental guarantors of peace in the borderlands. Under the Democratic-Republicans, they could assume a larger role as engines of American expansion. In the nineteenth century they would extend American influence, trade, and settlement into a frontier zone that was about to become much larger and even more tenuous.

3

Like So Many Armies

The Mississippi River formed the United States' western political boundary before 1803, and even after that year's Louisiana Purchase it constituted an intellectual veil beyond which American officials' knowledge did not extend. Ignorance of conditions in the western Mississippi Valley governed the War Department's initial choices about where to site the region's Indian factories, usually in older French trading towns near the river, and which to endow with the most resources. For the Native peoples of the Mississippi Valley, however, and for the private traders who worked with them, the river was neither a boundary nor a veil, merely a useful feature of the landscape. Some of the Indians who traded with the factories in Missouri and Arkansas, in fact, came from eastern Indian nations that also patronized the trading houses in Indiana and Mississippi, and most of the traders who competed with the Arkansas factory came from the east. The Trans-Mississippi West comprised the same kind of geopolitical domain as the Trans-Appalachian West: a region dominated by Indian communities and nations over which the American empire sought to extend its influence and authority. A borderland, in short.

Choices that factors and officials made in the Louisiana Territory resembled those their counterparts made in the east. Factories would have to shut down when overwhelmed by private competition, as Detroit had done and Arkansas would do. They would find themselves too far from Native American towns, like Coleraine (in the Upper Creeks' opinion, at least) or Bellefontaine, and have to move. They would do business in the commercial sphere of another empire and incur significant added costs from this "forward" position, such as those that the Saint Stephens factory and the Natchitoches trading house experienced. As in the east, moreover, accommodation remained more important for the factors than profits. They bought pelts they couldn't sell, accepted handicrafts for which there was little market but which their donors considered gifts, resolved disputes between their Indian trading partners, and gave presents to visitors.

The key difference between these factories and their predecessors was geopolitical: there were no American institutions in the Louisiana Territory before 1803, so the trading houses became important markers and manifestations of the new American frontier zone. Choices about their location, relocation, and maintenance became choices about where that frontier would stand and where American influence would spread. American officials made those choices, as before, in halting and intermittent dialogue with the peoples of the new borderland—with the Indian communities whom the factors served and the private traders with whom they competed.

IN 1800 THE VAST range of prairie, plain, and desert between the Mississippi and the Rockies, though ostensibly administered by Spain, actually belonged to several dozen Indian nations, to the Caddos and Osages and Sauks and others. In January 1803 President Jefferson suggested that American fur traders displaced by the Indian factories might profitably work in the Trans-Mississippi region. He asked Congress to send a discreet reconnaissance mission up the Missouri River to acquire commercial intelligence, more for the benefit of traders than as a prelude to territorial expansion.[1]

News that Spain had in 1800 ceded Louisiana (or its claim thereto) to France jolted American policy-makers. The Louisiana Purchase, whereby France sold the United States that vast province for $18 million, surprised American officials just as much. Robert Livingston and James Monroe had dramatically exceeded their mandate to purchase New Orleans, and their superiors did not know what to do with the massive new territory. While land developers celebrated the opportunities they expected Louisiana to bring, federal officials scrambled to gain intelligence about the new domain and secure those parts of it closest to the old Union.[2]

Between 1804 and 1806, Congress, the War Department, and the president extended the apparatus of American empire into a region that had always been Indian country, first and foremost, with little bureaucratic government. They sent four exploratory expeditions—the Corps of Discovery under Meriwether Lewis and William Clark being the most famous—to survey the new territory and contact its Indian peoples. Congress drafted territorial governments, the president appointed officials, and the Secretary of War garrisoned New Orleans and other strategic points. And, by the end of 1805, the War Department had opened three new Indian trading houses west of the Mississippi: at Bellefontaine on the Missouri River, Arkansas Post on the Arkansas, and Natchitoches on the Red.[3]

The story of these trading houses reveals the depth of the federal government's ignorance of demographic and economic conditions in its accidental empire. The War Department built its new factories at old European communities, rather than sites convenient to the Indians who dominated the Plains peltry trade. Consequently the factors stationed there could not compete with private traders willing to travel to their Indian partners. Territorial Governor James Wilkinson made a ham-fisted attempt to halt private trading on the Missouri and Arkansas Rivers, but in the face of Native American protests federal officials had to relent. Ultimately, the War Department shuttered two of its first three Trans-Mississippi factories, retaining only the post at Natchitoches, which ran a large loss. It took several years before the Secretary of War and the superintendents of Indian trade adjusted to new information on western Indian trading patterns and replaced one of the closed factories with more successful posts closer to Sauk and Osage towns. The Louisiana Territory remained Indian country, and the national government had to adapt to the patterns and protocols of its fur trade if it wanted to establish a presence there. To create an empire was far from an automatic process.[4]

Secretary of War Henry Dearborn selected Saint Louis as the site of the largest Trans-Mississippi factory almost automatically. Founded in 1764 by French fur traders, the town had become the commercial and administrative center of upper Louisiana under Spanish rule, and it commanded Indian trade on the Missouri and upper Mississippi Rivers. Moreover, in November 1804 William Harrison had negotiated a treaty with the Sauk and Mesquakie (or Fox) Indians, in which Quashquame and other chiefs exchanged 55 million acres of land for an annuity and a federal trading post. As these nations would receive their annuities at Saint Louis, it made administrative sense to build their factory there.[5]

In the spring of 1805 Dearborn advised James Wilkinson, the territorial governor, to build the new trading house on the lower Missouri River, outside of Saint Louis. Wilkinson chose a site twelve miles from town that featured ample timber and a large spring, the latter of which gave the factory its name, Bellefontaine. By year's end Wilkinson's soldiers had finished the storehouse and factor's residence, both log structures with planked floors and glass-paned windows. By December the factor, Rudolph Tillier, and his assistant, George Sibley, had arrived at the cantonment; several months later their goods followed. These comprised the largest quantity of merchandise yet delivered to any of the trading houses, almost $40,000 worth of wares. In December 1806, Tillier reported that the factory still had nearly $30,000 worth of inventory—hardware and tinware, crockery and saddlery, and nearly $10,000 worth of blankets. Most of it would sit there unsold for two more years.[6]

Like its predecessors in the east, Bellefontaine factory served throughout its short lifespan as an adjunct to federal Indian diplomacy or, more specifically, as a warehouse for gifts and annuity goods and a stopping point for Indian travelers. In 1806 the factory issued over $5,700 worth of presents and annuities at the request of the War Department or Governor Wilkinson. Tillier and Sibley also gave $200 worth of gifts to Quashquame, sent supplies to the Osages, and issued clothing to the Mandan chief Sheheke, who visited while traveling to Washington with Lewis and Clark.[7]

Regular trade at Bellefontaine, however, proved slow and improved very slowly. At the end of 1806, Factor Tillier reported that the factory had disposed of $8,400 worth of goods, but he also observed that sales to Indians, whether for pelts, cash, or credit, accounted for only 13 percent of this amount. Most (68 percent) of the rest of the year's merchandise sales he credited to the War Department as gifts and annuities. A September 1807 account of factory debts told a similar story: of $1,446 in outstanding debts, white soldiers, merchants, and officials owed $1,026 (71 percent), and Native Americans only $420.[8]

The goods that Indians and white traders sold the factory would probably not turn a profit in New Orleans or Philadelphia. Many of Tillier's regular customers were local farmers, and many of these were Delawares and Kickapoos who had settled in Missouri in the 1770s and 80s. They sold the factory a large quantity of "frontier-exchange" products: value-added items for which there was only local demand and which arguably functioned more as gifts than marketable commodities. These included wooden bowls and boards, woven baskets, and honey. Other, more salable goods included lead from the Sauks' mines in Illinois, locally grown tobacco, and tallow. In late 1807 traders also brought down a few buffalo hides and robes from the upper Missouri.[9]

Bellefontaine was poorly situated, however, to tap the rich peltry trade of the Missouri and upper Mississippi Valleys. Since the mid-1700s the Osages, a nation with over 1,000 mounted warriors, had dominated commerce on the lower Missouri River, and they preferred doing business with French traders willing to bring their wares to Osage towns. By the 1790s the Chouteau family had secured a near monopoly of the Osage trade, which they continued to dominate after the Americans occupied Saint Louis. Meanwhile, the Sauks and Mesquakies preferred to trade at Prairie du Chien with British merchants, who offered brandy (which federal law prohibited Tillier from selling) and ample credit (which Tillier issued grudgingly). After the war in Europe disrupted their British trading partners' supplies, Sauk and Mesquakie hunters complained that the Bellefontaine factory stood too far from their towns, a complaint the U.S. government could not safely ignore.[10]

As Tillier and other officials began to realize Bellefontaine's limitations, they compensated by sending factory goods out or bringing remote Indians in. During the factory's last year, the factor gave goods to Indian agent Maurice Blondeau, to trade with Sauk and Mesquakie communities in northern Illinois, and he did over $1,000 worth of business with a party of Ottawas and Sioux whom trader Louis Dorion brought to Bellefontaine. By then, however, Secretary Dearborn and Superintendent John Mason had concluded that Bellefontaine's location made it an impractical site for Indian trade and an inconvenient one for diplomacy. In April 1808 Dearborn decided to replace the flagging trading house with new posts on the Osage and Des Moines Rivers, which would split Bellefontaine's remaining inventory. William Clark agreed to serve as the new factories' agent in Saint Louis, responsible for forwarding peltry and manufactured goods.[11]

Rudolph Tillier would not serve as factor at either of the new houses. Officials acquainted with him praised the New Yorker's character and refinement but described him as "subject to gusts of passions and splenetic humors," one of which had caused him to fire his assistant, George Sibley, after a dispute over custody of the factory's books. Superintendent John Mason excused the factor's action, but rather than risk more altercations he allowed Tillier's commission to expire with his post. Tillier retired, and his abandoned factory rotted away; by 1819 floods had destroyed the remaining buildings.[12]

THE FIRST U.S. FACTORY in Arkansas, which opened the same year as Bellefontaine, suffered from many of the same disadvantages as its Missouri Valley counterpart. Its base community, Arkansas Post, was a 120-year-old French and Spanish settlement near the mouth of the

Arkansas River. Once the primary interethnic trading site in the Arkansas Valley, the town had seen its role change with the region's Indian population. As the Quapaws, whose towns stood only a dozen miles from Arkansas Post, declined in numbers, immigrants from larger Indian nations—Cherokees, Chickasaws, Delawares, and Osages—took over their hunting ranges and the Arkansas peltry business.[13]

White traders followed the newcomers into Arkansas to provide them with goods and credit. Arkansas Post changed from a fur-trading village into an outfitting center for trading expeditions up the Arkansas and White Rivers. By the time John Treat arrived to open the federal factory, the town harbored about a dozen independent and Detroit-based traders, along with Bright & Morgan, a well-financed firm with connections in New Orleans and Philadelphia. The company's founder, Jacob Bright, had previously operated a trading post at Chickasaw Bluffs, but he had left in 1804 and (unwittingly following Jefferson's plan) moved across the Mississippi to Arkansas. Neither Bright nor his partner, the banker Benjamin Morgan, intended to move again. By 1805 they had invested $25,000 in the Arkansas trade, a sum Treat could not afford to spend.[14]

In this competitive environment, the factor and his assistant struggled to attract regular trading partners. During his first year of operations, John Treat obtained permission from his superintendents to extend credit to Native American hunters and to sell goods that local Indians didn't want, like red-striped duffels, to white farmers. He built a cabin to accommodate Indian visitors "during the winter season," and he sold some items at a loss to attract customers. By April 1806 Treat had bought and shipped 61 packs of skins and furs, though private traders enjoyed an even better season—Bright & Morgan shipped 267 packs of deerskins and 1,500 pounds of beaver pelts to New Orleans. The U.S. factory was only the fourth-largest exporter of peltries from Arkansas Post that spring.[15]

Treat's business fluctuated over the next two years. In 1807 the factor purchased 13,400 pounds of deerskins from his trading partners, who included Choctaw and Delaware hunters and Cherokee emigrants, most of whom "prefer[red] . . . the factory" to its competitors. John Treat further enlarged his customer base by ordering his assistant, Joseph Waterman, to open a temporary post at the confluence of the White and Black Rivers. While Waterman made several hundred dollars' profit, Superintendent John Shee upbraided Treat for opening a subfactory without his permission, and the factor did not repeat the attempt. The next year

(1808) proved disappointing, as a hard winter deprived hunters of their catch and as traders from the new Mackinac Company moved into Arkansas with ample brandy and credit; Treat returned less than 4,000 pounds of deerskins to New Orleans that year. In total, the Arkansas factory purchased 34,000 pounds of deerskins during its first three years, compared with 53,000 pounds purchased by the Natchitoches factory.[16]

More problematically, Treat was proving a poor trader and skin handler. The factor diligently reported on local economic conditions, and he successfully mediated a dispute between Quapaws and Chickasaws in 1807. However, some of the basic details of running a fur-trading business lay beyond his competence. His customers sold him many poorly cleaned furs and skins, "loaded with flesh, pates, shanks, and . . . hoofs," which increased their susceptibility to rot. Treat often failed to preserve or pack his pelts properly, and they arrived at New Orleans or Philadelphia clotted with dirt or eaten by worms. Those that arrived in good condition proved difficult to sell, as private traders had glutted the domestic market and as the federal embargo had cut off American access to foreign markets. Superintendent Shee noted in 1807 that raccoon skins sold in Philadelphia for a penny and deerskins for 2.5 cents per pound. Such meager returns could not long justify the expense (sometimes over $1,000 per consignment) of supplying the remote factory.[17]

In 1809, despite an uptick in business, Superintendent John Mason warned that the trading house still could not support itself financially. A year later he closed the Arkansas establishment and moved its merchandise and its acting factor, Samuel Treat, to Chickasaw Bluffs. This inadvertently fulfilled Jefferson's 1803 prediction that federal factories would dominate the east bank of the Mississippi River, and that the private traders they displaced would control the fur trade to the west.[18]

It is unlikely that Arkansas Post's deficit convinced Mason to shutter the trading house, since other factories ran losses at the same time. The factory simply lacked political importance compared to other houses, because in the minds of federal officials the entire region between the Missouri and Red Rivers was marginal. Few white settlers lived in the Arkansas Valley, and the local Indian nations posed no threat to the United States. The Chickasaws, Choctaws, and Cherokees were already U.S. allies, the Quapaws were too few in numbers (only 550 men, women, and children), and private American traders had firmly bound the Arkansas Osages to the United States' interest.[19]

The Jefferson administration thus committed few resources to defending and administering the Arkansas country. Apart from the tiny Army garrison and rare visits by officials from Saint Louis, John Treat and James Waterman were the only federal employees in the Arkansas Valley. The assets of the Arkansas trading house reflected the district's low priority: at the end of 1809 it had only $7,400 worth of property, making it the eighth-largest of ten factories in operation.[20]

Absent significant federal intervention, private traders would inevitably control the peltry trade of the Arkansas Valley. The factory could not supply all of the region's Indians, the local garrison was too small to enforce federal trade restrictions, and there was no superintending official able to create an orderly and consistent trading policy. Territorial Governor James Wilkinson closed the Arkansas River to private commerce in 1805, but almost immediately thereafter he gave a two-year license to Bright & Morgan, probably expecting that the factory would thereafter become the local trading monopoly. John Treat then undercut Wilkinson's policy by issuing temporary licenses to Arkansas Post traders, who told him they needed to continue trading to recover past debts. Governor Meriwether Lewis further muddied the waters by licensing Saint Louis traders to operate in Arkansas, a measure that he took without consulting Treat, and that according to Lewis's secretary produced "derangement and confusion." He might as accurately have reported that, from the standpoint of Indian traders, the Arkansas region retained its old status as a contested borderland, and that the U.S. government had withdrawn from the contest.[21]

THE FEDERAL RETREAT from the Arkansas Valley coincided with the concentration of federal resources in the southernmost part of Louisiana, the Territory of Orleans. Orleans Territory had the largest non-Indian population in Louisiana—over 40,000 white and black inhabitants—a rich commercial economy based on sugar and cotton, and one of the continent's most important cities. It was also one of the most exposed provinces of the American empire, flanked by Spanish Texas and Florida and vulnerable to British attack from the sea. Initially the War Department sent 600 infantry to garrison the territory, to which Secretary William Eustis added another 2,000 in 1809. Meanwhile, the federal civil administration in Orleans Territory—legislators, judges, customs collectors—constituted the largest American civil establishment west of the Mississippi River.[22]

The Indian factory in Orleans Territory shared the district's importance. The War Department established the trading house in the 90-year-old French village of Natchitoches, the United States' extreme southwestern outpost, perched beside a neutral zone that the United States and Spain created between their territories in 1806. It was also the home of Doctor John Sibley, an American who had fled there ahead of his creditors, become the U.S. government's agent in the Red River Valley, and convinced Secretary Dearborn to open a local trading house. Serving as a conduit for furs, horses, and information, the new factory would help Sibley extend the United States' influence into Texas, the northeastern borderland of New Spain.[23]

In practice, most of the Natchitoches house's customers came from the American side of the border. Factor Thomas Linnard did not record the names and affiliations of all of his Native American trading partners, but of the eighteen he did list in his daybooks, Linnard identified ten as Choctaws, Chickasaws, and Creeks, two as Caddos, and one as a Pascagoula. Members of the first three nations either led hunting parties from the east side of the Mississippi River or lived in villages that southeastern emigrants had established on the Red River. The Pascagoulas and Caddoes were older Indian residents of the region, dwelling about fifty miles from Natchitoches.[24]

The eastern origins of the Natchitoches factory's trading partners did not inhibit their productivity. The Choctaws, Caddos, and others sold Linnard over 130,000 pounds of deerskins during his first six years in operation. In September 1809 the factor reported that he had almost $11,000 worth of pelts in his skin house. Linnard also purchased tallow, a few bison robes and tongues from the southern Plains buffalo range, and eight horses, bought for $10–40 each. These were all staples of the Plains trade, which suggests that Linnard's partners sold most of their horses and bison robes to private traders.[25]

Linnard's customers then purchased a conventional assortment of consumer goods: britannia and mamoodie cloth, strouds, blankets, kettles, and ammunition. Most of these were commodities that the Office of Indian Trade imported through Philadelphia or New Orleans, but some originated in North America: Linnard stocked lead from the mines on the upper Mississippi and gunpowder from Kentucky and Delaware. The Natchitoches trading house thus belonged to a small but growing intraregional economy. Like those who traded at the other southern factories, the Indians who patronized the Natchitoches house bought

Table 3.1 Selected Sales to the Natchitoches Factory, 1806–1811

	1806	1807	1808	1809	1810	1811	Total
Bear	396	321	207	948	932	582	3,386
Beaver		27	120	85	165	32	429
Bison robes		130	2	1	1	5	139
Deer	19,278	14,134	20,573	40,028	31,977	6,179	132,169
Raccoon	33	62	40	121	27	15	298
Tallow	747	31	58	562	769	355	2,522
Wax	41	165	18	110	121	99	554

Source: Daybooks for Feb.–Dec. 1806, Apr.–Dec. 1807, Jan.–March and July–Dec. 1808, Jan.–Dec. 1809, and Jan.–Dec. 1810, Misc. Accounts of the Natchitoche–Sulphur Fork Factory, 1805–1823.

Beaver, deer, tallow, and wax figures are in pounds; fractions are rounded to the nearest pound. Other figures refer to whole skins. This table does not include dressed or damaged deerskins, of which the factory purchased a small amount each year. The figures above exclude January 1806, January–March 1807, and April–June 1808, for which there are no extant daybooks. For 1807 and part of 1810, when Linnard measured his deer and beaver in whole skins, the author has assumed an average of two pounds per deerskin and 1.5 pounds per beaver pelt. (Kathryn Braund, *Deerskins and Duffels*, 69–70; Harold Innis, *Fur Trade in Canada*, 2–3.)

manufactured goods in bulk for redistribution or sale to their kinsmen. Some resold their factory goods to whites for cash or liquor, a practice that Linnard and Sibley found troublesome but hard to stop.[26]

While the Natchitoches factory enjoyed a very high volume of business, it also incurred substantial financial losses, totaling $11,719 for the period between December 1807 and September 1811—the largest loss in the system. Superintendent Mason attributed the shortfall in part to "the late depression in the price of deerskins," a problem it shared with Arkansas Post. Some of the Natchitoches factory's losses derived from its remote location, far up the Red River, and the consequent high cost of shipping its furs. For the years 1808–11 these expenses totaled $11,940, more than half of the market value of all the peltry sold or held by Natchitoches house during the same period.[27]

John Mason had closed the Arkansas factory in 1810 for incurring similar losses. Yet despite its even greater shortfall, Natchitoches factory stayed open until 1817. The strategic value of the Red River trading house—its ability to extend American influence deep into the southwestern borderland—outweighed its expense. The factory's cheap goods, and the factor's willingness to buy and store his customers' deerskins even when he could not market them, drew Indian customers away from Spanish-licensed traders in Texas. By 1809, chiefs from as far away as Matagorda Bay visited Natchitoches and promised that their hunters would "frequently visit" the factory in the future.[28]

Indeed, the Natchitoches trading house played a role in bankrupting one of the largest private fur-trading outfits in Texas, the Nacogdoches-based company of Barr and Davenport. Founded by Irish and American emigrants in 1798, the firm employed a "network of Indian traders" throughout the region. By 1809, however, the U.S. factory at Natchitoches had undermined Barr and Davenport's profitability, by drawing off some of the Indian customers who owed the company large debts. The business closed the next year.[29]

Even though most of its customers still came from Orleans Territory, the Natchitoches factory had demonstrated its ability to project American commercial power beyond the Sabine River. This made the trading house particularly valuable, for the U.S. government claimed Texas as part of the Louisiana Purchase and the Madison administration wanted to promote American influence in the region, especially after a Creole insurrection in Mexico (1810) undermined Spanish authority. Should the U.S. government wish to annex Texas by force, Native American friendship, secured by a convenient factory, would prove invaluable.[30]

What saved the Natchitoches factory from closure were the same factors whose absence had doomed the Bellefontaine and Arkansas houses: a high volume of business, stemming from a location convenient to the towns of local Indians, and a strategically useful position on a contested international border. That the Natchitoches trading house's benefits came at high financial cost reminds us again that the factory system's advocates never made profitability their central concern. What mattered instead to the secretaries of war and Superintendent Mason was securing the United States' newly established borders in Louisiana.

ONE OF THE PRINCIPAL questions that the divergent histories of the Arkansas, Bellefontaine, and Natchitoches factories raise was this: where and what were the United States' borders after 1803? The U.S. government could not answer these questions through international diplomacy, for France had left the boundaries of the Louisiana Purchase ill-defined, and Britain and Spain refused to recognize the cession. The Jefferson and Madison administrations thus had to define the new American frontiers for themselves through specific government actions, rather than by marking lines on a map.[31]

In the process, the federal government actually created several different frontiers: a military frontier, comprised of the Army's borderland garrisons; a jurisdictional frontier, defined by American territorial courts; and a commercial and diplomatic frontier, anchored by the United States' Indian factories. The War and State Departments could not define these frontiers arbitrarily, however. Numerous factors constrained their choices, including the expense of transportation, the locations of Native American and white settlements, and the objections of local leaders to the presence of American posts on contested soil. In short, the U.S. government had to align its new political borders with local realities—to treat its new domains as multi-dimensional borderlands, rather than one-dimensional frontier lines, and to mobilize its assets, rather than treat them as flags stuck in a map.[32]

The fate of the first U.S. Indian factories in the Louisiana Territory demonstrates that federal officials willingly, if slowly, undertook the difficult task of boundary adjustment. In the north, the secretary of war recognized that Bellefontaine stood within a powerful trading family's sphere of influence and too far from Indian communities, and replaced it with successor posts closer to the Sauk and Osage homelands. In the south, intelligence from local informant John Sibley allowed the War Department to select a suitable site for its Orleans Territory trading house—an old French town surrounded by Indian communities—on the first try. However, the advanced location that was the Natchitoches factory's great advantage also proved its greatest disadvantage, raising the cost of supplying the factory above its profit margin. Finally, in the Arkansas Valley, Secretary Dearborn and Superintendent Mason decided that their efforts to establish American authority could not succeed. The garrison at Arkansas Post could not protect the region's dispersed white settlements, and the trading house could not compete with a multitude of private traders. Rather than commit more resources to the region, policy-makers withdrew the garrison and factory, allowing the effective boundary of the United States to return, for the time being, to the Mississippi River.[33]

As president, Thomas Jefferson several times referred to the expanding United States as an empire, though he took care to describe it as a special kind of empire, bound together by constitutional government and commerce rather than military strength. In the Jeffersonian "empire of liberty," territorial legislatures and Indian factories would be more important guarantors of American imperium than legions. Jefferson said as much in a letter to Missouri Territorial Governor Meriwether Lewis: "As soon as the factories on the Missouri can be in activity they will have more powerful effects than so many armies." In practice, the War Department did manage the Trans-Mississippi trading houses like armies. The early history of these posts included deployment, intelligence-gathering, probing into enemy territory, advancement, and retreat. It should not surprise us that this was so. As French authorities had learned a century before, and as George Washington had recognized twenty-five years earlier, the North American Indian trade wasn't merely a commercial or diplomatic enterprise—it was also war by other means.[34]

4
The Commercial Ecology of the Indian Factory System

The United States' Indian factories stood as points on a (shifting) line, namely, the American commercial frontier, where they served as sites of interethnic diplomacy and projected U.S. government influence. They also became components of their local social geographies, governed by the habits and interests of local actors—hunters, farmers, traders, chiefs. There was, however, another dimension to the trading houses: they belonged to a web of trade that extended from the interior of North America through marketing centers on the seaboard to Europe. This web bound the factories into a system that exchanged resources with the outside world and internally reallocated them to achieve equilibrium (in this case, maintaining its original capital). Within this network, the factories became more than the sum of their parts.[1]

The factory system comprised many interlocking institutions and personnel, beginning with the trading houses and the Native American communities they served. Resource sites, such as hunting territories, lead mines, and maple forests, supplied the factories with peltry, lead, sugar, and other goods. Shipping agents in market towns like Saint Louis, aided by boatmen and teamsters, shipped Indians' wares to coastal cities and forwarded European merchandise to the factories. Merchants in New York and other cities bought the factories' furs at auction and sent them on to American buyers or to mercantile partners in Europe. Other urban merchants supplied the trading houses with manufactured goods, as did domestic manufacturers—weavers, smiths, wampum makers, gunpowder mills. The factories belonged to a single organic system, a kind of institutional animal, but one that depended on many symbiotes to supply it with resources and keep its lifeblood flowing.

Unlike individual organisms, the factory system had no purely automatic components. Its ingestion of manufactured goods required officials and local agents to hunt down importers and manufacturers in many different cities and towns. Factors also had to report what kinds of textiles, jewelry, and other wares matched the exacting preferences of their

Native American customers. The factories' transport system—the wagon and river routes that carried merchandise to the trading houses and peltry and other materials from them—required considerable effort to use. Overland travel was slow and expensive, and travel by water could prove dangerous. And marketing Native Americans' wares often taxed the patience and resourcefulness of officials at the new Office of Indian Trade. Some Indian goods, like food and moccasins, probably functioned more as gifts than salable commodities, and factors could only barter them locally. Others, like deerskins, had once been marketable in Europe but quickly glutted the factories when, in the first decade of the nineteenth century, European trade faltered. A few proved so valuable that officials had to ration them or they received protests about their monopolization of the supply. These difficulties made the factory system inefficient, but the U.S. government, which provided the factors' capital and salaries, had less interest in efficiency than in extending American influence into the interior of the continent, and it continued to support the trading houses as long as their reach continued to grow.

Given the adaptation and integrated decision-making the factory system required, the factories needed a central bureaucratic office, an institutional brain, to function and grow. Initially, however, the War Department prioritized neither the factories' systematic growth nor their institutional cogitation. During the 1790s, the factors at the Tellico and Georgia trading houses had no formal manager. Secretary of War James McHenry asked the factors for occasional updates but otherwise ignored them. John Harris, Keeper of Supplies for McHenry's department, assumed responsibility for supplying the posts, marketing their furs, and paying their bills, but he had many other responsibilities and sometimes neglected the factories. On one occasion Harris allowed the factories' Philadelphia agent, Andrew Tybout, to store thousands of deer and bearskins in his cellar until they rotted, then pitch the refuse onto the city commons.[2]

The trading houses acquired an attentive manager at the same time the Jefferson administration decided to triple their number, turning the Federalists' experiment into an ongoing institution. In the spring of 1801 Secretary of War Henry Dearborn made William Irvine the superintendent of the Schuylkill River arsenal, with the additional title of agent for the Indian factories. Irvine was no obscure functionary; he had served as a Continental Army officer, a Democratic-Republican Congressman, and a Pennsylvania official, and the administration invested considerable trust in him. General Irvine quickly took charge of the growing factory system. He drafted instructions for factors at the new houses, supervised their first shipments of goods, and found purchasers for these factories' pelts.[3]

Irvine's death in July 1804 left the factors without the manager on whom they were coming to depend. In April 1805 Dearborn appointed William Davy, a Philadelphia merchant who had served as the factories' agent for European sales, to succeed Irvine as the factories' principal agent. Davy continued to expand the responsibilities of the office, shutting down the Detroit factory and organizing auctions and sales in Philadelphia whereby he disposed of the trading houses' large output of furs and skins. The growing size of the factory system and its foreign market, however, drew the ire of American hatters and furriers. In December 1805 forty-six Philadelphia hatters asked Congress to intervene, claiming that Davy had engrossed the national fur trade and deprived American craftsmen of materials. Similar petitions from furriers in Baltimore, New York, and Boston persuaded the House Committee on Commerce and Manufactures to request from Secretary Dearborn an account of Davy's activities and an explanation of the authority under which Dearborn appointed him.[4]

Dearborn replied that he had created Davy's office under the "implied authority" of the 1796 factory law. William Davy responded more thoroughly, reporting that he had held several public auctions but could only sell therein a fraction of the tens of thousands of furs his office received. Most of the pelts he exported, Davy added, were not actually useful to hatters. The committee decided, however, to heed the petitioners' call for greater oversight of the factories, and it overhauled the system with a new bill, which Congress passed in April 1806. This formally created the office of Superintendent of Indian Trade, required him to take an oath and post bond as the factors did, and prohibited him from engaging in private trade or exporting pelts for his own profit. The new law also obliged the superintendent to hold at least six public auctions each year, with no more than two in any one state. Finally, the law increased the factories' capital to $260,000 and their annual salary pool to $10,000.[5]

After the passage of the new law, William Davy, who wished to continue his career as a merchant, tendered his resignation. Secretary Dearborn replaced Davy with a political appointee, General John Shee, who became the first official superintendent of Indian trade. Shee had little enthusiasm for the superintendency and served time until the president gave him a more lucrative office, Collector of Customs for Philadelphia, in October 1807. Shee's successor, John Mason, held the superintendent's office for the next eight and a half years, treating that position as a vocation. The son of Virginia statesman George Mason, John was an experienced merchant and prominent landowner, residing on Analostan Island (now Roosevelt Island) in the District of Columbia. As one of his first official actions, Mason moved the Office of Indian Trade to the District, specifically to Georgetown, where it remained for fifteen years.[6]

As superintendent, John Mason standardized the instructions issued to the factors and required them to submit quarterly accounts and annual inventories. He also lobbied Congress to remove the auction rules it had imposed in 1806 and to increase his office's funding. He argued that $10,000 did not suffice for twelve factors and their assistants, and that a limit of two auctions per state would prevent him from selling in the best market. Mason's requests highlighted the hybrid nature of the corporation he ran: he acknowledged that the factory system, unlike private companies, depended on outside funding, but also that he still had to generate enough profit to preserve its capital. In the end, Mason persuaded sufficient congressmen to accept his arguments, perhaps because he periodically entertained members of Congress at his home, just as his factors entertained Indians at their factories. In 1809 Congress increased the factories' capital to $300,000 and repealed the auction restrictions. That same year, Secretary of War William Eustis authorized Mason to name factors without the prior approval of the War Department, effectively making the Office of Indian Trade an autonomous unit.[7]

A subsequent act of March 1811 granted the rest of Mason's outstanding requests: it increased the factories' annual salary pool to $14,750, provided an automatic increase for each new factory, and gave the superintendent full discretion over peltry sales. The law also made the superintendent responsible for the distribution of Indian annuity goods, which, thanks to the Jefferson administration's many treaties, had become a large part of the War Department's budget. By 1812 Mason's office disposed of more than $22,000 worth of Indian annuities, not including special appropriations for treaty conferences. If gifts and trade made up the lifeblood of Indian diplomacy, the Office of Indian Trade had become the U.S. government's diplomatic heart.[8]

Mason's largest challenge when he took office was supplying his factories and selling their products during a serious disruption of American international trade. This disruption resulted from the new war between Britain and France, during which the Royal Navy had resumed its old practice of impressing English-born sailors from American ships at sea, and during which Britain and France blockaded their respective adversaries—most of Europe, actually. American efforts to reach a settlement with Britain failed, and in 1807 a skirmish between the U.S.S. *Chesapeake* and the H.M.S. *Leopard*, which left three American sailors dead and the United States humiliated, caused Congress to lay an embargo on American foreign trade.[9]

The embargo, which lasted until 1809, profoundly affected the Office of Indian Trade, because the factories principally sold imported goods. From the beginning the War Department's agent in London, William Murdock, had used the factories' exports to buy English "merchandise to suit the trade," a practice that continued during Irvine's and Davy's superintendencies. In addition, the factories' agents regularly purchased imports from merchants in Philadelphia. The house of Bryan & Schlotter sold the trading houses scarlet cloth and strouds. Alexander Henry, an Irish importer, sold bales of 2½- and 3-point blankets—thick blankets printed with short blue lines ("points") to denote their size and price. Robert Smith, one of Philadelphia's most prominent merchants, supplied chintz, nonesopretties, and sewing silk, while Charles Ellet, a hardware dealer, furnished the trading houses with flints, knives, and steel-topped thimbles.[10]

As the embargo dried up the supply of European goods in Philadelphia, John Mason cast a wider net of procurement. He bought from importers in Georgetown, New York City, and other market centers. The superintendent also patronized American manufacturers. Mason bought calico prints and shawls from Baltimore calico companies, ordered blankets from weavers in Maryland and Delaware, sent Jacob Varnum to New England to survey the production of woolen cloth, and sent textile samples to the Philadelphia Almshouse for the inmates to copy. He ordered rifles from gunsmiths in Philadelphia and Maryland, bought several thousand silver broaches from Carl Westphall of Philadelphia, and asked a German smith in Baltimore, Mr. Lamb, to make some sample beaver traps.[11]

Mason patronized American manufacturers out of patriotism and necessity, but they often proved unequal to the task of properly supplying the factories. They generally could not produce as much as Mason needed, and the quality of their manufactures did not meet Native Americans' high standards. Indians had always been highly discriminating customers and quality mattered greatly to them. The point blankets that Great Lakes Indians preferred to buy, for example, had to meet very exact specifications: 3-point blankets had to be white in color with "cross stripes of very dark blue," 6 feet by 5 feet 2 inches in size, and weigh four pounds. In buying jewelry, Indians sought specific decorative schemes—fish and animal engravings, or patterns of interlocking rings—and a silver content equivalent to that of Spanish dollars, being, Mason wrote, "very particular and suspicious on that score." Native American hunters, meanwhile, preferred high-quality powder for their firearms. These and other Indian goods required considerable skill to manufacture, and American craftsmen frequently lacked adequate proficiency. A sample Indian rifle that Mason ordered from Mr. Riser of Cumberland proved unsatisfactory, marred by shallow rifling, a stiff gunlock, and insecure mountings. Mr. Lamb's beaver traps also came out badly, with overly stiff springs and jaws that would not close.[12]

Americans could manufacture a few commodities as skillfully as Europeans. One was gunpowder, which John Shee had begun ordering from E. I. Dupont de Nemours in 1807, and which Superintendent Mason was soon buying by the ton. By 1810 Thomas Linnard could report from Natchitoches that "Dupont's is the best American powder that has ever been seen here and is preferred infinitely before any other by the Indians." Other choice American-made articles included rifles manufactured by the Philadelphia gunsmith Henry Deringer, which both factors and Indians found highly satisfactory, and wampum, the shell beads that the northern Indians had long used as decorations, gifts, and sacred tokens solemnizing diplomatic conferences. Mason noted Native Americans' "considerable consumption" of wampum—in one four-month period the superintendent ordered 250,000 from various sources—and he sought to minimize costs by purchasing the beads directly from the poor New Jersey families who made them.[13]

While the superintendents usually ordered and paid for merchandise by mail, they also employed local agents to maintain good relations with suppliers, inspect their wares, and help negotiate prices. These agents included Thomas Waterman in Philadelphia, Joseph Lopez Dias in New York, and George Mason's brother-in-law Reynaldo Johnson in Virginia, source of the trade office's tobacco. After buying factory goods, the agents shipped them to one of several American ports: New York City, Alexandria, Savannah, or New Orleans. From thence the superintendent or another agent forwarded the merchandise by boat and wagon to the trad-

Table 4.1 Selected Shipments from the Office of Indian Trade, 1803–1811

	1803	1804	1805	1806	1807	1808	1809	1810	1811	Total
Blankets	300	783	2,520	1,474	480**	694	1,394	670	868	9,183
Brass kettles	255	843	307	1,714	1,075	1,429	638	828		7,089
Calico	2,783	1,788	19,313	10,699	1,641	6,651	8,652	8,690	12,918	73,135
Guns	86	132	178	219	694	200	140	218	98	1,965
Gunpowder	2,500	7,600	9,600	1,400	4,000	7,975	6,900	4,000	7,200	51,175
Knives	432	72	9,672	2,232	288	1,776	1,008	576	2,668	18,724
Needles	*	2,000	50,000	24,000	3,000	100	2,000	16,000	8,300	105,400
Saddles	74	104	106	108	83	81	26	74	30	686
Shirts		663	1,537	1,106	250	538	653	894	1,060	6,701
Shoes			579	132	100				96	907
Strouds	136	205	557	450	152**	361	362	318	453	2,994
Tobacco	175		425	1,716	666	5,033	3,419			11,434
Total Value ($)	18,673	27,588	121,642	49,833	31,464	50,422	45,102	44,254	41,102	430,080

Source: 1803: Invoices Outward, 4: 1–24; 1804: ibid., 4: 25–50; 1805: ibid., 1: 1–106; 1806: ibid., 1: 107–75; 1807: ibid., 1: 177–224. 2: 250; 1808: ibid., 2: 1–80, 251; 1809: ibid., 2: 81–140, 162, 252; 1810: ibid., 2: 141–60, 164–194; 1811: ibid., 2: 195–249.

Blankets are 3-point blankets. Calico is measured in yards; brass kettles, gunpowder, and tobacco, in pounds (rounded to the nearest yard or pound). Several hundred pieces of calico in the 1805 invoices had no yardage listed; based on the remaining pieces shipped that year, the author has interpolated an average of 17.8 yards per piece. When kettles appear in invoices as individual items, the author estimates (based on weights in the 1808 invoices) an average of five pounds per kettle. Guns include all firearms. Needles include knitting and sewing needles. Shoes are measured in pairs. Strouds sometimes appear in yards in the invoices; the author estimates that one stroud measured 20 yards.

The 1808 figures do not include goods transferred from Bellefontaine to Fort Osage and Fort Madison.

"Total Value" is the total invoiced dollar value of all goods shipped that year, including many not listed in this selection. Sums are rounded to the nearest dollar. Freight costs and supplies shipped for factors' own use are not included.

* "2 dozen packages," each probably containing several hundred sewing needles.

** Does not include two bales of blankets and two bales of strouds.

ing houses. Shipments destined for the Great Lakes posts first traveled to Albany, where U.S. Military Agent Peter Gansevoort stored them during the winter, then hired boatmen to transport the freight to Buffalo, via the Mohawk River, Lake Ontario, and Niagara portage. Finally, lake sloops carried the supplies, for two dollars per barrel, from Buffalo to the northern factories.[14]

A second supply route snaked down the Ohio River, then up the Mississippi and Missouri Rivers to Bellefontaine and its successor posts (Fort Madison and Fort Osage), or down the Mississippi to Chickasaw Bluffs and Arkansas Post. William Davy and John Shee initially shipped goods by wagon from Philadelphia to Pittsburgh, then by boat to the West. In 1808 John Mason moved the eastern terminus of this route to Georgetown, whence supplies traveled up the Potomac River to Cumberland, then overland to Wheeling or Brownsville—cutting freight costs by $10 to $25 per ton compared with the trans-Pennsylvania route—and then by boat to Saint Louis. He made the latter town a supply depot for Forts Osage and Madison, with William Clark as his agent.[15]

The Ohio–Mississippi supply route could prove an arduous, even deadly passage, a lesson George Sibley learned during his first trip to Fort Osage in 1808. Sibley hired six men to take himself and $3,800 worth of merchandise from Pittsburgh to Saint Louis. The crew took thirty-four days, including a twelve-day layover at Wheeling, to descend the Ohio River to its mouth. Sibley and his oarsmen then spent twenty days ascending the Mississippi River to Saint Louis, averaging less than ten miles per day. Two days before the boat arrived in Saint Louis, one of Sibley's crewmen, John Spear, fell into the river and drowned; another, Bill Brooks, died trying to save Spear's life. Sibley took another month to transship his goods onto smaller boats and dispatch them up the Missouri River to Fort Osage, where he finally arrived on 2 September. The trip had taken twelve weeks and cost $400—and two human lives.[16]

Fort Osage and the factories near the Mississippi River exported their skins and furs through New Orleans, the city that also served as the port of entry for Natchitoches. Joseph Saul served as local agent for the Office of Indian Trade, in which capacity he received, stored, and shipped tens of thousands of pounds of deerskins and other peltries from the southern and western trading houses. The supply route for one southern factory, Saint Stephens, ran through West Florida rather than New Orleans, and both Saul and the Saint Stephens factors paid large fees for the use of Spanish Mobile. Moreover, in February 1809 Governor Vicente

Table 4.2 Freight Costs for Selected Factory Supply Routes, 1807–1810

Route	Cost per ton ($)	Distance (miles)	Ton-mile cost (cents)
Brownsville to Saint Louis	40	1,300	3
Pittsburgh to Chickasaw Bluffs	45	1,300	4
Saint Louis to Brownsville, Pa.	80	1,300	6
Albany to Buffalo	69	423	16
Saint Louis to Fort Osage	55	300	18
Saint Louis to Fort Madison	35	200	18
Brownsville, Pa., to Georgetown	55	200	28
Philadelphia to Pittsburgh	90	300	30
Georgetown to Wheeling	80	260	32
Savannah to Ocmulgee	80	240	33
Georgetown to Brownsville	65	200	33
Cincinnati to Fort Wayne	80	150	53

Sources on costs: Memorandum Book, 6–7, 37–38, 93–94; Receipt to Francis Johnston, 30 Sept. 1810, Misc. Accounts of the Fort Wayne Factory; Receipt to Andrew Kennely, ca. Jan. 1808, Misc. Accounts of the Cherokee Factory; Invoice of Peltry Forwarded to Levi Sheftall by Nicholas Byers, 18 March 1808, ibid.; Mr. Irwin's Account of Shipment of Goods, 28 October 1809, Misc. Accounts of the Chicago Factory. Ton-mile costs are rounded to the nearest penny.

Sources on travel distances: Dunbar, *History of Travel*, 1: 324–25; Blane, *Excursion*, 85–86; Barber and Howe, *Our Whole Country*, 2: 884, 1271; Beltrami, *Pilgrimage,* 2: 76, 136; Mr. Irwin's Account of Shipment of Goods, 28 October 1809, Misc. Accounts of the Chicago Factory; George to Samuel Sibley, 16 Sept. 1808, George Sibley Papers, Box 1–2, Folder 7.

Folch abruptly banned the importation of military stores through Mobile, impounding 4,500 pounds of gunpowder and lead destined for the Choctaw factory. Despite the pleas of the State Department, the governor refused to countermand the order. Most likely Folch believed the ammunition might wind up in the hands of white Americans with designs against Florida.[17]

With the partial closure of Mobile, Mason had to find an alternative route to Saint Stephens. In 1810, the superintendent decided to try an interior passage: via the Ohio and Tennessee Rivers to Colbert's Ferry and then over the Alabama hills to the Tombigbee River. To test the route's feasibility, Mason purchased several tons of gunpowder and lead from Lexington, Kentucky, and instructed George Gaines to transport these goods to Saint Stephens. In November 1810, the factor, with the help of Chickasaw packhorse handlers who carried the cargo eighty miles overland, completed the route.[18]

Gaines succeeded in his mission, but the Tennessee–Tombigbee route proved difficult and expensive. The factor took nearly two months to travel from Saint Stephens to Kentucky and back, "run[ning] several narrow chances of being drowned" as he swam across creeks. The cost of this first shipment exceeded $400, including $40 to replace a horse crushed by the load it carried. This translated to $135 per ton, equal to the expense of shipping cargo from Saint Louis to Georgetown. Gaines and Mason subsequently used the Tennessee–Tombigbee route to ship only a small amount of freight, and they discontinued it after the U.S. Army took Mobile in 1813.[19]

The last factory supply route began in Savannah. There a succession of agents, including Abraham Abrahams and Levi Sheftall, took charge of the goods bound for the Creek factory and of the skins and furs it exported. While the Creek trading house operated at Fort Wilkinson, on the Oconee River (1797–1806), its Savannah agents hired boatmen to carry its wares up the Savannah River to Augusta, then employed wagons to cover the remaining 90 miles overland. This route remained in use after the Creek factory moved to Ocmulgee Old Fields (1806–16), but the overland leg then increased by 30 miles and shipping costs to and from Savannah increased to $70 per ton.[20]

Savannah also served for a time as the supply port for the Cherokee factory. Originally, the War Department supplied the Tellico trading house by wagon from Philadelphia. When, at the request of Cherokee leaders, the factory moved to Hiwassee in southern Tennessee, the Office of Indian Trade rerouted its supply path to Augusta and Savannah. While this new route involved less overland travel than the old, it still proved expensive, bearing freight costs of up to $110 per ton. The construction of a federal road through Cherokee territory and northern Georgia, which the Cherokees had authorized, might have lowered these costs, but the Hiwassee factory closed before the road's completion.[21]

THE SAME AVENUES that brought manufactured goods to the trading houses also conveyed those factories' produce to market. Native Americans sold a wide array of goods at the factories, of which the single most plentiful type was deerskins. Between 1796 and 1812, the factories purchased over one million pounds of deerskins, about 85 percent of which came from the southern and southwestern houses—a rich haul, perhaps, but well below the output of the eighteenth-century trade, when the southern Indians collectively harvested up to 1.5 million pounds of deerskins each year.[22]

Two significant problems attended the factories' deerskin business. First, the skins were bulky and transporting them was expensive. The factors mitigated this problem by paying Indians and traders higher prices for skins they had shaved or dressed (trimmed, scraped, and preserved). A more serious problem, from the superintendents' perspective, was the uncertain market for deerskins, which were primarily an export commodity. During their first decade of operations, the factories' supervisors in Philadelphia sent most of their deerskins to London for sale. Between 1805 and 1808, the first years for which specific records exist, the superintendents of Indian trade sold about 58,000 pounds of deerskins in London and Bordeaux, and another 13,500 pounds in Amsterdam.[23]

The curtailment of American trade with Europe created a deerskin glut in the United States. Superintendent Mason noted the problem early in his term, calling the pelts "a millstone around the neck of" the Office of Indian Trade. He ordered the factors at the most active southern factories (Arkansas Post, Chickasaw Bluffs, Natchitoches, and Saint Stephens) to stop buying the unsalable skins, though the southern factors ignored him because refusal to buy would alienate their Indian partners. Mason also told his agents in Savannah and New Orleans to shave, treat, and store the skins they had on hand, rather than shipping them onward. Despite some spoilage, most of the deerskins sent to the southern ports of collection survived, and by February 1810 the Office of Indian Trade had nearly 109 tons of skins warehoused in New Orleans.[24]

With European trade still restricted by an 1809 Non-Intercourse Act, Superintendent Mason decided he had to dump these pelts on the market at any price he could get. In the summer of 1809 he authorized George Gaines, the factor at Saint Stephens, to approach John Forbes & Company about buying deerskins, either for cash or credit. Gaines apparently did not succeed. Next, Mason approached "a large dealer in furs and peltries" in New York City about buying his surplus deerskins below the usual market price. The dealer was John Jacob Astor, a German immigrant who had in the 1790s built a fur-trading network that extended from Leipzig to Saint Louis. In the early 1800s Astor had obtained the endorsement of President Jefferson to build trading posts in the Pacific Northwest. He now sought to strengthen his tie to the U.S. government by aiding its Indian trade office. Business, however, was business. Astor offered to buy all of Mason's deerskins for 4–10 cents per pound, representing a steep discount (30–40 percent) from market price. Mason tried to negotiate, but Astor held firm and the deal fell through. Finally, the superintendent obtained the permission of the secretary of war to sell surplus skins in New Orleans and New York for whatever the market would bear—"sacrifices we must hope [plan] to make," he glumly wrote. On 1 November, the Office of Indian Trade's New Orleans agent, Joseph Saul, managed to sell about 55 percent of his deerskin inventory to D. Clark and the firm of W. & Morris, for $40,460 in mercantile notes. And, by year's end, foreign trade had revived, and Mason auctioned new skins from the Great Lakes factories for 32–40 cents per pound.[25]

More lucrative than deerskins were "hatter's furs," thick furs suitable for coat linings, muffs, and hats. These comprised the second largest type of Indian wares sold at the factories. They included raccoon furs, of which the Office of Indian Trade sold 99,000 between 1805 and 1811; muskrat furs (29,000 sold); bearskins (nearly 9,000 sold), mainly purchased from the southern Indians; and beaver pelts (8,000 pounds sold), which at a market price of two to three dollars per pound numbered among the factories' most valuable products. Unlike deerskins, these furs were in demand in the United States, so much so that despite a congressional ban on their export, the Office of Indian Trade still ran short of them at its auctions. In October 1809 John Mason turned down a request for furs from Boston hatters because a hard winter had curtailed sales to the Great Lakes factories, and he had already sold the "miserable" proceeds of the season. In the same letter, Mason noted that he expected additional beaver, muskrat, and raccoon furs from Fort Osage and Fort Madison, but he had already arranged to sell all of them. Thus, while Mason and his factors labored under a glut of deerskins, they also faced such a shortage of hatter's furs that they had to ration them.[26]

Not as readily marketable as skins and furs were what one might label "domestic consumables." These Indian-made goods included animal tallow, useful for grease and candles; beeswax, a sealant and candlemaking material; mats, which Sauk and Mesquakie women wove from rushes and bound with bark twine; and snakeroot, a medicinal plant Indians used to treat pain and inflammation from snakebite. Factors and agents marketed these commodities in interior towns like Saint Louis, located close enough to the factories to make the transport of these less profitable items worthwhile.[27]

A subcategory of domestic consumables comprised goods that Indians and whites bought and sold at the factories, and which essentially remained bartered goods because the factors did not believe they could sell them in more distant markets. Examples included meat, corn, and groundnuts; moccasins, sometimes decorated with quillwork by the women who made them; and homespun cloth, which one factor bought from whites for resale to the Creeks. Perhaps the most voluminous of these products was maple sugar, which Great Lakes Indian women and their daughters prepared in the springtime from boiled maple sap. Sugar production belonged to the economic domain of women—they owned the maple groves and performed most of the labor associated with the good—and the finished product served both as an important subsistence food and a component of feasts and mortuary ceremonies. By the nineteenth century, it had also become a commodity: Native American women in the Great Lakes region produced up to 75,000 pounds of sugar a year, and factors used it as a medium of exchange, reselling it to Indians or shipping it to Detroit for local families.[28]

One might also label these bartered items *frontier-exchange* goods, akin to the wooden bowls and woven baskets that Mississippi Valley Indians sold to the Bellefontaine factory. It is likely that the Indians who bestowed these goods upon the factories regarded them simultaneously as gifts—tokens of esteem and good relations—and commodities, items one could exchange in distant markets. Many goods of this class, like meat and corn and sugar, were foodstuffs, and food played an essential part in everyday diplomacy, allowing different peoples to demonstrate their hospitality. One suspects Native American men and women wanted to return to the Americans some of the hospitality the factors had shown them, even if fulfilling that obligation also brought them access to factory merchandise. Food also elicited an important diplomatic metaphor for the Iroquois and Great Lakes Indians; eating from a "common dish" was an act that affirmed the common humanity of the participants and bound them together. From the factors' perspective, receiving foodstuffs and other frontier-exchange goods represented another accommodation to Indian norms, for this produce brought little immediate profit and usually came in quantities too great for the factors themselves to consume.[29]

The last category of Indian wares sold to and shipped from the factories was neither animal nor vegetable but a mineral, lead. Indians had been mining the metal in present-day Iowa and Illinois for nearly

Lakes Indian women, like those portrayed in this 1851 Seth Eastman painting, manufactured thousands of pounds of maple sugar every year; it became one of the factories' largest frontier-exchange products. *Sugar Camp*, from *American Aboriginal Portfolio* by Mary Eastman (1853), courtesy of the Rare Book Collection, Wilson Special Collections Library, University of North Carolina at Chapel Hill.

4,000 years, but lead did not become a major part of the region's economy until the late eighteenth century, when British traders convinced local Indians that a large market for it existed. In the early 1800s the Bellefontaine and Fort Wayne factories both bought lead mined by Native Americans, and according to agent Nicholas Boilvin, the Sauks and Mesquakies produced tons of the metal, "which . . . enabled them to clothe themselves better than with the proceeds of the chase." By late 1811, the Fort Madison factory had purchased over 130,000 pounds of lead, nearly all of which William Clark sold in Saint Louis.[30]

Women dominated Native American lead production, most likely because the Sauks, Mesquakies, and Ho-Chunks associated it with the earth and thus with female spiritual power. Female miners used hoes, shovels, and pickaxes to dig trenches or shafts, then hauled out the ore in baskets and bags. Men guarded the mines, smelted the ore, and marketed the finished product. In this respect, lead mining resembled a number of other Indian commercial activities, like deerskin processing, which required a joint application of male and female labor.[31]

While the factors often purchased the products of Native women's labor, they seldom encountered Indian women as customers. Of the several hundred persons identified by name as debtors or customers of the trading houses, one can only definitively identify a dozen or so as female. Native American women conducted some transactions with the factories, but the factors did not, as a rule, extend them credit or sell them large quantities of merchandise. This restricted the economic power of women in communities served by the factories, insofar as they depended on male relatives to buy them goods, like clothing and cookware, they once could make for themselves. The factors wanted to make Native Americans dependent on the United States, but they also reinforced new patterns of dependency within Indian towns and families.[32]

Most of the factories' peltry and other Indian goods found their way to New York, New Orleans, and other cities, where the Office of Indian Trade's agents sold it at auction or in smaller private sales. Between 1806 and 1812, the trade office sold nearly $215,000 worth of pelts, lead, and other goods. It concluded 70 percent of these sales (by dollar value) during the last three years of the period, between the end of the embargo and the start of the War of 1812. At least 140 individuals and partnerships took part in these sales and auctions, the majority (80 percent) either in New York City or Georgetown. Many, if not most, of these purchasers were merchants who intended to either export the peltry they purchased or retail it to hatters and furriers within the United States.[33]

Those who exported their purchases usually shipped their goods to London, during the brief period after 1809 when Congress made it legal to do so. Alternatively, they may have sold their skins and furs in Hamburg or Bremen, two German cities that had prospered from American trade in the eighteenth century and received dozens of American ships in the early 1800s. If they chose the latter market, they faced harassment by French officials enforcing Napoleon's Continental System and (after 1810) high import tariffs. Trade with Europe carried large risks, and arguably Congress did the Office of Indian Trade a favor by prohibiting it from exporting peltry on its own, instead transferring the risk to private parties.[34]

The factories' $30,000 average annual sales of peltry and Indian goods seems modestly impressive, considered in isolation, but it appears much smaller compared to the total proceeds of the American fur trade. In the

Table 4.3 Sales of Indian Wares by the Office of Indian Trade, 1805–1811

	1805	1806	1807	1808	1809	1810	1811	Total
Badger							6	6
Bear	202	962	484	427	1,461	4,290	1,155	8,981
Bear's oil							6b	6b
Beaver	872	494	1,048	706	758	2,712	1,687	8,277
B. robes							58	58
Candles		15					1,940	1,955
Cat	278	259	232	1,727	1,666	503	213	4,878
Deer	35,258	8,747	41,987	27,852	30,477	86,023	57,717	288,061
Dr. deer					457	759		1216
Sh. Deer		7,006		13,558		64,067	48,732	133,363
Elk	1			4	18		26	49
Feathers							661	661
Fisher	22	18	25	30	166	39		300
Fox	1,054	627	1,606	2,883	2,275	220	124	8,789
Hogskins							111	111
Lead						105,870	25,287	131,157
Martin				12	2	21	13	48

Mats							67	67
Mink	32	120	184	614	134	146	318	1,428
Muskrat	1,700	208	10,879	6,429	3,143	6,747	188	29,206
Otter	415	68	11	668	351	155	612	2,409
Panther	17			29	8			133
Rabbit				34				34
Raccoon	3,112	2,391	14,094	42,415	18,413	8,835	10,488	99,748
R. robes						9	9	9
Snakeroot		30	38	229	180			248
Tallow	672		230		145	934	5,177	7,387
Tiger				40	68			108
Wax		1,218	1,771	56	1,888	333+b	719	5,985+b
Wolf	16	39	147	126	88	239	130	785

Sources: *1805*: Invoices Outward, 1: 71–72, 103–6, 110–11; *1806*: ibid., 1: 136, 146, 157–58, 166, 169, 182, 187; *1807*: ibid., 1: 183, 206, 209–10, 217–18, 220, 225; Sales Books, 2: 1–4; *1808*: Invoices Outward, 1: 111; Sales Books, 2: 2–18; *1809*: Sales Books, 2: 19–29, 31, 35; *1810*: ibid., 2:30, 32–40; *1811*: ibid., 2: 41–56.

Abbreviations: "b": barrel; "B. robes": bison robes; "Dr. deer": dressed deerskins; "Sh. deer": shaved deerskins; "R. robes": raccoon robes.

Beaver, deer, shaved deer, feathers, lead, snakeroot, tallow, and wax figures are in pounds. All other entries are individual items. Bear, deer, and shaved deer entries include damaged skins. Bear includes cub skins. "Tiger" refers to wildcats or panthers. Where records list whole deerskins or list smaller pelts in pounds, the author assumes one deerskin weighed two pounds, and that one fisher, fox, mink, or muskrat fur weighed one pound. When two types of furs are combined in the records, the author has split the listing in half. All fractions are rounded to the nearest whole number.

1790s Montreal merchants annually exported £200,000 ($800,000) worth of furs to London, while during the first decade of the nineteenth century Americans exported an average of $540,000 worth of peltries each year. Since these figures do not include domestic fur and skin sales, the federal trading houses apparently accounted for less than 5 percent of the American peltry trade. If Congress hoped, and private traders feared, that the factories would become a monopoly, their hopes and fears were in vain.[35]

The factory system's great advantage lay in the irrelevance of trade volume and market share to its survival. The Indian trading houses did not belong to a closed system: a significant part of their budget came from a congressional appropriation that paid factors' salaries and subsistence. In addition, the Army provided free security for the factories, and the War Department supplied Indian annuity goods that helped draw regular Native American visitors. The factory system thus did not have to generate profits to pay its employees or give gifts to Indian customers. Shielded from the imperatives of a free-market enterprise, the factory system could simply maintain its economic equilibrium while competing companies went bust.

That equilibrium proved hard to maintain. The federal factories had to accommodate the material needs and wants of Native Americans, an undertaking both difficult and expensive. Indian communities and resource centers stood deep in the interior of the continent, which complicated transportation. Indians obliged the factors to buy produce that the factories could not easily sell in a larger market, like deerskins or maple sugar, leading to additional storage and preservation costs. They also demanded high-quality merchandise made according to exact specifications, goods that were difficult for Americans to make and difficult for them to import. It was to the credit of the superintendents, factors, and local agents that they overcame these obstacles: developing alternative supply routes, finding eventual purchasers for surplus deerskins, identifying Native Americans' particular tastes in goods, and locating manufacturers for those goods when imports dried up.[36]

Having dealt with these problems, all that the employees of the Office of Indian Trade had to do to preserve the factory system was justify it to Congress, the source of the factories' capital and their own salaries. And on the few occasions before the War of 1812 when Congress took an interest in the factories, the superintendents and secretaries of war convinced the legislature to strengthen rather than restrict the factory

Table 4.4 Sales by the Office of Indian Trade, by Market, 1805–1812

	1805	1806	1807	1808	1809	1810	1811	1812	Total
Baltimore		$524							$524
Georgetown					$1,463	$11,491	$18,753	$9,612	$41,319
London	£2,870								£2,870
New Orleans		$5,203	$654	$4,433	$1,060	$44,737	$32	$399	$56,518
New York		$806	$4,370	$9,825	$6,592	$5,381	$11,902	$30,413	$69,289
Philadelphia	$1,312	$3,569	$13,419	$5,225	$4,020			$1,214	$28,759
St. Louis					$2,094	$5,822	$8,391	$1,838	$18,145
Savannah			$1,439						$1,439
Total	$12,792	$10,102	$19,882	$19,483	$15,229	$67,431	$39,078	$43,476	227,473

Sources: Invoices Outward, 1:71–72, 103–6, 110–13, 136, 146, 157–58, 166–69, 182–83, 187, 206, 209–10, 217–18, 220–22, 225; Sales Books, 1 (n.p.), 2: 1–80.
    Where records distinguish between net and gross sale prices, the author has used the net price (4–5 percent lower than the gross price) or converted the gross price to net (by multiplying by 0.95). The location of domestic sales in 1805–6 is often unidentified, but the author assumes that all took place in Philadelphia. For London sales, the author uses a sterling-to-dollars exchange rate of 1:4. The 1805 domestic sale figures do not include 146 deer, 48 otter, 21 fisher, 11 mink, 4 wolf, 2 panther, 144 pounds. of beaver, 587 fox, and 339 raccoon.

system, to enlarge its capital and increase its superintendent's autonomy. Congress even gave the superintendent de facto control of Native American annuities, acknowledging the role that the Office of Indian Trade played in Indian diplomacy. As long as Indian-white relations remained important, as long as the U.S. government believed that commercial diplomacy could facilitate Indian land sales and solidify federal influence in the borderlands, then the superintendents would have little trouble justifying the factories' existence. And, as the United States entered a period of territorial expansion and strained international affairs, the "cheap" options of Native American diplomacy and trade became more important than they had been since the Revolution.

5

Negotiation, Manipulation, and Alliance-Building

Like most institutions, the American factory system took several years to mature. It appears to have entered its peak epoch about ten years after the first trading houses opened, and to have left it with the onset of the War of 1812. The twelve operational factories constituted, as we have noted, an extensive system that exchanged tons of deerskins, furs, and lead for thousands of yards of cloth, hundredweight of gunpowder, and packages of needles, using American rivers and roads and Atlantic sea-lanes as its circulatory apparatus. On a more human scale, the factories were individual centers of trade and diplomacy, entwined with local communities and embedded in local circumstances. Most of the people who used the factories did not ask "How can I help the system function effectively?" but rather "How can this trading house help me? My family? My town? My nation?" From the perspective of American officials and Native American men and women, these questions pointed toward the factories' ultimate function, which was not to circulate and exchange commodities but to bind Indians and Americans together. Intricate and important as its workings were, the factory system did not exercise agency; only its customers and managers did.

For their American patrons, the pre-1812 factories helped ensure more pliant Indian leadership in the southeast, procure land cessions from the Cherokees (until the cessions' opponents conducted a coup), and secure the military allegiance of the Choctaws and Chickasaws. They extended American influence across the Mississippi River, anchoring trading alliances with the Osage, Sauk, and Kansa Indians. For Native Americans, the trading houses served as banks, annuity collection centers, dumping sites for unsalable deerskins, places to socialize with servants of the American sovereign, alternatives to British trading centers upon which they did not want to depend, and sources of sophisticated consumer goods. There was an important difference between these two groups' perceptions of the factories. Indians valued them for the convenience, hospitality, and freedom of choice they offered, while American officials saw the trading houses as generators of influence and catalysts of Indian land sales. These officials therefore agreed to sustain the factories even during a period of American economic hardship, caused by deteriorating relations between the United States and Britain and by congressional trade sanctions. They continued to do so even when the factory system ran close to a loss.[1]

Native Americans who perceived the disparity in motives between the factories' customers and its patrons also recognized the factories' implicitly imperialist nature. Some believed that the trading houses' advantages and their own ability to maximize them superseded their white operators' shadier motives; some saw political benefits in building a closer relationship with the American empire. Others agreed with Thomas Jefferson that the factories acted like "so many armies," and they did not view them as utilities. They considered them military targets.

THE TRADING HOUSES that generated the least ire from Native Americans ran, not entirely coincidentally, the greatest financial losses. These were the southern factories. The oldest of them, the Creek trading house at Fort Wilkinson, recorded a 50 percent decline in peltry shipments early in the century, from 34,430 pounds of deerskins in 1802 to about 17,000 pounds in 1807–8. Sales fell further during the next five years. After 1808 the Office of Indian Trade received no more peltry from the Creek factory, though the house did purchase and store about $10,800 worth of furs and skins between 1809 and 1811. This only slightly exceeded the value of the shipments the factory had made in the single year 1802.[2]

One can partially attribute this decline in peltry sales to declining game populations in the Creeks' hunting preserves. White settlers and hard weather compromised the productivity of the old Creek hunting grounds in Georgia, and private traders poached the factory's customers, pressing any small advantage they could take. In 1804, for instance, the War Department neglected to fill Jonathan Halstead's requisition of goods, and the factor had to arrange for "the neighboring stores on the other side of the [Oconee] river" to supply his Creek customers. Many Creek hunters resorted to these stores the following year when they returned to sell their furs and hides, the factory's empty shelves having called Halstead's reliability into question. Moreover, private traders sold liquor, which an 1802 federal law prohibited the factors from selling. "Have it they will, let it cost what it may," the factor ruefully observed.[3]

Competition remained intense even after the War Department moved the Creek factory to Ocmulgee Old Fields, a Creek reservation on the

Ocmulgee River, in September 1806. The new site, chosen by Creek leaders in an 1805 treaty, stood thirty miles closer to the Creeks' towns, but its greater convenience did not prevent the Creeks from trading with Halstead's competitors—like John Forbes & Company, whose Pensacola store charged some of the same prices for merchandise as the factory. Some of the Creek factory's competitors enjoyed, moreover, the advantage of ethnic and kinship ties to their customers: Menawa, a Creek captain, maintained both a store for his kinsmen and a brisk deerskin trade with Pensacola, investing his profits in (eventually) several thousand head of livestock.[4]

Despite declining sales to his factory, Halstead met most of his expenses and maintained a moderate volume of business through the first decade of the century. He continued to order and stock thousands of dollars worth of light textiles, needles and thread, rifles and ammunition, sugar and hyson tea. Halstead also diversified the factory's transactions, selling groceries to the soldiers at Fort Wilkinson, using the Creeks' 1802 debt-settlement pledge to underwrite factory drafts, and trading goods to white settlers for cash or homespun cloth, the latter of which he sold to the Creeks.[5]

Halstead also "sold"—or, rather, credited—the Creek factory's wares and cash supply to the War Department, which used them for gifts and annuity payments. Benjamin Hawkins frequently had drawn on the factory for goods with which to pay the Creeks the stipend promised them by the Treaty of New York.[6] That stipend grew after the Creeks, in 1802 and 1805, ceded to the United States their lands between the Oconee and Ocmulgee Rivers, for which the U.S. government promised to pay them $16,000 per annum in goods and cash. Creek leaders drew both annuity goods from the Ocmulgee factory's shelves and cash from its till; some even used drafts on the factory, backed by the tribal annuity, to pay personal expenses. Effectively, the Creek factory functioned more like a bank than a trading post, benefiting the Creeks' leaders more than "common" hunters. Creek commoners took their business elsewhere; Creek chiefs observed in 1813 that their "poor[er]" kinsmen took their peltry and foodstuffs and other wares to white settlements in Tennessee, rather than to Ocmulgee.[7]

The Creek house's sister factory at Tellico had also come to focus on the interests of a small minority: the faction of Cherokee leaders who controlled that nation's relations with the U.S. government. Indeed, the War Department used the Tellico factory to bribe these leaders into selling the United States more land. The Cherokees already had made several land cessions, and after 1800, the Jefferson administration began seeking more. Tennessee settlers wanted the lands in the middle of their state, and the War Department wanted to build roads through Cherokee country. Cherokee leaders visiting Washington made it clear, however, that they preferred not to part with any more land, and the penurious Jefferson administration hesitated to pay them a large enough price to overcome their opposition. Short of violence, the government could only secure the cessions it wanted at the price it wanted (1–2 cents per acre) if it bribed leading Cherokees. This it proceeded to do.[8]

John Hooker, factor at Tellico from 1798 to 1804, took a leading part in the corrupt drama that ensued. The president himself supposedly asked Hooker to extend liberal credit to Cherokee leaders, then encourage them to sell their hunting grounds to retire their debts. "That is the way I intend to get their country," Jefferson purportedly told Hooker, "to get them to run in debt to the public store and they will have to give their land for payment." The story of Jefferson's request comes to us at fourth hand, and one suspects at least one person in the chain of evidence was exaggerating, but fictive or not the instruction conformed with the president's policy and his subordinates' subsequent actions.[9]

In April 1804 Secretary of War Dearborn authorized Hooker to give several hundred dollars' worth of goods or cash to the prominent Cherokee councilor James Vann, thereby securing Vann's good offices in forthcoming land negotiations. Vann owed the factory nearly $600, so the douceur may have had the desired effect: that October Vann joined nine other Cherokees in signing the second Treaty of Tellico, trading land in Georgia for factory goods. Factor Hooker died a month later, but his successor, Nicholas Byers, continued his policy of subornation. In the summer of 1805, Byers extended more than $500 in credit to the influential Cherokee leader Doublehead (Chuqualatague), with the understanding that Byers would cancel Doublehead's factory debts if the summer's "unfinished negotiations turn out favorabl[y]." As it happened, those negotiations proved highly favorable for the United States: Doublehead and 30 other Cherokees signed two treaties ceding five million acres of land in Tennessee, in return for a $3,000 increase in the Cherokee annuity and over $15,000 in goods.[10]

The War Department then brought some of the men who had signed the 1805 treaties, including Doublehead and Vann, to Washington, where federal officials wined, dined, and flattered them, inducing them (on

7 January 1806) to sign away another four million acres of land. The seventeen signatories left the capital with well-greased palms: the new treaty awarded them $2,000 for their personal use, and a special resolution reserved $8,000 of the Cherokees' annuity for payment of "debts due to the Traders in the nation."[11]

These corruptly executed land cessions generated fierce opposition from most Cherokees. Regional councils denounced the new treaties, and in mid-1807 a party from the nation's Upper Towns assassinated Doublehead. The murder rattled the Cherokees' agent, Return Meigs, but did not alter his determination to press for new cessions. In September 1807 Meigs met with a few Cherokee chiefs and asked them to alter the national boundary in the United States' favor. He offered to have Nicholas Byers cancel $1,800 of the Cherokees' factory debts if the chiefs agreed; the chiefs held out for $2,000, plus another $1,000 in cash and goods. Meigs recognized that he could more cheaply fill this demand than move the white families who had settled on the disputed lands, but he predicted his allies would "have their hands full" with their fellow countrymen's complaints.[12]

Meigs guessed correctly. The faction of Cherokees opposed to the recent land cessions gained control of the Cherokees' national council. In November 1808 this faction, headed by The Ridge and others, deposed the Cherokees' national leaders and asked President Jefferson to help them divide the nation into Upper Towns and Lower Towns sections (based in east Tennessee and northern Alabama, respectively). The proposal fell through, but the national council did subsequently revoke the citizenship of Lower Towns Cherokees who emigrated, and it also refused to make further land cessions.[13]

The Cherokee trading house did not long survive the Upper Towns chiefs' victory over Doublehead's faction. The factory's importance as a trading center had been declining since the turn of the century. Cherokee hunters brought in fewer pelts, and many preferred to deal with private traders, some of whom were themselves Cherokees. Between 1802 and 1806, deerskin shipments from Tellico fell 77 percent, bearskin shipments 96 percent, and beaver exports 97 percent. Meanwhile, the costs of shipping those pelts and supplying the factory remained high, and they rose higher in 1807 when, as Cherokee leaders requested, the Office of Indian Trade moved the factory to Hiwassee, 75 miles down the Tennessee River. The move brought a brief increase in peltry sales, but it also raised overland shipping costs (to Savannah) to $110 per ton.[14]

With the Cherokee factory's business in decline and its expenses rising, John Mason marked the house for closure. In January 1809 Mason asked Meigs "whether the object to the Indians of maintaining" the Hiwassee post justified "the extraordinary expense." Meigs could not say yes, because in his view the factory had mainly served as a source of bribes and subsidies for those Cherokees willing to sign land cessions. By 1809, that group had lost its leaders and its influence, and 1,100 Lower Towns Cherokees had left or had decided to leave for Arkansas. Nicholas Byers, who had supplied earlier Arkansas-bound parties, gave provisions to more departing Cherokees in 1810. This was the last service the Hiwassee house performed for Meigs, who then acquiesced in Mason's decision to close the factory.[15]

IN CONTRAST TO THE Creek and Cherokee factories, the trading houses for the Choctaws and Chickasaws witnessed steady trade and declining Indian debts from 1807 to 1811. George Gaines, the factor at Saint Stephens, shipped over 120,000 pounds of deerskins, 1,000 pounds of beaver, and 2,900 fox furs to Philadelphia and Georgetown in these years. Gaines also ordered and sold an abundance of manufactured goods: his orders for 1807–12 included 10,000 pounds of gunpowder and 5,000 pounds of lead, 2,000 yards of country cotton, 1,400 blankets, 650 shirts, and 800 axes, hatchets, and hoes. Business remained steady despite merchandise price increases occasioned by the 1807–9 embargo.[16]

Gaines's daybooks give some insight into the changes taking place in early nineteenth-century Choctaw material culture. Between 1808 and 1812 Choctaws bought from the factor 64 axes, 122 augurs and gimlets, and 168 saw files, indicating their growing investment in wooden houses and fences and their move toward individual farms. They also purchased cotton and wool cards (25 pairs), cowbells (89), hoes (334), and whips (144), all of which Choctaw women needed to raise livestock and cotton. Choctaw families made these changes to increase their self-sufficiency, and the federal government encouraged the transformation because land-intensive farmers could presumably sell their "extensive forests." At the same time, Choctaw men continued to buy merchandise reflecting their intention to rely on the fur trade as long as possible: powder and lead by the ton, blankets and finished garments by the bale. They and other factory customers also—contrary to Thomas Jefferson's wishes—used their proceeds to pay down their factory debts, which shrank about 6 percent between 1811 and 1812.[17]

Despite his government's stated commitment to Indian "civilization," Gaines went to some trouble to help Choctaw men remain hunters. In particular, he continued to buy great quantities of deerskins, for which he could find, at the moment, little market demand. Superintendent Shee noted in 1807 that deer sold in Philadelphia for only one-eighth the price that Gaines and his predecessor paid their Choctaw trading partners. Seven months later, Superintendent Mason ordered all the southern factors to store their deerskins until the end of the embargo. The factor had to enlarge his storehouse and hire additional beaters to keep his skins free of worms. Another burden related to supplying Choctaw hunters fell upon the factory in 1809, when Governor Folch closed Mobile to American lead and gunpowder, and Gaines had to open an expensive overland supply route through Chickasaw country. High transport costs eroded the Choctaw trading house's net worth, as did the ongoing depression in deerskin prices. The book value of Saint Stephens factory fell by $10,353 between 1807 and 1811—one of the largest declines in the system.[18]

No such extraordinary costs accrued to the trading house at Chickasaw Bluffs. Thanks to its location on the Mississippi River, the Chickasaw factory could receive goods by flatboat and export its furs through New Orleans duty-free. The Chickasaw Bluffs house did, however, run into periodic shortages, caused by the difficulty of trans-Appalachian freight haulage and the irregularities of river transportation. Two 1811 shipments of merchandise, for example, took a year to arrive from Georgetown.[19]

Such shortages also developed in consequence of the Chickasaw factory's high volume of business and the Chickasaws' steady demand for goods, which was probably greater per capita than the Choctaws'. For just one trading season (the winter of 1810–11), the factor at Chickasaw Bluffs requested, among other goods, 1,250 pounds of gunpowder, 175 blankets, 50 blue strouds, and 50 pairs of cotton cards. Factor John Treat, formerly of Arkansas Post, made it clear he already had buyers for these items: "The above articles are much wanted," he wrote the Office of Indian Trade, and "it is probable they would not be more than the winter and spring [trading] seasons would demand."[20]

Robert Bayly, who upon Treat's death succeeded him as factor, placed an equally large order in June 1812. This included 1,600 yards of calico and chintz and several dozen axes and hoes. The last two, along with Treat's cotton cards, indicate that some Chickasaws used the factory to support their adoption of "civilized" occupations, namely commercial agriculture and textile production. Rush Nutt, who visited the Chickasaws' towns in 1805, observed that Chickasaw families were raising grain and livestock and asserted that "the men have laid down their gun and tomahawk & taken up the implements of husbandry." The quantity of furs and skins Chickasaws sold the trading house somewhat belied Nutt's claim: between 1807 and 1811 the factors' trading partners sold several thousand beaver, fox, and raccoon furs, several hundred pounds of tallow, and at least 140,000 pounds of deerskins.[21]

The ample peltry they sold at Chickasaw Bluffs, combined with the modest prices the factors charged their Chickasaw trading partners—their markup generally ranged from 33 to 66 percent above Philadelphia prices—allowed the Chickasaws steadily to reduce their factory debts. Total debts owed the factory shrank 43 percent, from $5,928 to $3,376, between December 1807 and June 1812. Concurrently, the factory's large shipments of skins and smaller furs, combined with moderate transport costs, allowed Chickasaw Bluffs, alone of the southern factories, to post a four-year gain in net worth.[22]

The diminution of the Chickasaws' factory debts lowered the likelihood that their leaders would want to make a debt-for-land swap with the United States, particularly after they paid off their private debts to John Forbes & Company with the proceeds of their 1805 land sale. Moreover, the War Department had since 1795 provided the Chickasaws an annuity to assure itself of that nation's good offices, which it needed in order to keep the Natchez Trace open. The payments were small, but the U.S. government furnished them without demanding any territorial quid pro quo. This served as a further disincentive for the Chickasaws to cede more land to the United States: why do so when the nation enjoyed shrinking debts, favorable trading terms, and a free annuity?[23]

If President Jefferson hoped that the trading factories would induce Indians to sell off their "extensive forests," the Chickasaw and Choctaw factories must have disappointed him. After their cessions of 1805, neither nation would sign another treaty until 1816. To the extent that anyone benefited materially from these two trading posts, the southern Indians did, not the federal government.

Yet insofar as the factories existed to assure the United States of Native Americans' friendship and military assistance, both the Chickasaw and Choctaw factories became success stories. When after 1812 Americans found themselves embroiled in war with Britain and the Red Stick

Creeks, the Chickasaws and Choctaws proved their strongest allies in the southeast. The factories were hardly the only reasons why these nations' warriors threw in their lot with the United States, but the material benefits and diplomatic gifts they received from the trading houses almost certainly served as incentives.[24]

A HIGH VOLUME of business did not always translate into profitability for the factories, since so many of the furs and skins the factors purchased proved either unsalable or, when sold, barely worth the cost of transporting them. If, however, business volume also measured Indians' interest in and reliance on a particular factory, the new Trans-Mississippi trading posts at Fort Osage and Fort Madison clearly generated great interest from the start. Between 1809 (their first full year of operations) and 1813, the two new trading houses shipped to New Orleans 178,300 pounds of deerskins, 21,000 raccoon furs, 17,000 pounds of tallow, and 133,000 pounds of lead. Early reports by one house's factor suggested that the two factories had as many customers as they could handle: George Sibley, in his first month at Fort Osage, traded with at least 100 Kansa and Osage men.[25]

Sibley's factory originated with Secretary Dearborn's decision to close Bellefontaine house and move some of its inventory and personnel to Osage country. William Clark and Meriwether Lewis, the American officials most familiar with the Missouri Valley, selected for the factory site a bluff overlooking the Missouri River on Fire Prairie, 330 miles from Saint Louis and "convenient to" Osage and Kansa towns. In August 1808 Clark took six boats and 180 men to Fire Prairie, where the soldiers began building Fort Osage—ultimately a large wooden fort with five blockhouses—while Clark negotiated a treaty with Osage leaders. George Sibley, former assistant factor at Bellefontaine, arrived at the site and began trading with the Osages in September.[26]

Sibley's trading partners sold him a prodigious amount of Indian goods: nearly $27,000 worth in 21 months. Sibley shipped most of these downriver to Saint Louis and New Orleans, but the factor also purchased some goods he could only sell locally, like meat (5,500 pounds by mid-1810) and tallow. In return for the animal products they sold the factory, the Kansa and Osage Indians purchased blankets, calico, knives, silver earrings, and gunpowder. What Sibley's partners chose *not* to buy is, in some ways, as revealing as their purchasing decisions. The factor returned as "unsuitable for the trade" fishing tackle, cowbells, and beaver traps, among other articles. Some of these the Kansas and Osages, who did not rely on fishing or stock-raising, could not use; the last item the Osages found defective.[27]

While the Osage factory's book value grew, its overall business volume declined after its first year. By 1812, Sibley was shipping only 60 percent as many deerskins, half as many beaver pelts, and one-quarter as many bearskins per year as he had packed and shipped in 1809. The decrease in the quantity of goods the Indians sold the factory did not apply to all commodities. Sibley recorded increased purchases of tallow and raccoon, and in 1810 the factory temporarily acquired tallow candles, produced by a local white family at their home. (Mason sold them as curiosities.) Apart from these exceptions, the factory generally shipped fewer Indian wares with each passing year.[28]

It is difficult to deduce the reasons for this decline from factory records alone, but other sources suggest several causes. Sibley may have been following the superintendent's directive that he curtail his purchases of deerskins. Also, some of the factor's Indian trading partners had resumed business with private traders. William Clark initially prohibited fur traders from passing Fort Osage, but after the Kansas and Otos complained that the factory was too distant from their towns, Clark, now the governor of Missouri Territory, relented. By 1812 white traders had taken up residence with the Kansas, Osages, Otos, and Pawnees. Finally, the Indian nations who initially traded with the factory intermittently warred with one another during its first years of operation: the Kansas with the Pawnees and Otos, and the Osages with the Iowas and Sauks. Warriors' raids made long journeys to Fort Osage dangerous; for example, an unidentified war band robbed an Osage trading party as it left the fort in April 1812.[29]

The interethnic warfare that flared in the neighborhood of Fort Osage magnified the factory's importance as a diplomatic center, even as its trading volume declined. From his first year at the post, George Sibley affirmed his dual role as a trader and a diplomat by giving gifts to his trading partners and to other Indian visitors, a well-established policy Sibley found it prudent to retain. "Custom has established it as a law with the Osages," the factor wrote, "a practice of soliciting from traders and other white people . . . small presents of tobacco, paint, ribbon, calico &c" to mourn the death of a warrior, celebrate the arrival of guests, or mark the end of a hunt. "[I]t would look ill for the U.S. to disregard" this custom. The Osages enjoyed most, but not all, of Sibley's largesse: in 1809, for

Table 5.1 Indian Products Shipped by the Fort Osage Factory, 1809–1813

	1809	1810	1811	1812	1813	Total
Bear	2,495	326	317	623	375	4,136
Beaver	4,213	653	1,000	2,130	1,187	9,183
Bison horns		321	100	167	36	624
Bison robes		58	7	9	76	150
Candles		505	2,403			2,908
Cat	663	175	94	112	43	1,087
Deer	28,322	14,606	10,264	16,732	12,410	82,334
Elk		152	29	32	40	253
Elk Horns		36	100		155	291
Fox	39	25	9	18	2	93
Muskrat	663	25		170	36	894
Otter	338	99	105		127	669
Raccoon	1,350	971	874	2,184	1,507	6,886
Tallow*			8,500	5,726	1,904	16,130
Wolf	43	106	56	40	17	262

Sources: *1809*: Invoices Inward, 4:33, 35, 37, 38, 39, 41, and 49; *1810–13*: Journal and Invoices of Peltry Shipped, Misc. Accounts of Fort Osage, Box 1, Folders 1–5; Furs and Pelts Taken by the Factory, 1 Oct. 1808 to 30 June 1810, ibid., Box 1, Folder 1.

In this table, beaver, candle, deer, elk horn, and tallow figures are in pounds; all others represent individual furs or skins. Bear figures include cubs. Bear and deerskin covers, used to cover fur shipments, are not included, nor are a few badger and groundhog pelts and 90 gallons of bear's oil.

Deerskins appear in the factory's records as individual dressed skins and pounds of shaved skins; the author has grouped these two types together, assuming an average weight of 2 pounds per dressed skin. In 1809 the Office of Indian Trade received a parcel of 2,676 "cat, muskrat, and raccoon" furs from Fort Osage. Since the factory purchased 2,350 raccoon furs by mid-1810, the author has assumed that 1,350 furs from the 1809 shipment were raccoon and divided the remainder into 663 cat and 663 muskrat.

*Sibley bought over 4,300 pounds of tallow between 1808 and 1810, but apparently he sold or disposed of it locally.

example, he gave a laced coat, plumed hat, and silver armbands to a Pawnee chief and his son.[30]

Some of Sibley's Osage customers clearly indicated that they considered trading a form of mutual gift-giving. In September 1808 an elderly Osage man approached Sibley and begged him for "a little blue cloth to bury his wife in," giving the factor some animal skins. In return Sibley gave the man tobacco and two yards of cloth. On its face, this was a simple exchange of peltry for merchandise, but the Osage man's words and posture infused the trade with greater significance: his supplicatory pose made him an object of pity, while his reference to his deceased wife established an emotional bond between him and the factor. This sort of exchange affirmed the common humanity as well as the mutual utility of both trading partners. One suspects similar instances occurred but went unrecorded at other factories.[31]

The Osages also made it clear that they expected Sibley to extend hospitality to them regularly, even though he described himself and his clerk Isaac Rawlings as "utterly unfit to manage kitchen affairs" apart from beef and potatoes. "Frequently we are honored with an Osage chief or war captain to dine or sup with us," the factor wrote, "and very often are favored with the company of the princesses and young ladies of rank decked out in all the[ir] finery of beads red ribbons and vermilion, silver ornaments and scarlet blankets." As in Creek country, Osage women visited Fort Osage to affirm their kinsmen's good intentions; while they did not leave a record of formal diplomatic conversation, their very presence at the fort and factory spoke volumes.[32]

To his diplomatic roles as gift-giver and host, Sibley perforce added that of mediator. In 1810 the factor took depositions from one Osage warrior and two chiefs (Town Maker and John LeFoe) concerning the theft of property from an American, and he recorded their payment of beaver pelts as restitution. On a larger scale, in May 1811 Sibley left Fort Osage on a diplomatic mission to the towns of the Kansas, Pawnees, and Arkansas Osages. The factor distributed American flags and medals as symbols of amity; the Pawnees responded with a gift of thirty horses. Sibley also invited Kansa, Osage, and Pawnee leaders to a general meeting, in which he urged them to make peace with one another and to trade (or resume trading) at the Osage factory.[33]

The factor wanted to create a regional alliance that would extend the United States' commercial influence several hundred miles up the Missouri and Kansas Rivers. While the peace agreement which Sibley negotiated did not last, his mission probably helped stabilize the United States' relationship with the nations he visited. During the Anglo-American war that began the year after Sibley's return, the Kansa Indians remained neutral, even though British agents endeavored to recruit them. Osage warriors, once foes of American expansion, became American allies against British-allied Sauks.[34]

That only a portion of the Sauk nation allied with the British can be attributed, in part, to the U.S. government's commercial policy toward them, a policy centering on the establishment of a convenient factory for the Sauks and Mesquakies. William Harrison had promised them a trading house in 1804, but the Illinois Sauks, adequately supplied by the British, did not immediately press the issue. In 1807, however, some Sauk hunters and chiefs—recognizing the merits of having another supply center close to home—agreed that Bellefontaine stood inconveniently far from their towns. To accommodate them, Secretary of War Dearborn agreed to move part of Bellefontaine's merchandise to a successor factory at the confluence of the Des Moines and Mississippi Rivers, 200 miles from Saint Louis. Lieutenant Alpha Kingsley, surveying the site in the fall of 1808, thought it dangerously flood-prone, and he and his superiors decided to move the factory and garrison to a bluff in present-day southeastern Iowa.[35]

The Sauks' factor, John Johnson of Maryland (Superintendent Mason's brother-in-law), reached his post in October 1808. His factory, an oak-shingled building with nine rooms on three stories, remained under construction. Unfinished or not, the establishment received many Indian visitors over the next few years. In May 1809, for instance, "four hundred canoes" bearing Sauk and Mesquakie men and women stopped at the federal post, which had been named Fort Madison. Pausing en route from their winter hunting grounds to their summer villages, they paid the factor for goods they had bought on credit the previous fall. Johnson shipped over 36,000 pounds of deerskins and nearly 5,000 raccoon and muskrat furs to Saint Louis that year. By the end of 1811, he had purchased Indian wares with a total invoiced value of over $35,000, including several hundred bushels of maize—a hospitable gesture if not a salable commodity—and 112,000 pounds of lead. Native Americans residing in the upper Mississippi Valley mined many tons of lead, whose high "quality and quantity," noted Superintendent Mason, explained why Fort Madison posted a $10,000 gain in book value since its opening.[36]

With the credit Johnson advanced them for their lead and peltries, the Sauks and Mesquakies purchased the same sort of merchandise that the Osages bought at George Sibley's factory. During the early years of the Fort Madison factory, however, the quality of Johnson's wares was poor, because the embargo prevented the Office of Indian Trade from importing fresh goods from Europe. The fort's sutler, George Hunt, recalled that "It would seem that all the old goods of all our cities were bought up as good enough for wild Indians . . . The blankets were small and thin . . . the cloths . . . so narrow that two yards would not make a matchicota [mantle] for a squaw and the calico would not, from age, hold together." Both Johnson and his Indian customers complained about the "miserable" quality of the factory's merchandise.[37]

Since the Sauks and Mesquakies knew of the shoddy quality of American goods, and since traders at Prairie du Chien could sell them better British merchandise, one wonders why they did so much business with Johnson ($20,000 worth by the end of 1809). George Hunt opined that their interest stemmed from Johnson's willingness to extend credit: "No matter how inferior an article, if an Indian can obtain it on a credit he will take it." Perhaps some wanted to establish a good early trading relationship, in the hope that the factory's merchandise would later improve (as it did). Others likely wanted to maintain good relations with the U.S. government and, in accordance with the principle that "the trade and the peace . . . [are] the same thing," saw continued trade as a means to that end. The Sauk and Mesquakie Indians had maintained cordial relations with most of the belligerents in the American Revolutionary War (Britain, Spain, and the United States), a political balancing act which many Indian nations practiced to maximize their chances of survival. Apparently the Sauks and Mesquakies wanted to continue this practice and firm up their relationships with all of the European powers within their ambit.[38]

Not all of the Native American peoples of the northern Mississippi Valley wanted to demonstrate such political ambidexterity. The Ho-Chunks, along with a large faction of Sauks, opposed the new American post on the upper Mississippi River. In the spring of 1809, a Sauk war party tried to enter Fort Madison's stockade and kill its commander, but soldiers of the garrison drove them off. Later that year, Ho-Chunk captains and prophets, spiritual allies of the Shawnee prophet Tenskwatawa, advocated another attack on the fort, prompting Governor Lewis to reinforce the garrison.[39]

American officials attributed Sauk and Ho-Chunk hostility not to Native American grievances but to the intrigues of British traders and agents. Indeed, William Clark and agent Nicolas Boilvin believed that Indian prophets and proponents of confederation ultimately served Great Britain, gathering to defend their British "father" in the event of another Anglo-American war. While this belief was inaccurate, it is not surpris-

Table 5.2 Indian Wares Shipped by the Fort Madison Factory, 1809–1813

	1809	1810	1811	1812–13	Total
Bear	20	345	202	120	687
Bear's oil		488			488
Beaver	700	906	327	738	2671
Deer	36,299	18,362	12,916	203	67,780
Feathers		578		460	1,038
Lead		80,624	31,389	21,479	133,492
Mats		75		4	79
Muskrat	1,353	188	2,157	634	4,332
Otter	176	119	47	61	403
Raccoon	3,585	2,583	5,031	2,949	14,148
Tallow		479	256		735
Wax		235	700		935

Sources: Invoices Inward, 4:34, 55, 63, 78, 82, 83, and 86; Factory Inventories, 1 Jan. 1810, 1 April 1810, 1 July 1810, 31 March 1811, and 31 Dec. 1811, in Misc. Accounts of Fort Madison, Box 1, Folders 15 and 27.

Bear, mat, otter, and raccoon figures represent individual items. All other figures are in pounds. Bear and deerskin covers are not included, nor are several hundred bushels of maize, 732 pounds of maple sugar, or three bison robes. 1812–13 figures represent produce received by the Office of Indian Trade in 1813.

ing that U.S. officials held it, since their government had recently started a commercial war with Britain, embargoing that country's imports, barring British traders from the United States, and building factories like Fort Madison within Britain's zone of economic influence. No doubt they assumed Britons would show similar belligerence toward them.[40]

The success John Johnson enjoyed in attracting Britain's former trading partners led him to extend the factory's operations further afield. In September 1811 Johnson loaned merchandise to George Hunt and sent him to establish a subfactory at Toledo Mort in the Illinois lead-mining district (near modern Dubuque). Hunt and his three assistants erected warehouses and a store, and by October they were trading with up to fifteen Indian canoe teams each day. Within a few months, however, Hunt would learn just how vulnerable the Office of Indian Trade's expansionism had made him.[41]

FOR THE TRANS-MISSISSIPPI trading houses at Fort Madison and Fort Osage, the War Department chose previously unoccupied sites many miles from white settlements. By contrast, American officials sited the second generation of Great Lakes factories at well-established communities or trading rendezvous. The first of these posts opened in 1805 at Chicago, a Lake Michigan portage located near a Potawatomi and Ottawa town complex. The second, initially an outpost of the Fort Wayne factory, debuted in 1806 at Sandusky, a seventy-year-old Wyandot settlement. The third, scheduled to open in 1808, adorned Mackinac Island, an Ojibwa ceremonial center and the site of a British and American fort since the Revolutionary War.[42]

The U.S. government laid the legal groundwork for the Chicago factory in the Treaty of Greenville, wherein Great Lakes Indian leaders ceded to the United States a reservation at the mouth of the Chicago River. Army troops occupied the site eight years later and built Fort Dearborn, to which the secretary of war moved the moribund Detroit trading house. The new Chicago factory got off to a rocky start: one-third of its initial supply of goods perished in the 1805 Detroit fire, and its first factor, Ebenezer Belknap, lost his job for drunkenness and bad character. Belknap's assistant, Thomas Hayward, took charge of the trading house but did not see much business until late in his term; the factory did not begin to ship furs and skins to Philadelphia until 1807.[43]

Under Hayward's successors, Joseph Varnum—a War Department clerk and a congressman's son—and Matthew Irwin, the Chicago factory's business volume increased. Between 1807 and 1811, Potawatomi, Ho-Chunk, and other Great Lakes Indian hunters sold the trading house peltries (chiefly muskrat and raccoon) with a total invoiced value of $14,200. Additional Indian produce, of the "frontier-exchange" or diplomatic type, included corn, maple sugar, and moccasins. Since the factory mostly shipped "hatter's furs," which commanded good prices in New York and Philadelphia, and whose light weight kept transport costs low, Chicago posted a modest ($3,725) gain in book value by 1811.[44]

Varnum and Irwin's Indian clients received (in 1810) one dollar for every five muskrat furs, three mink furs, or pound of beaver pelts they sold the factory. That dollar would, in turn, purchase one and a half yards of calico cloth, five small knives, or ten ounces of gunpowder. While the Potawatomis considered the factory's goods fairly cheap, the factors also paid low prices for Indians' furs and skins. However, the Great Lakes Indians also had a comparatively limited demand for trade goods, so they usually settled their accounts by the end of each trading season. Indians owed the factory only $170 total in June 1809. Making up for Indians'

Table 5.3 Selected Shipments from the Chicago Factory, 1807–1811

	1807	1808	1809	1810	1811	Total
Cat	38	104	56	40	68	306
Deer	596	1,256	397	394	435	3,078
Fox	9	59	37	32	48	185
Mink	154	198	114	110	447	1,023
Muskrat	8,430	4,988	2,523	3,854	11,477	31,272
Otter	71	108	34	71	81	365
Raccoon	3,507	8,149	2,226	4,456	6,660	24,998
Wolf	46	101	53	185	88	473

Sources: Peltries Shipped, 6 June 1807, Misc. Accounts of the Chicago Factory; Statement of Account, 21 Dec. 1807, ibid.; Invoices Inward, 1796–1822, 3:54; 4:17, 43, 52, 68

All items in the table above (including deer) represent individual skins or pelts. Bear, beaver, fisher, and martin exports (collectively totaling about 100 furs) are not included. The 1807 figures do not include three shipments of peltry, on 24 July, 21 August, and 30 August, collectively invoiced at $1,798. The author has not located a detailed inventory of these shipments.

lower quantity of purchases, the local Indian agent, Charles Jouett, and the local military agent gave the factors additional business. Both bought trade goods and supplies from the factory and settled their accounts in cash or War Department drafts; the factory's balance sheet for 1807–11 credited it with nearly $6,000 in cash and drafts, a sum equaling almost 30 percent of its remittances.[45]

While the Chicago factory prospered, its contemporary on the other side of the lower Great Lakes, at Sandusky, enjoyed dimmer prospects. Henry Dearborn and William Davy established the Sandusky trading house in 1806 as an outpost of the Fort Wayne factory, in the hopes of drawing Wyandot and Ottawa customers, who needed ample supplies and could "make good pay." The Sandusky factory grew within two years into a multi-building complex with a staff of five. Its business grew less rapidly: between 1807 and July 1812, factor Samuel Tupper shipped to Georgetown about 22,300 raccoon and muskrat furs, among other peltries; his remittances had a total invoiced value of $9,000. By contrast, the Chicago factory remitted more than $20,000 in cash and peltries during the same period.[46]

The Sandusky factory's low volume of business caused it to lose nearly $3,400 in book value by the fall of 1811, making it the only northern factory to sustain such a loss. Its poor economic performance probably resulted, in part, from competition. At the time of its founding, several British traders lived and worked on the Auglaize River, and American traders operated in western Ohio. Also, Sandusky did not offer the same convenience to homebound Indian hunters as did Chicago and Fort Wayne, which adjoined portages connecting the Great Lakes with the rich hunting grounds of the upper Mississippi Valley.[47]

Sandusky's isolation did not indicate a lack of sophistication on the part of its Native American customers—quite the reverse. Sandusky's trading partners hailed from a complex of towns on the lower Sandusky River whose inhabitants included Ottawas, Wyandots, and Delawares, all of them long-time European trading partners. They demanded, and the factory stocked, an eclectic and sophisticated array of merchandise: consumables such as snuff, corn, and maple sugar; a wide array of textiles, including red flannel, osnabrig, and blue kersey; hunters' supplies, like flints and beaver traps; and hardware such as handsaw files and dutch ovens, which reflected the local Indians' adoption of carpentry and the cold local climate.[48]

Samuel Waterman (Tupper's predecessor) also identified more specialized goods as "very saleable," "in great demand," or "very necessary" at Sandusky. From Superintendent John Shee, Waterman requested saddle bags with locks, nests of trunks for personal possessions, mittens, ice skates, silver spoons stamped with the letters "U.S.", imported queensware and wine glasses, bed linen, tin-plated stovepipes, and woodworking tools. "All kinds of hardware and tools," the factor wrote, "will sell very well to the Wyandots, who are wishful to improve in building and the cultivation of land." Waterman might have added that the southeastern Great Lakes Indians also wanted to guard their stock of personal property; to take advantage of their sedentary communities by adorning their houses with heavy beds, stoves, and tableware; and to retain individual mobility (hence the ice skates) in a region with hard winters and few roads.[49]

The merchandise on the shelves at Sandusky included commodities forwarded to that factory from the third of the new Lakes trading houses, on Mackinac Island in the strait separating Lake Huron from Lake Michigan. Mackinac factory opened with high hopes for its success. The island and its environs, a major fur-trading center since the seventeenth century, remained one in the nineteenth; local fur traders and companies dispatched nearly 850 voyageurs from Mackinac between 1807 and 1817. Secretary Dearborn approved the Mackinac factory as a thrust against the British traders of the upper Great-Lakes region, and John Mason appointed an experienced factor, Joseph Varnum, to run it. When, after numerous delays, Varnum finally reached Mackinac in the fall of 1809, he found the factory—a 7,740-square-foot structure previously occupied by the garrison commander—in dismal repair, and the island cut off from customers by ice. Few Indians visited the new factory in the first winter, and by June 1810 Varnum had bought only 400 furs and skins. He also had to get rid of $2,800 worth of goods that the northern Great Lakes Indians would not buy:, white wampum (which they did not want), defective American-made beaver traps, and copper kettles and silver jewelry that local Indians found too heavy.[50]

Since the upper Great Lakes Indians preferred to stay in their villages that winter, Varnum made a virtue of necessity and gave "a few respectable persons" among the white trading community credit to buy his merchandise. These traders then resold Varnum's goods in Native American communities up to 300 miles away. By the end of 1810, the factor's "few respectable persons" grew to include 58 separate debtors, chiefly white and métis traders, who collectively owed the factory $4,836. "Sundry Indians" comprised only one line on the list.[51]

Varnum eventually did attract Indian trading partners, either directly or indirectly (through white traders), to the Mackinac factory. The factor bought few furs, but he accumulated and shipped to Detroit a prodigious amount of maple sugar—about 24,000 pounds in 1811—which he valued on the factory's balance sheet at nine cents per pound, though there was only a regional market for it. Between its sugar shipments, the crediting of unwanted goods to Chicago and Sandusky factories, and the cash and IOUs that local merchants paid for goods, Varnum's factory achieved a $3,085 net worth gain by 1811.[52]

Mackinac's gains proved much smaller, however, than those of the oldest federal trading house in the Lakes region, at Fort Wayne. Between 1807 and 1811, the Fort Wayne factory, under the direction of John Johnston, increased its net worth by $10,502, the largest gain of any of the ten factories in operation. The Fort Wayne factory's gains derived from a surge in Native American skin and fur sales that followed several years of lackluster business. Between 1808 and 1811, the trading house shipped $27,320 worth of peltries, most of them the "hatter's furs" prized by eastern buyers, whose light weight mitigated high transport costs.[53]

The annual merchandise orders that Factor Johnston submitted to the Office of Indian Trade make it clear which of the factory's wares his

Native American customers particularly wanted: rifles, ammunition, knives, needles, wampum, saddles, and twist tobacco. Johnston also ordered iron and steel for the fort's blacksmith, whom his Indian customers visited in order to repair their tools, traps, and rifles. Most importantly, the factor stocked and sold textiles: swanskin and baize cloth for men's leggings, russia duck (heavy linen) for tents, flannel, striped cotton cloth, calico, and blankets.[54]

Johnston's merchandise orders displayed keen attention to detail. Superintendent Mason had ordered the factor to provide him with a "particular" account of local Indians' wants and needs, and Johnston obliged him by including many specific details that he must have based on observation of Great Lakes Indian behavior and demands. For example, he requested a gross of sail needles, which the Indians used to "sketch skins with bark thread"; specified that trade rifles have brass mounting, maple stocks, and 47-inch-long barrels; and identified gray wampum, of which he ordered 30,000 one year, as "an essential article in the trade." In their specificity, Johnston's orders attest to his and Mason's desire to accommodate Indians' particular demands, thereby underscoring their government's desire to retain those customers' friendship. The orders also provide details about the economic culture of the Miamis, Ottawas, and Potawatomis who patronized the Fort Wayne trading house.[55]

First, not all of the factory's goods were strictly utilitarian. The Fort Wayne trading house stocked and sold two commodities with a diplomatic function, namely tobacco and wampum. Eastern and Plains Indians smoked tobacco at treaties as a "seal or memorial to an agreement of peace," while the Great Lakes Indians employed wampum not only for decoration but to remember diplomatic speeches and certify their sincerity. Apparently the Lakes Indians still regarded trade as a way of acquiring goods with ceremonial functions, and thus as a partly diplomatic rather than purely economic enterprise.[56]

Second, the Native Americans who traded with Johnston had not embraced the same dramatic economic changes as the contemporary southeastern Indians or the Delaware and Wyandot communities near Sandusky. Goods such as cowbells and spindles rarely appeared on Johnston's shelves. Instead, his Native American customers' marked demand for ammunition, fishhooks, and cloth indicates that they still based their local economies on hunting, fishing, subsistence agriculture, and trade, and that they planned to rely on the fur trade to provide the goods they required. Fort Wayne and posts like it would play an important role in their lives for the foreseeable future.[57]

For all Johnston's efforts to ensure that his Indian customers had access to the goods they wanted, they sometimes expressed dissatisfaction with the factor's wares. Johnston generally sold his goods at lower prices than those charged by private traders, but as at the Fort Madison and Mackinac factories, the merchandise on his shelves frequently proved "unfit for the Indian trade." In his official correspondence Johnston reported, for example, that the trade office had sent him unsalable jewelry. His Indian customers preferred gorgets engraved with "a fish or animal," small heart-shaped chest broaches, and ear wheels with patterns of four interlocking rings or flower petals—motifs, in short, that recalled clan totems, bodily images, or familiar natural elements. Johnston also observed that he could only sell American-made cloth to the Great Lakes Indians so long as his rivals had no British textiles for sale, for "their dry goods are such as the Indians have been accustomed to from time immemorial."[58]

Johnston had discovered what private traders had long known: Indians were discriminating consumers who wanted familiar and high-quality merchandise. Johnston struggled to meet their needs. If Indian hunters still found the Fort Wayne factory appealing, it was for reasons other than the quality of the factor's wares. These included the factory's convenient location, at the head of two important waterways; the factor's attentiveness to Indian demands, even when he couldn't always provide what they wanted; and the free repair services offered by Fort Wayne's blacksmith. Other reasons included the Miamis' and Potawatomis' desire to keep the peace with the United States and their association of the fort with treaty conferences and annuity distributions, an association strengthened by Johnston's appointment, in 1809, to the post of Indian agent.[59]

Some of the region's Indians, however, held unfavorable views of Fort Wayne and its factory. In 1805–06 the Shawnee brothers Tenskwatawa and Tecumseh had begun forming a pan-Indian confederacy to oppose land sales and assimilation of Euro-American culture. They and their many followers came to regard Fort Wayne as the site of several disgraceful land-cession treaties. Most notorious of these was an 1809 conference at which Delaware, Miami, and Potawatomi chiefs, their palms greased with factory goods and their throats lubricated with whiskey, ceded three million acres of land to the United States. This transaction induced Tecumseh to call for the execution of the signatory chiefs and to threaten war if the Americans attempted to occupy the cession.[60]

Also, Fort Wayne's garrison threatened the Indian confederates' efforts to obtain British assistance, since it could block communication between Upper Canada and Native American towns on the Wabash River. Yet despite the bad reputation that Fort Wayne had acquired among Tecumseh's followers, some may have joined the hundreds of Indians who came to the fort for rations after the hard winter of 1811–12. A few months later, on 17 June 1812, Tecumseh himself stopped at Fort Wayne on his way to Fort Amherstburg. He spent four days dining and conversing with factor Benjamin Stickney, whom he tried to convince of his confederates' peaceful intentions.[61]

On 18 June, Tecumseh's second day at Fort Wayne, U.S. Army Lieutenant Daniel Baker recorded the receipt, at Detroit, of thirty-seven packs of furs from the Fort Wayne factory. It was the last shipment. That same day, four hundred miles away in Washington City, the United States Congress declared war on Great Britain.[62]

BY THE ONSET OF THE WAR of 1812, the factory system had reached institutional maturity, insofar as the trading houses had spread throughout the Great Lakes region and Mississippi Valley, and had demonstrated both their strengths and shortcomings. Their principal weakness remained their inability to achieve any purely economic goals. The system as a whole barely broke even, despite large sales of valuable furs and lead from the northern factories. Nor could many of the trading houses compete with the private traders that the War Department wanted them to supplant. The Creek, Cherokee, and Osage factories all lost customers to private competitors, and the Mackinac factory came to rely on mobile fur traders to sell its wares. And, while President Jefferson had hoped that the factories would ensnare Indian chiefs in a web of debt that would make them more tractable in land negotiations, he only realized his hopes among the Creeks and Cherokees. Choctaws and Chickasaws actually reduced their debt loads at their trading houses, and Native American customers in the north avoided accumulating significant debts.

The factories' strong suit, as they repeatedly demonstrated between 1807 and 1812, remained their diplomatic utility. Superintendent Mason's instructions to one of his factors, David Hogg, stressed the centrality of diplomatic behavior to the factories' mission: "You will on all occasions so demean yourself toward the Indians . . . as to obtain & preserve their friendship, to be conciliatory in all your intercourse with them & by every proper means in your power to secure their attachment to the United States." Most of the factors worked diligently to accommodate their customers' demands: recording their consumer preferences, purchasing their less marketable wares, and even opening an expensive trail to one factory to keep its customers in gunpowder. Factors like George Sibley conducted "everyday" diplomacy in the form of gift-giving and hospitality, and they arranged interethnic peace councils backed with the promise of improved trade. Finally, the factories at Ocmulgee, Tellico, Chickasaw Bluffs, Sandusky, and Fort Wayne helped sustain good U.S.-Indian relations, or at least helped the U.S. government negotiate treaties, by supplying the Creeks, Cherokees, Chickasaws, Wyandots, Miamis, and Potawatomis with annuity goods and compensation for land.[63]

Ultimately, though, only one "metric" can gauge the success of a diplomatic initiative: whether it allowed a government to achieve goals that might otherwise have required military force. The success of the factories as diplomatic institutions rested on their ability to improve U.S.-Indian relations and facilitate the United States' acquisition of Indian land without war. The trading houses did play a part, if a limited one, in facilitating land cessions. The extent to which they "secured [Indians'] attachment to the United States" was about to be tested on the battlefield, as both the British and Americans sought allies in a war that would spread deep into the continent.

6

Ten Commercial Embassies in Wartime

The War of 1812 began on the United States' maritime frontier, where for nearly a decade the British navy had infringed upon the "detached sovereignty" of American ships, impressing sailors from their crews and seizing vessels bound for Napoleon's Europe. Congress and the Jefferson and Madison administrations regarded these as attacks on their nation's independence and honor. They responded with economic sanctions against Britain and France, including the 1807 embargo and a Non-Intercourse Act (1809), intended "to starve the offending nations" into respecting American neutrality. By 1811, it had become clear that these sanctions had failed.[1]

By then, too, American leaders had come to believe that Britain had extended its aggression against the United States to the nation's landward frontier, manipulating the Great Lakes Indians into a war with the Americans. This was a potent but misguided belief. The Americans' own man on the ground, Indiana Governor William Harrison, had actually instigated that war. Harrison's 1809 Treaty of Fort Wayne led to an angry confrontation with pan-Indian leaders Tecumseh and Tenskwatawa and their confederates. Harrison responded, in the fall of 1811, by leading 1,000 troops against the confederates' headquarters at Prophetstown. Harrison's force fended off an attack by Indian warriors at Tippecanoe Creek (7 November), then plundered and burned Prophetstown. Early the following year, Ho-Chunk warriors retaliated by attacking American outposts in Illinois and present-day Iowa, including George Hunt's outpost of the Fort Madison factory, which they burned. Ho-Chunks killed several soldiers outside Fort Madison itself later that spring. While small in scale, these attacks convinced American officials that a British-led Indian confederation now mobilized against the United States.[2]

American officials persuaded themselves that submission to British or (they believed) British-inspired Indian attacks would sully their nation's honor and call into question its ability to protect its citizens, whether sailors or frontiersmen. Hence Congress's declaration of war on Great Britain. Once the Anglo-American war began, its center of gravity quickly shifted to the continental interior, as the U.S. government organized an invasion of Canada (the one British possession within its army's range) and Britain sought to defend Canada and launch diversionary attacks on the United States' Atlantic and Gulf coasts. The Indian nations of the Great Lakes region and the Deep South held many of the keys to American success or failure, and the ability of Britain and the United States to recruit Native American allies became proportionally important. As it turned out, many warriors wanted to fight, some to sustain old alliances, others for individual prestige and wealth, still others to protect their land or sustain Tecumseh's confederation. Altogether, nearly 20,000 Native Americans fought in the War of 1812, 80 percent as British allies and the rest as American allies.[3]

The continental focus of the War of 1812 and the vital role that Indians played in its campaigns turned the conflict into a test of the Indian factories: could the United States now capitalize on the influence the trading houses had generated? Around the Great Lakes, Native American warriors answered that question by capturing, destroying, or otherwise neutralizing the four U.S. trading houses in the region. They thus acknowledged, in a backhanded way, the factories' significance, but they also prevented the Americans from using those factories to build wartime alliances. In the Mississippi-Missouri Valley, raiders forced the temporary closure of the Fort Madison and Osage trading houses, but the United States had enough Indian allies and thus enough security to relocate these factories, which continued to serve as centers of trade and diplomacy. In the Southeast, the factories from Ocmulgee to Natchitoches not only survived the war but served as supply and recruitment centers for American-allied warriors. The system as a whole survived both the wartime destruction of individual trading houses and the systemic shocks delivered by British maritime forces, whose blockade severed the supply lines of the Office of Indian Trade, and whose 1814 attack on Washington City forced Superintendent John Mason to close his office and submerge (literally) its assets. Whether the system would survive the peace that followed the war remained uncertain, as this survival depended less on the factories' passage of its wartime tests— securing U.S.-Indian alliances and neutralizing Anglo-Indian ones— than on the mixed motives of the Americans who would evaluate the test results.

THE DAY AFTER Congress declared war on Britain, Superintendent Mason warned the factors at Chicago, Fort Wayne, Mackinac, and

Sandusky that their factories were now vulnerable to attack and that they should take suitable defensive precautions. The warning had little effect, as British and Indian forces soon captured or destroyed all of these posts. The first to fall, Mackinac, did so just four weeks after Mason wrote his letter.[4]

Two circumstances accounted for the speed with which Britain seized Mackinac Island. Captain Charles Roberts, the British commandant of nearby Saint Joseph's Island, had early notice of the declaration of war courtesy of John Astor, who had alerted his Canadian business partners to the outbreak. Astor's colleagues, in turn, shared the news with Lieutenant Governor Isaac Brock, who notified Roberts and other garrison commanders. Captain Roberts quickly assembled a strike force of Northwest Company *voyageurs* and four hundred Ho-Chunk, Ojibwa, Ottawa, and Sioux warriors, and on 17 July they landed on Mackinac Island. The attackers mounted cannon on the heights overlooking Fort Mackinac and forced the commander of the island's garrison to surrender, thereby capturing Mackinac factory and assets worth nearly $13,000. Roberts gave the house's merchandise to his Indian allies for their services.[5]

The booty at Mackinac soon included some former property of the Chicago factory: nearly $6,000 worth of furs, which Matthew Irwin sent to Mackinac before learning of that island's capture. Irwin had shipped the furs on the orders of Nathan Heald, commandant of Fort Dearborn, who assumed the peltries would be safer at Mackinac than Chicago. Fort Dearborn had been on alert since April, when Ho-Chunk warriors killed two white farmers nearby. In the summer a faction of Potawatomis counseled with Ho-Chunk leaders, and some joined Tecumseh's confederacy; in late July Potawatomi gunmen fired on Fort Dearborn. Heald understood his command's parlous situation when the war began, and he probably expressed no surprise when on 9 August he received orders to evacuate his post, which the U.S. Army could no longer defend.[6]

Heald spent the next few days assembling Chicago's civilians for the evacuation and distributing the remaining factory goods to neutral Potawatomis. On 15 August about 55 American soldiers and 40 civilians assembled to depart. Later that day, as the evacuees made their way down the shore of Lake Michigan, five hundred British-aligned Miami and Potawatomi warriors intercepted them, killed more than half of the Americans, and took the survivors captive. The war party then destroyed what was left of Fort Dearborn. Another American post and factory had fallen.[7]

One day later the United States suffered another critical loss: the surrender of Detroit and more than 2,000 American troops to British forces
under Isaac Brock. The American commander, William Hull, had come
to Detroit in July to prepare an invasion of Upper Canada, but he had
lost his nerve after news arrived of the fall of Mackinac. When General
Brock arrived at Detroit with 1,600 soldiers and warriors, issuing a thinly
veiled threat to set his Indian allies against the town's civilians, Hull broke
down completely and raised the white flag. Brock's American prisoners
included Joseph Varnum, former factor at Mackinac, whom British
troops held for six months before paroling him.[8]

The collapse of American power on the Great Lakes continued into
late August with the fall of Upper Sandusky, whose American commander ordered its evacuation after learning of the capture of Detroit.
The new factor at Sandusky, Jacob Varnum (Joseph's brother), had
arrived at his post in late 1811 and enjoyed a modestly successful trading
season with the Wyandots and Ottawas. After receiving his evacuation
orders Varnum went to Delaware, Ohio, to hire wagons to remove his
post's merchandise. On 23 August, during the factor's absence, three hundred Canadian militia and Indian warriors came up the Sandusky River
and destroyed the fort and trading house. Varnum lost over $3,800 worth
of public property.[9]

The final act of the northern Anglo-Indian offensive began in late August, when Potawatomi leaders Winamac and Five Medals led an attack
on Fort Wayne. Potawatomi warriors killed acting factor Stephen Johnston as he traveled to Ohio; other raiders burned some of the fort's out-
buildings in early September. Winamac tried but failed to take Fort
Wayne by surprise during a parley with the commandant. On 5 September the five hundred warriors gathered outside the fort began assaulting
it with musket fire and flaming arrows, but the seventy soldiers within
the stockade doused the flames and returned fire. The defenders held
their own for a week, until the besieging warriors learned that an ap-
proaching American relief party would arrive before British reinforcements did. The Potawatomis and Miamis lifted their siege. Before they
did so, the Fort Wayne factory burned down; most likely the garrison
troops set the fire to deny cover to the Indians attacking the fort.
(Indian agent Benjamin Stickney later wrote that the trading house
was "burned for the safety of the fort.") Acting factor Stephen Johnston
had moved most of the merchandise into the stockade before his death,
but the factory still sustained $5,500 of losses.[10]

The battle at Fort Wayne, and a similarly abortive Native American attack on Fort Harrison (near modern Terre Haute) that same month, brought the Anglo-Indian campaign to a temporary halt. This did not, however, spell the end of trouble for the factories. Fort Madison came under attack on 5 September by two hundred Ho-Chunk and Sauk warriors, who during the next three days destroyed several boats and cabins, killed a soldier, and tried to burn the fort with flaming arrows. Worried that the Indians might use the factory to ignite the fort (by setting fire to it on a day when high winds would spread the flames), the garrison commander ordered his soldiers to destroy the building as a preventive measure. Factor Johnson moved or salvaged much of his inventory, but he and Mason estimated that the factory had lost $5,500 in other assets.[11]

Undaunted by the loss, Johnson and his assistant set up a temporary store at Portage des Sioux, which remained open through the winter of 1812–13 and bought ample peltry. The factor sent his remaining goods to Saint Louis, where George Sibley took some of them for the Osage factory and William Clark stored the rest. In 1813 Frederick Bates, acting governor of Missouri Territory, asked Johnson to give him his remaining merchandise and the Sauk and Mesquakie annuities, claiming those nations had "gone over to our enemies." When Johnson demurred, Bates simply seized the factory's goods.[12]

Bates misspoke about the Sauks and Mesquakies. Many members of these two nations remained neutral during the War of 1812, and the Mesquakies sought American protection when an interethnic war erupted between them and the Ho-Chunks. In April 1813 agent Nicholas Boilvin and trader Maurice Blondeau convinced Sauk and Mesquakie neutralists to move to the Des Moines River, hoping thereby to "quarantine" them from British-allied Sauks on the Rock River. The destruction of the Fort Madison factory, however, left these evacuees short of supplies. In September 1813 William Clark persuaded 1,500 Sauks and Mesquakies to move to temporary villages on the Missouri River, where the War Department could rebuild their factory. During the winter of 1813–14, the former Fort Madison trading house reopened at Little Manitou Creek, near the settlement of Sauk chief Quashquame. By the middle of 1814, it had accumulated over $10,000 worth of inventory, including about 10,000 skins and furs; by the end of the war, the Sauks' and Mesquakies' new factory had recorded an increase in book value greater than the losses the Fort Madison trading house had sustained.[13]

This photo displays a modern reconstruction of the factory building at Fort Osage. Courtesy of Fort Osage National Historic Landmark.

The War Department also went to some trouble to sustain Fort Madison's sister factory at Fort Osage, and for a similar reason: to maintain the Osages' good relationship with the United States in wartime. Factor Sibley strove to remain in the Osages' good graces: in October 1812 he advanced Osage and Oto hunters $540 to buy rifles, blankets, and other supplies, because their annuities had not arrived. The following year he distributed the Osages' 1812 and 1813 annuities from his factory's inventory. He also made small gestures of conciliation toward the Kansa Indians, whose neutrality the United States wanted to secure. Sibley provided food and transport to three Kansa men returning to their nation, and when one died of illness, he sent gifts to the man's relatives to cover the grave.[14]

U.S.-Osage relations undoubtedly cooled in the spring of 1813, when Governor Howard closed Fort Osage and its factory as a security measure. However, the factor soon reopened the trading house at a more defensible site: Arrow Rock on the Missouri River, near the towns of the Great Osages, where he resumed business in September. Sibley then displeased Osage leaders again by proposing to move their factory to Dardanelle Rock on the Arkansas River, near the towns of the Arkansas Osages. However, Osage chiefs reminded him of the treaty that guaranteed them a factory in their Missouri homeland. The Little Osages noted their disapproval even of the move to Arrow Rock, observing that they had moved their towns near Fort Osage five years earlier, only to find that the permanent "iron post" the Americans promised to erect there had become a transient "old wooden one."[15]

Sibley dropped the subject of moving the Osage factory, and the issue became academic the following year, as frontier security again deteriorated. In March 1814 Osages killed several whites in western Missouri, and that summer the American military position in the region collapsed when British troops and Indian warriors occupied Prairie du Chien. Emboldened Sauk and Kickapoo warriors raided American settlements west of Saint Louis, and George Sibley shut down the Arrow Rock post for good. The temporary factory at Little Manitou Creek also closed for the rest of the war.[16]

TO THE NORTHERN INDIAN factories, the War of 1812 brought destruction; to the western factories, dislocation; and to the southern factories, disruption. The southern United States saw little fighting during the first year of the war, apart from two filibustering expeditions— George Mathews' invasion of East Florida and José Gutiérrez and Augustus Magee's raid on Texas—occasioned not by the Anglo-American war but by the disintegration of Spanish rule in the Americas. Neither directly affected the southern trading houses, though the Gutiérrez-Magee expedition did use Natchitoches as its base. Mathews' incursion, meanwhile, caused the first sustained fighting between Americans and southern Indians in almost twenty years: the commandant of Saint Augustine recruited Seminole warriors to cut the filibusters' supply lines, and in retaliation U.S. troops destroyed several Seminole villages in Florida.[17]

The fighting between Seminoles and Americans alarmed and energized a large dissident faction among the Seminoles' Creek kinsmen. The dissidents had been growing in numbers for years, their discontent fed by land cessions, their chiefs' monopolization of annuity payments, and the growing disparity of wealth between the Creeks' traditionalist majority and their slave-owning elite. The divisions in the Creek nation widened in September 1811, when chiefs allowed the U.S. government to cut a road through Creek territory, and a party of northern Indians, led by Tecumseh, met five thousand Creeks at Tuckabatchee. Tecumseh urged his listeners there to depose their accommodating chiefs, refuse further land cessions, and return to their traditional ways of life.[18]

Tecumseh's visit to Creek country turned hundreds of dissident Creeks into militants, subsequently known as *Red Sticks* for their red-painted weapons. In 1812 some Red Stick Creeks went north to help the Great Lakes Indians fight American militia, while others killed a half-dozen whites in the Ohio Valley. The Creek national council punished these murders and other crimes against white settlers by executing a dozen Creek men and women. The executions, combined with the American attacks on Seminole villages in early 1813, turned the Red Sticks from militants into rebels. By the summer of 1813 over 2,500 Creeks had joined the Red Stick movement, killing chiefs, slaughtering cattle, and soliciting assistance from the Spanish. When American militia assaulted a party of warriors carrying munitions from Pensacola, and Red Sticks retaliated by killing 250 people at Fort Mims and Tensaw, the Creek civil war became a war with the United States.[19]

The Creek War, as the Americans called it, nearly destroyed the Creek nation. Beginning in November, 5,200 regulars, volunteers, and militia invaded Creek country from the north, south, and east. Joining them were numerous southeastern Indians: 700 Choctaw warriors under Pushmataha and Mushulatubbe, several hundred Chickasaws, and more than 500 Cherokees and "loyal" Creeks, who fought alongside General Andrew Jackson's forces. In a series of battles culminating in the storming of a Red Stick fort at Horseshoe Bend, the American invaders and their allies killed over 1,600 Creeks and destroyed about sixty Creek villages and towns, along with $300,000 worth of property.[20]

The Creek War and the concurrent Anglo-American war inhibited the operations of all four southern factories. The factory at Ocmulgee Old Fields felt the effects of the Creek War immediately. In July 1812 the Creek factory had on hand or in storage about $8,200 worth of peltry, including nearly 40,000 pounds of deerskins. This figure grew by 10 percent over the next nine months, then froze from April 1813 through April 1814, as the Creeks' civil war and the American invasion halted local trade. During the tumultuous third quarter of 1813 and the first quarter of 1814, factor Jonathan Halstead bought only 50 cowhides, 12 small furs, and about 200 pounds of deerskins from his trading partners.[21]

Meanwhile, the Creek trading house's inventory of goods dropped in value from $4,943 to $1,315, as Creek leaders cleared off its shelves—taking in particular as many rifles as they could—and as Halstead found it impossible to restock them. Between March 1814, when the Creek War ended, and the following March, Halstead and his successor Charles

Magnan did dispose of $2,300 worth of peltry, but their factory's supplies of merchandise and cash continued to shrink while debts owed the factory doubled, to $3,471. By the end of the War of 1812, the trading house at Ocmulgee Old Fields had nearly ceased to operate.[22]

The other factory in the Deep South, at Saint Stephens, also took a financial blow during the Creek and Anglo-American wars. Between April 1812 and April 1813, factor George Gaines purchased $5,400 worth of skins and furs and sold or distributed $7,800 worth of merchandise. The wars cut both of those figures in half: from 1813 to 1814 the Saint Stephens factory bought $2,500 worth of peltries and dispensed $3,700 worth of merchandise. Part of the decline resulted from wartime supply problems: Britain's blockade of the Atlantic seaboard prevented Superintendent Mason from obtaining point blankets and strouds for the factories, so he had to send less desirable substitutes. The blockade also made it difficult for Mason to supply Saint Stephens by sea, even though, with the American capture of Mobile in April 1813, the War Department had finally acquired the means to do so.[23]

Saint Stephens' business declined due to the Creek War, in which Choctaws became combatants and their factory a potential target. The Choctaws' national council had forbidden their countrymen, on pain of death, from joining Tecumseh's confederacy, and in 1812 Tecumseh's Red Stick allies threatened to attack settlements and shipping on the Tombigbee River, obliging Factor Gaines to reinforce the hulls of the boats carrying his gunpowder. In 1813, following the Red Sticks' attack on Fort Mims, Saint Stephens became a rallying point for Choctaw warriors who wanted to fight the Creeks. Pushmataha came to the trading house that fall to offer his nation's assistance, Gaines visited Choctaw towns to recruit warriors, and General Jackson drew supplies from the factory for his Choctaw allies.[24]

Business revived at the end of the Creek War. During the year ending 1 April 1815, Gaines took in about $5,600 worth of peltry and sold $6,400 worth of merchandise, the latter mostly on credit—indeed, factory debts rose steadily after the war. Meanwhile, John Mason made plans to move the trading house to a site further up the Tombigbee, and to combine its operations with those of another southern factory, at Chickasaw Bluffs.[25]

The Chickasaw factory, though distant from any fighting, witnessed similar problems. Supplies frequently ran low, due to shipping delays; a load of textiles that factor Robert Bayly ordered in the fall of 1812 did not reach Chickasaw Bluffs until May 1814, by which time Bayly had died. The only goods the factory received in 1813 were $222 worth of unwanted jewelry and moth-eaten clothing and blankets that Indians had pawned at the Arkansas Post factory. Undeterred, Chickasaw hunters continued to bring in skins and furs, and Bayly had to compensate most of his customers with IOUs. The house bought even more peltry (including 70,000 pounds of deerskins) and sold over $8,000 worth of goods in 1814. Concurrently, the Chickasaws aided the Americans' military efforts by providing food and fodder to American militia, and by scouting and fighting for American forces in the Creek War. Business and alliance prospered together.[26]

The last southern factory, in Natchitoches, felt the effects of the wars faintly but distinctly. In the summer of 1813, Red Stick emissaries brought war messages to the Alabama and Coushatta Indians, and Natchitoches's resident Indian agent, John Sibley, urged their and the Caddos' leaders to remain neutral. All agreed to reject the Red Sticks' appeal, and the "Caddo chief," probably Dehahuit, promised to "make common cause" with the United States. Fifteen months later, as New Orleans braced for assault by a British expeditionary force, Andrew Jackson directed Sibley to recruit Indian warriors for the defense of the city, and he asked factor Thomas Linnard to supply them with goods. Linnard forwarded Jackson nearly $4,600 worth of guns, ammunition, and other supplies, along with all of the factory's cash.[27]

Linnard had goods to spare because the Natchitoches factory, like those elsewhere in the South, conducted below-average business during the Anglo-American war. Between 1812 and 1814, the amount of deerskins and tallow that Linnard purchased fell by one-third, and the Office of Indian Trade could only sell $300 worth of the Natchitoches factory's Indian wares in 1813–14. Only one commodity, bear's oil—"a nasty article to trade in" but an abundant and locally salable one—brought any profit.[28]

The town of Natchitoches saw an increase in its trade during the war, when the Mexican Creole rebellion that had erupted in 1810 spread to Texas. The breakdown of royal government in that province opened the border to travel and commerce. By December 1811, John Sibley reported "considerable trade carried on from the Spanish country to this town," with Spanish mule trains bringing in silver and returning to Nacogdoches and San Antonio with consumer goods. Superintendent Mason asked Factor Linnard if he could import 20,000 pounds of Mexican wool through his factory, but Linnard found he could not obtain that commodity for a price the superintendent would accept.[29]

Despite the new opportunities that an open Spanish border provided them, Natchitoches's private Indian traders considered their business in jeopardy, and the factory as the greatest threat thereto. In December 1813 the local parish council, seconded by the town's Catholic church, petitioned Congress and President Madison to move the Natchitoches trading house to the Sabine River. Thomas Linnard attributed the petition to mere commercial jealousy, but Mason, wary of controversy, began planning to move the factory after the war.[30]

IN GEORGETOWN, hundreds of miles east of the United States' inland commercial frontier, Superintendent of Indian Trade John Mason struggled to preserve a normal routine, even though half of his factories had burned down and several of his factors languished in British custody. He continued to buy goods for the houses in the South and the temporary posts on the Missouri River, though this became difficult later in the war: between 1812 and 1814, the quantity of some commodities that Mason shipped to the factories, including calico, rifles, and strouds, fell by 50 to 66 percent. During the same period, the aggregate price of all the merchandise shipped to the trading houses rose by nearly 80 percent, due to wartime inflation. Furs and skins also became scarce, and the Indian trade office's sales and auctions became sporadic: Mason only held six sales (half of them in Georgetown) during the war. The quantities of most types of Indian produce sold by Mason's office dropped sharply, and total proceeds from these sales fell from $44,500 in 1812 to $15,000 in 1814.[31]

Mason's office experienced wartime hardships other than poor business. The Office of Indian Trade found itself short of personnel, owing to the enlistment of two of its three clerks in the Army and the superintendent's own service as commissary general for prisoners. Moreover, the office's headquarters became part of the war zone in August 1814, when a British force occupied Washington City. Superintendent Mason had already made contingency plans for a British attack on the District of Columbia, and when enemy troops reached the capital he ordered his clerk, James Bronaugh, to remove all the office's records from Georgetown. Then he loaded his trade goods onto boats and deliberately sank them in the Potomac River. Most of the merchandise survived the immersion.[32]

Table 6.1 Selected Shipments from the Office of Indian Trade, 1812–1815

	1812	1813	1814	1815	Total
Blankets (3-pt)	501	204	44	3,470	4,219
Calico	10,892	2,272	3,998	6,146	23,308
Guns	120			90	210
Gunpowder	6,000	10,000	6,750		22,750
Knives				612	612
Needles	2,500	3,000	2,000	9,000	16,500
Rifles	90	90	30	149	359
Saddles	43		22		65
Shirts	215		90	43	348
Strouds	163	139	81	40	423
Tobacco	495	155		1,402*	2,052
Total Value ($)	18,449	26,910	33,018	58,205	136,582

Source: *1812*: Invoices Outward, 2:253–63, 265–84, 302, 306; *1813*: ibid., 2:285–306; *1814*: ibid., 2: 307–33; *1815*: ibid., 2:334–44, 3:1–12, 17–40.

Calico is measured in yards, gunpowder and tobacco in pounds. Guns include all firearms except rifles. All quantities are rounded to the nearest whole number.

"Total Value" is the total invoiced dollar value of all goods shipped that year, including many not listed in this selection. Shipping charges are excluded. Sums are rounded to the nearest dollar.

* Does not include 600 pieces "cut and dry" tobacco shipped to northwestern factories.

The attack on the national capital, along with a September 1814 assault on Baltimore and British raids on the coast of New England, made it clear that in this war, enemies could target the Americans' core settlements as easily as their frontier outposts. The war also tested the U.S. government's ability to command the loyalty of both its core and peripheral populations. The most notoriously disaffected people within the United States were the inhabitants of Federalist New England, whose hostility to the administration in Washington led to talk of secession. African American slaves in the Chesapeake region were another such group; several thousand of them took refuge with British forces in 1813–14. And Native Americans, despite the U.S. government's efforts to cultivate their friendship, largely numbered among the United States' adversaries. While about four thousand Indian warriors fought alongside American troops in the War of 1812, fifteen thousand became allies or co-belligerents of Great Britain.[33]

Table 6.2 Office of Indian Trade Produce Sales, 1812–1815

	1812	1813	1814	1815	*Total*
Badger	179				179
Bear	845	797	480	1,501	3,623
Bear's oil	1b.				1b.
Beaver	1,799	1,500	2,523	1,940	7,762
B. horns	264	319			583
B. robes	5	6	73		84
Cat	1,402	101	122	157	1,782
Deer	88,558	355	10,181	259	99,353
Dr. deer	1,988	763	532		3,283
Sh. Deer	27,077	9,000			36,077
Elk		34	188	15	237
Elk Horns	291	238			529
Fisher	5	18	25	30	78
Fox	1,624	18	38	94	1,774
Groundhog		13			13
Hogskins			7		7
Lead	20,046		365		20,411
Mats	37		33		70
Mink	87		23	6	116
Muskrat	19,168	7,291	2,876	2,710	32,045
Otter	580	261	280	200	1,321
Panther	1			4	5
Raccoon	22,273	3,108	4,012	2,205	31,598
Snakeroot	22				22
Tallow	1,140	779			1,919
Tiger	33				33
Wax	3,009				3,009
Wolf	137	43	13	4	197
Total Value ($)	44,500	12,700	15,100	13,300	85,600

Source: Sales Books, Vol. 1 (n.p.); Vol. 2: 52, 57–73, 78.

Abbreviations: "B."=bison, "b."=barrel, "Dr."=dressed, "Sh."=shaved.

Beaver, deer, shaved deer, lead, snakeroot, tallow, and wax figures are in pounds; all others represent whole items. Bear skins include cub; deer skins exclude wrappers. Elk horns include some deer horns; the author assumes each horn weighed one pound. Where deerskins are recorded as whole skins, the author has estimated their weight as two pounds per skin. Where two categories are mixed in the records, the author has divided the aggregate total of the mixed record in half. All fractions are rounded to the nearest whole number.

"Total Value" is the total gross sale value of all goods sold by the Office of Indian Trade that year, rounded to the nearest hundred dollars.

Would this imbalance have been greater without the factories? Certainly, after the war began, the surviving trading houses did help the War Department arm or supply its Native American allies and manipulate neutrals. The Fort Madison, Fort Hawkins, and Natchitoches factories served as arsenals for American-allied Osages, for the "loyal" Creeks, and for Caddos who offered to aid Jackson's defense of New Orleans. Saint Stephens functioned like a recruiting center for Choctaws fighting in the Creek War. Meanwhile, the War Department used the promise of a new factory to draw Sauk and Mesquakie neutralists to Missouri and isolate them from British influence.[34]

It is hard to determine whether the trading houses were a factor in some Indians' decision to align themselves with the United States. (One might note that five of the seven Indian nations who received the most annuity goods from the Office of Indian Trade, specifically the Delawares, Miamis, Potawatomis, Shawnees, and Wyandots, contributed warriors to both sides of the conflict.) It seems likelier that the Americans' Indian allies either used the Anglo-American war as a pretext to fight old foes or benefited from another federal policy, the "civilization" program, and wished to defend their survival strategy of selective acculturation.[35]

Among the Native American allies of Great Britain, the prospect of capturing and plundering the northern factories probably helped draw some warriors into the forces that attacked Mackinac, Sandusky, and Fort Wayne. Ramsey Crooks, an employee of John Astor, argued in 1813 that the fall of the Great Lakes factories proved they had failed in one of their principal missions, "attaching [the Indians] unalterably to the United States." The trading houses allegedly "meliorate[d] . . . the condition of the Indians," but, Crooks caustically observed, "those very tribes who experienced in the greatest degree [this] fostering care . . . were the first to raise the tomahawk against the American settlements."[36]

Crooks's observation was not entirely accurate; the largest factories (measured by the quantity of goods they received from the Office of Indian Trade) generally served Indians who stayed neutral in the conflict or allied with the United States.[37] However, his letter does draw attention to another presumptive function of the factories: to "meliorate" Native American living conditions, by protecting them from unscrupulous private traders and supplying them with inexpensive goods. The administrators and supporters of the factory system had sidelined this philanthropic goal, focusing instead on details of administration and supply. During the war they had endeavored to turn the factories and the Indian communities they served into military assets. After the War of 1812, however, the "benevolent" purpose of the trading houses, which President Washington had stressed at the program's inception, came to the front of the War Department's justifications for retaining them.

As the U.S. government's fear of its Indian clients becoming involved with foreign powers slowly declined, the Office of Indian Trade instead began to link the trading houses to the Monroe administration's revived Indian "civilization" policy. A new superintendent, Thomas McKenney, began to argue that the factories could provide the setting and funds for schools that would teach Native American children the arts of Anglo American culture. To put it more crudely, the supporters of the factories had once claimed that the trading houses would attach Indians to the American interest; they now asserted that the factories could help turn Indians into Americans. Their ability to sell this argument to Congress, however, depended on the currency of the eighteenth-century idea that trade and civilization complemented one another. As these supporters would soon learn, in the nineteenth century white Americans no longer took that compatibility for granted.

7

Running Hard and Falling Behind

The War of 1812 inflicted great damage on the Indian factories. British and Native American war parties destroyed or disrupted six of the trading houses, while a British blockade and stalled inland transportation starved the rest of supplies. The outcome of that war posed an equally large threat to the factories' existence, as it dramatically reduced the power and independence of the Indian nations whose goodwill the trading houses cultivated. While the Treaty of Ghent, which restored peace between the United States and Britain, identified no clear victor of the War of 1812, American policy-makers moved quickly to turn the Indian combatants, regardless of the side they had taken, into the war's losers.[1]

Following the defeats of Tecumseh's confederation and the Red Stick Creeks, American officials began demanding large land cessions from the surviving Native American combatants. Andrew Jackson, for a start, extracted 22 million acres from the Creek confederacy in the Treaty of Fort Jackson (9 August 1814), and during the next six years the general acquired by treaty lands comprising three-fourths of modern Florida, one-third of Tennessee, and twenty percent of Mississippi. Speculators and settlers surged into the Southeast and the Great Lakes region, raising the Trans-Appalachian population of the United States to two million within five years. In the nation's western states, Native Americans comprised only five percent of the population by 1820.[2]

The Indians' former European allies also retreated from involvement in North American affairs. The British government declined to intervene on behalf of the King's Indian allies when Americans violated the Treaty of Ghent, which guaranteed Native Americans their prewar boundaries. Nor did British officials object when Congress barred foreigners, including Britons, from trading with Indians within the United States. Britain's government wanted rapprochement with the United States, not to redress the grievances of Native Americans. As for the Spanish, their position in Florida had become untenable in the wake of multiple Latin American revolutions, and in 1819 Spain sold Florida to the United States. For the eastern Indians, at least, the "modern Indian politics," by which they could play one Euro-American power against another, had come to an end.[3]

Despite this triple blow—to their physical plant, supply chain, and relevance—the factories survived the war and remained open for another seven years. Senator Benton would attribute this to bureaucratic inertia, but the system's survival owed more to the diligence of Superintendent of Indian Trade Thomas McKenney. McKenney located new suppliers and opened new supply routes for the trading houses, and he oversaw or planned the relocation of declining factories, to follow Indian communities that had moved or to evade private traders who dominated places like Green Bay. Even more importantly, Native Americans kept the factories in business, as they continued to view them as economic and political assets. Sauk and Menominee visitors traded furs, lead, and frontier-exchange goods to the Prairie du Chien trading house. The Osages, Kansas, and Caddos used Fort Osage and Sulphur Fork as diplomatic centers, places to feast and resolve disputes as well as trade. Choctaws flooded the new factory at Fort Confederation with both peltry and agricultural produce, while the Spadre Bluffs factory sold consumer goods and weapons to the Arkansas Cherokees, helping them preserve their "civilized" identity while fighting their Osage neighbors.

For McKenney's first boss, Secretary of War William Crawford, the ability of the factories to promote a more complex Native American material culture had become their most attractive feature. As President Madison's last secretary of war, Crawford wrote the first draft of postwar Indian policy. In 1816 he argued that the U.S. government now had the power to bring the Indians completely under its influence and complete its plan to convert them into literate, propertied commercial farmers. As Native Americans in the eastern United States could no longer resort to British or Spanish traders, and as American traders (supposedly) lacked enough capital to supply them, a rebuilt factory system would ensure the federal government's dominance of the Indians residing within its borders. Moreover, the factories could themselves advance the Indian civilization program by supplying Indians with goods that would promote "ideas of separate property," and by marketing their livestock and farm produce.[4]

Crawford's report helped set the agenda of the Office of Indian Trade for the next five years. It suffered, though, from two significant flaws. First, some Americans had begun to suspect that personal acquisitiveness and commerce were not necessarily compatible with civilized behavior, which they increasingly defined in terms of orderly habits and domesticity, and the social institutions that reinforced them. This suspicion undermined Crawford and McKenney's attempts to link the trading houses to the civilization program, calling the relevance of the factory system into question. Second, however limited their means before the war, private American fur traders rapidly increased in numbers and capital after 1815, and they proved more than a match for several of the reestablished factories. Indeed, one trader, John Jacob Astor of New York, marshaled more employees and capital than the Office of Indian Trade ever commanded. Within just a few years Astor would also have enough political capital to strike against the factory system at its heart, in Washington City.[5]

ASTOR DID NOT single-mindedly pursue the factories, particularly not while he was reviving his business right after the war. In fact, in April 1816 he wrote a letter of congratulations to Thomas McKenney, offering any information that might help the neophyte with his new job as superintendent. This gesture suggests the merchant hoped to reach an accommodation with the Indian trade office regarding separate spheres of operation.[6]

McKenney, a 31-year-old Maryland Quaker, had received his position through influential friends and an acquaintance with President Madison. He soon made it clear to Astor and to his superiors in the War Department that he had no interest in serving as a caretaker or lackey. The new superintendent soon set about reviving the trading houses and their business, a process that began with the factories' resupply. During his first year on the job, Superintendent McKenney shipped to the eight postwar factories over $65,000 worth of goods, including about 3,000 3-point blankets, 3,250 yards of calico, and 7,000 pounds of gunpowder. McKenney also assumed responsibility for supplying governors and Indian agents with annuity goods, to the amount of $51,800 in the year he took office. Many of these annuity goods came from a stock of low-quality merchandise John Mason had bought during the war, a stock so large, McKenney wrote, that the barrels into which his clerks packed them could have formed a line 1¼ miles long. The superintendent allowed the factors to sell the shoddy leftovers at a loss while he ordered new supplies from merchants in the District of Columbia.[7]

McKenney's supply network extended beyond the capital's mercantile community. The three dozen suppliers from whom he ordered merchandise during his first three years in office (1816–18) included wampum manufacturers from the New York City region; steelmakers from Pittsburgh; weavers from Baltimore; Henry Deringer of Philadelphia, from whom the superintendent ordered rifles and tomahawks; and James Morrison of Lexington, Kentucky, who furnished the factories with salt and gunpowder. However, most of his suppliers hailed from the District of Columbia, including one of the largest, John Cox, who sold McKenney over $100,000 worth of goods between 1817 and 1819. When a congressional committee asked why McKenney did so little business with out-of-town merchants, he replied that he preferred dealing with local suppliers because they allowed the selection and packing of goods "under the personal inspection of the superintendent." One suspects personal connections also played a part.[8]

The cost and difficulty of transporting goods from the District to the factories, and of bringing Indians' wares to Georgetown, remained high, as before the war. Mason and McKenney partially consolidated the factories' supply routes by sending most of their shipments by wagon from Georgetown to Pittsburgh, at a cost of $180–200 per wagonload. Freight bound to the Mississippi, Missouri, and Arkansas Valleys traveled from Pittsburgh by flatboat, while McKenney's Pittsburgh shipping agent, Abraham Wooley, sent goods bound for the Great Lakes to Erie and then by schooner to their final destinations. Only the three factories in the lower South retained independent supply lines: the Creek trading house received merchandise via Savannah, Natchitoches through New Orleans, and Fort Confederation by way of Mobile. Consolidation of the factories' supply routes did not, however, significantly reduce overall transportation costs, which, after including incidentals like warehousing fees, averaged over $7,000 per year. Much of the problem lay in the newer factories' growing distance from Georgetown, which McKenney had made not only his main supply center but also his "principal depot" for pelts. The remote trading houses at Prairie du Chien, Fort Osage, and Green Bay accounted between them for $20,800 in round-trip transport costs, while the Choctaw factory, though nearer the zone of American settlement, also generated large freight costs due to its high business volume and position upriver from Mobile.[9]

At the other end of the trading circuit, McKenney continued to organize regular sales of the factories' peltries, though he held only one or two auctions and a few smaller transactions each year. The Office of

Table 7.1 Selected Shipments from the Office of Indian Trade, 1816–1821

	1816	1817	1818	1819	1820	1821	Total
Blankets, 3-pt	3,914	1,995	917	1,080	586	649	9,141
Brass kettles	207	474	541	954	99	63	2,338
Calico	4,047	7,318	1,960	252	925	5,095	19,597
Cigars	14,500	3,500	8,600				26,600
Guns	30	129	256	140	40	18	613
Gunpowder	7,200	9,300	3,750	4,000	3,000	3,750	31,000
Knives	948	900	727		96		2,671
Needles	40,000	31,100			1,000	7,500	79,600
Rifles	153	116	195	110	120		694
Saddles	24	79	91	63	21	24	302
Shirts	231	448	50				729
Shoes		50	78	137	340	346	951
Strouds	337	349	183	93	125	250	1,337
Tobacco	*	3,220	1,500		1,223		5,943
Total Value ($)	86,738	62,649	52,826	37,138	28,025	33,926	301,302

Source: *1816*: Invoices Outward, 3: 13–16, 41–87, 134; *1817*: ibid., 3: 88–133, 135–36; *1818*: ibid., 3: 139–82; *1819*: ibid., 3: 183–216, 220; *1820*: ibid., 3: 217–19, 221–46; *1821*: ibid., 3: 247–78.

Calico is measured in yards; brass kettles, gunpowder, and tobacco, in pounds (rounded to the nearest pound). Guns include all firearms except rifles. Needles include knitting and sewing needles. Shoes are measured in pairs. Strouds sometimes appear in yards in the invoices; the author estimates that one stroud measured 20 yards.

The 1816 brass kettle figure does not include 50 individual, unweighed kettles. The 3-point blanket figure for 1817 includes one undifferentiated shipment of 246 3-point and 4-point blankets, which the author has divided in half.

"Total Value" is the total invoiced dollar value of all goods shipped that year, including many not listed in this selection. Sums are rounded to the nearest dollar.

* 288 pieces of "cut and dry" tobacco

Indian Trade's peltry sales from April 1817 to April 1818 yielded gross proceeds of about $42,000, slightly lower than those of the last year of the prewar era (1812). Subsequent auctions took place less frequently and generated declining returns, until by November 1820 McKenney's office received less than $9,000 from fur and skin sales. One must attribute this decline to the falling prices (30–70 percent for some kinds of furs in 1818–19) that followed the Panic of 1819. It certainly did not result from a shrinking supply. Between 1816 and 1819, the quantity of

Table 7.2 Sales of Indian Wares to All Factories, 1815–1819

	1815	1816	1817	1818	1819	Total
Bear	461	635	578	615	1246	3,535
Beaver	58	868	3,757	4,350	4,396	13,429
Cat	62	36	276	161	173	708
Deer	69,303	83,485	96,557	86,508	149,879	485,732
Feathers				834	980	1,814
Fisher		6	114	219	75	414
Fox		207	1,848	1,827	1,059	4,941
Lead				200,148	67,799	267,947
Marten		20	112		14	146
Mats		2	42	149	216	409
Mink		4	437	338	112	891
Muskrat		4,406	33,146	25,552	14,736	77,840
Otter	63	351	715	1,111	846	3,086
Raccoon	37	1,323	8,123	6,333	4,877	20,693
Sugar				3,098	1,996	5,094
Tallow	663	280	2,507	3,789	1,217	8,456
Wax	329	1,259	1,351	362	1,725	5,026

Source: Transactions at the Indian Trading-Houses since the Peace, 30 Apr. 1820, *ASPIA*, 2:208.

Beaver, deer, feathers, lead, sugar, tallow, and wax are measured in pounds; all others are whole items. The 1817–19 deer returns from Green Bay and Chicago were reported as whole skins, recorded here as two pounds each in weight.

Indian produce that the factors annually purchased increased dramatically: deerskins by 75 percent, muskrat by 300 percent, fox and beaver by 500 percent.[10]

The single largest source of Native American goods in the system was the Choctaw factory, which John Mason had moved to Fort Confederation in present-day Alabama. The post opened for business in 1816, and during the next four years its factors purchased more deerskins (184,065 pounds) and fox furs (4,300) than any other trading house. Fort Confederation's sales of Indian wares during this period generated nearly $30,000 in revenue. Meanwhile, between 1816 and 1822 the Choctaw house received over $71,000 worth of merchandise, a quantity sufficiently large, one clerk promised factor George Gaines, to "enable you to put down all opposition from private traders."[11]

As they had done before and during the war, Choctaws visiting Fort Confederation closed the gap between the low prices they were paid for their peltry and cotton and the higher prices of the merchandise they wanted by buying goods on credit. Total debts owed the factory rose from $7,500 in 1815 to $15,000 by December 1817, receded the following year, and then rose again. John Hersey, who became factor in 1819, pressed the Choctaws to pay their debts and threatened them with loss of their annuities if they didn't comply. His trading partners, however, didn't take his threat seriously, nor did they stop trading with Hersey. By 1822 they owed the factory $13,500.[12]

That Hersey and his superiors regarded the Choctaws' commercial debts as a problem, rather than an asset to exploit, reflected the U.S. government's belief that it no longer needed to use Indians' debts to pry land cessions from them. Instead, the War Department began pursuing those cessions openly and aggressively. In 1816 federal commissioners persuaded the Choctaws to sell their lands east of the Tombigbee River for $130,000. Eighteen months later, on the initiative of Secretary of War John Calhoun, the U.S. government began pressing the Choctaws to cede their remaining territory in Mississippi and move west. Choctaw chiefs stood firm against another cession until the fall of 1820, when, by the Treaty of Doak's Stand, they reluctantly traded five million acres of land in Mississippi for a Trans-Mississippi reserve, along with supplies for emigrants and funding for schools.[13]

Andrew Jackson and Thomas Hinds, the federal commissioners at Doak's Stand, initially believed they could secure their goal (namely, removal) by exploiting a factional split in the Choctaw nation between traditional hunters and proponents of Anglo American civilization. If the Choctaws did not cede their eastern lands and move west, Jackson warned, whites would seize and settle their Trans-Mississippi hunting ranges, forcing Choctaw hunters to stay in the east. There, unable to feed themselves, they would "become beggars and drunkards." Only uncharitable "half-breed" planters, Jackson and Hinds argued, would want their nation to refuse the U.S. government's generous offer.[14]

The commissioners, however, misunderstood the dynamics of cultural change in the Choctaw nation, where most families were incorporating Anglo American professions and skills into their economic strategy. By 1820 many Choctaws had begun to raise livestock to supplement or replace hunting, and many families had moved into the Tombigbee Valley in search of better pasturage. A smaller but still significant number of families raised cotton, which they sold or turned into homespun textiles. Moreover, while Choctaw hunters continued to hunt deer west of the Mississippi River, they did not comprise a separate interest group from farmers, because Choctaw families usually pursued both activities simultaneously: men hunted and traded, while women raised crops and livestock. The factory at Fort Confederation reflected the hybrid nature of the economy the Choctaws had created: it continued to receive furs and skins, but it also purchased cowhides and cotton—nearly 16,000 pounds of unginned cotton appeared in the factory's final inventory—and sold not only ammunition and blankets but also cotton cards and cowbells.[15]

Thus, most of the Choctaws who attended the Doak's Stand conference opposed an eastern land cession, which would deprive their families of cropland and pasturage. The Choctaw chief Puckshunubbee refused to negotiate with the commissioners after they rejected his counteroffer of a smaller cession. In the end, Jackson and Hinds could not obtain their ends through craft and division, so they resorted to threats and bribery. They warned Choctaw leaders that they must not "trifle . . . with" the United States, and that the government might convince those Choctaws who'd emigrated to Arkansas to cede their nation's eastern lands. The commissioners then promised a $1,000 increase in the Choctaws' annuity and an independent fund for Choctaw schools, assets that chiefs could use to increase their own prestige. They also distributed about $4,700 in cash to the men and women who had attended the conference.[16]

In their report to Secretary Calhoun, Jackson and Hinds noted that their treaty provided for the eventual liquidation of the eastern Choctaw nation. Those who stayed in the east would eventually "become so civilized and enlightened as to be made citizens of the United States," subject to its laws, while the treaty would encourage the rest to emigrate by providing them with a protected western hunting range and a factory in their new homeland. The federal government did not, in fact, make good on its promise of a Trans-Mississippi factory for Choctaw emigrants, since few Choctaws moved to Arkansas before Congress shuttered the trading houses for good.[17]

The Choctaws' neighbors, the Chickasaws, had already seen their factory closed and its stock moved across the Mississippi, though their business with that house had been declining for several years. The Chickasaw Bluffs factory's remittances shrank from 87,000 pounds of deerskins in 1815 to 13,200 by 1817. Business fell off in spite of the steady prices that factor Isaac Rawlings paid for furs and skins—the 25 cents he paid for a pound of deerskins matched the amount Thomas Peterkin had paid in 1806—and the lower merchandise prices he offered. Competition, both from the new trading house at Fort Confederation and from private traders, became the primary drain on Rawlings's customer base.[18]

While Rawlings's operation lasted, many of his customers were whites or "mixt breeds," or at least had the same Europeanized tastes as biracial Chickasaws. The specialized goods they purchased included sugar, coffee, fine cloth, and tableware. Like the Choctaws, the Chickasaws had undertaken a transition from subsistence agriculture to commercial stock-raising and home manufacturing, so Rawlings's customers also requested ploughs, hoes, cowbells, and cotton cards. After the Chickasaw Bluffs factory closed in 1818, they could continue to purchase these goods at Fort Confederation, or receive them from the U.S. government as part of its civilization program. They could also buy them from private traders, some of whom were Chickasaws themselves; indeed, McKenney closed the trading house in part because Chickasaw leaders wanted to "manage their own trade."[19]

Following the closure, Superintendent McKenney moved Chickasaw Bluffs's factor and stock across the Mississippi River, to a region from which the Office of Indian Trade had withdrawn a decade earlier: the Arkansas Valley. It returned with Native American allies, specifically Cherokee emigrants, for whom the U.S. government had created a reservation in 1817. Cherokee agent Return Meigs advised the War Department that a trading house for the Arkansas Cherokees would serve as a "rallying point" for them and other eastern Indian emigrants; would attach the United States to the Cherokees, Quapaws, and other local Indians "by the strongest ties"; and would turn these nations into "a permanent force on the frontier."[20]

Isaac Rawlings carried out this proposal in September 1818, when he took a keelboat full of goods to Illinois Bayou, near the homestead of Cherokee chief Tekatoka, and opened a temporary trading post for the Cherokees. The new factory drew numerous customers—forty-two Cherokees owed it money by 1820—and saw a fair volume of business, purchasing $6,805 worth of Indian wares in its first full year of operation (1819). Business grew in 1820, after Rawlings moved the factory twenty-five miles upriver to Spadre Bluffs. Extant daybooks from that year reveal that Barak Owens, Rawlings's successor as factor, bought

$4,071 worth of peltry and other goods between April and September, a monthly average exceeding that of Illinois Bayou. Then came the perhaps-inevitable decline: during the last six months of 1821 Matthew Lyons, who became factor that year, purchased a monthly average of $312 of produce. This likely resulted from the resumption of the Cherokee-Osage war and growing competition from private traders, who now numbered more than one hundred in the Arkansas country. A few of them patronized or owed money to the Spadre Bluffs factory, which made them less the factory's competitors than part of its trading network.[21]

Spadre Bluffs's merchandise sales resembled those of the other southern factories. The Cherokee emigrants who traded at Illinois Bayou and Spadre Bluffs purchased the usual staples of the trade—textiles and ammunition—as well as cotton cards, spoons, and sugar. These customers left little in their purchase records to distinguish them from contemporary Anglo American farmers. Indeed, the Arkansas Cherokees took pride in displaying a material culture similar to that of white Americans. Travelers visiting the Cherokees' settlements in Arkansas Territory remarked on the emigrants' fenced-in fields, herds of livestock, and frame houses, all of which set them apart from their Osage neighbors. Cherokee leaders used their nation's "civilized" self-image to support the Arkansas emigrants' land claims vis-à-vis the more "savage" Arkansas Osages, and to call on the United States government for support when their nation and the Osages went to war in 1817.[22]

The war stemmed from Osage objections to the land cession their chiefs had made to Cherokee emigrants. In 1816 and 1817 Osage warriors killed a dozen Cherokee men in the Arkansas Valley, and the Cherokees retaliated by organizing a 600-man war party and attacking the Osage village at Claremore Mound, killing or capturing more than 140 people. Federal officials brokered a truce in 1818, but the Cherokees and Osages continued to skirmish with one another periodically until 1820, when the war resumed with the deaths of three Cherokee men on the Poteau River. It would continue until 1822, when the exhausted Osages signed another treaty brokered by the War Department.[23]

The Arkansas Osages labored under three disadvantages in this war. First, the Cherokees' numbers were growing as new immigrants arrived from the east, and Osage numbers declined as Cherokee raiders attacked their villages. Second, the Cherokees enjoyed the protection of the federal garrison at Fort Smith, near which they had concentrated their settlements. Finally, the Cherokees carried better weapons: according to the *Arkansas Gazette*, the Cherokees and their allies had an ample supply of firearms and ammunition, while Osage warriors had to rely on bows and arrows. Many of the Cherokees' weapons came from the Office of Indian Trade: the nation's 1817 treaty with the United States promised each emigrant to Arkansas "one rifle gun and ammunition," which Thomas McKenney supplied. The factories at Illinois Bayou and Spadre Bluffs then sold the emigrants ammunition. Meanwhile, Matthew Lyons took pains to deprive the Osages of weapons: during one of the peak months of the war (April 1821) he and his assistant removed rifles and gunpowder from Spadre Bluffs to prevent Osage men from plundering them. Through its trade and removal policies, then, and its decisions on where to build forts and factories, the War Department threw its weight behind the Cherokees. The Cherokee émigrés, in turn, served—much as Meigs had proposed—as the sharp edge of American expansion into the Arkansas Valley. In time, American settlers would displace them as they had displaced the Osages.[24]

The Office of Indian Trade maintained one other factory in Arkansas Territory: the Sulphur Fork trading house at the confluence of the Sulphur and Red Rivers, deep in what American officials considered terra incognita. This post replaced the old factory at Natchitoches, whose business had deteriorated after the war and whose tenancy had come into dispute. Rather than fight the Catholic congregation that claimed the factory's land or continue subjecting his Indian clients to "the debauchery and excesses" of a frontier town, Thomas McKenney agreed to move the post. In the spring of 1817 John Fowler, who had succeeded Thomas Linnard as factor at Natchitoches, reconnoitered the upper Red River and selected a new factory site on the bank of the Sulphur River, a healthy and well-watered "situation" twenty miles from the future Texas-Arkansas border. The new location had a significant shortcoming: an immense logjam blocked its supply line to Natchitoches, making transport expensive. However, it was closer to the towns of the Caddo, Alabama, and Coushatta Indians, and close to the Texas border, allowing Fowler to contest Spanish influence in the region.[25]

The new factory, a complex of four pine log buildings, opened in the summer of 1818. Soon after the opening, Factor Fowler dispatched a messenger to the Arkansas Cherokees, inviting them to trade at the factory, and he distributed corn and salt to a visiting Delaware chief "and sundry Indians." Such diplomatic favors remained an important part of Fowler's business, on a frontier where the United States had almost no military presence (just nine soldiers remained at the nearby fort after 1819) and Native Americans held a preponderance of power. In subsequent months the factor gave blankets, tobacco, and shawls to Cherokee and Coushatta chiefs, arranged repairs for visitors' guns, resolved disputes between white traders and Indians, and helped locate stolen horses. It is possible that he also dined with or received gifts of food from Native American visitors; a midden near the factory site, excavated in the 1980s, contained peach pits and deer bones, perhaps the remains of foods provided by Indian townsmen. If so, they indicate that prandial diplomacy became a part of Fowler's routine.[26]

However expertly Fowler conducted diplomacy with Indian visitors, his trading post did only moderate business during its first two years. In 1819 Fowler shipped $5,650 worth of skins and furs, including 17,700 pounds of deerskins—fewer than Illinois Bayou or Fort Confederation shipped that year. Fowler made only one shipment the following year, invoiced at $1,091. An 1820 list of the factory's debtors suggests one reason for Sulphur Fork's anemic level of trade: only four Native Americans owed the factory money, and the largest debt ($50) belonged to "the Caddo chief," who according to Fowler had barred his kinsmen from the factory. The chief in question was almost certainly Dehahuit, the principal spokesman for the confederated Caddos, Coushattas, and Alabamas of the Arkansas-Louisiana borderlands. If he was in fact restricting access to Sulphur Fork to augment his influence at home—and Fowler did not identify any other Caddo debtors or customers in 1819–20—then Dehahuit had deprived the trading house of the custom of the largest Indian nation in the region.[27]

The Sulphur Fork factory also suffered from a structural flaw that prevented it from fully participating in the regional economy: the Office of Indian Trade's decision to forego the buying and selling of live animals, such as horses. During the second half of the eighteenth century, the powerful Comanche nation had expanded its sphere of influence into the Texas-Louisiana borderlands, making their trade in horses and mules—many of them captured in raids—the dominant component of the region's economy. The Comanches, their Caddo neighbors and clients, and the American traders who bought those nations' livestock found the horse and mule trade even more lucrative than the bison trade. In early 1817 a visiting Comanche gave the factories the chance to partake of this valuable traffic, offering to sell mules to the Natchitoches trading house and its Sulphur Fork successor. Fowler and McKenney declined his offer, however, on the grounds that the Comanches had stolen many of their animals, and that purchasing "plundered property" would only encourage theft from Spanish Texans and endanger U.S.-Spanish relations. American officials were willing to extend the factories' zone of influence into Spanish territory by trading with Indians who lived in Texas, but they drew the line at breaking treaties or promoting lawless behavior. That Fowler and McKenney characterized the Comanches as plunderers or bandits indicates a tension within their perceptions of this indigenous power: they knew of the Comanches' autonomy but refused to consider them sovereign, so they characterized the Comanches' imperial predation on Spaniards and other Indians—their collection of involuntary tribute, so to speak—as criminal.[28]

Many private American traders did not share these perceptions, and several of them operated on the Red River concurrently with the Sulphur Fork factory. Predation was part of their game, too: they sold the Cherokees and Coushattas whiskey for their peltry and cattle, cheated them in trade, and beat up customers who complained of being cheated. Fowler deplored his competitors' abuses, but he could not drive them off—the soldiers who might have enforced federal laws preoccupied themselves instead with pilfering from local settlers. In June 1820 Fowler, in poor health and fed up with the troops' misconduct, abandoned his post; he died six months later.[29]

Fowler's successor, William McClellan, arrived at Sulphur Fork the following spring to discover the furniture missing, the inventory moth- and worm-eaten, and the trading house's keelboat decayed almost to uselessness. The only good news was that Dehahuit had ended his monopoly, and the Caddos had sold many furs and skins to acting factor Larkin Edwards in the previous trading season. The new factor spent the summer of 1821 in repair and cleanup, then purchased enough peltry for another shipment to New Orleans. When Robert Johnson arrived at Sulphur Fork in 1823 to wrap up the factory's business, he reported that McClellan still had over $1,700 worth of Indian wares on hand and $1,055 worth of debts, indicating that trade had risen above its low 1820 level. However, the Sulphur Fork factory never became a major trading center. Its disadvantages—restrictive chiefs, exclusion from horse trading, unethical competitors, and exhausted administrators—proved too great.[30]

Sulphur Fork stood beyond the U.S. government's zone of commercial influence. By 1820, powerful regional actors had made the Red River borderland their own territory. The other western outrider of the factory system, Fort Osage, had its commercial field more to itself. The U.S. Army reoccupied Fort Osage shortly after the War of 1812, and Missouri Territorial Governor William Clark directed the garrison commander and the new agent to the Osages, George Sibley (who also retained his factorship), to restrict closely the passage of private citizens up the Missouri River. Private traders thus found it harder to do business with Missouri's Indians than with Arkansas's, and fewer sought to do so, since Missouri's fast-growing white communities offered "petty traders" more accessible markets than did its Indian population. Meanwhile, the Osage and Kansa Indians still needed trade goods and allies. The Osages worried about the Cherokees on their southern flank, while the Kansas wanted the United States to help them arrange a peace treaty with the Otos.[31]

With a dependent base of customers and little competition until 1819, the Fort Osage trading house became one of the three most productive factories in the postwar system. Between September 1815, when Sibley reopened for business, and the end of 1819, Fort Osage purchased nearly $55,000 worth of Indian wares, including 44 tons of deerskins and nearly 8,000 pounds of beaver. (Factor John Johnson's joking remark that Sibley would "turn out a second Colonel Boon[e]—spending a life in trying to obtain beaver fur" was not entirely off the mark.) The factory received in those years a nearly equal value of manufactured goods: $55,615 in merchandise, including 1,825 3-point blankets, 1,720 yards of calico, and 575 firearms. Sibley supplemented these staples with orders for ribbons, corn hoes, and light "squaw axes," the last two reminders that Osage and Kansa women continued to farm while men hunted. Notably absent from the factor's returns, meanwhile, were bison hides and robes, the staples of the Plains peltry trade, which his Native American customers most likely sold to traders like the Chouteaus. Sibley's factory did ample business, but it was not the only game in town.[32]

Sibley's competition increased markedly after 1819, when a financial panic spread economic depression throughout the United States. In Missouri Territory, men who had lost their investments in land now sought to recover their fortunes in the less expensive Indian trade. Both licensed and unlicensed traders flooded into the Missouri Valley, chasing, as it turned out, a limited market for their dry goods and liquor; at least four companies, for example, traded with the Kansa Indians, whose peltry sufficed only for one. The Fort Osage factory's business contracted; only a dozen Osages visited the post during the winter of 1819–20, and in May 1820 the factory returned only $3,600 worth of furs and skins to Georgetown. Sibley began devoting more attention to his own economic pursuits than his factorship.[33]

Until it lost its garrison (in 1819) and much of its trading business, Fort Osage remained a diplomatic center for the region's Indians. Sibley continued to repair Kansa, Osage, and Sauk visitors' tools, distributed rations to Indian visitors, and gave gifts to grieving family members, honoring the practice of "covering the dead." He urged his trading partners not to do business with the British, whom he believed had infiltrated the Missouri Valley. In September 1818 Sibley hosted a conference with several hundred Kansas and persuaded them to cede part of their nation's land claims in Missouri and modern Kansas. While the U.S. government declined to ratify the treaty, the preliminary agreement demonstrated the Kansas' desire for a closer alliance with the Americans, and it showed that they regarded Sibley and Fort Osage as the appropriate person and place to strengthen that connection.[34]

Meanwhile, the Osages, thanks to their war with the Cherokees, began to consider the fort dangerously far from their towns on the Osage River. In 1820, Secretary of War Calhoun approved a subfactory for them at Marais des Cygnes, near the modern Missouri-Kansas border. The post opened for business in 1821, and during its single year of operations factor Paul Baillio bought about $650 worth of peltries per month (during peak seasons) and made a profit of $3,200. Baillio also helped sustain friendly U.S.-Osage relations by supplying the Osages with their arrearages of annuities, and by giving them nearly $2,500 worth of merchandise in return for releasing the United States from Article II of its 1808 treaty. Despite growing private competition, then, the Osage factory, or a branch of it, remained active until the end of the factory system.[35]

Fort Osage and Fort Confederation were two of the three most productive establishments in the postwar factory system. The third stood at Prairie du Chien, an old trading rendezvous at the confluence of the Wisconsin and Mississippi Rivers. By 1815, when the factory opened, the town on this site had grown to 600 people, mainly French and British traders and their Native American kinfolk, and it served as a commercial center for several thousand Indians. American observers had noted the site's strategic importance and proposed building a trading house there before the War of 1812. In 1814 the U.S. Army tried to station a garrison at Prairie du Chien, to "slam . . . the British influence and fur trade with the Indians," but British troops and Indian warriors dislodged it. Shortly after the war Superintendent Mason made another attempt to establish American authority, sending veteran factor John Johnson to Prairie du Chien to begin taking control of its Indian commerce.[36]

Initially, the Prairie du Chien factory was something of a secondhand operation. Johnson rented a building for the trading house and, lacking customers of his own, advanced $2,000 worth of goods to Louis Dorion and Maurice Blondeau for trading ventures to the Iowas and Sauks. In 1816 Indian hunters began bringing their wares to Johnson's factory. Johnson sent his first peltries to New Orleans in March and distributed his first gifts to Native visitors in June.[37]

Johnson's business grew steadily as Sauk, Mesquakie, Menominee, and Ho-Chunk men and women learned of Johnson's hospitality and plentiful goods: between 1815 and 1821 the Prairie du Chien factory received over $73,000 worth of merchandise, more than any other house in the postwar system. In addition to textiles and firearms, the post received more specialized items: handkerchief cloth illustrated with the "House That Jack Built," snuffboxes stamped with the visages of George Washington, Thomas Jefferson, and Napoleon Bonaparte, and medicines such as antibilious pills and peppermint oil. The quantity and variety of Johnson's goods probably helped attract more customers, but the factory's business also grew through Johnson's continued recruitment of private traders, like François Boutilliers and Duncan Campbell, to undertake "winter adventures" to Indian towns.[38]

Between 1816 and 1819, the Prairie du Chien factory bought more than a quarter-million pounds of lead, nearly the entire supply of that mineral obtained by the Office of Indian Trade, as well as more than half (42,920) of the muskrat pelts and 25 percent (5,313) of the raccoon furs bought by all the factories. Johnson also obtained deerskins, rush mats, and animal tallow, retaining some of the latter for hospitality, "for the Indians to eat with their corn when they come to trade." At Thomas McKenney's request, Johnson in 1818 shipped to Georgetown a barrel of "Indian curiosities," principally apparel—a fox headdress, an ornamented bison robe, elk-leather leggings. The factor valued these items more for their exotic nature than their marketability, but some were frontier-exchange or diplomatic goods of the type that Johnson and his customers traded locally, like ornamented moccasins and knife scabbards.[39]

Wild rice, an aquatic grain harvested by Lakes Indian women, served as an important foodstuff in the upper Mississippi Valley. John Johnson accepted it in trade at the Prairie du Chien factory. Seth Eastman, *Gathering Wild Rice*, from *American Aboriginal Portfolio* by Mary Eastman (1853), courtesy of the Rare Book Collection, Wilson Special Collections Library, University of North Carolina at Chapel Hill.

Johnson's frontier-exchange commodities included several hundred bushels of corn and several hundred pounds of "wild oats." This last was actually wild rice, a high-protein food that Menominee and Ojibwa women harvested from aquatic grasses, using carved sticks to knock the plants' edible seeds from the stalks into their canoes. Indeed, many of the Prairie du Chien factory's purchases were the products of female labor: Indian women mined the lead, decorated the leather goods, wove the mats, and harvested the rice and corn that Johnson shipped or stocked. The factory's purchase of these wares did not necessarily empower Indian women, but its infusion of female-"gendered" produce, particularly plant foods, probably helped assure local Indians of Johnson's peaceable intentions, since he willingly received as well as extended hospitality.[40]

During its next—and, as it turned out, last—three years, the trading house's business fell off, particularly its purchases of lead and muskrat fur. Johnson's average annual shipments of lead fell 40 percent between the 1816–19 period and 1820–22, and average annual muskrat exports declined 25 percent. The total invoiced value of all goods shipped from the Prairie du Chien factory between 1820 and 1822 totaled about $20,250, an annual average of $6,750—well below the annual average of $11,300 for 1816–19. Johnson's purchases of raccoon did grow, and he also bought three tons of feathers (probably intended for mattress stuffing) and more Indian "curiosities," including a child's cradle. Overall, though, shipments were 40 percent smaller (by invoiced value) than they had been in the trading house's early years.[41]

Business declined at Prairie du Chien trading house thanks to a problem it shared with other factories: private competition from traders whom Johnson could not incorporate into his network. Increasingly this competition came from the employees of New York fur magnate John Astor, who in 1817 had merged the old British and American Southwest Company with his American Fur Company and expanded into the Mississippi Valley. By 1819 John Johnson reported that "Astor and his opposition fairly fills the [Mississippi] River from Fort Edwards to the River Saint Peters." In addition to their greater numbers, Johnson's private competitors enjoyed the advantage of extra-legally selling liquor to the northern Great Lakes Indians. The region's Indians considered alcohol a vital adjunct not merely of trade but of diplomacy; the Ojibwas, for instance, referred to liquor as "milk," the fundamental gift a parent gave to its child, and expected traders who claimed a fictive kin relationship with them to dispense it. Johnson's legal inability to do so undermined his status not only as a trader but as a parental official of a paternal government.[42]

Still, Johnson soldiered on, and with the help of his local traders and the liberal credit the factory gave them, the factor continued to move merchandise from his shelves to Native American homes. Debts owed the trading house grew to nearly $17,000 in April 1822, then shrank to $6,608 (as of 30 September) as debtors brought in goods and cash to pay their bills. The Prairie du Chien factory's business remained healthy in the last year of the system. As that business depended largely on mobile private contractors rather than public employees at a federal post, however, it is hard to say whether the factory was performing its main function: improving the U.S. government's reputation among the region's Native population.[43]

AT THE FOUR OTHER OUTPOSTS of the postwar factory system—Fort Edwards, Chicago, Green Bay, and Fort Mitchell—trade stagnated and

Indian visitors were few. The least inactive of these underperforming houses, at Fort Edwards in Illinois, opened in 1817 as an outpost of the Prairie du Chien factory, and it became a sickly copy of its parent. Superintendent McKenney commissioned the Fort Edwards house for the convenience of the Sauk and Mesquakie communities on Des Moines River, but few of these villages' inhabitants had returned home after the war. The subfactory McKenney opened on their behalf thus had few customers. In his first two shipments of produce to the Office of Indian Trade, factor Robert Belt packed 3,700 muskrat, raccoon, and beaver furs. This represented the factory's marketable yield for three years, and it compared very unfavorably with figures from Prairie du Chien: Fort Edwards's annual average acquisitions of raccoon, beaver, and muskrat only totaled 35 percent, 12.5 percent, and 7 percent of the parent factory's equivalents.[44]

From this low level, business declined further in 1820. The following year Superintendent McKenney ordered the closure of the Fort Edwards factory and moved its merchandise and factor to a new site: Fort Armstrong, at the mouth of the Rock River. The new trading house would be closer to the towns of its intended clients, the Sauks and Mesquakies, but it never conducted any business because Congress terminated the factory system before customers ever arrived.[45]

On the other side of the new state of Illinois, the federal trading house at Chicago, destroyed early in the war and rebuilt four years later, proved an equally inactive diplomatic and commercial center. Ill omens accompanied the Chicago factory's reopening: its merchandise became waterlogged during shipment, its military escort did not arrive until fall 1816, and its factor, Jacob Varnum, arrived in Chicago to find nothing but ruins and the bodies of wartime victims. Death remained Varnum's close companion for the rest of his factorship. His first wife, Mary Ann Aiken, died delivering a stillborn child in April 1817; his second wife's sister died in Chicago in 1820; and in September 1821, during his last year of service, the factor learned of the near-simultaneous passing of his father and his brother James.[46]

There was little at his post to distract Varnum from these melancholy events. "Traffic with the Indians" (Potawatomis, mostly) went well during his first year of business but diminished rapidly thereafter. In 1817 the factor bought $4,600 worth of Indian wares; in 1818 his take declined to $1,760 worth of peltry, and in 1819 it dropped to $520. By September 1820 he had less than $200 worth of skins and furs on hand. Varnum attributed his shrinking business to the usual suspects—private competitors who sold the Indians alcohol—but his chief regional competitor, the American Fur Company, fared as badly as he did.[47]

Apart from distributing gifts and annuities to the Indians, Factor Varnum found little to do in the spring and summer but "fight mosquitoes," tend his garden, and go on disappointing hunting trips that yielded only birds and a few deer. Varnum's poor yield from his hunting excursions does help explain the Chicago factory's declining business, for both resulted from changes in the local environment. The Lake Michigan shorelands had suffered depletion of game before the War of 1812, and while the deer population recovered during the war it collapsed with the return of peace. White hunters began clearing out the Illinois prairies and woods, and within a few years Potawatomi men began returning from their hunts without meat for their families. Under these straitened circumstances, southern Great Lakes Indians who wanted to work as commercial hunters had to find more distant fields for their labor, and other trading posts stood nearer those grounds. In 1821, Varnum suggested moving the Chicago factory to the upper Lakes, and Superintendent McKenney authorized him to shift the establishment several hundred miles northwest, to Saint Peter's River (the modern Minnesota River). The relocation never took place, however, because Congress terminated the factories before Varnum finished packing.[48]

The Saint Peter's factory, had it opened, would have been the northernmost postwar U.S. trading house. That geographic honor went instead to the factory at Green Bay, which had, like the prewar establishment on Mackinac Island, opened with high hopes for its productivity. Green Bay had been a multiethnic settlement and trading center since the seventeenth century, and the War Department had been planning a trading house there since 1805. When the Office of Indian Trade finally opened a factory at the bay in 1815, Superintendent Mason invested $15,700 worth of merchandise in the new post—with another $12,000 to follow by 1820—and sent veteran factor Matthew Irwin to staff it. The returns on these investments, however, proved meager. From 1816 to 1819, the trading house purchased only $1,750 worth of Indian goods, chiefly muskrat pelts and maple sugar. As a trading post, the Green Bay factory performed quite badly, receiving barely enough commodities to cover Irwin's subsistence allowance.[49]

In another part of the factory's balance sheet, however, lay evidence that Irwin actually did a fair amount of business: Green Bay's cash receipts for 1815–19 totaled $9,250, putting it in fourth place among the factories in volume of cash sales. The factory's debt records point to the sources of Irwin's business: soldiers from nearby Fort Howard, and white traders like Thomas James and Louis Rouse, who bought or borrowed merchandise to sell in nearby Indian communities. Irwin contracted with these traders to counter two of the largest disadvantages he labored under as Green Bay's factor. Deep snow during the winter discouraged many Ojibwas, Ho-Chunks, and Menominees from traveling to Green Bay, and in the warmer months resident British traders monopolized trade with the Indians who came there. Finding himself in much the same position Joseph Varnum had been in at Mackinac, Irwin adopted Varnum's strategy. However, his first experiment in contracting out the Green Bay factory's business did not go well: Irwin's partners could only buy 34 packs of furs (about 30 percent of the 1817–18 season's total harvest) at Winnebago Lake and Wisconsin River, and they could not subsequently repay the debts they owed the trading house.[50]

Factor Irwin sent out one more remote trading mission: in 1821 he sent Jacques Vieux to Milwaukee with $2,200 worth of goods for the Potawatomis. By then Irwin had run a deficit for several years, and when he submitted his returns for the last quarter of 1820 he suggested relocating the factory to a location with fewer competitors. In July 1821 Superintendent McKenney proposed closing the Green Bay house and "consolidat[ing]" its merchandise with the Chicago factory's at Saint Peter's. Secretary Calhoun approved, but the factories closed before the move could occur.[51]

While the Chicago and Green Bay trading houses generated disappointing returns, it took Thomas McKenney five years to conclude they no longer merited the expense of maintaining them. The superintendent needed less time to decide that the factory at Fort Mitchell had outlasted its usefulness. Constructed during the Creek War, Fort Mitchell stood "in the heart of the [Creek] nation," 90 miles west of the old factory at Fort Hawkins. McKenney agreed to move the Creek factory to the new site after the "rickety" Fort Hawkins house suffered heavy financial losses in 1816. Business at the new factory, however, ground to a halt by the third year: factor Daniel Hughes reported a balance of $1,123 at the end of 1817, $495 by the end of the following year, and $27 in December 1819. The Fort Mitchell factory, grumbled the superintendent, was not "doing anything besides losing money."[52]

McKenney exaggerated, somewhat. The Creeks had built up a $35,000 surplus in their annuity account, and Creek leaders continued to draw annuity goods from the Creek factories during and after the war. After McKenney finally ordered Daniel Hughes to close the Fort Mitchell house and sell its assets, a group of Creek chiefs used the rest of their annuity account, in January 1820, to buy the store and its goods. One of those chiefs, Little Prince, resided near Fort Mitchell and owned part of a tavern and store there. He and his political allies had opposed moving the factory from Fort Hawkins in the first place, and doubtless they appreciated the opportunity to buy out one of Little Prince's competitors.[53]

As with so many other factories, private competition caused the Creek trading house's evaporating business. After the Creek War of 1813–14, sutlers attached to new military posts in Creek country began trading with their Indian neighbors. Accompanying them were unlicensed traders who offered Creek hunters "the coarsest and cheapest kind of goods," innkeepers who opened stores on the road between Fort Mitchell and Fort Hawkins, and Creek agent David Mitchell, who in 1817 opened a store at the Creek agency. Mitchell encouraged Creek leaders to buy goods at his emporium with credits they had earned for service in the Creek War, or with advances from the large national annuity ($30,000 a year between 1817 and 1821). Hughes believed that the agent personally sought "to destroy the factory ... and monopolize the whole of the Indian trade" in the Creek nation, and he may have been right. Mitchell certainly intended his store to replace the factory as the Creeks' chief supplier, and his influence as the Creeks' agent and the distributor of their annuities and claims payments made him a formidable competitor.[54]

"It appears to be your misfortune," McKenney wrote Hughes in 1817, "to have a more than ordinary share of the opposition made by private traders against ... our factories." Hughes's opponents were extraordinary not only in determination but in kind: many were federal contractors (the sutlers) and employees (Agent Mitchell). One is tempted to see here an example of the corruption of the public sector by private interests. Then again, it had been many years since the Creek factory served anyone but a small Creek elite, so one might more accurately characterize its dissolution as the replacement of one set of private interests with another.[55]

VIEWING THE POOR BUSINESS at the Chicago, Fort Edwards, Fort Mitchell, and Green Bay trading houses, one might describe the entire factory system as moribund by 1820. Certainly, some scholars have reached this conclusion; Herman Viola, in particular, argued that the War of 1812 dealt the factories a blow from which they never recovered. However, several of the postwar factories, notably those at Fort Confederation, Fort Osage, and Prairie du Chien, did ample business, and the new Superintendent of Indian Trade and his factors infused healthy change into a supposedly dying system. Thomas McKenney consolidated the factories' supply routes and centralized his purchases and auctions in Georgetown. He and Secretary Calhoun moved the declining factories at Chickasaw Bluffs and Fort Edwards to more profitable locations, and they scheduled the consolidation and relocation of the dormant Chicago and Green Bay trading houses. The factors at Green Bay and Prairie du Chien, surrounded by private competitors, hired some of those competitors to undertake trade missions on their behalf, thereby extending their houses' range. And while the factories' influence over Native Americans no longer mattered as much as before the war, the trading houses at Spadre Bluffs and Marais des Cygnes did help extend federal political power west of the Mississippi, the former by solidifying a de facto alliance between the United States and the Arkansas Cherokees, the latter by securing the loyalty of the Osages.[56]

The factory system retained both political relevance and competent administrators. The greatest threat to it had become private, domestic competition, which had grown considerably since the war. The competitors included Indians who now worked both sides of the fur trade, Red River horse traders, Saint Louis merchants, and the American Fur Company. These competitors drew off the factories' customers in part because they sold alcohol, which federal laws prohibited factors from offering, and purchased horses, which diplomatic considerations barred factors from purchasing. The factories' business thus tended to flag even as their expenses remained high. This ensured the trading houses remained dependent on their patron, the Congress of the United States. Since many members of Congress considered the factory system obsolescent, their support for it could only be lukewarm.[57]

Superintendent McKenney did not see himself as the caretaker of an obscure and stagnant trading establishment. He planned to reinvigorate the factories by making them the wellspring of publicly funded Indian schools that would "civilize" Native American children while the factors mitigated the iniquities of the fur trade. In this way McKenney would tie his office both to the U.S. government's Indian civilization program, whose primacy Secretary Crawford had asserted, and to the growing number of Protestant mission societies that had begun to spring up earlier in the century. In the process, though, the superintendent intensified the determination of the factories' foes to destroy their public competitor, which they now saw as a "pious monster" they had to slay before it recovered its strength. Their efforts, in turn, revealed that in the minds of some national leaders, one could no longer reconcile the spirit of commerce with the mandates of civilization. Thus, the domestic fur trade could no longer constitute a legitimate utility for a government that wanted to develop, not merely control, its western borderlands.[58]

8

Civilization versus Commerce

The factory system was clearly flagging by the 1820s, but some of the houses continued to see steady business, and Thomas McKenney and John Calhoun had drawn up plans for expansion. Congress abruptly derailed those plans when it ordered the remaining factories closed and appointed independent commissioners to liquidate their assets. The national legislature's decision, and the testimony and speeches Congress heard before making it, grew from genuine animosity. This unfavorable sentiment, in turn, arose from a perception that trade, far from uplifting and civilizing people, had become a rather sordid and venial endeavor, of which a high-minded Congress should wash its hands. This attitude surfaced in public commentary on the Panic of 1819 and the ensuing depression. Congress, slashing its expenses in the depths of that depression, had probably come to view a public trading enterprise like the factories as particularly worthy of liquidation.

General anti-factory sentiment had grown in Congress during the trading houses' last few years. A handful of men fanned this sentiment into flame in 1821–22. These were the proprietor and officers of the American Fur Company (AFC) and their allies in the War Department and Congress. That a private company had acquired such influence over the federal government seems noteworthy, even if a story of private corruption strikes modern readers as drearily familiar. From John Jacob Astor's perspective, the story becomes more complicated. The American Fur Company came under federal scrutiny and regulation, and it shared with the national government a common interest (namely, encouraging Indians to trade with American traders). Its partners, particularly Astor, saw themselves as nearly adjuncts of the national government, doing a risky and grubby job that benefited the nation-state but earned them only minimal respect. When Thomas McKenney implicitly criticized them as sharpers needing tighter regulation, while at the same time declaring that his own factories could, through a partnership with Christian missionaries, uplift and civilize his Indian clients, it proved the last straw. Anger at McKenney's interference, self-righteousness, and apparent hypocrisy drove Astor's lieutenants, and the officials and Congressmen who sympathized with them, to mount a documentary and legislative assault on the factory system. It succeeded, and then Astor moved in to pick some of the more valuable pieces from the rubble.

THE MOST FATAL YEAR for the Indian factories was 1819. Two events in that year created the preconditions for the demise of the factory system: a nationwide depression that caused Congress to cut public spending, and the passage of a law that, ironically, sprang from the mind of Thomas McKenney, but which in its final form isolated the factories from the mainstream of national Indian policy. Lacking dedicated congressional supporters, dependent on Congress for funds, and caught in a wave of retrenchment, the factory system staggered, then collapsed when attacked by determined foes.

The depression that began in 1819 originated in the worldwide deflation that followed the Napoleonic Wars. The United States initially escaped this contraction because postwar crop failures in Europe created demand for American produce. Produce and real estate prices rose sharply in North America, particularly in western districts that the U.S. government had just purchased from hard-pressed Native Americans. Easy credit, extended by hundreds of banks and backed by the new Second Bank of the United States (BUS), pushed those prices to giddy heights.[1]

Then the bubble burst. European farmers recovered from the destruction of the Napoleonic Wars, and as food supplies increased crop prices fell. British bankers called in their American loans, while the new director of the BUS, Langdon Cheves, also contracted his loans to meet a federal demand for specie (to pay an installment on the Louisiana Purchase). The resulting shortage of gold and silver nearly killed the American banking industry; Missourian George Tompkins noted a "general crash of banks" by July 1819. Commerce and industry also faltered, squeezed by deflation and lack of credit. By 1820 three-fourths of Philadelphia's laborers and 65 percent of Pittsburgh's industrial workers were unemployed, much of the real estate in Cincinnati went into foreclosure, and in Kentucky, where forty banks closed, "the times for money [were] alarming and frightful."[2]

As the economy imploded, the federal government responded with austerity measures. During its 1820–21 session Congress reduced the size of the army by 40 percent and cut naval and Indian Department expenditures in half. The retrenchment program addressed the budget deficit caused by shrinking tax revenue, but it also had a basis in ideology, in the old "republican ideal" of frugality, economy, and stoicism. Newspaper publisher Hezekiah Niles expressed this ideal when he hoped that the depression would purge the national economy of inflation and return the country to "the old times of honesty and leather breeches." Given that ideology fueled their retrenchment campaign, it is unsurprising that members of Congress rooted out expenditures wherever they could find them—Thomas Benton recalled that "even the abolition of a clerkship of $800 . . . was not deemed an object below the attention of Congress." In this climate, a $300,000 factory system whose function newer congressmen could not understand would not easily escape the budgetary axe.[3]

The other event that imperiled the factory system was more obscure than the panic and the depression, but arguably it mattered more to Native Americans and makers of federal Indian policy: the Civilization Act of 1819. This law created an annual appropriation of $10,000 for Native American education, which the president would distribute to missionaries and philanthropists willing to open schools for Indian children. The act represented a significant expansion of the U.S. government's thirty-year-old Indian civilization program, whose designers had sought, through technical assistance and schooling, to convert Native Americans into English-speaking commercial farmers. Through this program, policy-makers hoped to achieve several significant, if possibly contradictory, goals: persuading Indian leaders to create tribal governments that federal agents could manipulate, persuading Indians to sell "surplus" lands they no longer needed (since farmers needed less land than hunters), and persuading foreigners that the United States treated its Indian peoples honorably.[4]

The civilization policy originated with colonial American efforts to convert Native peoples to Christianity. In the 1790s the War Department placed Indian children with Quaker families charged with their education, and it included clauses in laws and treaties that promised free plows, looms, and mills to several Indian nations. After 1800 the Democratic-Republicans enlarged their Federalist predecessors' policy. Congress authorized annual gifts of livestock and hardware to the Indians in the Trade and Intercourse Act of 1802, and the War Department funded mission schools and teachers for the Cherokees, Kaskaskias, and southern Great Lakes Indians. Several factors also participated, in a modest way, in the civilization program, selling farm equipment and cloth-making supplies at their stores.[5]

The link between the factory system and the civilization program remained tenuous until 1816, when Secretary of War Crawford explicitly defended the trading houses as civilizing influences. When Thomas McKenney assumed the superintendency of Indian trade a month later, he strengthened the bond between the troubled factory system and the more promising civilization initiative. McKenney asked the factors to supply him with lists of "the particular instruments of husbandry" requested by would-be Indian farmers, and he urged them to set a good example for aspiring cultivators by raising gardens near their factories. This latter proposal mirrored, and perhaps borrowed, the educational methodology of Indian agent Benjamin Hawkins, who had built a farm and smithy at his agency "to serve as a model and stimulus" for Creek farmers.[6]

McKenney soon received an opportunity to tie the factories even more closely to the civilization project. In December 1816 Isaac Thomas, the chair of the House Committee on Indian Affairs, asked the superintendent to help him review existing Indian trade regulations and design legislation to further "the work of civilization." In his reply, McKenney observed that many Native Americans had begun to adopt "the pursuits of civilized life," tilling the soil, making their own clothing, and displaying "discipline" (presumably frugality) in their trading practices. However, avaricious private traders threatened to halt this progress, as they plied Indians with liquor and defrauded them with counterfeit money. Only positive action, McKenney argued, could counter these malefactors' corrupting influence.[7]

Noting the extent of the United States' territory and the size of its Indian population, McKenney proposed a bold program. He first recommended the construction of between four and eight new factories, each capitalized at $20,000. The new infusion of capital into the system would help factors compete with better-financed private companies. Then, to minister to what McKenney considered the Indians' longer-term needs, the government would open a schoolhouse near each factory, where Indian children could learn the arts of "civilized" society. Each school would require $1,000 to build and equip, and the War Department could use factories' profits to hire missionary teachers. Older students would help by serving as monitors and drill leaders under the Lancastrian system of instruction.[8]

The proposed reforms would provide new justification for the factories, making them centers of Indian civilization and development, and would augment McKenney's own official duties. They would also create

Thomas McKenney, third and last superintendent of Indian trade, is portrayed here in his later years as a public official. Behind him, three Indians discuss their affairs without, apparently, McKenney's input or awareness. Portrait of Thomas McKenney, courtesy of the State Historical Society of Missouri.

a new "constituency" for the trading houses, in the form of Protestant mission societies. McKenney himself had been raised a Quaker, within a denomination that had been evangelizing Indians for a century, so he probably felt more of an affinity for missionaries than did his predecessors. Nor would the public employment of missionaries as teachers have seemed unusual to McKenney and his superiors, for the federal government had done so in the recent past and now would have new opportunities to employ them.[9]

Most American missionaries had been slow to express interest in educating Indians. At the end of the first decade of the nineteenth century, though, as the domestic religious revivals known as the Second Great Awakening began to swell American church membership, a new generation of Protestant seminary students began organizing foreign mission societies, like the American Board of Commissioners for Foreign Missions (ABCFM). They sought to harness the spiritual enthusiasm of the newly enlarged laity, and to use the romance of overseas missionary adventures to attract donations and recruit future ministers. British colleagues of these young American missionaries reminded them of the "not less destitute tribes" of non-Christians in their own homeland, and once the War of 1812 had ended the ABCFM and other groups began sending agents to Indian country. The ABCFM was the first of these mission societies to ask the War Department for assistance; thanks to McKenney's help, it would not be the last.[10]

In 1817 McKenney incorporated his program into a draft bill he presented to the House Committee on Indian Affairs. The bill proposed eight new factories, with a combined capital of $160,000, and a $10,000 annual Indian school fund drawn from the factories' profits. The committee warmly received the bill and recommended it to Congress as "an act of humanity . . . [and] sound national policy." In April 1818, however, the House of Representatives voted it down.[11]

The superintendent remained undeterred. Since he began his second year in office, McKenney had been developing a network of correspondents among American missionaries and evangelizing denominations. In July 1817 he distributed to several Indian agents and territorial governors a pamphlet printed by the Kentucky Mission Society, to demonstrate the civilizing "spirit gone forth amongst many tribes." In 1818 McKenney sent a confidential circular to several dozen churches and religious associations, asking them to help secure passage of an Indian education act. He then advised Secretary Calhoun, whom Congress had asked to start liquidating the trading houses, that the federal government should instead expand the factory system, not only to maintain Native Americans' goodwill, but also to promote "benevolence and reform"—synonyms for the civilization policy.[12]

The correspondence paid off. In December 1818 Secretary Calhoun recommended that Congress retain the factories to "hasten [the Indians'] ultimate civilization." Meanwhile, memorials from several religious societies arrived in Washington, supporting the expansion of the factory system and the use of its profits to fund Indian schools. Several of these petitions came from frontier states and districts, where white settlers knew traders' sharp practices firsthand, and where churches often provided the only schooling of any kind. The Blue River Baptist Association of Indiana and the Mississippi Baptist Association asserted that private traders sought only to "defraud" and "debauch" their Native clients, and they asked Congress to supply Indians with an "honorable trade" via the factories. Several Quaker meetings urged Congress to protect the "helpless and oppressed" Indians and appealed to national pride—something that the United States' survival of the War of 1812 had enhanced—by asserting that "righteousness exalteth a nation."[13]

The members of Congress decided to give Calhoun, McKenney, and their religious allies half a loaf. The two chambers agreed to renew the factory system for at least one more year, and the Senate Committee on Indian Affairs, whose members came from some of the same frontier states as the petitioners, drafted another Indian education bill in January 1819. To prevent the "future decline and final extinction" of Indian nations, the Civilization Act, as some later called it, appropriated $10,000 per annum for training in "the habits and arts of civilization." With these funds the president would hire "capable persons of good moral character" to teach English literacy, arithmetic, and European-style agriculture. The bill passed both houses of Congress two months later, and President James Monroe signed it into law.[14]

It would prove, however, a setback for McKenney and the Office of Indian Trade. The Civilization Act included no provision for new factories, and it took the annual fund for Indian schooling from the Treasury, rather than factory profits. This deprived McKenney of both control of the Indian school fund and one of his best arguments for retaining and expanding the factory system. The new law instead advanced the institutional fortunes of American mission societies, to whom in the fall of 1819 Calhoun sent a circular letter inviting them to apply for a share of the new school fund. The ABCFM, the United Foreign Missionary Society, and other groups soon responded. The number of schools for Native Americans in the United States rose from four to twenty-one, with 800 enrolled students, by 1824.[15]

The Civilization Act codified a new concept that had been gathering followers since the turn of the century: civilization was a form of moral acculturation best taught by ministers and "moral teachers," not by secular government agents. Commerce, which had appeared to eighteenth-century philosophers and policy-makers as the "cement" of society, no longer seemed fully compatible with civility. Quaker missionaries had been tacitly making this argument for years, insofar as they emphasized subsistence farming and material self-sufficiency as the bases of civilization. The Quakers shared with others this anti-commercial asceticism:

during the late eighteenth and early nineteenth centuries, American statesmen periodically attributed to trade such moral excesses as avarice, laziness, and luxury. After the Panic of 1819, several congressmen blamed the economic meltdown on Americans' "undue relish for speculation and trade" and urged them to return, in the words of a Southern political meeting, to the "simple habits of republicanism." Hard times made it harder for Americans to consider commerce morally uplifting, and easier for them to see it as a threat to republican civilization. In this intellectual climate, one would find it difficult to persuade congressmen that trade could promote Indian civilization, and easy to convince them that withdrawing the federal government from the former would not endanger the latter. The Civilization Act reinforced this belief by interposing a legislative barrier between the factories and the federal government's Indian civilization project. Once this wall had arisen, it cut off the factory system from one of its last justifications for survival.[16]

McKenney gamely defended the factories as essential components of the civilization project. In a November 1820 report to Congressman Henry Southard, he described "a well-devised system of trade" as an invaluable "auxiliary in promoting the benevolent scheme of [Indian] civilization," noting that "thousands of our most respectable citizens" supported that scheme. He made a telling choice of words: McKenney no longer viewed the trading houses as the financial support of the civilization program, but a mere "auxiliary" to it. Moreover, by the time the superintendent made his request, more powerful men had concluded that even a diminished factory system threatened them, and they prepared to demolish it. Among these were the merchant John Astor and his lieutenant, Ramsey Crooks.[17]

Astor's economic fortunes had suffered during the War of 1812, when the British seized his trading posts on Mackinac Island and at Astoria in the Oregon country. His political fortunes, however, prospered. Astor helped raise loans for the Treasury Department, and later he became a shareholder in the Second Bank of the United States, which he had urged President Madison and Congress to charter. He also became the creditor of several prominent federal officials, loaning money to Henry Clay ($20,000) and James Monroe ($9,000) and taking charge of the finances of former secretary of the treasury Albert Gallatin. Astor generally treated these loans as simple business investments, but he did occasionally remind his debtors of their obligations when he needed political favors.[18]

Astor came to need political preferment after the war, as he began building his American Fur Company into the powerhouse it eventually became. In 1816 he purchased the assets of the Montreal-based Southwest Company and expanded his trading operations into the southern Great Lakes region. By 1817 he had reorganized his firm into a joint-stock company with 125 employees under three field managers, one of whom was Ramsey Crooks. Thirty-year-old Crooks had more than a decade's experience as a trader and owned shares of the company he now managed.[19]

As few of the AFC's employees held U.S. citizenship, Astor viewed with alarm President Monroe's efforts to tighten a law barring foreign traders from American territory, and in 1817 he persuaded the president to loosen it. Shortly thereafter, the merchant prince complained to Secretary Calhoun that the Army had arrested two of his company's employees because the Indian agent at Mackinac had given them invalid trading licenses. Reviewing this and other complaints against the agent, Calhoun fired him.[20]

One can view these episodes as evidence of Astor's influence on the federal government, and of the ability of a wealthy private citizen to defeat adverse regulations and interfering regulators. For a large-scale fur trader in the early nineteenth century, however, the reverse was more nearly true. Astor's company fell squarely within the federal government's sphere of interest and under its power. It operated in a sensitive borderland, the Great Lakes region, which the United States and Britain had just been contesting, and in which the United States sought to reestablish its influence by building or rebuilding six forts. The American Fur Company employed foreign workers whom Congress had technically barred from the fur trade, and its business came under the U.S. government's constitutional authority. If anyone held the whip hand in this relationship, the U.S. government did, not the AFC. If Astor received special favor from officials, he did so, arguably, because they saw him as nearly a public official himself.[21]

While Astor viewed the factories as a threat, he could not afford to move against them too swiftly. In October 1815 Astor did fire an initial salvo at the factory system. In correspondence with Albert Gallatin, Astor argued that private traders would not invest more capital in the fur trade until Congress shut down the factories. He asked that Gallatin, through President Madison, recommend closure of the trading houses to Congress, but while Gallatin discussed Astor's business with the president that fall, Madison made no such recommendation. The War Department instead began reviving the factory system under Superintendent McKenney.[22]

Astor subsequently adopted a more cautious strategy of undermining his public rival. He directed his traders to undersell the factories on certain goods, which the employees of a company with one million dollars in capital could do, and he received permission from the War Department to sell liquor to the Indians, which the factors could not do. Moreover, Astor resumed seeking allies within the federal government. He developed a cordial relationship with Lewis Cass, the governor of Michigan Territory, whom he persuaded to join his campaign against the factory system. Cass argued in an 1818 letter to Calhoun that the factories "render the government obnoxious and contemptible to the Indians," and he urged their abolition.[23]

Additional allies soon presented themselves. The community of Saint Louis fur traders, with whom Astor had developed business relations, objected to the expansion of the factory system into the upper Mississippi valley. One of their principal mouthpieces, the *St. Louis Enquirer*, published editorials blasting the factors for incompetence, profiteering, and shoddy merchandise. The editor of the *Enquirer* was Thomas Hart Benton, a lawyer and aspiring politician who had moved to Missouri in 1815 and become one of the region's boosters. He had become friends with one of Saint Louis's leading fur-trading families, the Chouteaus, and with their in-law Charles Gratiot, an Astor trading partner. Given Benton's connections, it is not surprising that Astor hired him to sue Talbot Chambers, the officer who had arrested American Fur Company employees in 1816. Nor is it surprising that when the Missouri legislature appointed Benton to the U.S. Senate, he would lead the drive to abolish the factories.[24]

By the time Senator Benton joined his colleagues in Washington, congressional support for the factories had fallen to its lowest level. The slow decline had started even before the retrenchment movement of the early 1820s. At the end of the War of 1812, Congress renewed funding for the trading houses for two years, but in its 1817 reauthorization it shortened the renewal period to fourteen months. In 1818 Congress renewed factory funding for eleven months, with the Senate stipulating that it would henceforth confirm all factors' appointments, and the House of Representatives asking Secretary Calhoun to prepare a "system" for replacing the factories with private traders. Calhoun, on McKenney's advice, instead submitted a report that identified the factories as incubators of Indian civilization.[25]

Congressional objections to the trading houses receded far enough to allow three more renewals of the system's funding. In March 1819 the superintendent even expressed the hope that Congress would soon "enlarge" the factory system, as he had advocated. The House of Representatives, however, soon began placing the factories under more scrutiny, pressing the War Department to document their debts and receipts. In early 1821 Henry Southard, chair of the House Committee on Indian Affairs, asked McKenney to address reports that the factors had been defrauding their Indian customers or shaking them down for bribes.[26]

Stoking House members' suspicions about the factories were several traders, including Ramsey Crooks, who had come to Washington to oppose a restrictive new trade-licensing bill. Crooks had by now become one of the factory system's ardent opponents. Two years earlier he and American Fur Company manager Robert Stuart had shared with Astor their opinion that the U.S. government had no business competing with fur traders, and their hope that Congress would close the factories before they destroyed all private competition. They did suggest that the company could coexist with the Office of Indian Trade if the government moved its trading houses west of Lake Superior, away from the AFC's ambit. In 1820, though, Crooks withdrew this concession after McKenney published, in the *National Intelligencer*, a report denouncing private traders as "pernicious" whiskey-peddlers, and after Secretary Calhoun urged Congress to give McKenney control of trading licenses and increase traders' bonds to $10,000.[27]

Crooks and his allies viewed this bill as an effort to destroy the private fur trade, and they remained in Washington to lobby the House of Representatives—successfully—against it. It is likely that these men spread the rumors of malfeasance that Southard brought to McKenney's attention. The superintendent made short work of the charges, noting that the Office of Indian Trade's invoicing system made fraudulent accounting impossible, and that his employees had certified their honesty by posting bonds for good behavior. His reply mollified the House Committee on Indian Affairs, but apparently not the rest of the chamber.[28]

In February 1821 Southard's committee reported a bill to the House to renew the factories' funding for another year. On 24 February, Congressman Christopher Rankin moved to return the factories bill to committee with instructions to prepare plans for "wind[ing] ... up the present establishments" by 1 September. Southard and Representative

Felix Walker opposed the motion, calling the trading houses vital to the civilization and protection of the Indians, but their colleagues overruled them. Representatives Albert Tracy and John Floyd (the latter a friend and hotel-mate of Benton and Crooks) argued—reasonably enough—that the factories kept Native Americans "in the hunter state." They also alleged that the factors had made unauthorized profits, perhaps a reference to the earlier allegations of fraud. In the end, the House members, who had just made major spending cuts in the War and Navy departments, saw no reason to spare the factories, and they supported Rankin's motion by a 50-vote majority. However, the trading houses were saved by the bell, or more specifically by the adjournment of Congress to attend James Monroe's second presidential inauguration. Ramsey Crooks opined that, absent the early adjournment, the factories would surely have closed in 1821.[29]

Superintendent McKenney initially agreed with Crooks's assessment, writing that "the system will die of itself soon, by the very policy of the Congress." He did believe congressional opposition to the factories rested on a weak base, informing George Sibley that only five House members had marshaled the vote to terminate the trading houses. In mid-1821 he announced that Congress would soon hear "the voice of the people," who favored Indian civilization and believed the factories could protect Native Americans from the "artifices of private traders." By "the people," McKenney meant the Protestant mission societies that supported the Indian civilization program, and that had in the recent past petitioned Congress in support of the Civilization Act and the factories. Anglo American officials had long tended (when it suited them) to conflate small groups of petitioners with a more general *vox populi*, but if McKenney's missionary and philanthropic supporters did not represent the entire American public, they at least outnumbered the employees of the major fur companies.[30]

McKenney began writing his missionary allies for assistance in the spring of 1821, but his efforts acquired new urgency that December, when the House of Representatives approved a resolution by Congressman Floyd to alter the existing Indian trade system. The petitions the superintendent requested began to arrive in Washington over the summer, signed by inhabitants of Pennsylvania, Maryland, and Ohio, along with institutional groups like the Trustees of Dickinson College. Congress received eleven memorials in favor of retaining the factories, collectively bearing over 850 signatures. Most copied a boilerplate memorial that Reverend Philip Milledoler, a prominent New York minister, had prepared and circulated to his contacts. This overwrought document argued that the interests of private traders had "ever been at war with Indian happiness," and that the federal government could protect Indians from their corrupting influence only through the interposition of its factories. If it did so, missionaries' work of teaching Indians could continue, but if it closed the trading houses, "war and bloodshed" and "a cruel destiny" for the Indians would result. A similar but independently authored petition from "Citizens of the State of Ohio" concurred, denouncing private traders and supporting additional funding for the factories.[31]

The memorials revived McKenney's hopes. He wrote to one of the factors that "I do not think the factory system will be broken up"; he probably hoped that a new report he had prepared for the Senate Committee on Indian Affairs, which had opened its own investigation into the factories, had won him some supporters on that side of the capitol. McKenney larded this report with pathos and paternalism. He asserted that Indians had reached "a state of . . . absolute dependence" on the fur trade, and that their "incompeten[ce]" to determine their own interests ensured that "the keen and adventurous trader, skilled in the arts of deception" would frequently cheat them unless the federal government intervened. The trading houses, McKenney continued, would allow the United States to maintain "friendly intercourse" with Native Americans and pursue its civilization program; meanwhile, private traders could still buy peltry from the Office of Indian Trade. Both groups, Indians and traders alike, would benefit from the U.S. government's continued involvement in the fur trade, but if it ended, Indians faced "bereavement, and suffering, and death."[32]

The Senate committee, however, had also solicited hostile testimony on the factories from Indian agents John Bell, John Biddle, and Benjamin O'Fallon, as well as Ramsey Crooks, who delivered a long and eloquent broadside. Drawing chiefly on their knowledge of the northern factories, which had been doing poor business for years, the agents declared that the trading houses had become "useless" and that Indians viewed them with "sickly indifference." Biddle and Crooks called the factors' Indian customers "competent judges" of their own interests, and they argued that the poor quality and high prices of the factories' merchandise drove Indians to trade with private businessmen. Crooks drew on popular stereotypes when he described some of the factories' goods as too refined for mere Indians, "unless the committee should be of the opinion that men's and women's coarse and fine shoes, worsted and cotton hose, tea, glauber salts, alum, and antibilious pills, are necessary to promote the comfort or health of the aborigines." Clearly, Crooks argued, the factors did much of their business with whites. Finally, the respondents asserted that the trading houses would not "encourage civilization in the Indian population" because the factors' interest lay in keeping Indian men in their hunting ranges rather than putting them behind a plow or a desk. "The desperate efforts which the factors make . . . to prop the questionable pecuniary credit of the whole system," Crooks concluded, could prove "but little favorable to that serenity of mind, mildness of disposition, and . . . strictly moral deportment" necessary for a moral leader. Commerce, it seemed, now made men too competitive and amoral to promote their own or others' cultural progress. McKenney's professed interest in Indian civilization, claimed an editorial in Senator Benton's newspaper, was "merely a stalking horse to gain more substantial ends."[33]

One month later, the Senate Committee on Indian Affairs completed a bill to close the factories. The proposed statute gave the superintendent a year to sell off the trading houses' assets, and it created a new position for McKenney—superintendent of Indian affairs—with authority over Indian agents and regulatory authority over private traders. The committee's generosity infuriated Senator Benton, who had the testimony of Crooks and the three Indian agents printed for the members of the Senate, and he used that testimony to support a damning speech against the factories on the Senate floor.[34]

Benton began by moving an amendment to the closure bill that appointed special agents to liquidate the factories' stock, on the grounds that Congress could no longer trust the Office of Indian Trade. He followed the motion with a passionate denunciation of the factory system. He estimated that Congress had spent $600,000 on the trading houses since their inception, and that the system now only reported $32,000 in annual gross returns. He accused McKenney of selling the factories' furs and pelts well below market value, and of buying inferior-quality merchandise from his Georgetown cronies well above market rates.[35]

The senator also charged the superintendent with stocking inappropriate merchandise at the factories. His scornful remarks on this subject revealed that he held stereotypical views both of Indians' wants and of how those wants changed as human beings progressed toward civilization, a state Native Americans had supposedly not reached. Indians, Benton asserted, had no need for sophisticated goods like coffee or morocco shoes. He dismissed McKenney's explanation that he stocked these items for "half-breeds" and Indians "desirous of imitating the whites." The senator reserved particular abuse for one item in the factories' inventories: Jews' harps. He sardonically declared that McKenney had ordered these instruments as part of his civilization plan, "to draw [the Indians] from the savage and hunter state" and carry them to "the first state" after savagery, "the pastoral" stage. In this era the "tawny-colored Corydons and the red-skinned Amaryllises, '*recubans sub tegmine fugi*,' upon the banks of the Missouri and Mississippi, could make no progress in the delightful business of love and sentiment" without music.[36]

With these satirical remarks, Benton exploited a "stadial theory" of human development that Anglo American philosophers had developed in the previous century. According to this theory, which enjoyed much currency by Benton's day, human beings advanced from "savagery" to civilization through discrete stages: pastoral, agricultural, and commercial. The senator argued that Indians could not simultaneously occupy several of these rungs on the ladder of cultural development, and that a federal policy which let them do so would inevitably fail. It was folly to expect trading posts to lead Indians to pasturage and agriculture, since they (in Benton's view) depended upon Native Americans' continuing to hunt and on traders' confining themselves to buying and selling. It was equally foolish to stock sophisticated goods for Indians, since simple hunters had no need of the accoutrements of an advanced commercial civilization. If McKenney did these things, Senator Benton concluded, incompetence or corruption must explain his actions.[37]

Several members of the Senate rose after Benton's speech to defend the superintendent. Henry Johnson praised McKenney and his employees and defended their integrity. Both he and Richard Johnson argued that the Senate should focus on the efficacy and expense of the factory system, not the behavior of its managers and employees. However, no one in the Senate would speak on behalf of the factories themselves. Walter Lowrie and Nathaniel Macon argued that the government simply lacked the specialized competence to engage in the fur trade: the United States' "Indian border" was too extensive, the logistics involved too complicated, and the federal government's other concerns too many. Several senators still objected to Benton's plan to kill the trading houses immediately, but in the end the Missourian's diatribe reflected the general mood and opinion of the chamber. On 28 March, the Senate not only approved

Benton's immediate-liquidation amendment (17-11) but also agreed to strip the draft factory bill of any reference to superintendents of Indian affairs or private trade regulations. In this form the factory closure bill passed the Senate on 1 April.[38]

The debate over the factories then passed into the press, thanks to the *National Intelligencer*'s reprinting of Benton's speech. Both McKenney and veteran factor George Sibley published responses to Benton. McKenney observed that he had always supplied the factories according to the Indians' wants, rather than merely sending the cheapest merchandise; he also rebutted Benton's claim that he'd sold furs and skins in the worst markets, noting that his Georgetown auctions yielded sale prices 84 percent higher than their equivalents in Saint Louis. Sibley elaborated upon McKenney's theme of accommodation, noting that the factors' primary mission had always been diplomatic: to supply the Indians, develop "intimate knowledge" of Native American nations, maintain a "dignified and correct deportment" toward their leaders, and by these means keep the peace. He agreed with Senators Lowrie and Macon, however, that the factory system had become "quite inefficient and useless," describing his own factorship at Fort Osage as a waste of time. Sibley sought to redeem the reputations of his fellow factors rather than save the factory system, which he believed beyond salvation.[39]

In this, Sibley proved correct. The House of Representatives approved the factory closure bill in May without debate. While President Monroe expressed dismay at Senator Benton's attack on McKenney, he signed the closure bill and appointed nine commissioners to liquidate the factories. Between June 1822 and December 1823, these agents inventoried the property of the Office of Indian Trade, which they initially valued at $286,000: $131,000 worth of trade goods, $85,000 worth of debts, $17,000 worth of buildings, and the rest fairly equally divided between Indians' wares and cash. They then sold off what they could, at a large loss: by the end of 1823 they had sold the factories' material assets at a $69,000 loss, and had written off $76,000 worth of debts. Such was the price of shuttering the trading houses so peremptorily, and selling their contents during a depression.[40]

The U.S. government would, of course, save the $15,000 it spent each year on salaries and subsistence payments for Office of Indian Trade employees, and it would thereby make good its losses from the liquidation in about ten years. The larger significance of the factories' closure lies not, however, in the savings the federal government realized, but in the changes in the American nation-state and its relationship with American Indians that turned congressmen against the program, twenty-five years after its inception. The factory system had grown from colonial precedents, namely the government-run truck houses of Massachusetts, South Carolina, and other provinces, which in turn originated with those colonies' understanding that they could not survive without Indian allies and the trade that cemented alliance. As Native Americans began to rely on European goods in the eighteenth century, European settlers began to use trade and gifts to recruit warriors and employ them in their conflicts with other European empires. Native American allies gave the French a defensible claim to the North American interior, and they allowed Britain and Spain to challenge the United States' claim to the same region until 1815.[41]

The fledgling U.S. government, after a failed experiment with intimidation in the 1780s and an expensive war in the 1790s, decided to copy its European predecessors' Indian policy. Hence the establishment of the factories, which Indians used as trading centers, as bursaries for annuity goods, and as homes away from home. The factors and other officials, in turn, put the factories to their own uses, some foreseen by the system's founders and some not. Trading houses like those at Fort Wilkinson and Fort Wayne served as diplomatic conference centers, where federal commissioners used factory merchandise—and, in a few cases, factory debts—to secure land cessions. Factors compiled intelligence on distant Indian communities and tried to persuade their inhabitants to become their customers, thereby projecting American influence into the borderlands of Spanish Texas and British Canada. Finally, during the War of 1812, the factories acted as arsenals for the United States' Indian allies, and as inducements for groups like the Osages to take the American rather than the British side in the conflict. The trading houses, in short, served both as embassies and outposts of empire, and they performed these functions cheaply—for an average of $21,600 a year in salaries and capital costs.[42]

If the factory system inconvenienced anyone, it burdened the factors and superintendents, whose success depended on their ability to conciliate their Native American customers and satisfy their demands. To the Superintendent of Indian Trade fell the responsibility for supplying Indians with the high-quality, finely detailed merchandise they desired, even during wars and trade embargos, and in the absence of skilled domestic manufacturers. To the factors and local agents fell the burden of accepting hard-to-sell Indian wares like deerskins and maple sugar, lest they alienate their Indian partners, and of storing these commodities until they could be sold. To the factors and their assistants fell the tasks of entertaining Native American guests, dining with them, giving them presents, listening to their demands and grievances, and condoling with them when they lost loved ones.

The factors also faced the challenge of private traders, who competed with the factories everywhere they stood. The employees of the Office of Indian Trade met this challenge in creative ways, refuting the argument that public officials were too complacent or hidebound to embrace innovation. While the factors could not avoid one crucial restriction on their trade, namely the ban on liquor sales to Indians, they could and did offer Native visitors other forms of hospitality. While they did not initially offer credit, they ignored this restriction once it became clear that credit served as a more important commercial lubricant than alcohol. And while the factories' fixed locations impeded their business, the factors found ways around this problem. They opened subfactories closer to Native communities, or they loaned goods to private traders willing to undertake remote trading missions, thereby turning one of the factories' problems (private competitors) into a solution. If other expedients failed, their superiors in the War Department and Office of Indian Trade moved unprofitable posts to new locations, something they did at least ten times during the system's tenure.[43]

Safely removed from the burdens of the factory system, and mindful of its benefits, congressmen supported the program for two decades, steadily increasing the resources invested therein. The War of 1812, however, brought a sea change in federal Indian policy. The war demonstrated that, even with foreign support, eastern Indians could no longer overpower American troops, and therefore they could no longer credibly maintain independence from American rule. Moreover, the war largely ended American leaders' fears that foreign powers would intervene in U.S.-Indian relations. Britain, seeking an entente with its former adversary, did not protest when the United States extorted huge land cessions from King George's Indian allies or excluded British traders from American territory, and Spain's control over its North American borderlands collapsed with the mainland Spanish Empire.

The political realities that had midwifed the factory system no longer existed. The United States' frontier settlements no longer depended on the goodwill of Native Americans to survive; it was the other way around, now that white settlers outnumbered Indians twenty to one east of the Mississippi River. Americans' need for Native American alliances had largely vanished, as neighboring European empires retrenched or collapsed. The U.S. government's need for special resources, like trading debts, to leverage Indian land cessions had also diminished, as federal commissioners could now rely on the threat of force or of white settlers' overrunning Indian lands to persuade reluctant chiefs. The factories, already damaged by the war, now seemed an anachronism, and Congress put the Office of Indian Trade on a tighter leash while it reevaluated the need for it. When the Panic of 1819 forced Congress to reduce expenditures, and lobbyists for the private fur trade alleged factorial misconduct, Congress concluded that the time had come to end the antiquated factory system.[44]

In their twilight years, the federal trading houses did not lack their defenders, chief among them Superintendent of Indian Trade Thomas McKenney. Well connected and well protected, McKenney rebuilt the factory system and endeavored to give it a new mission, making it a component of the federal government's Indian civilization policy. To do so, he tried to persuade congressmen that commerce, properly managed, could help Indians develop orderly and civilized habits, and that the proceeds of the public fur trade could finance schools for Native American children. The latter part of McKenney's proposal became a dead letter in 1819, when Congress decided to create an Indian school fund drawn from general revenues, rather than factory profits. The former depended on congressmen's willingness to associate commerce with civilization, and therefore with the federal government's mission in Indian country. This association had diminished by 1822. Unlike their eighteenth-century predecessors, nineteenth-century congressmen viewed trade not as a generator of gentle habits but of competitiveness, and the fur trade as an impediment to Indian civilization, insofar as it discouraged Native American men from leaving the hunter "stage" of social development. Traders, even those in government employ, could not possibly civilize Indians; only preachers and teachers could do so. Private traders, whom McKenney had antagonized, readily endorsed this belief. Let the government attend to the Indians' cultural needs, ran the argument of men like Ramsey Crooks, and the American Fur Company would satisfy their material wants.

Still, the separation of the public from the economic sphere in Indian country was far from complete. In February 1824, while the House

Committee on Indian Affairs wrapped up the factories' business, Senator Benton rose on the other side of the Capitol to denounce British traders for intriguing with the Indians of the Missouri Valley. He requested federal intervention there, in the form of treaties with the region's Indians and troops to protect private trading posts. Congress did not take the British threat very seriously, but it did recognize the economic importance of the Plains bison trade, appropriating $20,000 to send commissioners and soldiers to the upper Missouri. In the summer of 1825, Henry Atkinson and Benjamin O'Fallon negotiated treaties with leaders of the Sioux, Crow, and other nations. The Americans smoothly coordinated military and commercial power: 500 soldiers accompanied them upriver, and they held several of their conferences at American Fur Company posts. The Native American treaty signatories agreed to exclusive relations with American traders, relations which Benton's old employer, the AFC, would soon monopolize.[45]

By 1826, Ramsey Crooks had bought out the American Fur Company's major competitors on the Missouri River, and within a few years the company had built an extensive "hierarchy of trading posts" that allowed it to dominate the northern Plains trade until 1860. The company's domination rested not only on its superior organization and high capitalization, but on access to government resources—specifically, diplomatic resources. By the 1830s the AFC had acquired a federal contract to supply the upper Missouri Indian nations with their annuities, and American Fur Company forts provided federal Indian agents with supplies and bases of operation. Some Native Americans regarded Indian agents almost as company employees. The old connection between diplomacy and trade that underlay the federal factory system persisted, but it now benefited a private firm rather than sustaining a public utility.[46]

In the Great Lakes country, meanwhile, the AFC began to perform one of the functions Thomas Jefferson had once prescribed for the factories: using commercial debts to leverage Indian land sales. By the 1830s American Fur Company traders had spread throughout the Old Northwest, marrying into Native American families, using liquor and gifts to ingratiate themselves with their Indian customers, and extending ample credit—at interest rates of up to 100 percent. Then the bills came due, as the AFC and other private traders pressed their trading partners to settle their accounts, and as federal commissioners pressed the Great Lakes Indians for land cessions, arguing that this would allow them both to pay their debts and benefit American settlers. In 1832–33, for instance,

Potawatomi leaders agreed to sell their nation's remaining lands in the region for 2.3 million dollars, of which $285,000 went to pay debts to the AFC and other traders. Private traders also placed themselves front and center when nations like the Menominees gathered to collect annuities owed them for prior land cessions. One traveler characterized these claimants as "vampires . . . [and] leeches," and an Army officer, Zachary Taylor, described the American Fur Company's employees as "the greatest scoundrels the world ever knew." The administration of President Andrew Jackson, if asked, would probably have used different adjectives: "helpful," even "invaluable." After all, the American Fur Company's credit, manpower, and resources helped the U.S. government do something its own factories had never accomplished: persuading Great Lakes Indians to exchange debts for land.[47]

What had happened to commercial diplomacy in the Louisiana Territory and the Great Lakes region presaged future public-private relations throughout the western United States. Missouri Valley Indian treaties came to resemble straightforward "business contracts" drawn up for the benefit of the American Fur Company. The removal policy of the 1830s and 40s generated large profits for speculators in southeastern cotton lands. The grants of land and credit that the federal government made to railroad companies in the 1860s and 70s helped make those companies the largest and wealthiest corporations in the world. By the end of the nineteenth century, a sociologist could straightforwardly characterize the U.S. government itself as "a huge commercial company" working hand in glove with private firms to develop and exploit the resources of a continent. One might say the capitalists, not the United States government, had won the struggle for North America, but it was becoming increasingly hard to tell the one from the other.[48]

Notes

Abbreviations Used in the Notes

For citations from the *Annals of Congress*, the author first identifies the specific Congress and Session, divided by a slash mark, and then the column number. For citations from microfilm, the author gives the reel number, then the volume (if any), identified by a capital letter, then the page number.

AC	Gales, Joseph, comp. and ed. *Annals of the Congress of the United States.* 42 vols. Washington, D.C.: Gales and Seaton, 1834–56.
ASPIA	Lowrie, Walter, and Walter Franklin, eds. *American State Papers,* "Indian Affairs." 2 vols. Washington, D.C.: Gales and Seaton, 1834.
BFP	Labaree, Leonard Woods, Ralph L. Ketcham, Whitfield J. Bell, Helen C. Boatfield, Helene H. Fineman, eds. *The Papers of Benjamin Franklin.* Vols. 4–5. New Haven, Conn.: Yale University Press, 1961–62.
CSHSW	State Historical Society of Wisconsin. *Collections of the State Historical Society of Wisconsin.* 40 vols. Madison, Wisc.: The Society, 1888–1931.
HCPSM	Michigan Pioneer and Historical Society. *Historical Collections of the Pioneer and Historical Society of Michigan.* 40 vols. Lansing, Mich.: The Society, 1876–1912.
JCC	Ford, Worthington, Gaillard Hunt, John Clement Fitzpatrick, Roscoe R Hill; Kenneth E Harris, and Steven D. Tilley, eds. *Journals of the Continental Congress, 1774–1789.* 34 vols. Washington, D.C.: U.S. Government Printing Office, 1907–34.
LB, Creek	Letter Book of the Creek Trading House, 1795–1821. Records of the Office of Indian Trade. Microfilm, M-4. National Archives, Washington, D.C.
LDC	Smith, Paul Hubert, and Ronald M. Gephart, eds. *Letters of Delegates to Congress, 1774–1789.* 26 vols. Washington, D.C.: Library of Congress, 1976–2000.
LRSW	Letters Received by the Office of the Secretary of War Relating to Indian Affairs, 1800–23. Microfilm, M-271. National Archives, Washington, D.C.

LSSIT	Letters Sent by the Superintendent of Indian Trade, 1807–22. Records of the Office of Indian Trade. Microfilm, M-16. National Archives, Washington, D.C.
OSW, LSIA	Records of the Office of the Secretary of War Relating to Indian Affairs. Letters Sent, 1800–23. Microfilm, M-15. National Archives, Washington, D.C.
Recs. Choctaw TH	Records of the Choctaw Trading House, 1803–24. Records of the Office of Indian Trade. Microfilm, T-500. National Archives, Washington, D.C.
ROIT	Records of the Office of Indian Trade. National Archives, Washington, D.C.
TPUS	Carter, Clarence, and John Porter Bloom, eds. *The Territorial Papers of the United States*. 26 vols. Washington, D.C.: U.S. Government Printing Office, 1934–73.
WGW	Fitzpatrick, John C., ed. *The Writings of George Washington from the Original Manuscript Sources*. 39 vols. Washington, D.C.: U.S. Government Printing Office, 1931–44.

Introduction

1. Wesley, "Government Factory System"; Prucha, *Great Father*, 35–40.

2. Proceedings of 25 Mar. 1822, *AC*, 17th Congress, 1st Session, 38: 317–18, 327–31 (first four quotes); Proceedings of 26 and 28 Mar. 1822, ibid., 38: 339–43, 353–54; Benton, *Thirty Years' View*, 1:20–21 (last two quotes). Georgetown was the headquarters of the Office of Indian Trade from 1808 to 1822.

3. Turner, *Fur Trade in Wisconsin*, 59–60; Coman, "Government Factories," esp. 379–83; Way, "United States Factory System," esp. 228–29; Quaife, *Chicago*, 302–4, 309 (quote); Quaife, "Experiment of the Fathers." Cf. Edgar Wesley, who argued that the factories only "failed" because Congress bowed to pressure from private traders. ("Government Factory System," esp. 503–8.)

4. Peake, *History of the Indian Factory System*, esp. 204–56; Plaisance, "U.S. Government Factory System;" Morris, "Traders and Factories"; and five articles by Magnaghi: "Sulphur Fork Factory," "Bellefontaine Indian Factory," "Michigan's Indian Factory at Detroit," "Michigan's Indian Factory at Mackinac," "Sandusky Indian Factory."

5. Benton, *Thirty Years' View*, 1:21; Horsman, *New Republic*, 122–37, 220–53; Dangerfield, *Awakening*, 1–20.

6. Banning, *Jeffersonian Persuasion*, esp. 126–60, 208–45, 273–302; Wesley, "Government Factory System," 492–94; Quaife, "Experiment."

7. Berkhofer, *White Man's Indian*, 145 (quote); Calloway, *American Revolution*, 46–64; Horsman, *Expansion*, 3–31; Anderson and Cayton, *Dominion of War*, 168–76, 192–95. The author has extrapolated the expense of the Northwest Indian War from congressional military appropriations for 1793–94, which included $2,580,000 for the expenses of the army on the frontier. (Act Making Appropriations for the Support of Government, 28 Feb. 1793, Peters, *Statutes*, 1:328; Act Making

Appropriations for the Support of the Military Establishment, 21 Mar. 1794, ibid., 1:346–47.)

8. Calloway, *New Worlds*, 43–47, 115–33; Dorothy Jones, *License for Empire*, 155–56, 185–86.

9. Richter, *Ordeal*, 29 (first quote); Dalton, ed., *Primitive, Archaic, and Modern Economies*, 7–9, 12 (second quote), 87–89, 197–201; Sahlins, *Stone Age Economics*, 180; White, "'Give Us a Little Milk'"; Merrell, "'Customes of Our Countrey,'" 131–38; Choquette, "Center and Periphery," 197.

10. Return Meigs to Secretary William Crawford, 30 Nov. 1815, *ASPIA*, 2: 87 (quote). The nine conferences took place at Coleraine (1796), Tellico (1798, 1804, and 1805), Fort Wilkinson (1802), Fort Wayne (1803 and 1809), Hoebuckintoopa (Saint Stephens, 1803), and Choctaw Trading House (1816). The treaties are in *Indian Affairs*, Kappler, 2:46–50; 51–55, 73–74, and 82–84; 58–59; 64–65 and 101–3; 69–70; and 137, respectively.

11. Heyrman, *Commerce and Culture*, 361–64; Bell, *First Total War*, 73–74; Montesquieu, *Spirit of the Laws*, 316 (first quote); Matson and Onuf, *Union of Interests*, 17 (second quote); McCoy, *Elusive Republic*, 86–87 (third quote 87).

12. McCoy, *Elusive Republic*, 87–90, 219; Washington to Marquis de Chastellux, 25 Apr./1 May 1788, *WGW*, 29:485 (quote); Matson and Onuf, *Union of Interests*, 15–29, 67–100.

13. Wolf, *Europe and the People without History*, 239–46; Calloway, *New Worlds*, 43–48; Eccles, "Fur Trade and Eighteenth-Century Imperialism"; Weber, "Bourbons and Bárbaros," 83–86.

14. Journal of Richard Butler, 31 Oct. 1785, in *Olden Time*, Craig, 2:459; Report of Great Miami Treaty Commissioners, 19 June 1786, *JCC*, 30:350; George Washington to the Senate, 4 Aug. 1790, *ASPIA*, 1:80; John Doughty to Henry Knox, 17 Apr. 1790, Harmar Papers, 12:83; Fifth Annual Message to Congress, 3 Dec. 1793, *WGW*, 33:168; Treaty of Amity, Commerce, and Navigation between His Britannic Majesty and the United States, 19 Nov. 1794, Peters, *Statutes*, 8:117–18.

15. William Panton and John Leslie to the Baron de Carondelet, 2 May 1794, in "Georgia-Florida Frontier," ed. Corbitt, 24:150–52; John Forbes to Carondelet, Fall 1796, ibid., 24:267; Matthew Ernest to the Secretary of the Treasury, 1 Nov. 1802, *ASPIA*, 1: 684. One might hesitate to apply the word "empire" to the United States, but Jürgen Osterhammel has suggested that the early American republic resembled an empire more than a nation-state. Its borders were often ambiguous; it had peripheral populations whom the state and federal governments had not fully incorporated (Indians, African American slaves, French Louisianans); and its central government legitimized itself through symbols and services (like trading factories) and by pursuing a "civilizing mission" in the peripheries. Ilya Vinkovetsky, citing Osterhammel, notes another feature of empires: they often found themselves contesting territories and subject peoples with other empires. This contest, resolved through war or negotiation, gave leverage to peripheral peoples able to play the rivals against one another. (Osterhammel, *Transformation*, 412–15, 448–50; Vinkovetsky, *Russian America*, 9–10; Cayton, "Radicals in the 'Western World.'"

16. Adelman and Aron, "From Borderlands to Borders"; Ned Blackhawk, *Violence over the Land*, esp. 26, 57–58, 70–72, 79, 112–13, 120, 133–36, 168–70, 193; Hämäläinen and Truett, "On Borderlands"; and see also the DuVal, Barr, and Hämäläinen sources cited in n.18, below.

17. Speech of Little Turtle to the President, 4 Jan. 1802, cited in *John Johnston and the Indians*, Hill, 16; Frederick Bates to Henry Dearborn, 22 Oct. 1807, in *Life and Papers*, ed. Marshall, 1:222; Bates to Meriwether Lewis, 7 Nov. 1807, ibid., 1:230; Balances Due, 1 Oct. 1807, Recs. Choctaw TH, ROIT, 1:439; Debts Outstanding at St. Louis Trading House, 30 Sept. 1807, Misc. Accounts Bellefontaine Factory, ROIT; Price to James Byers, 28 June 1797, LB, Creek, ROIT, 70 (first quote); George to Samuel Sibley, 12 Feb. 1811, Sibley Papers, Box 1-2, Folder 9 (second quote); Inventories, 31 Mar. 1817 and 30 June 1817, Misc. Accounts Prairie du Chien Factory, ROIT, Box 3, Folder 2; Magnaghi, "Michigan's Indian Factory at Detroit," 174–75. On Native Americans as aristocrats see Liebersohn, *Aristocratic Encounters*, esp. 23–24, 37–43, 58–59, 104–5, 133–34.

18. John Mason to John Johnston, 19 Jan. 1808, LSSIT, ROIT, 1:A:36; Report on Deerskins Received at New Orleans, 1 Feb. 1810, Memorandum Book, ROIT, 67–8; McKenney to John Fowler, 30 June 1817, LSSIT, ROIT, 4:D:350; John Mason to James Moore, 29 July 1812, ibid., 3:C:24–26; Silverware Received from John Johnston, 7 Dec. 1808, Memorandum Book, ROIT, 31–33; Articles Wanted for the Factory at Sandusky, 17 Feb. 1807, Misc. Accounts Sandusky Factory, ROIT. On borderlands as "Native grounds" see DuVal, *Native Ground*, 9–12; Barr, *Peace Came*, 7–10; Hämäläinen, *Comanche Empire*, 3–12.

19. Horsman, *Expansion*, 41, 57–58, 60–62, 105–6, 108–10; Sheehan, *Seeds of Extinction*; Hume, "Of Commerce," *Essays*, Part II, Essay 1; Cheney, "False Dawn," 472; Speech of Rep. John Swanwick, 8 Jan. 1796, *AC*, 4/1, p. 230; Henri, *Benjamin Hawkins*, 120, 130; Jonathan Halstead to William Irvine, 25 June 1803, LB, Creek, ROIT, 248–49; Articles Wanted for the Indian Trade for 1810, Recs. Choctaw TH, ROIT, 1:17; Daybooks of Choctaw Trading House, 1808–1810 and Mar. 1812, ibid., Reel 4; Thomas McKenney to George Sibley, 21 Oct. 1816, LSSIT, ROIT, 4:D:153 (quote).

20. McKenney to Isaac Thomas, 14 Dec. and 23 Dec. 1816, LSSIT, ROIT, 4:D:203–8 and 4:D:211–13; Memorial of the Blue River Association of Indiana, 14 Sept. 1818, Records of the U.S. House of Representatives, HR15A-G6.1; Memorial of the Mississippi Baptist Association, 12 Jan. 1819, ibid.; Porter, *John Jacob Astor*, 2:708–14; Wesley, "Government Factory System," 504–5, 507–8.

21. Act Making Provision for the Civilization of the Indian Tribes, 3 Mar. 1819, *Statutes at Large*, 3:516–17; Report of Ramsey Crooks to the Senate, 23 Jan. 1822, *ASPIA*, 2:331.

22. John Mason to William Eustis, 13 May 1809, *TPUS*, 14:273–74; Edward Price to Henry Gaither, 10 Apr. and 30 May 1798, LB, Creek, ROIT, 129–33, 144; Jonathan Halstead to William Simmons, 8 Mar. 1804, ibid., 257; Wesley, "Government Factory System," 502–3; Mason to John Johnson, 20 May 1808, *TPUS*, 14:185–87; Price to R. Thomas, 19 July 1797, LB, Creek, ROIT, 74.

23. Jefferson to William Harrison, 27 Feb. 1803, in *Writings of Jefferson*, Lipscomb et al., 10:370; Treaty of Fort Wilkinson, 16 June 1802, in *Indian Affairs*, Kappler,

2:58–59; Nicholas Byers to Return Meigs, 4 Aug. and 16 Aug. 1805, Records of Cherokee Indian Agency, Reel 3; Resolutions of the Cherokee Delegates Relating to Their Funds, Annuity, etc., 5 Jan. 1806, ibid.

24. Berkhofer, *White Man's Indian*, 148–49.

25. Haeger, *John Astor*, 102–3, 110, 177, 179, 199, 207–13.

26. Murrin, "Great Inversion," 423–28.

Chapter 1

1. Benton, *Thirty Years' View*, 1: 20–21.

2. Entry of 19 Oct. 1770 in *Diaries of Washington*, ed. Jackson and Twohig, 2:292–93 (quote).

3. Anderson and Cayton, *Dominion of War*, 27–28; Hall, *Zamumo's Gifts*, 5, 52–53, 118.

4. Ward, *Breaking the Backcountry*, 48–58, 72; Nichols, *Red Gentlemen*, 1, 24–25.

5. Salisbury, "Indians' Old World," esp. 447–48; Miller and Hamell, "New Perspective," 315–26.

6. Wolf, *Europe and the People*, 158–61; Braudel, *Structures of Everyday Life*, 181–82, 443; Quinn, *North America*, 347–68; Turgeon, "French Fishers."

7. Parry, *Age of Reconnaissance*, 207–28; Quinn, *North America*, 465–89; Salisbury, *Manitou and Providence*, 76–100, 110–40; Richter, *Before the Revolution*, 125–27; Jarvis and van Driel, "Vingboons Chart," 386, 388.

8. Eccles, *Canadian Frontier*, 103–31; Ray, *Indians in the Fur Trade*, 11–14, 58; Taylor, *American Colonies*, 415–16; Crane, *Southern Frontier*, 108–12, 116–17; Curtin, *Cross-Cultural Trade*, 4; Innis, *Fur Trade*, 1–4; Carlos and Lewis, *Commerce by a Frozen Sea*, 5, 17–23, 40–42; Braund, *Deerskins and Duffels*, 87–88.

9. Trigger, "Early Native American Responses," 1204–9; Trigger, *Children of Aataentsic*, 424–25; Calloway, *New Worlds for All*, 45–46, 49–50.

10. Innis, *Fur Trade in Canada*, 6–7; Jaenen, "Role of Presents," 239, 249; Witger, "Rituals of Possession," esp. 646–47, 655–60, 664–65n18, and 667n35; Carlos and Lewis, *Commerce by a Frozen Sea*, 73; Taylor, *American Colonies*, 93, 379; Brown, *Strangers in Blood*, 51–80; Braund, *Deerskins and Duffels*, 83–85; Van Doren, ed., *Travels of Bartram*, 170, 200–201, 216–18, 283–84, 356–57.

11. Calloway, *New Worlds for All*, 42–48; Jennings, *Invasion of America*, 86–94; Reid, *Better Kind of Hatchet*, 27–41; Braund, *Deerskins and Duffels*, 121–38.

12. "A Key into the Language of America," in *Complete Writings of Roger Williams*, 1:175 (first quote); Calloway, ed., *Dawnland Encounters*, 194, 197; Cronon, *Changes in the Land*, 97–156; White, *Middle Ground*, 488–93; Silver, *New Face*, 90–101, 173–79.

13. White, "'Give Us a Little Milk'"; Mancall, *Deadly Medicine*, 62–129, 163; John Minot to Lt. Gov. Dummer, 20 Apr. 1725, in *Documentary History of Maine*, ed. Baxter, 10:252–53; Van Doren, ed., *Travels of Bartram*, 214–15; Speech of Scarouyady, 3 Oct. 1753, *BFP*, 5:97 (quote).

14. Jones, *Native North American Armor*, 58–63; Richter, "War and Culture," 538.

15. Crosby, "Virgin Soil Epidemics," 290–97; Fenn, *Pox Americana*, 144–258, 270–75. Cf. Jones, "Virgin Soils Revisited," 703–42.

16. Richter, "War and Culture," 539–47; Ray, *Indians in the Fur Trade*, 13–23; Anderson, *Kinsmen*, 1–28.

17. Gallay, *Indian Slave Trade*, 127–54, 259–344; Ethridge, "Introduction," in *Mapping the Mississippian Shatter Zone*, Ethridge and Shuck-Hall, 1–62, esp. 11–14; Christina Snyder, *Slavery in Indian Country*, 48–63.

18. Taylor, *American Colonies*, 96–97, 417; Gallay, *Indian Slave Trade*, 297, 350–54; Perdue, *Cherokee Women*, 74–75; Ray, *Indians in the Fur Trade*, 125–36; Calloway, *Dawnland Encounters*, 212; Innis, *Fur Trade*, 59–61.

19. Brackenridge, *Journal*, 59 (quotes); Richter, *Ordeal*, 22.

20. Anderson, *Kinsmen*, 29–57; Sahlins, *Stone Age Economics*, 185–230; Braund, *Deerskins and Duffels*, 26–28; Richter, *Trade, Land, Power*, 60–61, 63.

21. Entry of 28 Oct. 1770, *Diaries of Washington*, 2:304 (quote); Taylor, *American Colonies*, 92–93.

22. Trelease, *Indian Affairs*, 61; Eccles, *Canadian Frontier*, 42–43.

23. Trelease, *Indian Affairs*, 309; Shannon, *Indians and Colonists*, 28–30; Gallay, *Indian Slave Trade*, 216–17 (quote 216); Crane, *Southern Frontier*, 148–53, 202–3.

24. Havighurst, *Alexander Spotswood*, 45–52, 61–65, 75–76; Crane, *Southern Frontier*, 194–99; Merrell, *Indians' New World*, 80–82; Merrell, " 'Very Seat,' " 34, 40–41; Jordan, ed., "Journal of James Kenny," 7, 17, 24–25, 30–34, 37–38, 40, 46, 154, 156, and 172.

25. MacFarlane, "Massachusetts Bay Truck-Houses"; Calloway, *Dawnland Encounters*, 191, 199; Proceedings in Council, 9 June 1744, in *Documentary History of Maine*, ed. Baxter, 12:5; James Bowdoin to Benjamin Franklin, 12 Nov. 1753, *BFP*, 5:111–12.

26. Bushnell, "Gates, Centers, and Peripheries," 20; Choquette, "Center and Periphery," 197–98; Eccles, *Canadian Frontier*, 113, 145–48; Eccles, *France in America*, 172.

27. "Journal of Captain Phineas Stevens' Journey to Canada," in *North Country Captives*, ed. Calloway, 34–35 (quote 35); Eccles, "Fur Trade and Imperialism," esp. 342, 355.

28. Essington, "French Claims to the Ohio Valley," 373–75; Jennings, *Empire of Fortune*, 26–37, 49–53; White, *Middle Ground*, 186–222; Journal of Conrad Weiser, 8 Sept. 1748, in *Early Western Journals*, ed. Thwaites, 29–30; Hurt, *Ohio Frontier*, 33–39; Speech of Miamis, 3 Oct. 1753, *BFP*, 5:95.

29. Jennings, *Empire of Fortune*, 191–93; Anderson, *Crucible of War*, 236–37, 257–58.

30. White, *Middle Ground*, 231–248; Ward, *Breaking the Backcountry*, 183 (quote).

31. Franklin to James Parker, 20 Mar. 1751, *BFP*, 4:117, 120–21; Shannon, *Indians and Colonists*, 73–75, 110, 243; Dickerson, *American Colonial Government*, 339–42; Flexner, *Mohawk Baronet*, 19–25, 63–92, 160–61; Jacobs, ed., *Appalachian Indian Frontier*, 77–95.

32. Oliphant, *Peace and War*; Anderson, *Crucible of War*, 457–71; White, *Middle Ground*, 256–68.

33. White, *Middle Ground*, 269–314; Dowd, *War under Heaven*, 114–73; Dowd, *Spirited Resistance*, xviii–xxi, 16–33; Jordan, ed., "Journal of James Kenny," 171–72, 175, 188; Richter, *Facing East*, 191–99.

34. Plan for the Future Management of Indian Affairs, 10 July 1764, *Pennsylvania Archives*, Ser. 1, 4:182–88; Sosin, *Whitehall*, 52–78; Sosin, *Revolutionary Frontier*, 30–31; Richter, *Trade, Land, Power*, 177–201; Snapp, *John Stuart*, 17–18; Pressly, "Scottish Merchants," 152–53.

35. Sosin, *Revolutionary Frontier*, 12; Larry Nelson, *Man of Distinction*, 58–59; Ray, *Indians in the Fur Trade*, 125–26; White, *Roots of Dependency*, 71, 74–75; Snapp, *John Stuart*, 44; Thomas Gage to Sir William Johnson, 31 Mar. 1773, in *Papers*, Johnson, 8:749; Johnson to Gage, 13 Apr. 1773, ibid., 8:764; Pressly, "Scottish Merchants," 153.

36. Sosin, *Revolutionary Frontier*, 13–15; Dowd, *War under Heaven*, 233–46.

37. Richter, *Facing East*, 178–79; Bailyn, *Voyagers*, 26–28.

38. Jones, *License for Empire*, 108–10, 116–19; Sosin, *Whitehall*, 145–47, 161–62, 198–210; Corkran, *Creek Frontier*, 281; Pressly, "Scottish Merchants," 153–54, 162; Snapp, *John Stuart*, 41–42; Act for Establishing Trade with the Indians, April 1757, in *Statutes at Large*, ed. Hening, 7:116–18.

39. Dowd, *War under Heaven*, 243–45; Sosin, *Whitehall*, 240–49.

40. Dunmore to Lord Dartmouth, 24 Dec. 1774, in *Documentary History of Dunmore's War*, ed. Thwaites and Kellogg, 368–95, quotes 371, 376, 378; McConnell, *Country Between*, 258–59, 270–79; Hammon and Taylor, *Virginia's Western War*, xviii–xxxiv.

41. Holton, *Forced Founders*, 148; Frazier, *Mohicans of Stockbridge*, 198–99.

42. Calloway, *American Revolution*, 26–64. "Civil Indian" is from Callahan, *Henry Knox*, 41.

43. Horsman, *Expansion*, 23–24, 30–42; Dowd, *Spirited Resistance*, 90–115.

44. Downes, *Council Fires*, 183–84; Resolution of the Continental Congress, 1 July 1775, *JCC*, 2:123; Diary of Richard Smith, 27 Jan. 1776, *LDC*, 3:162; Instructions for Silas Deane, 2 Mar. 1776, ibid., 3:321–22.

45. Resolution of 27 Jan. 1776, *JCC*, 4:96–98; Draft Articles of Confederation, 17 June 1776, *LDC*, 4:251 (first two quotes); Adams' Notes of Debates, 26 July 1776, ibid., 4:546–47; Committee Report of 19 Aug. 1776, *JCC*, 5:669–70.

46. Committee Report of 7 Oct. 1776, *JCC*, 5:852; Downes, *Council Fires*, 226–27; Carp, *To Starve the Army*; Buel, *In Irons*, 77–133; Marinus Willett to George Washington, 21 July 1782, Papers of George Washington, Reel 86 (Ser. 4, Vol. 202), p. 45 (quote).

47. Seaver, *Narrative of the Life*, 50–51; O'Donnell, *Southern Indians*, 90, 101 (quote); Nichols, *Indians in the U.S. and Canada*, 134.

48. Higginbotham, *War of American Independence*, 321–31; Silver, *Our Savage Neighbors*, 227–60; Downes, *Council Fires*, 265–76; Waring, *Fighting Elder*, 105–34.

49. Richter, *Facing East*, 224–25; Horsman, *Expansion*, 3–15.

50. Nichols, *Red Gentlemen*, 19–54; Jones, *License for Empire*, 155–56.

51. Hinderaker, *Elusive Empires*, 232–34; Shannon, "Native American Way of War," 146; Merrell, "Declarations of Independence," 201–3.

52. Allen, *British Indian Department*, 29–35; Horsman, *Matthew Elliott*, 53–56; Nelson, *Man of Distinction*, 150–57; Weber, *Spanish Frontier*, 282–84.

53. Statement of Indebtedness of John Askin, 20 Dec. 1786, in *Askin Papers*, ed. Quaife, 1:274–75; Cangany, *Frontier Seaport*, 30; Coker and Watson, *Indian*

Traders, 49–92; Journal of Richard Butler, 31 Oct. 1785, in *Olden Time*, ed. Craig, 2:459; Report of William North, 23 Aug. 1786, ibid., 164:2:25–26; Nichols, *Red Gentlemen*, 74; Arthur St. Clair to Henry Knox, 1 May 1790, *ASPIA*, 1:87.

54. Hopewell Treaty Journal, 29 Nov. 1785, *ASPIA*, 1:43; John Pittslaw to William Davenport, 5 Sept. 1786, Creek Indian Letters, 1:136; William Blount to Richard Caswell, 19 July 1787, *LDC*, 24:364; O'Brien, "Conqueror Meets the Unconquered," 60–61, 68–69; Resolution of 16 July 1787, *JCC*, 32:354–55.

55. Matson and Onuf, *Union of Interests*, 82–100 (first quote 95); McDonald, *Novus Ordo Seclorum*, 143–83; Edling, *Revolution in Favor*, 73–100, 115–28, 149–74, 219–29.

56. Ward, *Department of War*, 89–91; Reports of the Secretary at War to Congress, 10 July 1787, 18 July 1787, 20 July 1787, and 18 July 1788, in *JCC*, 32:327–32 (quote 328), 32:365–69; 33:388–91, and 34:342–44, respectively; Knox to Josiah Harmar, 19 Dec. 1789, Harmar Papers, 11:113–14.

57. Treaty of Fort Harmar (9 Jan. 1789), in *Indian Affairs*, Kappler, 2:18–23; Nichols, *Red Gentlemen*, 118–24; Treaty of Holston (2 July 1791), in *Indian Affairs*, Kappler, 2:29–32.

58. Nichols, *Red Gentlemen*, 104–5, 114–18, 124 (quote), 139–40, 154–58; Nelson, *Man of Distinction*, 157–58; Denny, ed., *Military Journal*, 146–49, 164–68; Sugden, *Tecumseh*, 69–72.

59. Act Making . . . Provision for the Protection of the Frontiers, 5 Mar. 1792, in *Statutes*, Peters, 1:241–43; Horsman, *Expansion*, 90–98; Henry Knox to the Commissioners, 26 July 1793, *ASPIA*, 1:341–42 (quote 342); Knox to James Seagrove, 31 Oct. 1792, ibid., 1:260; Downes, "Creek-American Relations," 368–70; Additional Article to the Treaty of Holston, 17 Feb. 1792, in *Indian Affairs*, Kappler, 2:32–33; Blount to James Robertson, 5 Jan. 1792, *TPUS*, 4:110.

60. Downes, "Creek-American Relations," 371–73; Blount to Knox, 14 Jan. 1793, *ASPIA*, 1:432; Symonds, "Failure of America's Indian Policy," 37–44; Reply of the Sixteen Nations to the Commissioners, 16 Aug. 1793, *ASPIA*, 1:356–57; Anthony Wayne to Henry Knox, 14 Aug. and 28 Aug. 1794, ibid., 1:490; Treaty of Greenville (3 Aug. 1795), in *Indian Affairs*, Kappler, 2:39–45.

61. Washington to James Duane, 7 Sept. 1783, *WGW*, 27:133–34; Onuf, "Liberty, Development, and Union"; Indian Trade and Intercourse Act, 19 May 1796, Peters, *Statutes at Large*, 1:469–74; Nichols, *Red Gentlemen*, 182–85; William Harrison to Henry Dearborn, 15 July 1801, in *Governors Messages*, ed. Esarey, 1:25–27; Washington to Timothy Pickering, 1 July 1796, *WGW*, 35:112.

62. Larson, "'Wisdom Enough,'" 228–33; Washington to the President of Congress, 17 June 1783, *WGW*, 27:17; Washington to James Duane, 7 Sept. 1783, ibid., 27:134–39; Nichols, *Red Gentlemen*, 80–82; Report of the Secretary at War to Congress, 11 May 1786, *JCC*, 30:257–58.

63. Josiah Harmar to John Doughty, 15 July 1790, Harmar Papers, H:6–7; Nichols, *Red Gentlemen*, 113; Treaty of New York, 7 Aug. 1790, in *Indian Affairs*, Kappler, 2:26–28; Wright, "Creek-American Treaty," 395–97.

64. Memorandum, Nov. 1793, *WGW*, 33:60 (first quote); Fifth Annual Message to Congress, 3 Dec. 1793, ibid., 33:168 (second & third quotes); Sixth Annual Message, 19 Nov. 1794, ibid., 34:36; Sheehan, *Seeds of Extinction*, 224–26.

65. *JCC*, 31:490–93; Peters, *Statutes*, 1:137–38 and 329–32; Report of Committee on Indian Affairs, 1 Dec. 1794, *ASPIA*, 1:524; *AC*, Third Congress, 2nd Session, 1262–64 (quote 1263) and Fourth Congress, 1st Session, 232–33, 240, 283–84.

66. Elkins and McKitrick, *Age of Federalism*, 417–22, 441–49; Peters, *Statutes*, 9:117–18.

67. Report of John Askin, Jr. on Mission to Greenville, 19 Aug. 1795, in *Askin Papers*, Quaife, 1:560–65; Partnership for Purchase of the Michigan Peninsula, 27 Sept. 1795, ibid., 1:568–71; *AC*, 4/1, 166–95, 200–229, 230–31, 243–45; J. V. Campbell, "Account of a Plot," *HCPSM*, 8:406–10; Baumann, "John Swanwick," 138–39, 158–61, 168–69.

68. *AC*, 4/1, pp. 45, 230 (quote), 285; Act for Establishing Trading Houses with the Indian Tribes, 18 April 1796, in *Statutes*, Peters, 1:452–53.

69. Calloway, *American Revolution*, 292–301; Countryman, "Indians, the Colonial Order," esp. 354–62.

Chapter 2

1. *AC*, 3/2, 1276, 1282; *AC*, 4/1, 152; Peters, *Statutes*, 1:443; Report of the Secretary of War, 12 Dec. 1795, *ASPIA*, 1:583.

2. Report of the Secretary, 12 Dec. 1795, *ASPIA*, 1:583; Braund, *Deerskins and Duffels*, 170–88; Calloway, *American Revolution*, 267–68.

3. Prucha, *Sword*, 48; Blount to Knox, 3 Nov. and 10 Nov. 1794, *TPUS*, 4:362 (quote), 366–69; Pickering to Blount, 23 Mar. 1795, ibid., 4, 392; Polhemus, *Archaeological Investigation*, 1–4, 6–7, 9, 15, and 37.

4. Wright and Macleod, "William Eaton," 388, 395–96, 397–400 (quotes 398). On the eighteenth-century Seminoles, see Calloway, *American Revolution*, 246–49, 269–70.

5. Wright and Macleod, "William Eaton," 388–89, 391–92; Edward Price to Tench Francis, 26 Dec. 1795 and 11 Jan. 1796, LB, Creek, ROIT, 4–6; Price to Col. Henry Gaither, 24 Dec. 1796, ibid., 33–34; Price to James McHenry, 24 Jan. and 3 Apr. 1797, ibid., 41 and 49; Price to John Harris, 6 Mar. 1797, ibid., 47; Price to Samuel Allenson, 11 June 1797, ibid., 64.

6. Price to McHenry, 24 Jan. and 3 Apr. 1797, LB, Creek, ROIT, 41, 49 (first quote); Price to James Byers, 28 June 1797, ibid., 70 (third quote); Eaton to Samuel Lyman, 28 Feb. 1796, in "William Eaton," Wright and Macleod, 392 (second quote); Plaisance, "U.S. Government Factory System," 84; Braund, "Guardians of Tradition"; Rountree, "Powhatans and Other Woodland Indians," 27–29.

7. Price to Tench Francis, 30 Dec. 1795 and 11 Jan. 1796, LB, Creek, ROIT, 5–6; Price to McHenry, 2 Jan. and 15 June 1797, ibid., 35 and 65–66; Price to John Harris, 20 Jan. and 9 June 1797, ibid., 39–40 (quote), 62; Price to Timothy Barnard, 18 May 1797, ibid., 55.

8. Coleraine Treaty Journal, 23 June, 27 June, and 4 July 1796, *ASPIA*, 1:601, 608, and 611–12; Price to James Byers, 28 June 1797, LB, Creek, ROIT, 70; Eighth Annual Message to Congress, 7 Dec. 1796, *WGW*, 35:310–11; Price to Timothy

Barnard, 12 Apr. 1797, LB, Creek, ROIT, 53; Price to McHenry, 15 June 1797, ibid., 65; Price to E. Bullard, 19 June and 9 July 1797, ibid., 68 and 71.

9. Price to John Harris, 11 July 1797, LB, Creek, ROIT, 72; Coleraine Treaty Journal, 21 and 24 June 1796, *ASPIA*, 1:599–600, 604; Journal of Benjamin Hawkins, 26 Jan. 1797, in , *Letters, Journals, and Writings*, ed. Grant, 39; Davidson, *History of Wilkinson County*, Chapter 16.

10. Price to Gaither, 10 Apr. and 30 May 1798, LB, Creek, ROIT, 129–33, 144; Price to McHenry, 25 Aug. 1797 and 9 May 1798, ibid., 8–9; Samuel Lewis to Price, 26 Sept. 1797, ibid., 8; Mattison, "Creek Trading House," 175–76; Jonathan Halstead to William Irvine, 9 Oct. 1802, LB, Creek, ROIT, 229–30; Halstead to William Simmons, 8 Mar. 1804, ibid., 257; Henry Dearborn to Irvine, 11 Apr. 1803, OSW, LSIA, 1:A:339.

11. Nichols, "Land, Republicanism, and Indians," 214–18; Price to Benjamin Hawkins, 22 Aug. 1798, LB, Creek, ROIT, 157; Price to the Secretary of War, 1 Oct. 1798, ibid., 162–63 (quotes); Mattison, "Creek Trading House," 176. Price died sometime before 21 February 1799—see the Georgia factory invoice of that date, Invoices Inward, ROIT, 1:55.

12. Peltry Shipped from the Georgia Factory, Invoices Inward, ROIT, 1: 8, 16–20, 22–24, 27–30, 32–35, 54–55, 57, 61–62, and unpaginated Fort Wilkinson invoices of 20 Feb. and 4 April, 1801; Price to William Wallace, 10 Aug. 1797, LB, Creek, ROIT, 76; Price to Robert Grierson, 30 Aug. 1797, ibid., 81; Henri, *Benjamin Hawkins*, 120; Georgia Factory Account Book, 11 Nov. 1801, *ASPIA*, 1:654; Fort Wilkinson Conference Journal, 11 June 1802, ibid., 1:676; Braund, *Deerskins and Duffels*, 72, 177.

13. Price to John Harris, 20 Sept. and 1 Nov. 1797, LB, Creek, ROIT, 89 (first quote) and 95; Price to William Wallace, 6 Oct. 1797, ibid., 91; Benjamin Hawkins to Price, 26 Nov. 1797, cited in "Benjamin Hawkins," Harmon, 149; Report of William Irvine, Agent for the Indian Factories, 11 Nov. 1801, *ASPIA*, 1:653 (second quote); Fort Wilkinson Factory Daybooks, 1–12 May 1802, Records of the Creek Factory, 1795–1821, ROIT; Price to R. Thomas, 19 July 1797, LB, Creek, ROIT, 74; Price to Tupicco Mico, 24 Sept. 1797, ibid., 89; Peake, *History of the Indian Factory System*, 110–11. Stroud was cloth made from woolen rags, usually dyed blue or scarlet and sold in 18-inch-wide bolts. (Braund, *Deerskins and Duffels*, 122–23.)

14. Timothy Pickering to Price, 26 Nov. 1795, in "William Eaton," ed. Wright and Macleod, 398–400 (quote 398); Benjamin Hawkins to James McHenry, 6 Jan. and 1 Mar. 1797, in *Letters, Journals, and Writings*, ed. Grant, 1:63, 87; Hawkins to Timothy Barnard, 7 Mar. 1797, ibid., 1:91–92; Harmon, "Benjamin Hawkins," 148–51; Ethridge, *Creek Country*, 130–31.

15. James Madison, Albert Gallatin, and Levi Lincoln to Thomas Jefferson, 26 Apr. 1802, in *Republic of Letters*, Smith, 2:1221–24; James Durouzeaux to Benjamin Hawkins, 26 Sept. 1801, Letters Received by the Secretary of War, 1:42; Fort Wilkinson Conference Journal, 9 and 13 June 1802, *ASPIA*, 1:674–75, 679; Report of the Fort Wilkinson Treaty Commissioners, 15 July 1802, ibid., 1:669; Treaty of Fort Wilkinson, 16 June 1802, in *Indian Affairs,* Kappler, 2:58–59 (quote 59); Henry Dearborn to Jefferson, 11 Jan. 1805, *TPUS*, 7:256.

16. Invoices Inward, ROIT, 1: 8, 11–15, 17–18, 20, 22–25, 31, 36–41, 49–53, 58–60, 64–66, and unpaginated Cherokee factory invoices of 27 Jan.,12 Aug., 14 Oct., and 31 Dec. 1801 Misc. Records of Cherokee Trading House, ROIT; Polhemus, *Archaeological Investigation*, 8–9; Perdue, *Cherokee Women*, 78.

17. Louis-Philippe, *Diary*, 79–82; Perdue, *Cherokee Women*, 115–34; McLoughlin, *Cherokee Renascence*, 68; Henri, *Benjamin Hawkins*, 120–22, 130.

18. Invoice of 31 July 1797, Misc. Records of Cherokee Trading House, ROIT; Polhemus, *Archaeological Investigation*, 9, 206–9, 212–13, 246–48.

19. Tellico Factory Daybooks, 16–18 May 1798, Misc. Records of Cherokee Trading House, ROIT; John Sevier to William Blount, 29 Jan. 1797, quoted in *Hawkins*, Henri, 114; Prucha, *American Indian Policy*, 154–55; Louis-Philippe, *Diary*, 99.

20. Louis-Philippe, *Diary*, 79–82; Factory Invoice, 30 Jan. 1797, Misc. Records of Cherokee Trading House, ROIT; War Dept. in Account with Tellico Factory, ibid.

21. Tellico Conference Minutes, 25–28 Apr. 1797, in *Letters, Journals, and Writings*, ed. Grant, 1:80–84; Waring, *Fighting Elder*, 183–88; Treaty of Tellico, 2 Oct. 1798, in *Indian Affairs*, Kappler, 2:51–54; McLoughlin, *Cherokee Renascence*, 28, 46.

22. Plaisance, "U.S. Government Factory System," 91; House Resolutions of 10 Feb., 1 May, and 9 May 1800, *AC*, 6/1, 518, 689, 707; Committee on Reviving the Trading House Act, 22 April 1800, *ASPIA*, 1:643; Senate Resolution of 14 May 1800, *AC*, 6/1, 183; Bradley, "William C. C. Claiborne," 271–73.

23. House Resolution of 2 Dec. 1800, *AC*, 6/2, 732–33; Committee Report of 5 Feb. 1801, *ASPIA*, 1:646 (quotes); Bradley, "William C. C. Claiborne," 274–75. On the Jefferson–Burr tie, see Weisberger, *America Afire*, 258–77.

24. Elkins and McKittrick, *Age of Federalism*, 691–754; Weisberger, *America Afire*, 227–57, 287–88.

25. Report of William Irvine, 1 Nov. 1801, *ASPIA*, 1:653–54; Report of the Secretary of War, 8 Dec. 1801, ibid., 1:654–55.

26. Peters, *Statutes*, 2:173, 207, 403–4; Henry Dearborn to William C. C. Claiborne, 7 June 1802, in *Official Letter Books*, ed. Rowland, 1:150; Dearborn to William Harrison, 29 July 1802, *TPUS*, 7:63; Dearborn to Jefferson, 17 Jan. 1803, *ASPIA*, 1:684; Report of the Superintendent of Indian Trade, 12 Apr. 1810, ibid., 1:768.

27. First Annual Message to Congress, 8 Dec. 1801, *AC*, 7/1, 13; Wallace, *Jefferson and the Indians*, 207–12.

28. Thomas Jefferson to Henry Dearborn, 12 Aug. 1802, *TPUS*, 7:69–70 (first and third quotes); Confidential Message of the President, 18 Jan. 1803, *Journal of Executive Proceedings*, 1:438 (second quote); Jefferson to William Harrison, 27 Feb. 1803, in *Writings of Thomas Jefferson*, Lipscomb et al., 10:37.

29. Dunbar and May, *Michigan*, 45–51, 59–62, 88–89, 98; Speech of Peleaswa, 8 Nov. 1785, Papers of the Continental Congress, 69: 275; Innis, *Fur Trade*, 190.

30. Dunbar and May, *Michigan*, 103–4; Farmer, *History of Detroit*, 336; Weld, *Travels*, 169–71, 182–85; Cangany, *Frontier Seaport*, 143; Tanner, *Atlas*, 98–99, 101–2.

31. Pelt stock on hand, 5 Sept. 1803, Misc. Records Detroit Factory, ROIT; Magnaghi, "Michigan's Indian Factory at Detroit," 172, 176; Daybooks for Feb. and

Mar. 1804, Misc. Records of Cherokee Trading House, ROIT; Daybooks for June 1804, Misc. Records Detroit Factory, ROIT; Dowd, *Spirited Resistance*, 120; White, *Middle Ground*, 488–89; Innis, *Fur Trade*, 189–90; Editor's Note on Jacques Porlier, *CSHSW*, 18:462n.

32. Isaac Waterman to William Irvine, 10 Aug. 1802, Irvine–Newbold Family Papers, Box 9, Folder 9; Detroit Factory Daybooks for 15–31 Dec. 1802, Jan., Feb., Apr. 1803, 15–22 Sept. 1803, and June 1804, Misc. Records Detroit Factory, ROIT; Proceedings of 25 Mar. 1822, *AC*, 17th Congress, 1st Session, 38:320; Cangany, *Frontier Seaport*, 64–67. For Canadians' markups, see White, "Balancing the Books," 182–83.

33. Dearborn to Ebenezer Belknap, 12 Apr. 1805, *TPUS*, 7:281–82; Dearborn to Robert Munro, 13 Apr. 1805, ibid., 7:282; Prucha, *Sword*, 40; *Scioto Gazette*, 15 July 1805.

34. Ohio Enabling Act, 30 April 1802, in *Statutes*, Peters, 2:173–75; Act to Divide the Indiana Territory, 11 Jan. 1805, ibid., 309–10; Magnaghi, "Michigan's Indian Factory at Detroit," 178.

35. Cayton, *Frontier Indiana*, 5, 25–28, 143–45, 163–64, 203–4; James McHenry to Arthur St. Clair, 29 Mar. 1799, St. Clair Papers, Reel 4:658; St. Clair to the Secretary of War, 7 Apr. 1800, ibid., 5:27.

36. Thornbrough, ed., *Letter Book*, 12–13 (quote); Henry Dearborn to William Harrison, 23 Feb. 1802, *TPUS*, 7:49–50; Contingent Expenses of the Fort Wayne Factory, 3 May 1803–3 May 1804, Daybooks of the Fort Wayne Factory.

37. Griswold, *Fort Wayne*, 20–21; Daybooks for May–Dec. 1803, May–Sept. 1804, and Jan.—Oct. 1805, Daybooks of Fort Wayne Factory, ROIT; Daybook for 31 Jan. 1804 and Household Expenses for Feb. 1805, ibid.; Cayton, *Frontier Indiana*, 187–89; Owens, "Jeffersonian Benevolence," 409–12.

38. Owens, "Jeffersonian Benevolence," 418–24; Daybooks for 1–7 June 1803, 24 Aug 1804, 21–25 June 1805, 5 Oct. 1813, and 13 Oct. 1805, Daybooks of Fort Wayne Factory, ROIT; Harrison to Henry Dearborn, 16 Sept. 1805, in *Governor's Messages*, Esarey, 1:165; Dearborn to William Davy, 25 Feb. 1806, OSW, LSIA, 2:B:175; Johnston to Davy, 3 July 1806, *TPUS*, 7:363. The treaties are in *Indian Affairs*, Kappler, 2:64–68, 70–78, 80–82, 89.

39. John Gibson and Francis Vigo to Harrison, 6 July 1805, in *Governor's Messages*, Esarey, 1:145; Harrison to Dearborn, 10 July and 16 Sept. 1805, ibid., 1:148–49, 165; Johnston to Harrison, 28 Feb. 1806, *TPUS*, 7:343–44; Griswold, *Fort Wayne*, 21.

40. Treaty between Great Britain and the United States, 19 Nov. 1794, Peters, *Statutes*, 8:117–18; Harrison to Dearborn, 15 July 1801, in *Governors Messages*, ed. Esarey, 1, 27; Johnston to N. J. Vischer, 18 Sept. 1805, cited in *John Johnston*, Hill, 23.

41. Dearborn to Ebenezer Belknap, 12 Apr. 1805, *TPUS*, 7:281–82; Dearborn to William Davy, 22 Nov. 1805, OSW, LSIA, 2:B:136 (second quote); Dearborn to Davy, 30 Dec. 1805, *CSHSW*, 19:311 (first quote).

42. Innis, *Fur Trade*, 241; Lavender, "Some American Aspects," 32; Johnston to William Davy, 18 July 1806, *TPUS*, 7:370–71 (quote).

43. Dowd, *Spirited Resistance*, 120; Furs and Peltries Forwarded, 10 Mar., 9 Apr., and 25 May 1808, Misc. Accounts Fort Wayne Factory, ROIT; Clayton, "Growth and Economic Significance," 67; Cayton, *Frontier Indiana*, 203 (quote).

44. See chapter 1.

45. Treaty between the United States and the King of Spain, 27 Oct. 1795, in *Statutes*, Peters, 8:138–153; Prucha, *Sword*, 55–56; Mississippi Government Act, 7 Apr. 1798, in *Statutes*, Peters, 1:549–550; McLoughlin, *Cherokee Renascence*, 78.

46. Cuming, *Sketches*, 292–95; Coker and Watson, *Indian Traders*, 198–99, 201, 230.

47. Dearborn to Thomas Peterkin, 30 July 1802, OSW, LSIA, 1:256; Dearborn to W. C. C. Claiborne, 28 July 1802, in *Official Letter Books*, ed. Rowland, 1:181–82; Plaisance, "Chickasaw Bluffs Factory," 43; *Memorial of Sundry Manufacturers*, 15; George Colbert to Dearborn, 24 Feb. 1806, OSW, LSIA, 2:174; Factory Daybooks for 21 Jan., 20 Mar., and 24 Mar. 1807, Daybooks of Chickasaw Bluffs Factory, ROIT; John Treat to Henry Dearborn, 15 Nov. 1805, *TPUS*, 13:277, 280.

48. Statement of the Amount of Invoices of Goods Forwarded to the Several Factories, 11 Jan. 1806, *Memorial of Sundry Manufacturers*, 13. Prices compiled from factory daybooks for Apr.–June 1806; top textile sales from the Jan. 1807 daybooks. Skin prices are from the Daybook entries of 21 Jan., 20 and 24 Mar. 1807. An experienced eighteenth-century hunter could kill 50–100 adult deer in a good season; each pelt weighed about 2 pounds (McLoughlin, *Cherokee Renascence*, 6; White, *Roots of Dependency*, 93; Braund, *Deerskins and Duffels*, 69–72.)

49. General Abstract of Debts Due Panton Leslie & Co. by the Creek, Cherokee, Chickasaw and Choctaw Nations, 20 Aug. 1803, LRSW, 1:222; Debts Due the Factory, 30 June 1807, Daybooks of Chickasaw Bluffs Factory, ROIT.

50. Coker and Watson, *Indian Traders*, 233–36, 243–46, 250, 257–58, 265; Silas Dinsmoor to Henry Dearborn, 19 Aug. 1803, LRSW, 1:219–21; Treaty of 23 July 1805, in *Indian Affairs*, Kappler, 2:79–80 (second quote).

51. Calloway, *American Revolution*, 221, 223, 227–34; Treaty of Chickasaw Bluffs, 24 Oct. 1801, in *Indian Affairs*, Kappler, 2:55–56; George Gaines to Henry Dearborn, 29 Jan. 1808, *TPUS*, 5:601; Coker and Watson, *Indian Traders*, 257–58.

52. Debts Due the Factory, 30 June 1807, Daybooks of Chickasaw Bluffs Factory, ROIT; Sahlins, *Stone Age Economics*, 205–8; Hudson, *Southeastern Indians*, 90, 223, 295–97.

53. Plaisance, "U.S. Government Factory System," 49–52; Minutes of the Fort Adams Treaty Conference, 15 Dec. 1801, *ASPIA*, 1:662; Dearborn to Wilkinson, 7 and 14 Sept. 1802, ibid., 1:682; White, *Roots of Dependency*, 103–12; Plaisance, "Choctaw Trading House," 395–96.

54. Plaisance, "Choctaw Trading House," 396–97; Invoices of Deerskins Forwarded from Choctaw Trading House, 19 Jan. and 2 Feb. 1807, Recs. Choctaw TH, ROIT, 1:422, 424; Statement of the Amount of Invoices of Goods Forwarded to the Indian Factories, 11 Jan. 1806, *Memorial of Sundry Manufacturers . . . in Philadelphia*, 13; List of Goods Ordered, 8 Apr. 1805, Indent Book, Recs. Choctaw TH, ROIT, 1:5–6; Articles Wanted for 1808 (Compiled 7 Sept. 1807), Indent Book, ibid., 1:13; Carson, *Searching*, 67.

55. White, *Roots of Dependency*, 103–12; Daybooks for 16–18 Oct. 1807, Recs. Choctaw TH, ROIT, 1:443, 446–47.

56. Balances Due Factory, 1 Oct. 1807, Recs. Choctaw TH, ROIT, 1:439; John Treat to Henry Dearborn, 15 Nov. 1805, *TPUS*, 13:277; White, *Roots of Dependency*, 91–92. On credit-worthiness see Daybook Entry for 16 Oct. 1807, Recs. Choctaw TH, ROIT, 1:443.

57. Silas Dinsmoor to Henry Dearborn, 19 Aug. 1803, LRSW, 1:219–21; Treaties of 17 Dec. 1801, 17 Oct. 1802, 31 Aug. 1803, and 16 Nov. 1805, in *Indian Affairs*, Kappler, 2:56–58, 63, 69–70, and 87–88; Indent Book, 22 Jan. 1806, Recs. Choctaw TH, ROIT, 1:8.

58. Kappler, *Indian Affairs*, 2:87; General Abstract of Debts Due the House of Panton Leslie & Co., 20 Aug. 1803, LRSW, 1:222; Coker and Watson, *Indian Traders*, 255–56, 264–65.

59. William Claiborne to Henry Dearborn, 30 June 1802, in *Official Letter Books*, ed. Rowland, 1:134–35; Dearborn to James Wilkinson, 14 Sept. 1802, *TPUS*, 5:176–77; Wilkinson to Juan Morales, 6 July 1803, LRSW, 1:213–15; Claiborne to Gov. Folch, 7 Mar. 1804, *American State Papers*, "Foreign Affairs," 2:678.

60. Wilkinson to Dearborn, 31 Aug. 1803, *TPUS*, 5:237; Folch to Claiborne, 15 Mar. 1804, *American State Papers*, "Foreign Affairs," 2:678; Protest of Joseph Chambers, 13 Apr. 1804, ibid., 2:679; Account of Charges Paid by Joseph Saul and Joseph Chambers on Merchandise Forwarded from Philadelphia, 1805, Recs. Choctaw TH, ROIT, 1:171; President's Annual Message to Congress, 3 Dec. 1805, AC, 9/1, 13–14; Malone, *Jefferson the President*, 69–74, 91–94.

Chapter 3

1. Message of the President to the Senate, 18 Jan. 1803, *Journal of Executive Proceedings*, 1:439; Wallace, *Jefferson and the Indians*, 241–43.

2. Kukla, *Wilderness*, 225–83; Kastor, *Nation's Crucible*, 41–45.

3. Goetzmann, *Exploration and Empire*, 3–8, 41–53; Act Organizing Orleans Territory and Louisiana District, 26 Mar. 1804, *TPUS*, 9:202–13; Act Organizing Louisiana Territory, 3 Mar. 1805, Peters, *Statutes*, 2:331–32; Prucha, *Sword*, 68–73; Indian Trade and Intercourse Appropriations Act, 3 Mar. 1805, in Peters, *Statutes*, 2:338; Report of John Mason, 12 Apr. 1810, ASPIA, 1:768.

4. Proclamation by Governor Wilkinson, 10 July 1805, *TPUS*, 13:160; Wilkinson to Henry Dearborn, 8 Sept. 1805, ibid., 13:199; Statement of Gain and Loss on the Indian Factories, 31 Dec. 1807–30 Sept. 1811, ASPIA, 1:784; Magnaghi, "Bellefontaine Indian Factory," 414–16.

5. Weber, *Spanish Frontier*, 202, 291; Treaty of St. Louis, 3 Nov. 1804, in *Indian Affairs*, Kappler, 2:74–77; Henry Dearborn to Thomas Jefferson, 11 Jan. 1805, *TPUS*, 7:256–57.

6. Dearborn to Wilkinson, 19 Apr. 1805, *TPUS*, 13:116–17; Dearborn to Rudolph Tillier, 24 May 1805, ibid., 13:131–32; Wilkinson to Dearborn, 27 July, 29 Oct., and 10 Dec. 1805, ibid., 13:167–68, 248, and 299; Prucha, *Sword*, 76; Magnaghi, "Bellefontaine Indian Factory," 401–3, 405; Isenberg, "Market Revolution,"

449; Statement of the Amount of Invoices of Goods Forwarded to the Factories, 11 Jan. 1806, *Memorial of Sundry Manufacturers*, 13; Property on Hand, 31 Dec. 1806, Misc. Accounts Bellefontaine Factory, ROIT; Factory Inventory, 30 June 1807, ibid.

7. Brief of Merchandise Disposed of at the U.S. Factory to 24 Nov. 1806, Misc. Accounts Bellefontaine Factory, ROIT; Magnaghi, "Bellefontaine Indian Factory," 406–9, 412; Bakeless, ed., *Journals of Lewis and Clark*, 372, 384. On Sheheke, see Fenn, *Encounters*, 250–57.

8. Merchandise Sold to 24 Nov. 1806, Misc. Accounts Bellefontaine Factory, ROIT; Debts Outstanding at St. Louis Trading House, 30 Sept. 1807, ibid.; Debts Owed by Indians, 30 Sept. 1807, ibid.; John Mason to Dearborn, 13 Dec. 1808, LSSIT, ROIT, 1:A:276.

9. Calloway, *One Vast Winter Count*, 358–59; Faragher, "'More Motley Than Mackinaw,'" 305–11; Debts Owed by Indians, 30 Sept. 1807, Misc. Accounts Bellefontaine Factory, ROIT; Invoice of Peltry Shipped on 19 Mar. 1807, ibid.; Peltry on Hand, 30 June 1807, ibid.; Factory Daybooks, Oct.–Dec. 1807, Oct. 1808–Feb. 1809, ibid. The author has adapted the adjective "frontier-exchange" from Usner, *Indians, Settlers, and Slaves*.

10. George Peter to James Wilkinson, 8 Sept. 1805, *TPUS*, 13:231–32; Calloway, *One Vast Winter Count*, 362–64; LeCompte, "Pierre Chouteau," 25–26; Innis, *Fur Trade*, 189–90; Frederick Bates to Henry Dearborn, 22 Oct. 1807, in *Life and Papers of Frederick Bates*, ed. Marshall, 1:222; Bates to Meriwether Lewis, 7 Nov. 1807, ibid., 1:230.

11. Account of Factory with John Mason, 31 Dec. 1808, Misc. Accounts Bellefontaine Factory, ROIT; Factory Daybook, Oct. 1808, ibid.; Dearborn to Acting Governor Thomas Hunt, 17 May 1808, *TPUS*, 14:184; John Mason to William Clark, 31 Dec. 1808, ibid., 14, 247; Magnaghi, "Bellefontaine Indian Factory," 408, 414–16; Foley, *Wilderness Journey*, 177–78, 188.

12. James House to Frederick Bates, Oct. 1807, in *Life and Papers*, ed. Marshall, 1:225 (first quote); Bates to Henry Dearborn, 7 Nov. 1807, *TPUS*, 14:151 (second quote); John Mason to Rudolph Tillier, 12 Apr. 1808 and 20 Apr. 1808, LSSIT, ROIT, 1:A:152–54; John Mason to Rudolph Tillier, 27 May 1808, TPUS, 14:188, 188n; Magnaghi, "Bellefontaine Indian Factory," 412, 415–16.

13. John Treat to Henry Dearborn, 15 Nov. 1805, *TPUS*, 13:277–81; Plaisance, "Arkansas Factory," 192–93; Morris, "Traders and Factories," 36–37; Calloway, *One Vast Winter Count*, 248–49, 361, 364–65, 382; DuVal, *Native Ground*, 160.

14. Treat to Dearborn, 15 Nov. 1805, *TPUS*, 13:277; Treat to John Shee, 8 Jan. 1807, Letter Book of Arkansas Trading House, ROIT, 156; Plaisance, "Arkansas Factory," 186–88. For Bright and Morgan, see Bearss, *"Montgomery's Tavern,"* Chapter II, Sections A.1–4 and B.3.

15. John Treat to William Davy, 15 Nov. 1805, Letter Book of Arkansas Trading House, ROIT, 35; Davy to Treat, 14 Feb. 1806, ibid., 75; Treat to Davy, 24 Feb., 13 Apr., and 1 July 1806, ibid., 50–51, 61–62, and 106 (quote).

16. Arkansas Factory Daybook, 70–110; John Shee to John Treat, 14 Feb. 1807, Letter Book of Arkansas Trading House, ROIT, 176–77; Treat to Shee, 15 July

1807, ibid., 186–87 (quote); John Treat to Joseph Waterman, 13 Dec. 1806, ibid., 143–45; Expenditures and Receipts of Temporary 1807 Establishment on White River, Arkansas Factory Daybook, ROIT, n.p.; Plaisance, "Arkansas Factory," 192–93, 198–99; Abstract of Peltries Forwarded by the Trading Houses to Joseph Saul, Dec. 1807–Dec. 1809, ASPIA, 1:722; Wayne Morris, "Traders and Factories," 33. On the ethnicity of the factory's debtors, see Arkansas Factory Daybooks, ROIT, 81, 92, 104, 111, 119, 122, 130; Debts Due the Factory, 31 Mar. and 30 June 1810, Misc. Accounts of Arkansas Factory, ROIT.

17. DuVal, *Native Ground*, 192–93; Joseph Saul to Treat, 20 Jan. 1807, Letter Book of Arkansas Trading House, ROIT, 164; John Shee to Treat, 20 July and 8 Aug. 1807, ibid., 198 (quote) and 203–4; Thomas Davy and Jonathan Roberts to William Davy, 4 Aug. 1806, LRSIT, ROIT, 11.

18. Introduction, Letter Book of the Arkansas Trading House, ROIT, iv; Arkansas Factory Daybook, ROIT, n.p. (entries for 1809, following p. 130); Abstract of Peltries Forwarded by the Trading Houses, ASPIA, 1:722; John Mason to James Treat, 23 May 1809, LSSIT, ROIT, I:A:391–92; Plaisance, "Arkansas Factory," 199–200.

19. Treat to Dearborn, 15 Nov. 1805, TPUS, 13:278; Treat to Dearborn, 7 Jan. 1808, ibid., 14:164; DuVal, *Native Ground*, 199–200; Ryan, ed., "Bright's Journal," 511–20.

20. Report on the Military Force of the United States, 4 Feb. 1805, *American State Papers*, Military Affairs, 1:176. Factory assets as of 31 Dec. 1809 are in ASPIA, 1:770.

21. Treat to Dearborn, 15 Nov. 1805, TPUS, 13:278; Treat to Dearborn, 27 Dec. 1805, Letter Book of Arkansas Trading House, ROIT, 43; Treat to William Davy, 27 Feb. 1806, ibid., 52; Plaisance, "Arkansas Factory," 189–90; Frederick Bates to William Eustis, 28 Sept. 1809, in *Life and Papers*, ed. Marshall, 2:88–89 (quote).

22. Rohrbough, *Trans-Appalachian Frontier*, 86–87, 106–7; Rothman, *Slave Country*, 73–117; Prucha, *Sword*, 68–69, 73, 97–98; Kastor, *Nation's Crucible*, 86–101.

23. Calloway, *One Vast Winter Count*, 257–58; Prucha, *Sword*, 69–73; Hatfield, *William Claiborne*, 216–23; Haggard, "Neutral Ground"; Garrett, ed., "Doctor John Sibley," *Southwestern Historical Quarterly* 45 (Jan. 1942): 286–92; Barr, *Peace Came*, 80–85, 212–13, 223–24.

24. The individually identified Indians were Auchalaudavit (Choctaw); Bohie, Caddo Chief; Chaufalauby (Chickasaw); an unnamed Creek; Ettaene; John Hommo (Chickasaw); one of the Laures brothers; John Louis (Choctaw); Linton Nancarrow; a Natchitoches Indian; Nockhoomah; Pascagoula Chief; Phockako; Charles Rollins (Choctaw); Tamboly (Choctaw); Tushkatoka (Choctaw); and White Meat (Choctaw). (Daybooks of the Natchitoches Factory, Feb.–Dec. 1806, July–Dec. 1807, and Jan.–Mar. 1808, Misc. Accounts Natchitoches–Sulphur Fork Factory, ROIT; Debts Due, 30 Sept. 1808, 30 Sept. 1809, 30 June 1810, and 30 June 1811, ibid.) See also John Sibley to William Eustis, 30 Nov. 1810, in "Doctor John Sibley," Garrett, ed., 48 (July 1944): 67–69. On the northwestern Louisiana Indian population, see Sibley to Eustis, 8 May 1809, ibid., 47 (Jan. 1944): 319–21.

25. Factory Inventory, 30 Sept. 1809, Misc. Accounts Natchitoches–Sulphur Fork Factory, ROIT. Deerskin figures compiled from Table 3-1; for Jan.–Mar. 1807

and Apr.–June 1808, the author has interpolated estimates based on the average catch for the other nine months of those years.

26. Invoices of Goods for Natchitoches Factory, 18 Nov. 1805, 23 June 1810, and 31 Dec. 1811, Misc. Accounts Natchitoches–Sulphur Fork Factory, ROIT; Factory Daybook for 7 Nov. 1808, ibid.; John Mason to William Linnard, 28 Dec. 1807, LSSIT, ROIT, 1:A:23; Thomas Linnard to Mason, 1 Nov. 1810, Letter Book of Natchitoches–Sulphur Fork Factory, ROIT, p. 16; List of Articles Wanting at Natchitoches for the Following Year, 6 Feb. 1811, ibid., 22–24; Brandt, ed., "Letter of Sibley," 374–375. Mamoodie was muslin or fine linen; britannia was plain, high-quality linen woven in Brittany.

27. Thomas Linnard to John Mason, 26 Aug. 1809, Letter Book of Natchitoches–Sulphur Fork Factory, ROIT, 2–3; Statement of Gain or Loss on the United States' Indian Factories, 31 Dec. 1807 to 31 Dec. 1811, *ASPIA*, 1:784; Statement of Account of the Indian Factory at Natchitoches, 31 Dec. 1807 to 30 Sept. 1811, ibid., 1:790 (quote).

28. John Sibley to William Eustis, 5 July 1809, in "Doctor John Sibley," ed. Garrett, 47 (Jan. 1944): 323–24 (quote).

29. LaVere, "Edward Murphy," 382–90 (quote 387); Brandt, ed., "Letter of Sibley," 374–75; J. Villasana Haggard, "The House of Barr and Davenport," esp. 76–77.

30. D. W. Meinig, *Shaping of America*, Vol. II, 36; Kastor, *Nation's Crucible*, 123–27; John Sibley to William Eustis, 30 Nov. 1810 and 9 Feb. 1811, in "Doctor John Sibley," ed. Garrett, 48 (1944–45): 69–70 and 547–49.

31. Adelman and Aron, "Borderlands to Borders," 816–17, 839–41; Meinig, *Shaping of America*, Vol. II, 58–59; Lewis, *Louisiana Purchase*, 76–77.

32. On these different classes of frontier, see Eccles, *Canadian Frontier*, 2.

33. John Mason to Rudolph Tillier, 12 Apr. 1808, LSSIT, ROIT, I:A:153; James McFarlane to Gov. Meriwether Lewis, 11 Dec. 1808, *TPUS*, 14:268. William Eustis's report of 30 Jan. 1810 indicates the Arkansas garrison had been withdrawn (*American State Papers*, Military Affairs, 1:249–53.)

34. Onuf, *Jefferson's Empire*, 3–17; Lewis, *Louisiana Purchase*, 84; Jefferson to Meriwether Lewis, 21 Aug. 1808, *TPUS*, 14:220 (second quote).

Chapter 4

1. On systems generally and fur-trading systems particularly, see Berkhofer, *Behavioral Approach*, 171–83; Wishart, *Fur Trade*, 10, 18.

2. Edward Price to John Harris, 24 Dec. 1796, 20 Jan. 1797, 9 June 1797, and 1 Nov. 1797, LB, Creek, ROIT, 34–35, 39–40, 62, and 93, respectively; Henry Dearborn to William Irvine, 11 May 1801, Irvine–Newbold Papers, Box 9, Folder 4; Isaac Waterman to Wm. Irvine, 2 Nov. 1801, ibid., Box 9, Folder 6; Plaisance, "U.S. Government Factory System," 36–37.

3. Account of the Public Services of General Irvine, n.d., Irvine–Newbold Papers, Box 10, Folder 13; Instructions to General Irvine, 11 May 1801, ibid., Box 9, Folder 4; Draft Instructions for John Johnston, 1802, ibid., Box 9, Folder 7;

Dearborn to William Irvine, 9 July 1802, OSW, LSIA, 1:A:247; Jonathan Halstead to Irvine, 9 Oct. 1802, LB, Creek, ROIT, 229–30; Timothy Barger to William Irvine, 9 Aug. 1802, Irvine–Newbold Papers, Box 9, Folder 9; William Irvine to Callender Irvine, 24 May 1804, ibid., Box 9, Folder 17.

4. Henry Dearborn to William Davy, 26 Mar. 1805, OSW, LSIA, 2:B:57–58; Dearborn to Ebenezer Belknap, 12 Apr. 1805, TPUS, 7:281–82; Gillingham, "Calico and Linen Printing," 109–10; Plaisance, "U.S. Government Factory System," 77; Statement of the Amount of Invoices of Goods Forwarded to the Several Factories, 11 Jan. 1806, Memorial of Sundry Manufacturers, 13; Furs and Pelts Received from the Several Indian Factories from Jan. 1st to Dec. 31st 1805, ibid., 17–18; Dearborn to Davy, 30 Dec. 1805, CSHSW, 19:311; Memorial, 6 Dec. 1805, in Memorial of Sundry Manufacturers ... in Philadelphia, 3–5; Memorial of Sundry Manufacturers of Hats in Easton, PA, 12 Dec. 1805, Records of the U.S. House of Representatives, 9th Congress, Microfilm M-1709, Reel 6, File 9A-F23; Memorials [from] New York, 17 Dec. 1805, Baltimore, 23 Dec. 1805, Boston, 2 Jan. 1806, Reading, Pa., 20 Jan. 1806, all ibid.; Jacob Crowninshield to Dearborn, 7 Jan. 1806, Memorial of Sundry Manufacturers ... in Philadelphia, 6.

5. Dearborn to Crowinshield, 17 Jan. 1806, Memorial of Sundry Manufacturers ... in Philadelphia, 8 (quote); William Davy to Dearborn, 18 Dec. 1805, ibid., 8–10; Act for Establishing Trading Houses with the Indian Tribes, 21 Apr. 1806, in Statutes, Peters, 2:402–4.

6. Dearborn to Davy, 29 Apr. 1806, OSW, LSIA, Indian Affairs, 2:B:207; Newman Dorland, "Second Troop," 93–94, 169–70, 184–85; Rowland, Life of Mason, 2:351, 464–65; Broadwater, George Mason, 246–48; Mason to Dearborn, 31 Oct. 1807, LSSIT, ROIT, 1:A:1; Mason to Directors of the Bank of Columbia, 3 Dec. 1807, ibid., 1:A:7.

7. Mason to David Hogg, 12 Dec. 1807, LSSIT, ROIT, 1:A:14–15; Circular Letter to Agents, 23 Dec. 1807, ibid., 1:A:19; Mason to John Johnson, 20 May 1808, ibid., 1:A:144–47; Mason to Rudolph Tillier, 8 July 1808, 1:A:180; Mason to Dearborn, 18 Jan. 1808, ibid., 1:A:42–43; George to Samuel Sibley, 23 Apr. 1812, George Sibley Papers, Box 1-2, Folder 13; Act Supplemental to the Act Establishing Trading Houses, 3 Mar. 1809, in Statutes, Peters, 2:544–45; Eustis to Mason, 13 May 1809, cited in Plaisance, "U.S. Government Factory System," 156.

8. Act Establishing Trading Houses with the Indian Tribes, 2 Mar. 1811, in Statutes, Peters, 2:652–55; Statement of Merchandise Prepared for Indian Annuities, 26 June 1812, LSSIT, ROIT, 3:C:6–7; Malone, Jefferson the President, 59–60, 95–117, 395–438, 451–90; Hickey, War of 1812, 9–21.

9. Malone, Jefferson the President, 59–60, 95–117, 395–438, 451–90; Hickey, War of 1812, 9–21.

10. Isaac Waterman to William Irvine, 2 Nov. 1801, Irvine–Newbold Papers, Box 9, Folder 6; Furs and Pelts Exported to Europe, May 1805, Memorial of Sundry Manufacturers ... in Philadelphia, 17; Dearborn to William Davy, 26 Mar. 1805, OSW, LSIA, 2:B:57–58; List of Goods Ordered and of Whom Purchased, 8 Apr. 1805, Recs. Choctaw TH, ROIT, 1:5–6; John Mason to Joseph Lopez Dias, 27 Nov. 1809, LSSIT, ROIT, 2:B:76; Winslow, Biographies, 58, 132–35, 181–83; Gambrel, ed.,

Memoirs of Mary Ellet, 9–15; Thompson and Anderson, eds., *Tribute*, 145–46. Chintz was printed and glazed cotton cloth; nonesopretties were colored ribbons, usually sold by the gross.

11. Mason to George Sibley, 26 Feb. 1808, LSSIT, ROIT, 1:A:69–70; Mason to Thomas Waterman, 28 Mar. 1808, ibid., 1:A:109; Mason to John Teackle, 4 Apr. 1808, ibid., 1:A:114; Mason to Thomas Waterman, 21 Nov. 1807, ibid., 1:A:5; Mason to Caleb Kirk, 16 Jan. 1808, ibid., 1:A:33; Mason to Jonathan Wilson, 16 Jan. 1808, ibid.; Mason to Louis and P. Lanney, 26 Feb. 1808, ibid., 1:A:68; Mason to K. Owen, 21 Feb. and 1 Mar. 1809, ibid., 1:A:316 and 321, respectively; Mason to Arthur McGill, 29 July 1812, ibid., 3:C:23–24; Invoices for Goods Shipped to John Treat, 23 Apr. 1810 and 26 July 1811; Misc. Accounts of the Chickasaw Bluffs Trading House, ROIT; Mason to Waterman, 27 Feb. and 31 Dec. 1808, LSSIT, ROIT, 1:A:73–74 and 291; Mason to Henry Derringer, 27 June 1809, ibid., 2:B:18; Mason to George Sibley, 16 Mar. 1808, ibid., 1:A:96–97; Mason to Roger Perry, 16 Apr. 1808, ibid., 1:A:120.

12. John Mason to James Moore, 29 July 1812, LSSIT, ROIT, 3:C:24–26 (first quote); Mason to Thomas Warner, 26 Apr. 1808, ibid., 1:A:126–27 (second quote); Goods Wanted for the Fort Wayne Trading House, 1 Dec. 1807, Misc. Accounts Fort Wayne Factory, ROIT; Richter, *Facing East*, 175; Carlos and Lewis, *Commerce by a Frozen Sea*, 96–100; Mason to Roger Perry, 16 Apr. 1808, LSSIT, ROIT, 1:A:120; Mason to George Sibley, 16 Mar. and 21 Mar. 1808, ibid., 1:A:96 and 1:A:108; Mason to John Lamb, 3 June 1808, ibid., 1:A:165; William Clark to George Sibley, 19 Aug. 1809, Sibley Papers, Box 1-2, Folder 8.

13. Mason to I. E. Dupont de Nemours, 19 Jan. 1808, 23 Mar. 1808, and 4 June 1808, LSSIT, ROIT, 1:A:37, 107, and 169, respectively; Mason to William Linnard, 28 Dec. 1807, ibid., 1:A:23; Mason to Henry Dearborn, 21 Oct. 1808, ibid., 1:A:246; Thomas Linnard to Mason, 1 Nov. 1810, Letter Book of Natchitoches–Sulphur Fork Factory, ROIT, p. 16 (first quote); Mason to Thos. Waterman, 9 Feb. 1810, LSSIT, ROIT, 2:B:90; Mason to Henry Deringer, 27 June 1809 and 10 Aug. 1812, ibid., 2:B:18 and 3:C:31; Invoices for Deringer, 23 Dec. 1811, 4 Apr. 1812, and 8 Jan. 1813, Invoices Inward, ROIT, 3:263, 268, and 281; George Sibley to Jeremiah Bronaugh, 19 Sept. 1813, Sibley Papers, Box 1-2, Folder 14; Mason to Anthony Bleeker and Sons, 15 Mar. 1808, LSSIT, ROIT, 1:A:92–93; Mason to Joseph Lopez Dias, 30 May and 8 July 1808, ibid., 1:A:159–60 (second quote) and 179; Mason to Dias, 22 Nov. 1809, ibid., 2:B:73. On wampum's diplomatic significance, see Shell, *Wampum*, 42, 52–55, 81–82.

14. Mason to Dearborn, 8 Jan. and 18 Apr. 1808, LSSIT, ROIT, 1:A:26–27 and 121; Mason to Reynaldo Johnson, 20 Feb. 1808, ibid., 1:A:57–58; Mason to Thomas Waterman, 27 Feb. and 7 Mar. 1808, ibid., 1:A:81; Mason to Joseph Lopez Dias, 9 Apr. 1808, 22 Apr. 1808, and 30 June 1810, ibid., 1:A:116, 1:A:124–25, and 2:B:164; Mr. Irwin's Account of Shipment of Goods, 28 Oct. 1809, Misc. Accounts Chicago Factory, ROIT. The cost of shipping goods from Detroit to Fort Wayne was $60 per ton (Memorandum Book, ROIT, 93).

15. Dearborn to William Davy, 2 Oct. 1805, OSW, LSIA, 2:B:115; Mason to Jacob Bowman, 11 and 21 Apr. 1808, LSSIT, ROIT, 1:A:117 and 122; Mason

to William McMahan, 11 and 16 Apr. 1808, ibid., 1:A:118–20; Mason to William Pratt, 10 May 1808, ibid., 1:A:136; Mason to George Sibley, 24 May 1808, ibid., 1:A:147–48; Mason to William Clark, 31 Dec. 1808, ibid., 1:A:292–93; Foley, *Wilderness Journey*, 177–78, 188. Dearborn estimated the freight cost from Pittsburgh to Saint Louis at $40 per ton.

16. George Mason to George Sibley, 24 May 1808, LSSIT, ROIT, 1:A:147–50; Bond of Joseph Ogden et al., 9 June 1808, George Sibley Papers, Box 1-2, Folder 7; George Sibley to Gen. O'Hara, 6 Aug. 1808, ibid.; George to Samuel Sibley, 16 Sept. 1808, ibid.

17. Joseph Saul to John Treat, 18 Apr. 1806, Letter Book of Arkansas Trading House, ROIT, 88; Entry for 21 Jan. 1807, Daybooks of Chickasaw Bluffs Factory, ROIT; John Mason to Joseph Saul, 9 Mar. 1808 and 13 Aug. 1808, LSSIT, ROIT, 1:A:85–86 and 202; Mason to William Eustis, 8 Aug. 1810, ibid., 2:B:173–74; Mason to William Clark, 13 Aug. 1810, ibid., 2:B:178; Account of Charges Paid by Joseph Saul et al. on Merchandise Forwarded from Philadelphia, 1805, Recs. Choctaw TH, ROIT, 1:171; Harry Toulmin to the President, 25 Feb. 1809, *TPUS*, 5:705–7; Toulmin to Vincent Folch, 21 Feb. 1809, ibid., 5:710; John Mason to George Gaines, 17 June 1809, ibid., 5:747. Folch's fears were not groundless: American filibusters raided West Florida in 1805 and captured part of the province in 1810. (Kastor, *Nation's Crucible*, 71–72, 124–27.)

18. Mason to James Morrison, 22 Aug. 1810, LSSIT, ROIT, 2:B:183; Mason to George Gaines, 28 Aug. 1810, ibid., 2:B:189–93; Plaisance, "Choctaw Trading House," 410–12; Leftwich, "Cotton Gin Port," 267–68; Account of Payment to George Colbert, 17 Nov. 1810–10 Jan. 1811, Recs. Choctaw TH, ROIT, 2:59–60.

19. Account of George Gaines' Journey, 9 Nov. 1810–4 Jan. 1811, Recs. Choctaw TH, ROIT, 2:65–69 (quote 69); Receipt for Payment to Ellman Simpson, 8 Jan. 1811, ibid., 2:5; Receipt for Payment to Benjamin Curridges, n.d., ibid., 2:9; Receipt to Mr. Kincade for Services Packing Gunpowder, 18 Feb. 1811, ibid., 2:55; Account of Payment to George Colbert, 17 Nov. 1810–10 Jan. 1811, ibid., 2:59–60; Plaisance, "Choctaw Trading House," 412–13.

20. Jonathan Halstead to Joseph Clay, 24 Mar. 1803, LB, Creek, ROIT, 242; Halstead to Abraham Abrahams, 24 July 1805, ibid., 273; Halstead to Levi Sheftall, 29 Sept. 1807, ibid., 308; John Mason to Levi Sheftall, 31 May 1808, LSSIT, ROIT, 1:A:162–63; Mason to William Simmons, 16 Dec. 1808, ibid., 1:A:278; Edward Price to John Harris, 11 July 1797, LB, Creek, ROIT, 72; Memorandum Book, ROIT, 6–7, 93–94. The seaborne freight cost from Philadelphia to Savannah was $1.00 to $1.25 per barrel, roughly $10 per ton.

21. Polhemus, *Archaeological Investigation*, 9; Treaty of Tellico, 25 Oct. 1805, in *Indian Affairs*, Kappler, 2:82–83; Receipt to Andrew Kennely, ca. Jan. 1808, Misc. Accounts of Cherokee Factory, ROIT, Folder 4; Memorandum Book, ROIT, 6–7; McLoughlin, *Cherokee Renascence*, 279–80.

22. Chapters Two, Three, and Five; Arkansas Factory Daybook, 1805–1810, ROIT (which reports 24,000 pounds purchased 1809–10); Invoices Inward, ROIT, Vol. 1 (unpaginated invoices for Tellico, 31 Dec. 1801–5 Nov. 1804; Ft. Wilkinson and "Georgia Factory," 15 Jan. 1802–20 March 1805; Detroit, 5 Sept. 1803 and 14

Aug. 1804; Chickasaw Bluffs, 20 Jan. - 30 March 1804; and Choctaw House, Spring 1804 and 30 March 1804), 2:19–21, 61, 66, 81, 114, 120, 122, 128, 130, 137, 145; 3:24–25; 4:5, 16, 29; Braund, *Deerskins and Duffels*, 71–72. The factors usually separately identified shaved or dressed deerskins, for which they paid a higher price. The figures included in this calculation from Natchitoches and Arkansas Post are deerskins purchased; other factories' figures are deerskins shipped. The Great Lakes factories shipped only 11,807 deerskins prior to the War of 1812. (Invoices Inward, ROIT, Vol. 1 [unpaginated invoices for Detroit, 5 Sept. 1803 and 14 Aug 1804]; 2:66–67, 158; 3:20, 54; 4:1, 9, 17, 18, 23–26, 42, 43, 45, 52–53, 64, 66, 68, 75.)

23. John Mason to William Clark, 29 June 1810, LSSIT, ROIT, 2:B:159–60; Isaac Waterman to William Irvine, 2 Nov. 1801, Irvine–Newbold Papers, Box 9, Folder 6; William Davy to Henry Dearborn, 11 Jan. 1806, *Memorial of Sundry Manufacturers . . . in Philadelphia*, 11; Invoices Outward, ROIT, 1:110–11, 113; Sales Books, ROIT, 2:9.

24. Braund, *Deerskins and Duffels*, 42–43, 87–88; John Mason to John Johnston, 19 Jan. 1808, LSSIT, ROIT, 1:A:36 (quote); Mason to Thomas Linnard, et al., 18 Mar. 1808, ibid., 1:A:99; Mason to Thomas Waterman, 13 May 1808, ibid., 1:A:137–38; Mason to Levy Sheftall, 3 June 1808, ibid., 1:A:166; Mason to Jonathan Halstead, 15 Jan. 1810, ibid., 2:B:83; Mason to William Eustis, 3 Feb. 1810, ibid., 2:B:87–88; Deerskins Received at New Orleans, 1 Feb. 1810, Memorandum Book, ROIT, 67–68.

25. Mason to Gaines, 14 Aug. 1809, LSSIT, ROIT, 2:B:48; Mason to Eustis, 3 Feb. 1810, ibid., 2:B:88 (quote); Haeger, *John Astor*, 51–57, 75–78, 81–82, 104–7; Mason to Eustis, 3 Feb. and 12 Feb. 1810, LSSIT, ROIT, 2:B:88–89 and 91, respectively; Mason to Saul, 3 Mar. 1810, ibid., 2:B:101–2 (quote); Mason to Astor, 20 Mar. 1812, ibid., 2:B:110; Sales Books, ROIT, 1807–1822, 2:31–34, 36–38, 39–40. The price quoted in the November 1810 sale was net of commissions, duties, and advertising. The buyers paid 14–28 cents per pound.

26. Table 4-3; Clayton, "Growth and Economic Significance," 64–67; Lawson, *New Voyage*, 122–23; Mason to Henry Dearborn, 9 Oct. 1809, LSSIT, ROIT, 2:B:63–65; Mason to William Clark, 29 June 1810, ibid., 2:B:159–60. Beaver prices (for 1808–11) are from Sales Books, ROIT, 2:14–52.

27. Murphy, "Autonomy," 78–79; Calloway, *New Worlds*, 29. For sales of produce in New Orleans and Saint Louis, see Sales Books, ROIT, 2:26, 31, 35, 40, 51, 53–54, 58–59, and 78.

28. Jonathan Halstead to William Irvine, 18 Aug. 1802, LB, Creek, ROIT, 225; Cangany, "Fashioning Moccasins," 268–70; Friend Palmer, *Early Days in Detroit*, 572; Wadc, "Indigenous Women and Maple Sugar," 16, 18, 30–31, 36–38, 55–56.

29. Williams, *Linking Arms*, 126–29; Usner, *Indians, Settlers, and Slaves*, 89–90, 195–98; and see Chapter Three.

30. Murphy, "To Live Among Us," 288–89; Articles Wanted for Fort Wayne Trading House for the Year 1809, Misc. Accounts Fort Wayne Factory, ROIT; Russell Magnaghi, "Bellefontaine Indian Factory," 410–11; Boilvin to William Eustis, 11 Feb. 1811, *TPUS*, 14:440 (quote); Sales Books, ROIT, 2: 40, 53–54, 78.

31. Murphy, "Autonomy," 81–82; Murphy, "To Live among Us," 290–91; Dowd, *Spirited Resistance*, 6–9; Braund, "Guardians of Tradition," 244–45.

32. The exceptions were General Colbert's wife and mother-in-law (Daybook for 12 April 1806 and Debts Due on 30 June 1807, Daybooks of Chickasaw Bluffs Factory, ROIT); Mrs. McIntosh (Debts Due, 30 June 1807, ibid.); Molly Glover (Sept.–Dec. 1813, ibid.); White Raccoon's Mother (Oct. 1806, Daybooks of Fort Wayne Factory, ROIT); Elizabeth Whitaker (Debts Due, 31 Dec. 1809, Misc. Accounts Sandusky Factory, ROIT); "sundry Osage squaws" from whom George Sibley purchased firewood (Contingent Account, 15 Feb. 1813, Misc. Accounts Osage Factory, ROIT); Thomas Maw's Sister (Journal, Sept. 1819, Misc. Accounts Spadre Bluffs Factory, ROIT); and Tollantuskee's widow, Polly (Debts Due, 31 Dec. 1821, ibid.). On the peltry trade's erosion of women's economic power, see Perdue, *Cherokee Women*, 70–78.

33. See Table 4-4 and the sources listed for Table 4-3. The author has matched nineteen of the forty-six men and partnerships who bought factory produce in New York with at least the family names of persons in the 1805 city directory. Of these nineteen, fourteen were merchants. (Invoices Outward, ROIT, Vol. 1; Sales Books, ROIT, Vol. 2; *Longworth's American Almanack*, 128, 136, 140–46.)

34. Haeger, *John Astor*, 78; Oddy, *European Commerce*, 2:146, 163, 171–72; Rabruzzi, "Cutting Out the Middleman," 188–90, 193; Mustafa, *Merchants and Migrations*, 117–19, 195–97, 200–203, 212–16.

35. Haeger, *John Astor*, 70–72; *American State Papers*, "Commerce and Navigation," 1: 488, 506, 542, 588, 668, 693, 719, 736, 813, 867.

36. Upon their closure, the factories still had over 15,000 pounds of sugar on hand. Final Inventories, 1822–23, ROIT, pp. 25–31, 43–49, 186.

Chapter 5

1. Smelser, *Democratic Republic*, 163–80; Hickey, *Don't Give Up*, 28–30. In January 1812 Mason reported that the ten extant factories had increased their collective book value by $14,471 over the previous four years. This represented an average gain of $350 per year per factory. (Statement of Estimated Gain or Loss on the United States' Indian Factories, 31 Dec. 1807–30 Sept. 1811, *ASPIA*, 1:764.)

2. Invoices Inward, ROIT, 1796–1822, Vol. 1 (unpaginated invoices for Ft. Wilkinson and "Georgia Factory," 15 Jan. 1802–20 March 1805;); 2:114, 122, 128, 145; 4:16; Jonathan Halstead to Levi Sheftall, 29 and 30 Sept. 1807, LB, Creek, ROIT, 308–9; Statement of Account of the United States' Indian Factory at Fort Hawkins, 31 Dec. 1807–30 Sept. 1811, *ASPIA*, 1:785. The invoiced value of the peltry Halstead shipped in 1802 was about $9,670.

3. Fort Wilkinson Conference Journal, 9 June 1802, *ASPIA*, 1:674–75; Saunt, *New Order*, 205–6; Jonathan Halstead to George Ingels, 9 Nov. 1804, LB, Creek, ROIT, 267 (first quote); Halstead to William Davy, 20 Sept. 1805, ibid., 278 (second quote).

4. Halstead to John Shee, 4 Nov. 1806, LB, Creek, ROIT, 299; Treaty of Washington, 14 Nov. 1805, in *Indian Affairs*, Kappler, 2:85–86; Piker, *Okfuskee*, 200, 203.

5. Halstead to William Irvine, 18 Aug. 1802, 9 Oct. 1802, 26 June 1803, and 4 Sept. 1804, LB, Creek, ROIT, 225, 229–30, 248–49, and 264, respectively; Halstead to

William Simmons, 8 Mar. and 11 Aug. 1804, ibid., 257, 261; Halstead to Benjamin Hawkins, Sept. 1806, ibid., 295; Halstead to John Shee, 2 Apr. 1807, ibid., 302; Halstead to John Mason, 10 Mar. 1808, ibid., 314.

6. Treaty of New York, 7 Aug. 1790, in *Indian Affairs*, Kappler, 2:26. For examples of stipend disbursements, see Orders for Creek Stipend Drawn on Edward Price, 1797–1798, in *Collected Works*, ed. Foster, 324–25; Creek Factory Daybooks, Records of the Creek Factory, ROIT, Reel 3, Vols. 1:28, 39, 41 and 2:2, 14, 26.

7. Halstead to Henry Dearborn, 8 Dec. 1807, LB, Creek, ROIT, 311; Saunt, *New Order*, 221; Chiefs of the Upper Creeks to Benjamin Hawkins, 26 Apr. 1813, *ASPIA*, 1:841. The 1802 and 1805 treaties are in *Indian Affairs*, Kappler, 2:58–59 and 2:86.

8. Treaty of Philadelphia, 26 June 1794, in *Indian Affairs*, Kappler, 2:33–34; Treaty of Tellico, 2 Oct. 1798, ibid., 2:53; Minutes of a Conference Holden at the War Office, 30 June and 3 July 1801, OSW, LSIA, 1:A:73–74, 79–80; Horsman, *Expansion*, 117–18; McLoughlin, *Cherokee Renascence*, 77–78.

9. Samuel Riley to Return Meigs, 29 Nov. 1806, Records of Cherokee Indian Agency, Reel 3 (quote); Thomas Jefferson to Henry Dearborn, 12 Aug. 1802, *TPUS*, 7:69–70; Jefferson to William Harrison, 27 Feb. 1803, in *Works of Jefferson*, ed. Ford, 10:370.

10. Dearborn to Hooker, 23 Apr. 1804, OSW, LSIA, 2:B:2; Factory Debts, 1 Apr. 1804, Misc. Accounts of Cherokee Factory, ROIT; Treaty of Tellico, 24 Oct. 1804, in *Indian Affairs*, Kappler, 2:73–74; Return Meigs and Daniel Smith to Henry Dearborn, 31 Oct. 1804, Documents Relating to the Negotiation of the Treaty of October 24, 1804 with the Cherokee Indians, in Documents Relating to the Negotiation of Ratified and Unratified Treaties, Reel 1, Item 42; Nicholas Byers to Return Meigs, 4 Aug. and 16 Aug. 1805, Records of Cherokee Indian Agency, Reel 3; Snyder, *Slavery in Indian Country*, 189–90; Treaties of Tellico, 25 Oct. and 27 Oct. 1805, in *Indian Affairs*, Kappler, 2:82–84; Daniel Smith and Return Meigs to Henry Dearborn, 29 Oct. 1805, Misc. Accounts of Cherokee Factory, ROIT, Folder 2.

11. Brown, ed., *Plumer's Memorandum*, 347–49, 361–62; Resolutions of the Cherokee Delegates Relating to Their Funds, Annuity, Etc., 5 Jan. 1806, Records of Cherokee Indian Agency, Reel 3; Treaty of Washington, 7 Jan. 1806, in *Indian Affairs*, Kappler, 2:90–92; McLoughlin, "Thomas Jefferson," 558.

12. Willstown Council to Return Meigs, 19 Sept. 1806, Records of Cherokee Indian Agency, Reel 3; James Phillips to Meigs, 15 Aug. 1807, ibid.; McLoughlin, "Thomas Jefferson," 558, 560–61; Wilkins, *Cherokee Tragedy*, 37–41; Convention between the United States and the Cherokee Nation, 11 Sept. 1807, in Documents Relating to the Negotiation of Ratified and Unratified Indian Treaties, Reel 1, Item 53; Return Meigs to Henry Dearborn, 28 Sept. 1807, Records of Cherokee Indian Agency, Reel 3 (quote).

13. Jefferson to the Deputies of the Cherokee Upper Towns, 9 Jan. 1809, in *Writings of Jefferson*, ed. Lipscomb et al., 15:455–58; McLoughlin, "Thomas Jefferson," 562–63, 567–80; McLoughlin, *Cherokee Renascence*, 143–45; Wilkins, *Cherokee Tragedy*, 42–51.

14. McLoughlin, *Cherokee Renascence*, 279–80; Invoices Inward, ROIT, 1796–1822, Vol. 1 (unpaginated invoices for Tellico, 31 Dec. 1801–5 Nov. 1804); 2:66, 81,

and 128; Polhemus, *Archaeological Investigation*, 9; Henry Dearborn to William Davy, 26 Sept. 1805, OSW, LSIA, 2:B:112; Treaty of Tellico, 25 Oct. 1805, in *Indian Affairs*, Kappler, 2:82–83. Peltry shipments from the Hiwassee factory in 1808 included 10,215 pounds of deerskins, 358 pounds of beaver, and 130 bearskins. Sales fell again in 1809. (Invoices Inward, ROIT, 4:16, 29; Daybooks for 1809, Misc. Accounts of Cherokee Factory, ROIT, Folder 6.) For freight rates, see Receipt to Andrew Kennely, ca. Jan. 1808, Misc. Accounts of Cherokee Factory, ROIT, Folder 4; Invoice of Peltry Forwarded to Levi Sheftall by Nicholas Byers, 18 Mar. 1808, ibid.; Memorandum Book, ROIT, 93–94.

15. John Mason to Return Meigs, 10 Jan. 1809, LSSIT, ROIT, 1:A:305 (quote); Mason to Nicholas Byers, 18 June 1810 and 17 July 1812, ibid., 2:B:152–54 and 3:C:18; Goods Forwarded to Meigs for Distribution to Indians Emigrating to Arkansas, 25 Sept. 1807, Misc. Accounts of Cherokee Factory, ROIT, Folder 3; McLoughlin, "Thomas Jefferson," 578–79.

16. Invoices of 19 Jan. and 2 Feb. 1807, Recs. Choctaw TH, ROIT, 1:422 and 424; Invoices Inward, ROIT, 1796–1822, 3:25 and 4:3, 11, 13, 30–31, 58, 72; Articles Wanted for the Indian Trade for 1807, 1808, 1810, and 1812, Recs. Choctaw TH, ROIT, 1:233–55, 1:13, 1:16–17, and 1:19, respectively; Daybooks for 18 May 1808, May 1809, May 1810, May 1812, and July 1812, ibid., Reel 4 (n.p.). Gaines' orders for 1807 and 1808 included seven bales of blankets; the author estimates that each bale contained fifty blankets of varying sizes. (See Plaisance, "U.S. Government Factory System," 345.)

17. Carson, *Searching*, 67–68; Daybooks of the Choctaw Trading House, Jan. 1808–Dec. 1812, Recs. Choctaw TH, ROIT, Reel 4; Articles Wanted for the Indian Trade for 1810, ibid., 1:17; Wallace, *Jefferson and the Indians*, 203–5, 225–26; Jefferson to William Harrison, 27 Feb. 1803, in *Works of Jefferson*, ed. Ford, 10:370 (quote). On debts, see Factory Balance Sheet, 31 Mar. 1811, Recs. Choctaw TH, ROIT, 2:136–37; Factory Debts, 31 Mar. 1812, ibid., 2:264.

18. John Shee to John Treat, 8 Aug. 1807, Letter Book of Arkansas Trading House, ROIT, 203–4; Receipt for Goods Received from Joseph Chambers, 1 Oct. 1807, Recs. Choctaw TH, ROIT, 1:368; Plaisance, "Choctaw Trading House," 405–6, 409–410; Plaisance, "U.S. Government Factory System," 50; Statement of Gain and Loss on the United States' Indian Factories, 31 Dec. 1807 to 30 Sept. 1811, *ASPIA*, 1: 784; Statement of Account of the Indian Factory at Fort St. Stephen's, ibid., 1:787; and see Chapter Four.

19. Memorandum Book, ROIT, 93–94; Plaisance, "Chickasaw Bluffs Factory," 42–43, 47. Due to the expense of trans-montane transportation, it cost $110 per ton to ship cargo to Chickasaw Bluffs from Georgetown.

20. Invoice of Goods Immediately Necessary to Supply the Factory, 13 Oct. 1810, Misc. Accounts Chickasaw Bluffs Factory, ROIT. Treat's predecessors at Chickasaw Bluffs were Thomas Peterkin (1802–7) and David Hogg (1808–10). (Plaisance, "Chickasaw Bluffs Factory," 43–45.)

21. Articles Wanted to Supply the Factory at Chickasaw Bluffs, 30 June 1812, Misc. Accounts Chickasaw Bluffs Factory, ROIT; Usner, *Indians in the Lower Mississippi Valley*, 83; Jennings, ed., "Rush Nutt's Trip," 49 (quote); Invoices Inward,

ROIT, 1796–1822, 3: 27–29 and 4: 5, 14, 36, 40, 47, 59, 63; Receipt for Factory Inventory, 1 Nov. 1811, Misc. Accounts Chickasaw Bluffs Factory, ROIT; Factory Accounts for 31 Dec. 1812, ibid.; Plaisance, "Chickasaw Bluffs Factory," 45–47.

22. Inventory, 31 Dec. 1807, Misc. Accounts Chickasaw Bluffs Factory, ROIT; Debts Due the Factory, 30 June 1812, ibid.; Statement of Gain and Loss on the United States' Indian Factories, 31 Dec. 1807 to 30 Sept. 1811, *ASPIA*, 1:784; Statement of Account of the United States' Indian Factory at Chickasaw Bluffs, ibid., 1:786. The author has extrapolated the markup rate from the Invoice for Goods Shipped 26 July 1811, Misc. Accounts Chickasaw Bluffs Factory, ROIT.

23. Statement of the Annuities . . . Payable Each Year under Indian Treaties to the Year 1819, *ASPIA*, 2:215–216; Invoice of Sundry Articles to Be Delivered . . . to the Order of James Neelly, Esq., Indian Agent, 4 June 1811, Misc. Accounts Chickasaw Bluffs Factory, ROIT.

24. DeRosier, *Removal of the Choctaw*, 34–36; Gibson, *Chickasaws*, 95–99.

25. Tables 5-1 and 5-2; George to Samuel Sibley, 16 Sept. 1808, Sibley Papers, Box 1-2, Folder 7; Gregg, "History of Fort Osage," 445. Five thousand Kansa and Osage Indians visited Fort Osage in the fall of 1808, to "settle their differences" with the Americans; if at least 2% of the visitors traded with Sibley, he would have had 100 customers. (Diary of George Sibley, 26 Sept. and 12 Oct. 1808, Lindenwood College Papers, Box 11; Gregg, 445.)

26. Henry Dearborn to Acting Gov. Thomas Hunt, 17 May 1808, *TPUS*, 14:184; Meriwether Lewis to Dearborn, 1 July 1808, ibid., 14:196; William Clark to Dearborn, 23 Sept. 1808, ibid., 14:224–27; Kate Gregg, "History of Fort Osage," 439–45; George Sibley to Samuel Sibley, 16 Sept. 1808, Sibley Papers, Box 1-2, Folder 7; Diary of George Sibley, 21 Sept. 1808, Lindenwood College Papers, Box 11.

27. Furs and Pelts Taken by the Factory from 1 Oct. 1808 to 30 June 1810, Misc. Accounts Osage Factory, ROIT, Box 1, Folder 1; Goods Sold to Indians, 1 July 1809 to 30 Sept. 1809, ibid.; Articles Unsuitable for the Indian Trade, 2 Oct. 1810, ibid., Box 1, Folder 2; Factory Journal, 29 Aug. 1810, ibid., Box 1, Folder 2.

28. Statement of Gain and Loss on the United States' Indian Factories, 31 Dec. 1807 to 30 Sept. 1811, *ASPIA*, 1:784; Table 5-1; Diary of George Sibley, 27 Dec. 1810 and 9 Jan. 1811, Lindenwood College Papers, Box 11; John Mason to Sibley, 2 July 1811, *TPUS*, 14:458; Gregg, "History of Fort Osage," 453.

29. John Mason to George Sibley, 2 July 1811, *TPUS*, 14:458–59; Mason to William Clark, 29 June 1810, LSSIT, ROIT, 2:B:159–60; William Clark to Henry Dearborn, 23 Sept. 1808, *TPUS*, 14:226; Deposition of Paul Louise, 16 July 1810, Misc. Accounts Osage Factory, ROIT, Folder 1-2; Pierre Chouteau to William Eustis, 14 Dec. 1809, *TPUS*, 14:344 (quote); Officers of Fort Osage to Secretary William Eustis, 16 July 1812, *TPUS*, 14:587–89; Unrau, *Kansa Indians*, 87–94; Gregg, "History of Fort Osage," 448–50.

30. Factory Journal, 30 Sept. 1810 (quote) and 12 Sept. 1809, Misc. Accounts Osage Factory, ROIT, Folder 1-2; William Clark to George Sibley, 19 Aug. 1809, Sibley Papers, Box 1-2, Folder 8. On gift-giving in time of mourning ("covering the dead"), see Meriwether Lewis to Nicholas Boilvin, 14 May 1808, *TPUS*, 14:217.

31. Diary of George Sibley, 24 Sept. 1808, Lindenwood College Papers, Box 11.

32. George to Samuel Sibley, 12 Feb. 1811, Sibley Papers, Box 1-2, Folder 9. On women and diplomacy, see Barr, *Peace Came*, 1–15, 247–87, and Chapter Two.

33. Deposition of Towogohe, Wawchawawhe, and Shomecassetunga, 5 Apr. 1810, Sibley Papers, Box 1-2, Folder 8; Diary of George Sibley, 1 and 11 May 1811, Lindenwood College Papers, Box 11; George Sibley to William Clark, 22 July 1811, Sibley Papers, Box 1-2, Folder 9; Notes of an Official Expedition from Fort Osage to the Kansas–Pawnees–Osages, May–July 1811, ibid., Box 1-2, Folder 11.

34. Isenberg, "Market Revolution," 456–58; Unrau, *Kansa Indians*, 91–94; Stephen Aron, *American Confluence*, 115, 140, 155–56.

35. Chapter Three; Van Der Zee, "Fur Trade Operations," 491, 494; Henry Dearborn to Thomas Hunt, 17 May 1808, *TPUS*, 14:184; Prucha, *Sword*, 100.

36. John Mason to Henry Dearborn, 18 Apr. 1808, LSSIT, ROIT, 1:A:121; Mason to Meriwether Lewis, 10 June 1808, *TPUS*, 14:194 (first quote); Valuation of Factory Houses at Fort Madison, 20 Jan. 1810, Misc. Accounts Fort Madison, ROIT, Box 1, Folder 18; Labor Performed by Soldiers, Jan.—Mar. 1810, ibid., Box 1, Folder 10; [George Hunt], " Personal Narrative," *HCPSM*, 8:665 (second quote); Accounts of the U.S. Indian Factory at Fort Madison, 23 Aug. 1808 to 30 Sept. 1811, *ASPIA*, 1:789; Murphy, "To Live Among Us," 288–89; Estimated Gain and Loss on the United States' Indian Factories, 31 Dec. 1807 to 30 Sept. 1811, *ASPIA*, 1:784 (third quote).

37. Merchandise to be Delivered to Fort Madison Trading House for 1811, Misc. Accounts Fort Madison, ROIT, Box 1, Folder 25; [Hunt], "Personal Narrative," *HCPSM*, 8:663 (quotes).

38. Van Der Zee, "Fur Trade Operations," 502–3, 505–6; Calloway, *One Vast Winter Count*, 370; Richter, *Facing East*, 166; Nichols, *Red Gentlemen*, 8; John Mason to Henry Dearborn, 12 Nov. 1808, LSSIT, ROIT, 1:A:262; [Hunt], "Personal Narrative," 8:664. Black Hawk recalled that Johnson refused to give credit to Indians (Jackson, *Black Hawk*, 63). However, his memory apparently failed him—see Mason to John Johnson, 11 Nov. 1808, *TPUS*, 14:233; Skins Received from Indians to Repay Debts, 1 July–30 Sept. 1810, Misc. Accounts Fort Madison, ROIT, Box 1, Folder 11.

39. Jackson, *Black Hawk*, 57–58; [Hunt], "Personal Narrative," *HCPSM*, 8:665–67; Clark to Secretary William Eustis, 5 Apr. 1809, *TPUS*, 14:260.

40. Clark to Eustis, 29 Apr. 1809 and 28 Sept. 1810, *TPUS*, 14:265–66 and 415; John Sugden, *Tecumseh*, 176; Jefferson to Meriwether Lewis, 21 Aug. 1808, *TPUS*, 14:220–21; Van Der Zee, "Fur Trade Operations," 496–97.

41. [Hunt], "Personal Narrative," 667–68.

42. Tanner, *Atlas*, 40, 93; McConnell, *Country Between*, 62; Featherstonhaugh, *Canoe Voyage*, 1:137–43. Mackinac Island did not become a major trading center until the nineteenth century, but Michilimackinac, on Michigan's Lower Peninsula, had been one since the 1680s. Some documents confuse the two places. (White, *Middle Ground*, 31–32; Hickey, *Don't Give Up*, 253–54.)

43. Kappler, ed., *Indian Affairs*, 2:40; Quaife, *Chicago*, 129, 131–36, 296–97; John Mason to William Eustis, 13 May 1809, *TPUS*, 14:274; Henry Dearborn to William Hull, 23 July 1805, ibid., 10:24; Dearborn to William Davy, 31 Aug. 1805,

OSW, LSIA, 2:B:104; Personal Account of Thomas Hayward, Fall 1805–Jan. 1806, Misc. Accounts Chicago Factory, ROIT.

44. Quaife, *Chicago*, 297–99; "The Fur Trade and the Factory at Green Bay, 1816–1821," *CSHSW*, 7:269–70; Table 5-3; Statement of Account of the U.S. Indian Factory at Chicago, 30 Sept. 1807–30 Sept. 1811, *ASPIA*, 1:792; Peltries Purchased from the Indians, Apr.–June 1808 and Jan.–Aug. 1809, Chicago Factory Waste Book, ROIT; Indian Goods Sold, Jan. 1809, ibid.; George Mason to John Sibley, 2 July 1811, *TPUS*, 14:458–59; Statement of Gain and Loss on the U.S. Indian Factories, 31 Dec. 1807–30 Sept. 1811, *ASPIA*, 1:783. Transport and "contingent costs" for Chicago totaled about $1,100 per annum (per Statement of Account, above).

45. Furs and Peltries Received, 1 Jan.–31 Mar. 1810, Chicago Factory Waste Book, ROIT; Goods Purchased, May 1810, ibid.; Debts due the Factory, 31 Dec. 1807, 30 Mar. 1809, and 30 June 1809, Misc. Accounts Chicago Factory, ROIT; Thomas Forsyth to the Secretary of War, 13 Apr. 1815, *CSHSW*, 11:337; White, *Middle Ground*, 479–84, 487–89; Dowd, *Spirited Resistance*, 130–31; Account of Military Agent at Chicago with the Factory, 26 Aug. 1807, Misc. Accounts Chicago Factory, ROIT; Statement of Account of the United States' Indian Factory at Chicago, 30 Sept. 1807 to 30 Sept. 1811, *ASPIA*, 1:792.

46. Russell Magnaghi, "Sandusky Indian Factory," 174, 176; Henry Dearborn to William Davy, 25 Mar. 1806, OSW, LSIA, 2:B:184–85; John Mason to Samuel Tupper, 18 Aug. 1809, LSSIT, ROIT, 2:B:54; Invoices Inward, ROIT, 3:20 and 4:1, 18, 45, 53, 66, and 75; Statement of Account of the U.S. Indian Factory at Sandusky, 31 Dec. 1807 to 30 Sept. 1811, *ASPIA*, 1:793.

47. Statement of Gain or Loss on the United States' Indian Factories, 31 Dec. 1807–30 Sept. 1811, *ASPIA*, 1:784; Journal Entries for 17 and 19 Apr. 1804, in "Plowshares and Pruning Hooks," ed. Joseph Walker, 399, 401; Hill, *John Johnston*, 23–24; T. Tackle to the Earl of Bathurst, 24 Nov. 1812, *CSHSW*, 20:2–3.

48. Tanner, *Atlas*, 106 (Map 21); Magnaghi, "Sandusky Indian Factory," 174–75; Articles Sold, 1 July–11 Aug. 1812, Misc. Accounts Sandusky Factory, ROIT. Osnabrig was coarse linen, used for trousers and sacking; kersey was a coarse British cloth.

49. Articles Wanted for the Factory at Sandusky, 17 Feb. 1807, Misc. Accounts Sandusky Factory, ROIT (quotes). On Northwest Indian consumerism, see Sugden, *Blue Jacket*, 54, 80, 230–31; Richter, "Believing That Many," 614–16; Sadosky, "Rethinking Gnaddenhutten," 199.

50. Russell, *Michigan Voyageurs*, 1–3; Goods Forwarded from Michilimackinac, 30 Apr. 1810, Misc. Accounts Sandusky Factory, ROIT; Magnagni, "Michigan's Indian Factory at Mackinac," 22–25; John Mason to Joseph Varnum, 10 Sept. 1808, *TPUS*, 10:233–35; Mason to William Eustis, 18 Apr. 1809, ibid., 10:277–78; Varnum to Eustis, 10 Nov. 1809, ibid., 10:284–85; Invoices Inward, ROIT, 1796–1822, 4:52; Accounts of the U.S. Indian Factory at Mackinac, 31 Dec. 1807–30 Sept. 1811, *ASPIA*, 1:794; Unsaleable Articles, 30 Sept. 1811, Misc. Accounts Mackinac Factory, ROIT; Varnum to Mason, 30 Sept. 1810, *TPUS*, 10:330–32; Mason to Matthew Irwin and Varnum, 9 Sept. 1808, *CSHSW*, 19:327–28.

51. Varnum to Mason, 30 Sept. 1810, *TPUS*, 10:330; Debts Owed the Factory, 31 Dec. 1810, Misc. Accounts Mackinac Factory, ROIT (quote); Purchase Order of Mssrs. Porlier and Berthelot, 14 Aug. 1811, *CSHSW*, 19:341.

52. Inventory, 31 Mar. 1811, Misc. Accounts Mackinac Factory, ROIT; Inventory, 30 June 1811, ibid.; Statement of Gain and Loss on the United States' Indian Factories, 31 Dec. 1807–30 Sept. 1811, *ASPIA*, 1:784. Varnum also purchased Indian corn and beans, which he probably sold locally.

53. Statement of Gain and Loss on the United States' Indian Factories, 31 Dec. 1807 to 30 Sept. 1811, *ASPIA*, 1:784; Furs and Peltry Forwarded, May 1809, May–June 1810, and Apr.–June 1811, in *Fort Wayne*, Griswold, 563–64, 580–81, and 661–62; Invoices Inward, ROIT, 4: 42, 51, 64; Mason to Henry Dearborn, 9 Oct. 1809, LSSIT, ROIT, 2:B:63–64; Statement of Account of the Indian Factory at Fort Wayne, 31 Dec. 1807 to 30 Sept. 1811, *ASPIA*, 1:791; Hill, *John Johnston*, 22–23.

54. Goods Wanted for the Fort Wayne Trading House, 1 Dec. 1807, 29 Dec. 1808, 14 Jan. 1810, and 24 Feb. 1812, all in Misc. Accounts Fort Wayne Factory, ROIT. See also Daybooks of Fort Wayne Factory, ROIT, for Aug. 1804, Mar.–May 1805, July 1805, and July 1806.

55. John Mason to John Johnston, 19 Jan. 1808, LSSIT, ROIT, 1:A:35–36 (first quote); Goods Wanted for the Fort Wayne Trading House, 1 Dec. 1807 (second quote) and 29 Dec. 1808 (third quote), Misc. Accounts Fort Wayne Factory, ROIT. On the ethnicity of Johnston's customers, see Daybooks of Fort Wayne Factory, ROIT, for Aug. 1804, Jan. 1805, and Oct. 1806.

56. Springer, "Ethnohistoric Study," 222 (quote); Smith, "Wampum."

57. Inventory of Goods on Hand at Fort Wayne Trading House, 31 Mar. 1810, Misc. Accounts Fort Wayne Factory, ROIT. Fishhooks appear in Johnston's merchandise order of 29 Dec. 1808 (ibid.).

58. Harrison to Dearborn, 10 July 1805, in *Governors Messages*, ed. Esarey, 1:150 (first quote); Goods Wanted for the Fort Wayne Trading House, 1 Dec. 1807, Misc. Accounts Fort Wayne Factory, ROIT; Memorandum on Silverware Received from Johnston, 7 Dec. 1808, Memorandum Book, ROIT, 31–33 (second quote); Hill, *John Johnston*, 23; Reports of John Johnston, 10 Sept. 1807 and 29 Dec. 1808 (third quote), Misc. Accounts Fort Wayne Factory, ROIT; Goods Returned to the Superintendent of Indian Trade, 25 May 1808, ibid.; Goods Wanted for the Fort Wayne Trading House, 29 Dec. 1808, ibid; White, *Middle Ground*, 19–20; Shoemaker, *Strange Likeness*, 127–28.

59. T. Tackle to the Earl of Bathurst, 24 Nov. 1812, *CSHSW*, 20:4; Sugden, *Tecumseh*, 212, 258; Henry Dearborn to Johnston, 7 Jan. 1809, Johnston Papers, Reel 1 (Box 1, Folder 2).

60. Griswold, *Fort Wayne*, 51, 55; Dowd, *Spirited Resistance*, 136–40; Journal of Proceedings at the Indian Treaty at Fort Wayne, 1 Sept.–3 Oct. 1809, in *Governors Messages*, ed. Esarey, 1:362–78, esp. 376; Treaty of Fort Wayne, 30 Sept. 1809, in *Indian Affairs*, Kappler, 2:101–2; Owens, *Mr. Jefferson's Hammer*, 200–203; Sugden, *Tecumseh*, 106–7, 182–87, 198–202.

61. Sugden, *Tecumseh*, 171, 258, 270, 274–75; William Wells to William Harrison, 22 July 1812, in *Governors Messages*, ed. Esarey, 2:76–77.

62. Receipt of Lt. Daniel Baker, 18 June 1812, Misc. Accounts Fort Wayne Factory, ROIT.

63. John Mason to David Hogg, 12 Dec. 1807, LSSIT, ROIT, 1:A:17.

Chapter 6

1. Hickey, *War of 1812*, 9–24; Heaton, "Non-Importation"; Jefferson to Albert Gallatin, 8 Apr. 1808, in *Writings of Jefferson*, ed. Lipscomb et al., 11:27 (second quote). "Detached sovereignty" is from Diener and Hagen, *Borders*, 74.

2. Tecumseh's Speech to Governor Harrison, 20–21 Aug. 1810, in *Governors Messages*, ed. Esarey, 1:463–69; Harrison to Secretary of War William Eustis, 13 Aug. and 8 Nov. 1811, ibid., 1:554–55 and 614–15; Sugden, *Tecumseh*, 218–20, 228–36; Extract of a Letter from Captain N. Heald, 15 Apr. 1812, *ASPIA*, 1:806; Extract of a Letter from William Clark, 13 Feb. 1812, ibid., 1:807; [Hunt], "Personal Narrative," *HCPSM*, 8:667–68; John Mason to John Johnston, 14 Sept. 1812, LSSIT, ROIT, 3:C:55; Van Der Zee, "Fur Trade Operations," 508–11; Extracts from a Letter by William Wells, 1 Mar. 1812, *ASPIA*, 1:806.

3. Cleves et al., "Interchange," 544, 554; Risjord, "1812"; Hickey, *Don't Give Up*, 176–78.

4. John Mason to Matthew Irwin, Stephen Johnston, Joseph Varnum, and Jacob Varnum, 19 June 1812, LSSIT, ROIT, 2:B:496.

5. Matthew Irwin to Thomas McKenney, 18 June 1818, Records of the U.S. House of Representatives, HR17A-C12.1, Folder 2; Haeger, *John Astor*, 146–47; Lossing, *Pictorial Field Book*, Chapter 13; Letter from Captain Roberts, 12 July 1812, *HCPSM*, 15:101–2; Roberts to Major Brock, 17 July 1812, ibid., 15:108; Roberts to Colonel Baynes, 17 July 1812, ibid., 15:109; John Askin, Jr. to Unknown, 18 July 1812, ibid., 15:112–13; Estimate of Losses Sustained by the Late Factory at Michilimackinac, 17 July 1812, *ASPIA*, 2:59; Matthew Irwin to John Mason, 16 Oct. 1812, cited in Plaisance, "U.S. Government Factory System," 211.

6. Estimate of Losses Sustained by the Late Factory at Chicago, *ASPIA*, 2:59; Quaife, *Chicago*, 298–300; Edmunds, *Potawatomis*, 184–86. Irwin was captured at Mackinac in July. (Plaisance, "U.S. Government Factory System," 199.)

7. Ferguson, *Illinois in the War*, 61–73; Estimate of Losses Sustained by the Late Factory at Chicago, *ASPIA*, 2:59; Edmunds, *Potawatomis*, 185–88.

8. Hickey, *War of 1812*, 80–84 (quote 82); Sugden, *Tecumseh*, 290–305; Col. Henry Proctor to Major General Brock, 11 Aug. 1812, *HCPSM*, 15:129–130; Brock to Sir George Prevost, 16 Aug. 1812, ibid., 15:132; Mason to Secretary of State James Monroe, 29 Jan. 1813, LSSIT, ROIT, 3:C:124; Peake, *History of the Indian Factory System*, 161.

9. Plaisance, "U.S. Government Factory System," 190; Statement of the Amount of Property Taken or Destroyed by the British, Misc. Accounts Sandusky Factory, ROIT; Deposition of Jacob Varnum, ca. 1812–13, ibid.; Magnaghi, "Sandusky Indian Factory," 177–78.

10. Thornbrough, ed., *Letter Book*, 101n, 173n, 180n; Gov. Harrison to the Secretary of War, 12 Aug. 1812, *TPUS*, 8:189–93; Edmunds, *Potawatomis*, 189–91; Stickney to Secretary William Crawford, 1 Oct. 1815, in *Letter Book*, Thornbrough, 233–34

(quote); Stephen Johnston to Mrs. Stephen Johnston, 24 Aug. 1812, Misc. Papers Mrs. Forest Wilson; Losses Sustained by the United States' Indian Factory at Fort Wayne, *ASPIA*, 2:59.

11. Sugden, *Tecumseh*, 315–16; Van Der Zee, "Fur Trade Operations," 511; Prucha, *Sword*, 111–12; Bennett, "New Perspective," Part Two, 13–15; Inventory, 30 Sept. 1812, Misc. Accounts Fort Madison Factory, ROIT, Box 2, Folder 4; Estimate of Losses Sustained by the Late Factory at Fort Madison, *ASPIA*, 2:59.

12. Plaisance, "U.S. Government Factory System," 235–36; Inventory, 30 June 1813, Misc. Accounts Fort Madison Factory, ROIT, Box 2, Folder 8; Invoice of Goods Delivered to George Sibley, 8 Sept. 1813, ibid., Box 2, Folder 10; Balances Due, ibid., Box 2, Folder 11; Bates to Governor Benjamin Howard, 27 Feb. 1813, *TPUS*, 14:638 (quotes); Pierre Chouteau to the Secretary of War, 20 May 1813, ibid., 14:671–72.

13. Hagan, *Sac and Fox*, 53–58 (first quote 54); William Clark to Unknown, 2 Feb. 1814, *TPUS*, 14:740; Tanner, *Atlas*, 106, 119; Inventory, Factory on Little Manitou, 31 Mar. and 30 June 1814, Misc. Accounts Fort Madison Factory, ROIT, Box 2, Folder 16; Invoice of Furs and Pelts Shipped from Little Manitou, [received] 5 July 1814, ibid., Box 2, Folder 17; Balance Sheet, Des Moines Trading House, 31 Mar. 1813 to 1 Apr. 1814, *ASPIA*, 2:60.

14. Factory Journal, 18 Oct. 1812, Misc. Accounts Osage Factory, ROIT, Folder 1-4; Accounts Current, 31 Dec. 1813, ibid., Folder 1-5; Factory Journal, 30 Sept. and 30 Nov. 1813, ibid.

15. George Sibley to William Clark, 9 July 1813, Sibley Papers, Box 1-2, Folder 14; George to Samuel Sibley, 25 Sept. 1813, ibid.; Factory Journal, Sept.–Oct. 1813, Misc. Accounts Osage Factory, ROIT, Folder 1-5; Contingent Account, 31 Dec. 1813, ibid., Folder 1-5; Sibley to John Mason, 21 June 1814, *TPUS*, 14:774–75; John Mason to William Clark, 31 Aug. 1812, LSSIT, ROIT, 3:C:40–41; Sibley to William Clark, 28 Nov. 1813, ibid., *TPUS*, 14:712–14 (quotes).

16. William Clark to George Sibley, 17 Mar. 1814, Sibley Papers, Box 1-2, Folder 15; Governor Edwards to the Secretary of War, 26 July 1814, *TPUS*, 16:451–52; Hagan, *Sac and Fox*, 62–76; Tanner, *Atlas*, 119–20; George to Samuel Sibley, 12 Aug. 1814, Sibley Papers, Box 1-2, Folder 15.

17. Stagg, "Madison Administration"; John Sibley to William Eustis, 24 June 1812, in "Doctor John Sibley," ed. Garrett, *Southwestern Historical Quarterly* 49 (Jan. 1946): 407–10; Nugent, *Habits of Empire*, 111–16.

18. Dowd, *Spirited Resistance*, 146–57; Saunt, *New Order*, 168–85, 215–21; Estimate of the Stipend of the Creeks, 24 Apr. 1813, *ASPIA*, 1:840; Sugden, *Tecumseh*, 243–51; Nugent, *Habits of Empire*, 117.

19. Dowd, *Spirited Resistance*, 157, 171, 184–85; Martin, *Sacred Revolt*, 125–26; Andrew Jackson to George Colbert, 5 June 1812, in *Correspondence*, ed. Bassett, 1:227; Saunt, *New Order*, 249–72; Davis, "'Remember Fort Mims."

20. Anderson and Cayton, *Dominion of War*, 231–33; Remini, *Jackson and His Indian Wars*, 62–79; Speech of Mushulatubbe, 31 Dec. 1813, *TPUS*, 6:442; George Smith to Andrew Jackson, 22 Nov. 1813, in *Correspondence*, ed. Bassett, 1:358–59; Jackson to John Lowry, 7 Nov. 1813, ibid., 1:342; Thomas Pinckney to Jackson, 9 Jan. 1814, ibid., 1:439; Jackson to Pinckney, 28 Mar. 1814, ibid., 1:489; DeRosier,

Removal of the Choctaw, 34–36; Owsley, *Struggle for the Gulf*, 49, 62; Saunt, *New Order*, 270; Saunt, "Taking Account," 738–46; Sheldon, "Archaeology, Geography," 208–9.

21. Annual Accounts of the Indian Trade Carried on at Fort Hawkins, 31 Mar. 1811–1 Apr. 1812, 31 Mar. 1812–1 Apr. 1813, and 1 Apr. 1813–1 Apr. 1814, all in *ASPIA*, 2:42, 47, and 50; John Mason to James Fulton, 7 July 1812, LSSIT, ROIT, 3:C:12; Daybooks of the Creek Factory, July 1812, July–Sept. 1813, and Jan.–Mar. 1814, Records of the Creek Factory, ROIT, Reel 5.

22. Annual Accounts Particular of the Indian Trade Carried on at Fort Hawkins, 1 Apr. 1813–1 Apr. 1814 and 31 Mar. 1814–1 Apr. 1815, *ASPIA*, 2:50 and 54, respectively; Daybooks of the Creek Factory, 4 July 1813, Records of the Creek Factory, ROIT, Reel 5; Mattison, "Creek Trading House," 183.

23. John Mason to George Gaines, 19 Jan. 1813 and 21 May 1813, LSSIT, ROIT, 3:C:120 and 164; Walter Nugent, *Habits of Empire*, 116; Daybook for 8 Apr. 1814, Recs. Choctaw TH, ROIT, Reel 5. The author has extrapolated merchandise and peltry sales from the annual changes in the factory's capital stock, plus accounts of merchandise received and unsold peltries in storage, in Annual Accounts of Indian Trade Carried on at the Choctaw Trading House, 31 Mar. 1811–1 Apr. 1812, 31 Mar. 1812–1 Apr. 1813, and 31 Mar. 1813–1 Apr. 1814, all in *ASPIA*, 2:38, 43, and 48.

24. Cushman, *History of the Choctaw,* 317–18; Contingent Expenses, 21 July and 15 Aug. 1813, Recs. Choctaw TH, ROIT, Reel 4; Daybooks for 2 May, 9 May, 18 May, 21 May, 23 May, 27 May, 6 June, 20 June, and 29 Oct. 1814, ibid., Reel 5; Plaisance, "Choctaw Trading House," 412–13; Harry Toulmin to John Graham, 10 Mar. 1812, *TPUS*, 6:283; Governor Holmes to the Secretary of War, 29 June 1812, ibid., 6:297; Lossing, *Pictorial Field Book*, Chapter 34; Plaisance, "U.S. Government Factory System," 285–87.

25. Daybooks for 27 June and 7 Oct. 1814, Recs. Choctaw TH, ROIT, Reel 5; Annual Accounts Particular of the Indian Trade Carried on at Choctaw Trading House, 31 Mar. 1813–1 Apr. 1814 and 31 Mar. 1814–1 Apr. 1814, *ASPIA* 2:48 and 52; John Mason to George Gaines, 24 Sept. 1814 and 14 Aug. 1815, LSSIT, ROIT, 3:C:243 and 414–15, respectively; Plaisance, "Choctaw Trading House," 415–17.

26. John Mason to Robert Bayly, 20 May 1813, LSSIT, ROIT, 3:C:160–61; Factory Journal, 10 May 1814, Misc. Accounts Chickasaw Bluffs Factory, ROIT; Articles Wanted for Fall 1812, ibid.; Receipt for Merchandise Left by Indians as Pledges at Arkansas Factory, 6 Dec. 1813, ibid.; Chickasaw Bluffs Factory Accounts, 31 Dec. 1812, 30 June 1813, and 30 Sept. 1814, ibid.; Factory Journal, 6 May–31 Dec. 1814, ibid.; Plaisance, "Chickasaw Bluffs Factory," 47–49; Gibson, *Chickasaws*, 97–98. The author has estimated 1814 peltry purchases by subtracting the peltries received by Isaac Rawlings upon his arrival at the factory from those shipped to New Orleans in Mar. 1815. (Inventory of Public Peltries . . . Delivered to Isaac Rawlings, 10 May 1814, Misc. Accounts Chickasaw Bluffs Factory, ROIT; Daybooks for 4, 13, and 28 Mar. 1815, ibid.)

27. John Sibley to John Armstrong, 4 Sept., 3 Oct., and 6 Oct. 1813, in "Doctor John Sibley," ed. Garrett, 49 (Apr. 1946): 599–603; Thomas Linnard to John

Mason, 14 Oct. 1813, Letter Book of Natchitoches–Sulphur Fork Factory, ROIT, 62–63 (quote); Linnard to Mason, 9 Apr. 1815, cited in "U.S. Government Factory System," Plaisance, 339. On Dehahuit, see Smith, "Dehahuit," 155.

28. Annual Account of Indian Trade Carried on at Natchitoches, 31 Mar. 1813–1 Apr. 1814, *ASPIA*, 2:50; Thomas Linnard to John Mason, 8 Dec. 1813, Letter Book of Natchitoches–Sulphur Fork Factory, ROIT, 65 (quote); Mason to Linnard, 12 Sept. 1814, 14 Dec. 1814, and 20 Feb. 1815, LSSIT, ROIT, 3:C:242, 274, and 298, respectively; Daybooks for Jan.–Dec. 1812, Jan.–Mar. and July–Dec. 1813, Jan.–Dec. 1814, and Jan.–Sept. 1815, Misc. Accounts Natchitoches–Sulphur Fork Factory, ROIT, Box 1, Folder 4 and Box 2, Folder 1. Linnard bought 10,000 pounds of bear's oil in 1813–14.

29. John Sibley to William Eustis, 9 Feb., 17 July, and 31 Dec. 1811, in "Doctor John Sibley," ed. Garrett, 48 (Apr. 1945): 547–49, 49 (July 1945): 116–19, and 49 (Jan. 1946): 403–5, respectively; Mason to Thomas Linnard, 2 Dec. 1812, LSSIT, ROIT, 3:C:102–3; Linnard to Mason, 14 Feb. 1811, Letter Book of Natchitoches–Sulphur Fork Factory, ROIT, 24; Linnard to Mason, 1 Feb. and 8 July 1813, ibid., 47–48, 57.

30. Thomas Linnard to Mason, 8 Dec. and 15 Dec. 1813, Letter Book of Natchitoches–Sulphur Fork Factory, ROIT, 65, 69; Mason to Linnard, 14 Dec. 1814, LSSIT, ROIT, 3:C:274.

31. Mason to John Johnston, 19 Jan. 1813, LSSIT, ROIT, 3:C:118; Ramsey Crooks to John Astor, 1 Dec. 1813, *CSHSW*, 19: 349; Sales Books, ROIT, Vol. 1, n.p.; 2: 65–73; Plaisance, "U.S. Government Factory System," 369; and see Tables 6-1 and 6-2.

32. Plaisance, "Factory System," 379–81; Hickey, *War of 1812*, 153–54, 176, 197–201; Mason to John Johnston, 12 Sept. 1814, LSSIT, ROIT, 3:C:242; List of Balances Due the Superintendent of Indian Trade, 31 Mar. 1815, *ASPIA*, 2:35.

33. Hickey, *War of 1812*, 194–95, 201–4, 257–78; Horsman, *War of 1812*, 153–64; Banner, *To the Hartford Convention*, 294–350; Taylor, *Internal Enemy*, 245–73; Hickey, *Don't Give Up*, 176.

34. LaVere, *Caddo Chiefdoms*, 134–35.

35. Edmunds, "Loyal Shawnee"; Saunt, *New Order*, 264–72; Dowd, *Spirited Resistance*, 131–35, 149–61, 181–85; Statement of Merchandise Prepared for Annuities, 26 June 1812, LSSIT, ROIT, 3:C:6–7.

36. Edmunds, *Potawatomis*, 185–86; Crooks to Astor, 1 Dec. 1813, *CSHSW*, 19: 350 (quotes).

37. Between 1803 and 1811, the top five factories receiving the most merchandise from the Office of Indian Trade were Chickasaw Bluffs, Saint Stephens, Natchitoches, Bellefontaine, and Fort Osage. All but Bellefontaine served nations whose warriors allied with the United States.

Chapter 7

1. The Treaty of Ghent (24 Dec. 1814) is in *Statutes*, Peters, 8: 218–24.

2. Howe, *What Hath God Wrought*, 74–76; Prucha, *American Indian Treaties*, 135–55; Rohrbough, *Trans-Appalachian West*, 130, 163, 188.

3. Article Nine of the Treaty of Ghent, in *Statutes*, Peters, 8: 223–24; Act . . . to Regulate Trade and Intercourse with the Indian Tribes, 29 Apr. 1816, ibid., 3: 332–33; Calloway, "End of an Era," 3–4, 7, 10–11; Weeks, *John Quincy Adams*, 43–46; Howe, *What Hath God Wrought*, 74–75, 96–97, 107–9; Nugent, *Habits of Empire*, 120–29.

4. Report of the Secretary of War, 13 Mar. 1816, *ASPIA*, 2: 26–27.

5. Ryan, *Cradle*, 65–144; Bloch, "Gendered Meanings"; Richter, " 'Believing That Many.' "

6. Haeger, *John Astor*, 176–78, 184–86; Thomas McKenney to John Astor, 29 Apr. 1816, LSSIT, ROIT, 4:D:28.

7. Viola, *Thomas McKenney*, 2–5; McKenney, *Memoirs*, 22, 26–28; McKenney to George Graham, 20 Apr. 1816, LSSIT, ROIT, 4:D:8; Invoices Outward, ROIT, 3: 43, 45–87, 134; McKenney to George Gaines, 6 Aug. 1817, LSSIT, ROIT, 4:D:387; and see Table 7-1. The figures cover goods shipped between April 1816 and April 1817. Some recipients received payment in cash—see McKenney to John Johnston, 22 May 1816, LSSIT, ROIT, 4:D:44.

8. Invoices Inward, ROIT, 5: 1–98; Invoices Outward, ROIT, 3: 65, 133; McKenney to Joseph Lopez Dias, 10 Dec. 1816 and 6 May 1817, LSSIT, ROIT, 4:D:179 and 297; Abstracts of Merchandise Purchased and Packed for the Factories at Chicago, Green Bay, and Fort Osage, 11 July 1817, Misc. Accounts Green Bay Factory, ROIT, Folder 1; McKenney to Simpkins and Usher, 17 June 1816, ibid., 4:D:61; McKenney to Henry Deringer, 31 July 1816, ibid., 4:D:91; Russell Magnaghi, "Sulphur Fork Factory," 178; McKenney to Jeremiah Bronaugh, 22 Apr. 1816, LSSIT, ROIT, 4:D:9; McKenney to Israel Pickens, 26 Feb. 1817, ibid., 4:D:249–52 (quote 250); Plaisance, "U.S. Government Factory System," 531–32, 535–37.

9. McKenney to W. M. Rich, 9 May 1817, LSSIT, ROIT, 4:D:300; McKenney to Wooley, 15 Apr. 1816, ibid., 4:D:3; McKenney to Daniel Hughes, 28 Oct. 1816, ibid., 4:D:160; McKenney to Joseph Saul, 28 Aug. 1816, ibid., 4:D:125; Invoice of Indian Stores Forwarded to the Factor at Green Bay, 18 June 1818, Misc. Accounts Green Bay Factory, ROIT, Folder 1; Plaisance, "U.S. Government Factory System," 538; Plaisance, "Choctaw Trading House," 418–19; McKenney to George Gaines, 19 Apr. 1817, LSSIT, ROIT, 4:D:283 (but cf. McKenney to Gaines of 10 Sept. 1817, ibid., 4:D:401–2); Statement Showing Transactions at the Indian Trading-Houses since the Peace, 30 Apr. 1820, *ASPIA*, 2:208.

10. Sales Books, ROIT, Vol. 1; Viola, *Thomas McKenney*, 20; Plaisance, "U.S. Government Factory System," 545; Table 7-2. In these sales deerskins were sold by the pack, the author has assumed that one pack weighed 100 pounds.

11. John Mason to George Gaines, 14 Aug. 1815, LSSIT, ROIT, 3:C:414–15; Statement Showing the Transactions of the Indian Trading-Houses, *ASPIA*, 2:208; Invoices Outward, ROIT, 3: 53, 60, 80–87, 113–23, 173–79, 181, 207–11, 213–16, 220, 238–44, 264–72, 277; Jeremiah Bronaugh to Gaines, 6 Aug. 1817, *TPUS*, 18:135 (quote).

12. Thomas McKenney to John Hersey, 13 Oct. 1819, *TPUS*, 18:713–15; Plaisance, "U.S. Government Factory System," 498–99, 502–4; Final Inventory of the Choctaw Factory, 1 Oct. 1822, Final Inventories, ROIT, 66–70.

13. Treaty of Choctaw Trading House, 24 Oct. 1816, in *Indian Affairs*, Kappler, 2:137; Treaty of Doak's Stand, 18 Oct. 1820, ibid., 2:191–95; DeRosier, *Removal*, 37, 48–52; Remini, *Jackson and His Indian Wars*, 195–205.

14. Andrew Jackson to John McKee, 22 Apr. 1819, *ASPIA*, 2:229; Jackson and Thomas Hinds to the Chiefs and Warriors of the Choctaw Nation, 10 Oct. 1820, ibid., 2:235–37 (quotes); White, *Roots of Dependency*, 113–15.

15. White, *Roots of Dependency*, 105–6, 114–16; Carson, *Searching*, 77–79, 83; Factory Daybooks for 1816, Recs. Choctaw TH, ROIT, Reel 5; Final Inventory of the Choctaw Factory, 1 Oct. 1822, Final Inventories, ROIT, 51–65.

16. Doak's Stand Treaty Conference Journal, 15 and 17 Oct. 1820, *ASPIA*, 2:239–41 (quotes 240); Andrew Jackson and Thomas Hinds to the Secretary of War, 21 Oct 1820, ibid., 2:241–43; List of Donations, 21 Oct. 1820, ibid., 2:244; Carson, *Searching*, 90.

17. Treaty of Doak's Stand, in *Indian Affairs*, Kappler, 2:193–94 (quote); Jackson and Hinds to the Secretary of War, 21 Oct. 1820, *ASPIA*, 2:243. On pre-1830 Choctaw emigrants, see John Jamison to the Secretary of War, 16 June 1819, *TPUS*, 19:77.

18. Daybooks, 4, 13, and 28 Mar. 1815, Misc. Accounts Chickasaw Bluffs Factory, ROIT, Folder 3; Goods Shipped to Joseph Saul and Thomas McKenney, 16 Feb., 21 Mar., and 23 Apr. 1816, ibid., Folder 5; Daybooks, 7 and 29 Mar. 1817, ibid., Folder 5; Journal, 5 Feb. 1818, ibid.; Daybooks, 1 Jan.–31 Mar. 1817, ibid.; McKenney to Isaac Rawlings, 8 Apr. 1817, LSSIT, ROIT, 4:D:274; Nuttall, *Journal of Travels*, 88; and Chapter Two. Deerskin amounts have been rounded to the nearest hundred.

19. List of Goods Wanted for the Indian Trade for the Year 1816, 18 July 1815, Misc. Accounts Chickasaw Bluffs Factory, ROIT, Folder 5 (second quote); List of Goods Wanted for 1817, 30 Sept. 1816, ibid. (first quote); Gibson, *Chickasaws*, 95; Thomas McKenney to Abraham Wooley, 20 Aug. 1816, LSSIT, ROIT, 4:D:118; McKenney to John Calhoun, 17 Mar. 1818, *TPUS*, 15:361–62 (last two quotes); Invoices Outward, ROIT, 2:334–36; ibid., 3:12, 30–31, 42, 52, 61–65, 109–12, 132, 135–36, 158–60, and 182. On "mixed-bloods" see Perdue, *"Mixed-Blood" Indians*, 33–71.

20. Plaisance, "Chickasaw Bluffs Factory," 50–51; Treaty of Cherokee Agency, 8 July 1817, in *Indian Affairs*, Kappler, 2:140–44; Arkansas Cherokee Chiefs to the President, 3 Aug. 1819, *TPUS*, 19:92; Return Meigs to William Crawford, 17 Feb. 1816, ibid., 15:123 (quotes).

21. Receipt to James Davis, David Welch, and Looney Price, 19 Sept. 1818, Misc. Accounts Spadre Bluffs Factory, ROIT, Folder 1; James, *Account*, 4:23–24; List of Debts Due the Indian Factory Near Spadre Bayou, 30 June 1820, Misc. Accounts Spadre Bluffs Factory, ROIT, Folder 3; Factory Journals for Jan.–Dec. 1819, 1 Apr.–30 Sept. 1820, and 1 July–31 Dec. 1821, ibid., Folders 2, 3, and 4, respectively; Factory Journal, Jan.–Sept. 1822, ibid., Folder 5; Factory Debts, 31 Dec. 1821, ibid., Folder 4; Plaisance, "Chickasaw Bluffs Factory," 51–53; Morris, "Traders and Factories," 41–43.

22. Goods Purchased for Peltries, Oct. 1819, Misc. Accounts Spadre Bluffs Factory, ROIT, Folder 2; Goods Traded for Peltry, June 1820, ibid., Folder 3; List of

Indian Debts Due, 1 Apr. 1820, ibid., Folder 3; List of Debts Due the U.S. Indian Factory, 30 June 1820, ibid.; List of Debts Due, 31 Dec. 1821, ibid., Folder 4; Nuttall, *Journal of Travels*, 174, 181; James, *Account*, 4:17–18; DuVal, "Debating Identity," 39–47.

23. William Clark to George Sibley, 14 Apr. 1816 and 11 Nov. 1817, George Sibley Papers, Box 1-2, Folders 16–17; Morris, "Traders and Factories," 40; LaVere, *Contrary Neighbors*, 48–49; DuVal, *Native Ground*, 217, 219, 224; Nuttall, *Journal of Travels*, 191–92; James, *Account*, 4:19–21; William Bradford to the Secretary of War, 4 Feb. 1819 and 4 Mar. 1820, *TPUS*, 19:33–34 and 151; Gov. Miller to the Secretary of War, 24 Mar. 1820, ibid., 19:154.

24. DuVal, *Native Ground*, 223–24, 237–42; LaVere, *Contrary Neighbors*, 50; Matthew Lyons to the Secretary of War, 7 Apr. 1821, *TPUS*, 19:338; Treaty of Hiwassee, 8 July 1817, in *Indian Affairs*, Kappler, 2: 143 (quote); Thomas McKenney to George Graham, 25 Aug. 1817, *TPUS*, 18:137; "Account of the Osage-Cherokee War," 8 Apr. 1821, *TPUS*, 19:344.

25. McKenney to William Crawford, 24 June 1816, LSSIT, ROIT, 4:D:67–69 (quote 68); McKenney to John Calhoun, 16 Feb. 1818, ibid., 4:D:496; Contingent Expenses for the Quarter Ending 31 Dec. 1818, Misc. Accounts Natchitoches–Sulphur Fork Factory, ROIT, Box 2, Folder 4; William McClellan to Thomas McKenney, 4 June 1821, *TPUS*, 19:295; McCrocklin, "Site of Sulphur Fork Factory," 53–56; Magnaghi, "Sulphur Fork Factory," 168–71; Shuck-Hall, *Journey*, 107–8, 135.

26. Magnaghi, "Sulphur Fork Factory," 172–74, 178–80; Daybooks, 22–23 July 1818, Misc. Accounts Natchitoches–Sulphur Fork Factory, ROIT, Box 2, Folder 4 (quote); Receipt to O'Riley Colton, 29 July 1818, ibid.; Daybooks for 6 Apr. 1819 and 4 Aug. 1818, ibid., Folders 3 and 4, respectively; John Fowler to McKenney, 22 Dec. 1819, *TPUS*, 19:130; McCrocklin, "Site of Sulphur Fork Factory," 57–59.

27. Daybooks for 3 Feb. and 2 June 1819, Misc. Accounts Natchitoches–Sulphur Fork Factory, ROIT, Box 2, Folder 3; Daybooks for 31 Mar. 1820, ibid., Box 2, Folder 5; Balances Due the Factory, 31 Mar. 1820, ibid.; Fowler to John Jamison, 16 Apr. 1819, *TPUS* 19:70–71; LaVere, *Caddo Chiefdoms*, 135–39; Shuck-Hall, *Journey*, 118–19.

28. Hämäläinen, *Comanche Empire*, 149–50, 170–75; McKenney to John Fowler, 30 June 1817, LSSIT, ROIT, 4:D:350 (quote). On autonomous Indians described as bandits, see also Nichols, *Red Gentlemen*, 42–43, 82–84, 105, 119, 125, 158.

29. Fowler to McKenney, 14 June and 22 Nov. 1819, *TPUS*, 19:73 and 122, respectively; Fowler to John Jamison, 1 June 1819, ibid., 19:76; Fowler to Robert Coomb, 29 Dec. 1819, ibid., 19:134; Thomas McKenney to the Secretary of War, 8 Jan. 1821, ibid., 19:254 and 254n54; Magnaghi, "Sulphur Fork Factory," 179–80.

30. Magnaghi, "Sulphur Fork Factory," 181–82; Inventory, 31 Mar. 1820, Misc. Accounts Natchitoches–Sulphur Fork Factory, ROIT, Box 2, Folder 5; McKenney to William McClellan, 17 Feb. 1821, *TPUS*, 19:266; McClellan to McKenney, 20 May and 4 June 1821, ibid., 19:293–94 and 295–96; Abstract of Property Received by Robert Johnson, n.d., Misc. Accounts Natchitoches–Sulphur Fork Factory, ROIT, Box 2, Folder 5.

31. George Graham to Daniel Bissell, 4 Aug. 1815, *TPUS*, 15:75; William Clark to George Sibley, 14 Apr. 1816 and 23 Sept. 1817, Sibley Papers, Box 1-2, Folders 16–17; George to Samuel Sibley, 14 Jan. 1816, 26 July 1816, and 10 July 1817 (quote), ibid., Box 1-2, Folders 16–17; Wolferman, *Indomitable Mary Sibley*, 57–58; Aron, *American Confluence*, 158–59, 169; Unrau, *Kansa Indians*, 93–94, 97–99.

32. Statement Showing Transactions at the Indian Trading-Houses since the Peace, 30 Apr. 1820, *ASPIA*, 2:208; John Johnson to George Sibley, 1 Mar. 1819, Sibley Papers, Box 1-2, Folder 19 (quote); Invoices Outward, ROIT, 3: 1–11, 44–45, 51, 58–59, 66–69, 105–8, 130, 133–35, 140, 146–52, 183–88, 201; Articles Necessary to Supply Indian Demands for the Year 1817–18, Misc. Accounts Osage Factory, ROIT, Box 2, Folder 4; Plaisance, "U.S. Government Factory System," 483–84; Isenberg, "Market Revolution," 155; Christian, *Before Lewis and Clark*, 215–16, 251.

33. George Tompkins to George Sibley, 30 July 1819, Sibley Papers, Box 1-2, Folder 19; George Sibley to Samuel Sibley, 10 July 1819, ibid.; Wishart, *Fur Trade*, 47–48; Weber, *Mexican Frontier*, 128; Unrau, *Kansa Indians*, 95–96; Plaisance, "U.S. Government Factory System," 489–90; Viola, *Thomas McKenney*, 48; Invoice of Furs and Peltries Forwarded from the U.S. Trading House at Fort Osage, 16 May 1820, Misc. Accounts Osage Factory, ROIT, Box 2, Folder 7; Isenberg, "Market Revolution," 459.

34. William Clark to George Sibley, 11 Jan. 1817 and 29 Apr. 1819, Sibley Papers, Box 1-2, Folders 17 and 19; Sibley Diaries, 22 Dec. 1817, Lindenwood College Papers, Box 11; Provisions Drawn from the Fort Osage Contractor, 23 Dec. 1817–11 Feb. 1819, in Sibley Diaries, Vol. 10, Lindenwood College Papers, Box 11; Gifts Presented to Kansas, 28 May 1818, in Sibley Diaries, Vol. 10, ibid.; Sibley to Clark, 2 Feb. 1819, ibid.; Preliminary Arrangement for the Purchase and Sale of Lands Made . . . with the Chiefs and Headmen of the Kansas Nation, 20 Sept. 1818, Sibley Papers, Box 1-2, Folder 18.

35. Wolferman, *Indomitable Mary Sibley*, 53, 58, 66–67; Calhoun to William Clark, 20 July 1820, *TPUS*, 15:627–28; McKenney to Paul Baillio, 9 Dec. 1820, LSSIT, ROIT, 6:F:84–85; Factory Journals for Apr.–Aug. 1822, Misc. Accounts Osage Factory, ROIT, Box 2, Folder 7; Factory Journal for 31 Aug., 6 Sept., and 10 Oct. 1822, ibid.; Plaisance, "U.S. Government Factory System," 489–90; Invoices Outward, ROIT, 3:256–60.

36. Murphy, "Women, Networks, and Colonization"; Murphy, *Great Lakes Creoles*, 30–33, 45; Davis, *Frontier Illinois*, 134; Nicholas Boilvin to William Eustis, 11 Feb. 1811, *TPUS*, 14:439; Plaisance, "U.S. Government Factory System," 454; Taylor Berry to James Taylor, 9 July 1814, Taylor Berry Letters (quote); Prucha, *Sword*, 120–21; John Mason to William Clark, 24 Mar. 1815, *TPUS*, 15:19; Contingent Account, 8 July 1815, Misc. Accounts Prairie du Chien Factory, ROIT, Box 3, Folder 1.

37. Receipt to Paul Guitard, 8 July 1815, Misc. Accounts Prairie du Chien Factory, ROIT, Box 3, Folder 1; Factory Journal, 25 July and 25 Sept. 1815, ibid.; George Sibley to Samuel Sibley, 14 Jan. 1816, Sibley Papers, Box 1-2, Folder 16; John Johnson to George Sibley, 28 Apr. 1817, ibid., Box 1-2, Folder 17; Prucha, *Sword*, 125–26; Statement Showing Transactions at the Indian Trading-Houses since the

Peace, 30 Apr. 1820, *ASPIA*, 2:208; Plaisance, "U.S. Government Factory System," 463–64.

38. McKenney to John Johnson, 29 Apr. 1817, LSSIT, ROIT, 4:D:295; Invoices Outward, ROIT, *1815*: 2:337–44, *1816*: 3:13–16, 41–43, 49–50, 69–76, 134, *1817*: 98–104, 132, 135, *1818*: 139, 153–57, 180, *1819*: 189–93, 202, *1820*: 217, 232–36, *1821*: 251–55; Ramsey Crooks and Robert Stuart to John Astor, 24 Jan. 1818, *CSHSW*, 20:28; Factory Journal, 1 Apr. 1822, Misc. Accounts Prairie du Chien Factory, ROIT, Box 1, Folder 5.

39. Statement Showing the Transactions at the Indian Trading-Houses since the Peace, 30 Apr. 1820, *ASPIA*, 2:208; Circular Letter to Factors, 22 July 1817, LSSIT, ROIT, 4:D:376–77; Factory Journal, 31 Dec. 1817, Misc. Accounts Prairie du Chien Factory, ROIT, Box 3, Folder 2 (first quote); Factory Journal, 30 June 1818, ibid., Box 3, Folder 3 (second quote); Cash Book for Quarter Ending 30 June 1820, ibid., Box 1, Folder 1.

40. Plaisance, "U.S. Government Factory System," 467; Inventories, 31 Mar. 1817 and 30 June 1817, Misc. Accounts Prairie du Chien Factory, ROIT, Box 3, Folder 2; Birk, ed., *John Sayer's Journal*, 35–37, 46, 49–50; Nelson, *First Years*, 56, 104–5; Murphy, "Autonomy and Economic Roles," 78–79; Child, *Holding Our World*, 24–26.

41. Factory Journal, 5 June 1820, 16 June 1821, 28 May 1822 and 11 June 1822, Misc. Accounts Prairie du Chien Factory, ROIT, Box 1, Folders 2, 3, and 5, respectively; Accounts Current, 1 Apr.–20 Dec. 1820, ibid., Box 1, Folder 1; Statement Showing Transactions at the Trading-Houses since the Peace, *ASPIA*, 2:208. Where only a cash value was given for 1820–21 lead remittances, the author has assumed a value of five cents per pound.

42. Haeger, *John Astor*, 128, 134, 144, 178, 185–86, 196–97; John Johnson to George Sibley, 1 Mar. 1819, Sibley Papers, Box 1-2, Folder 19 (quote); Viola, *Thomas McKenney*, 79–81; White, "'Give Us a Little Milk,'" 66–71.

43. Factory Journal, 1 Apr. 1822, Misc. Accounts Prairie du Chien Factory, ROIT, Box 1, Folder 5; Abstract of Property Received by Daniel Garrett, 30 Sept. 1822, ibid.

44. Thomas McKenney to James Monroe, 5 Feb. 1819, *CSHSW*, 20:101–2; Plaisance, "U.S. Government Factory System," 475–79; Aron, *American Confluence*, 184–85, 206; Thomas Forsyth to the Secretary of War, 2 Apr. 1818, *TPUS*, 15:379; Tanner, *Atlas*, 140–41; Factory Journal, 31 Aug. 1819 and 25 Aug. 1820, Misc. Accounts Fort Edwards Factory, ROIT, Folder 1; Transactions at the Trading-Houses since the Peace, *ASPIA*, 2:208. The author has estimated that beaver pelts weighed 1.5 pounds each.

45. Factory Journals, Apr.–June 1820 and Apr.–June 1821, Misc. Accounts Fort Edwards Factory, ROIT, Folders 2 and 3; Produce Account, July–Sept. 1820, ibid., Folder 1; Transcript of Journal, July–Sept. 1821, ibid., Folder 1; Invoices Outward, ROIT, 3:161–66, 182, 194–96, 203, 210, 227–28, 247–250; Plaisance, "U.S. Government Factory System," 479–80.

46. Quaife, ed., *Development*, 71–72, 76–77, 80.

47. Ibid., 77–78 (quote); Transactions at the Trading-Houses since the Peace, *ASPIA*, 2:20; McKenney to Jacob Varnum, 19 May 1818, LSSIT, ROIT, 5:E:38;

Plaisance, "U.S. Government Factory System," 439; Varnum to McKenney, 12 July 1818, Records of the U.S. House of Representatives, HR17A-C12.1; Ramsey Crooks to John Astor, 23 June 1817, 21 July 1817, and 21 June 1819, Crooks Letter Book, American Fur Company Ledgers, 18:28–29, 33–34, and 193, respectively.

48. Quaife, ed., *Development*, 78 (quote), 80; Delivery of Indian Articles on Orders of the Agent, 1 July–30 Sept. 1819, Misc. Accounts Chicago Factory, ROIT, Folder 4; Edmunds, *Potawatomis*, 215; Prucha, *Sword*, 147–49; Final Inventory of the Chicago Factory, 15 Oct. 1822, Final Inventories, ROIT, 25–31.

49. Tanner, *Atlas*, 30, 39; Henry Dearborn to William Davy, 30 Dec. 1805, *CSHSW*, 19:311; Invoices Outward, ROIT, 3:17–24, 46–47, 54, 88–92, 133, 167–69, 221–22; Transactions at the Trading-Houses since the Peace, *ASPIA*, 2:208.

50. Transactions at the Trading-Houses, *ASPIA*, 2:208; Plaisance, "U.S. Government Factory System," 449–50; Matthew Irwin to McKenney, 10 Mar. 1817, 2 Aug. 1817, 29 Sept. 1817, and 10 June 1818, Records of the U.S. House of Representatives, HR17A-C12.1, Folder 2; Ninian Edwards to James Monroe, 3 Mar. 1816, *CSHSW*, 19:401; Miller, "Military Occupation," 552.

51. Matthew Irwin to McKenney, 1 Dec. 1819 and 6 Oct. 1821, Records of the House of Representatives, HR17A-C12.1, Folder 2; McKenney to Irwin, 19 May 1821 and 20 Nov. 1821, *CSHSW*, 20:198–99, 233–34; John Calhoun to McKenney, 18 Oct. 1821, ibid., 20:219.

52. Chambers, "Creek Indian Factory," 6 (first quote), 20, 37–38; McKenney to Daniel Hughes, 26 May 1817, *TPUS*, 18:103–4; McKenney to George Graham, 25 Aug. 1817, ibid., 18:137 (second quote); Plaisance, "U.S. Government Factory System," 493–95; McKenney to Hughes, 14 Apr. 1818, LSSIT, ROIT, 5:E:16 (third quote).

53. Daniel Hughes to McKenney, 28 Dec. 1817, *TPUS*, 18:282–83; Chambers, "Creek Indian Factory," 23–31, 40–41, 52; Plaisance, "U.S. Government Factory System," 496; David Mitchell to the Secretary of War, 3 Feb. 1818, *TPUS*, 18:242.

54. Hughes to McKenney, 28 May 1817, *TPUS*, 18:279–80; William Bowen to Hughes, 22 Jan. 1817, ibid., 18:49–50 (first quote 49); Hughes to McKenney, 28 Dec. 1817, ibid., 1:282–83 (second quote 283); Chambers, "Creek Indian Factory," 52; Green, *Politics*, 53, 56–57.

55. McKenney to Hughes, 17 June 1817, *TPUS*, 18:112.

56. Viola, *Thomas McKenney*; Harmon, *Sixty Years*, 128–29.

57. Quaife, *Development*, 81.

58. Ramsey Crooks to Thomas Benton, 1 Apr. 1822, quoted in *American Fur Trade*, Chittenden, 1:15n2.

Chapter 8

1. Dangerfield, *Awakening*, 74–80; Rohrbough, *Land Office Business*, 89–112; Haeger, *John Astor*, 139–44.

2. Dangerfield, *Awakening*, 73–75, 83; Howe, *What Hath God Wrought*, 142–44; Tompkins to George Sibley, 30 July 1819, Sibley Papers, Box 1-2, Folder 19 (first

quote); Wilentz, *Rise of Democracy*, 207–8; Wade, *Urban Frontier*, 166–67, 171–72; Cunningham, *Presidency of Monroe*, 83 (second quote).

3. Benton, *Thirty Years' View*, 1:11 (third quote); Cunningham, *Presidency of Monroe*, 84 (second quote), 111, 118–19; Ammon, *James Monroe*, 462 (first quote), 469–70; Larson, *Market Revolution*, 42–45; Skeen, "Calhoun, Crawford, and Retrenchment," 150–51.

4. Horsman, *Expansion*, 57–59, 108–10, 173; Green, *Politics*, 36–38; Nichols, *Red Gentlemen*, 133–34.

5. Nichols, *Red Gentlemen*, 121–22, 177–78, 194; McClinton, ed., *Moravian Springplace Mission*, 1:342; Thomas Jefferson to James Madison, 7 Dec. 1809, *TPUS*, 10:300–301.

6. Circular Letter of Thomas McKenney to the U.S. Indian Factors, 18 June 1816, LSSIT, ROIT, 4:D:63 (first quote); McKenney to Abraham Wooley, 20 Aug. 1816, ibid., 4:D:118; McKenney to George Sibley, 21 Oct. 1816, ibid., 4:D:153; Martin, *Sacred Revolt*, 94–95 (second quote).

7. Message of Pres. James Madison to Congress, 3 Dec. 1816, in *Messages and Papers*, ed. and comp. Richardson, 2:560–61; McKenney to Isaac Thomas, 14 Dec. 1816, LSSIT, ROIT, 4:D:200–203 (quotes 202).

8. McKenney to Thomas, 14 Dec. 1816 (quote), 23 Dec. 1816, and 3 Jan. 1817, LSSIT, ROIT, 4:D:205–9, 210–14, and 218–22. For Lancastrian instruction, see Berkhofer, *Salvation*, 26–27, 38–39.

9. Herman Viola, *Thomas McKenney*, 33–35.

10. Bloch, "Battling Infidelity"; Andrew, *Rebuilding*, 7–8, 17–24, 36–37, 82–86; Phillips, *Protestant America*, 12–14 (quote), 57–64; Annual Report of the Prudential Committee for 1816, *Panoplist and Missionary Magazine* 12 (Oct. 1816): 451.

11. Bill for Establishing Trading Houses with the Indian Tribes and for the Organization and Encouragement of Schools, 22 Jan. 1818, Records of the U.S. House of Representatives, HR15A-B1; Report of the House Committee on Indian Affairs, 22 Jan. 1818, *ASPIA*, 2:51; Viola, *Thomas McKenney*, 39–40.

12. Circular Letter of the Superintendent of Indian Trade to James Jamieson et al., 7 July 1817, LSSIT, ROIT, 4:D:372–73; McKenney, *Memoirs, Official and Personal*, 35; Viola, *Thomas McKenney*, 41–42; McKenney to John Calhoun, 19 Aug. 1818, *Papers of Calhoun*, 3:36–53.

13. Report of the Secretary of War to Congress, 5 Dec. 1818, *Papers of Calhoun*, 3:349 (first quote); Howe, *What Hath God Wrought*, 192–93; Memorials of the Blue River Association, 14 Sept. 1818 (second through fourth quotes), the Religious Society of Friends of New York, 18 Oct. 1818 (last two quotes), the Religious Society of Friends of Ohio, Indiana, Illinois, and Adjacent Parts of Pennsylvania and Virginia, 20 Nov. 1818, the Yearly Meeting of Friends of Baltimore, (received) 16 Dec. 1818, and the Religious Society of Friends of Pennsylvania, New Jersey, Delaware, and Eastern Maryland, 1 Jan. 1819, all in Records of the U.S. House of Representatives, HR15A-G6.1; Memorial of Mississippi Baptist Association, (received) 12 Jan. 1819, ibid., HR15A-G6.2.

14. Report of the House Committee on Indian Affairs, 15 Jan. 1819, *ASPIA*, 2:185–86; Draft "Act Making Provision for the Civilization of the Indian Tribes,"

AC, 15/2, 1:246–47. The members of the Senate Committee on Indian Affairs were Thomas Williams (Mississippi), John Williams (Tennessee), Waller Taylor (Indiana), John Crittenden (Kentucky), and Jeremiah Morrow (Ohio). (Proceedings of 18 Nov. 1818, *AC*, 15/2, 1:20.)

15. Circular Letter of the Secretary of War, 3 Sept. 1819, *ASPIA*, 2:201; Report of the Secretary of War to Congress, 15 Jan. 1820, ibid., 2:200; Report of the House Committee on Indian Affairs, 23 Mar. 1824, *ASPIA*, 2:457–59.

16. Richter, "'Believing That Many,'" 616–18; Watts, *Republic Reborn*, 140; Sellers, *Market Revolution*, 104, 119–21 (quotes 121, 104).

17. Report of the Superintendent of Indian Trade to the House Committee on Indian Affairs, 30 Nov. 1820, *ASPIA*, 2:223.

18. Ronda, *Astoria and Empire*, 293–301; Haeger, *John Astor*, 139–40, 148–51, 199–200; Remini, *Henry Clay*, 176–77; Ammon, *James Monroe*, 670n23; Gallatin to James Madison, 16 Apr. 1816, in Gallatin, *Writings*, 1:697.

19. Haeger, *John Astor*, 184–86; John Astor to Ramsey Crooks, 17 Mar. 1817, *CSHSW*, 19:451; Ronda, *Astoria and Empire*, 202, 239; Lavender, *Fist*, 1–2.

20. George Graham to William Puthuff, 5 June 1816, *CSHSW*, 19:419; Haeger, *John Astor*, 192, 195–97, 206; McKenney to Acting Secretary of War George Graham, 19 Mar. 1817, *CSHSW*, 19:452; Lavender, *Fist*, 276–77.

21. The forts were Detroit, Chicago, Green Bay, Prairie du Chien, Fort Edwards, and Fort Saint Anthony (later Fort Snelling). See Prucha, *Sword*, 125–28, 147–49.

22. John Astor to Albert Gallatin, 9 Oct. 1815, cited in *Life of Albert Gallatin*, Henry Adams, 555; Gallatin to Astor, 5 Aug. 1835, in *Writings*, Gallatin, Vol. 2; Haeger, *John Astor*, 179.

23. Viola, *Thomas McKenney*, 50–51; Porter, *Astor*, 2:708–12; Haeger, *Astor*, 209–10; Lewis Cass to John Calhoun, 14 Sept. 1818, *Papers of Calhoun*, 3:126 (quote). See also Ninian Edwards to William Crawford, Nov. 1815, *ASPIA*, 2:63–66.

24. Harmon, *Sixty Years*, 124–25; Lavender, *Fist*, 278–79; Haeger, *Astor*, 176–77; Thomas Benton to William Preston, 27 Apr. 1817, Benton Collection, Box 1; Astor to Charles Gratiot, 8 Apr. 1814 and 24 Apr. 1815, John Astor Papers; Aron, *American Confluence*, 180, 193–94; Gitlin, *Bourgeois Frontier*, 39, 69–70, 130; Ramsey Crooks to Benton, 28 July 1819, Crooks Letterbook, American Fur Company Ledgers; Mueller, *Senator Benton*, 77–78, 90.

25. Acts to Continue in Force . . . An Act for Establishing Trading Houses with the Indians, 3 Mar. 1815 and 3 Mar. 1817, in *Statutes*, Peters, 3:239 and 363; Act Directing the Manner of Appointing Indian Agents Etc., 16 Apr. 1818, ibid., 3:428; House Resolution of 4 April 1818, *AC*, 15/1, p. 1675; Thomas McKenney to John Calhoun, 19 Aug. 1818, *Papers of Calhoun*, 3:46–51; Lewis Cass to Calhoun, 1 Oct. 1818, ibid., 3:178; William Trimble to Calhoun, 27 Nov. 1818, ibid., 3:310; Report of Secretary Calhoun to Henry Clay, 5 Dec. 1818, ibid., 3:344–45.

26. Peters, *Statutes*, 3:514, 544, and 641, respectively; McKenney to Daniel Hughes, 29 Mar. 1819, LSSIT, ROIT, 5:E:250; Calhoun to Henry Clay, 12 Apr. 1820, *ASPIA*, 2:207; McKenney to Calhoun, 14 Apr. 1820, ibid., 2:247; Calhoun to Rep. John Taylor, 18 Jan. 1821, ibid.; McKenney to Henry Southard, 28 Feb. 1821, *CSHSW*, 20:190–92.

27. Lavender, *Fist*, 294; Stuart and Crooks to Astor, 24 Jan. 1818, *CSHSW*, 20:26–29; Viola, *Thomas McKenney*, 60–61.

28. William Woodbridge to Lewis Cass, 20 Mar. 1820, *TPUS*, 11:20–21; Lavender, *Fist*, 303–4; Viola, *Thomas McKenney*, 61–63; Haeger, *Astor*, 210; McKenney to Henry Southard, 28 Feb. 1821, *CSHSW*, 20:190–92.

29. Proceedings of 24 Feb. 1821, *AC*, 16/2, p. 1227; Ambler, *Life and Diary*, 53–54; Lavender, *Fist*, 312.

30. McKenney to Sibley, 21 June 1821, *TPUS*, 15:734–35 (quotes); Morgan, *Inventing the People*, 209–33.

31. Viola, *Thomas McKenney*, 64–65; Proceedings of 10 Dec. 1821, *AC*, 17/1, p. 529; Memorial of the Genesee Annual Conference of the Methodist Episcopal Church, 25 July 1821, Records of the U.S. House of Representatives, HR17A-F6.1; Petitions of the Citizens of the State of Ohio, received 24 Dec. 1821, 15 Jan. 1822, 21 Jan. 1822, and 12 Feb. 1822, ibid.; Petition of the Inhabitants of the State of Maryland, 7 Jan. 1822, ibid., Petition of the Trustees of Dickinson College and the Inhabitants of Carlisle, 11 Jan. 1822, ibid.; Petitions of the Inhabitants of Pennsylvania, 14 Jan. 1822, ibid. (first four quotes).

32. McKenney to John Johnson, 22 Jan. 1822, *CSHSW*, 20:240 (first quote); Report of McKenney to Henry Johnson, 27 Dec. 1821, *ASPIA*, 2:261–64 (remaining quotes).

33. Testimony of John Biddle, 19 Jan. 1822, *ASPIA*, 2:326–27 (first quote); Testimony of Benjamin O'Fallon, 22 Jan. 1822, ibid., 2:328; Testimony of John Bell, 23 Jan. 1822, ibid., 2:329 (fourth quote); Testimony of Ramsey Crooks, 23 Jan. 1822, ibid., 2:330–31 (second, third, and fifth quotes); *Missouri Enquirer*, 27 Apr. 1822 (last quote).

34. Senate Bill S.57, Bills and Resolutions of the Senate, 17th Congress, 1st Session (1822); Proceedings of 25 Feb., 8 Mar., 21 Mar. 1822, *AC*, 17/1, 235–37, 279, 313–14.

35. Speech of Thomas Benton, 25 Mar. 1822, *AC*, 17/1, 317–18, 322–28.

36. Ibid., 318–20 (quotes 318–19). The Latin quote, "reclining beneath the cover of a spreading beech," is from Virgil, *Eclogues*, I.1. Corydon and Amaryllis were from the same source.

37. Lucas, "Civilization or Extinction"; Griffin, *American Leviathan*, 29–30, 41, 254–55, 347n58.

38. Proceedings of 26–28 Mar. and 1 Apr. 1822, *AC*, 17/1, 339–43 (quotes 342), 351–52, 354–55, 357.

39. Viola, *Thomas McKenney*, 69; *National Intelligencer*, 18 Apr. 1822 (quotes) and 3 May 1822.

40. Proceedings of 4 May 1822, *AC*, 17/1, 1787; McKenney, *Memoirs*, 25; Act to Abolish the United States' Trading Establishment with the Indian Tribes, 6 May 1822, in *Statutes*, Peters, 3:679–80; General and Consolidated Statements of Property Received, *ASPIA*, 2:514; Abstract of Payments Made by George Graham, 15 June 1822–1 Dec. 1823, ibid., 2:516; Report of the Committee on Indian Affairs, 25 May 1824, ibid., 2:513. At its closure, the Office of Indian Trade had net assets (gross assets minus its own debts) of $269,000.

41. List of Persons Employed in the Indian Trade Department, 1 Apr. 1818, *ASPIA*, 2:163.

42. Statement of Appropriations and Expenditures of Trading-Houses, 4 Mar. 1789 to 31 Dec. 1819, *ASPIA*, 2:211.

43. Edwards to William Crawford, Nov. 1815, *ASPIA*, 2:63–66. Ora Peake made some of these points in her *History*, 218–30.

44. Ninian Edwards to William Crawford, Nov. 1815, *ASPIA*, 2:63–66; Wesley, "Government Factory System," 494. On the Indian population of the United States east of the Mississippi, see Speech of Thomas Metcalfe, 4 May 1822, *AC*, 17/1, 194.

45. Binnema and Dobak, "'Like the Greedy Wolf,'" 431–38; Act to Enable the President to Hold Treaties, 25 May 1824, in *Statutes*, Peters, 3:35–36; Report of Henry Atkinson and Benjamin O'Fallon, 7 Nov. 1825, *ASPIA*, 2:605–8; Fenn, *Encounters*, 283–85.

46. Wishart, *Fur Trade*, 52–54 (quote 53); Sunder, *Fur Trade*, 27–28.

47. Prucha, *American Indian Treaties*, 187–92, 221; Humins, "Fur, Astor, and Indians," 30; Wyman, *Wisconsin Frontier*, 167–69 (first quote); Dolin, *Fur, Fortune, and Empire*, 275–78 (second quote 278).

48. Gitlin, "Private Diplomacy," quote 90; Young, *Redskins, Ruffleshirts, Rednecks*; White, *Railroaded*, 17–36; Emile Boutmy, *Studies in Constitutional Law*, quoted in *The Frontier in American History*, Frederick Turner (New York, 1953), 211.

Bibliography

Archival Sources

Astor, John Jacob, Papers. Photostats and Typescripts of Originals in Baker Library, Harvard University. Missouri Historical Society Library and Research Center, Saint Louis.

Benton, Thomas Hart, Collection. Manuscript. Missouri Historical Society Library and Research Center, Saint Louis.

Berry, Taylor, Letters. Manuscript. Filson Historical Society, Louisville, Kentucky.

Creek Indian Letters, Talks, and Treaties. Typescript. Georgia Dept. of Archives and History, Atlanta.

Crooks, Ramsey, Letterbook, 1816–20. American Fur Company Ledgers, American Fur Company Ledgers. Papers of the Saint Louis Fur Trade. Microfilm, Reel 18. Missouri Historical Society Library and Research Center, Saint Louis.

Documents Relating to the Negotiation of Ratified and Unratified Treaties with Various Indian Tribes, 1801–1869. Microfilm, T-994. National Archives, Washington, D.C. Online via http://digicoll.library.wisc.edu/History /subcollections/IndianTreatiesMicroAbout.html (Accessed 27 April 2009).

Harmar, Josiah, Collection. Manuscript. Clements Library, Ann Arbor, Michigan.

Irvine–Newbold Family Papers. Manuscript. Historical Society of Pennsylvania, Philadelphia.

Johnston, John, Papers, 1801–1860. Microfilm, MIC 125. Ohio Historical Society, Columbus.

Letters Received by the Office of the Secretary of War Relating to Indian Affairs, 1800–1823. Microfilm, M-271. National Archives, Washington, D.C.

Lindenwood College Papers. Manuscript. Missouri Historical Society Library and Research Center, Saint Louis.

Miscellaneous Papers of Mrs. Forest Wilson, 1810-ca. 1840. Manuscript, VFM 482. Ohio Historical Society, Columbus.

Papers of the Continental Congress, 1774–1789. Microfilm. National Archives, Washington, D.C.

Records of the Cherokee Indian Agency in Tennessee, 1801–1835. Microfilm, M-208. National Archives, Washington, D.C.

Records of the Office of Indian Trade. National Archives, Washington, D.C.

Arkansas Factory Daybook, 1805–1810. Manuscript, Entry 28.

Chicago Factory Waste Book, 1808–1810. Manuscript, Entry 35.

Day Books of the Chickasaw Bluffs Factory, 1806–1807. Manuscript, Entry 38.

Day Books of the Fort Wayne Factory, 1803–1812. Manuscript, Entry 57.

Final Inventories, 1822–23. Manuscript, Entry 24.

Invoices Inward, 1796–1822. 5 volumes. Manuscript, Entry 15.

Invoices Outward, 1803–24. 4 volumes. Manuscript, Entry 17.

Letter Book of the Arkansas Trading House, 1805–1810. Microfilm, M-142.

Letter Book of the Creek Trading House, 1795–1821. Microfilm, M-4.

Letter Book of the Natchitoches—Sulphur Fork Factory, 1809–1821. Microfilm, T-1029.

Letters Received by the Superintendent of Indian Trade, 1806–1824. Microfilm, T-58.

Letters Sent by the Superintendent of Indian Trade, 1807–1822. Microfilm, M-16.

Memorandum Book, 1807–1813. Manuscript, Entry 6.

Miscellaneous Accounts of the Arkansas Factory, 1805–1810. Manuscript, Entry 32.

Miscellaneous Accounts of the Bellefontaine Factory, 1805–1809. Manuscript, Entry 33.

Miscellaneous Accounts of the Chicago Factory, 1805–1822. Manuscript, Entry 37.

Miscellaneous Accounts of the Chickasaw Bluffs Factory. Manuscript, Entry 39.

Miscellaneous Accounts of the Fort Edwards Factory, 1818–23. Manuscript, Entry 55.

Miscellaneous Accounts of the Fort Madison Factory, 1808–1815. Manuscript, Entry 56.

Miscellaneous Accounts of the Fort Wayne Factory. Manuscript, Entry 58.

Miscellaneous Accounts of the Mackinac Factory, 1808–1812. Manuscript, Entry 60.

Miscellaneous Accounts of the Natchitoches—Sulphur Fork Factory, 1805–1823. Manuscript, Entry 68.

Miscellaneous Accounts of the Osage Factory, 1808–1823. Manuscript, Entry 69.

Miscellaneous Accounts of the Prairie du Chien Factory, 1815–1822. Manuscript, Entry 71.

Miscellaneous Accounts of the Sandusky Factory, 1806–1812. Manuscript, Entry 72.

Miscellaneous Accounts of the Spadre Bluffs (Illinois Bayou) Factory, 1818–1824. Manuscript, Entry 73.

Miscellaneous Records of the Cherokee Trading House, 1796–1810. Manuscript, Entry 34.

Miscellaneous Records of the Detroit Factory, 1802–1804. Manuscript, Entry 54.

Records of the Choctaw Trading House, 1803–1824. Microfilm, T-500.

Records of the Creek Factory, 1795–1821. Microfilm, M-1334.

Sales Books, 1807–1822. 2 volumes. Manuscript, Entry 20.

Records of the Office of the Secretary of War Relating to Indian Affairs. Letters Sent, 1800–1823. Microfilm, M-15. National Archives, Washington, D.C.

Records of the United States House of Representatives. National Archives, Record Group 233, Washington, D.C.

St. Clair, Arthur, Papers. Microfilm. Ohio Historical Society, Columbus.

Sibley, George Champlain, Papers. Manuscript. Missouri Historical Society Library and Research Center, Saint Louis.

The Papers of George Washington. Microfilm. Library of Congress, Washington, D.C.

Newspapers

The Missouri Enquirer, 27 Apr. 1822
The National Intelligencer, 18 Apr. and 3 May 1822
The Panoplist and Missionary Magazine, Oct. 1816
The Scioto Gazette, 15 July 1805

Other Published Primary Sources

Ambler, Charles. *The Life and Diary of John Floyd*. Richmond, Virginia: Richmond Press, 1918.

Bakeless, John, ed. *The Journals of Lewis and Clark*. New York: New American Library, 1964.

Bassett, John Spencer, ed. *Correspondence of Andrew Jackson*. 7 vols. Washington, D.C: Carnegie Institute, 1926–1935.

Baxter, James, ed. *Documentary History of the State of Maine*. 25 vols. Portland, Maine: Fred L. Tower Company, 1876–1916.

Beltrami, Giacomo C. *A Pilgrimage in Europe and America, Leading to the Discovery of the Sources of the Mississippi*. 2 vols. London: Hunt and Clark, 1828.

Benton, Thomas Hart. *Thirty Years' View*. 2 vols. New York: D. Appleton and Company, 1854.

Birk, Douglas A., ed. *John Sayer's Snake River Journal, 1804–05: A Fur Trade Diary from East Central Minnesota*. Minneapolis: Institute for Minnesota Archaeology, 1989.

Blane, William. *An Excursion through the United States and Canada during the Years 1822–23*. London: Baldwin, Craddock, and Joy, 1824.

Brackenridge, Henry Marie. *Journal of a Voyage up the River Missouri in 1811*. In *Early Western Travels, 1748–1846*, edited by Reuben Gold Thwaites. Vol. 6. Cleveland, Ohio: A.H. Clark, 1904.

Brandt, Penny, ed. "A Letter of Dr. John Sibley, Indian Agent." *Louisiana History* 29 (Fall 1988): 365–87.

Brown, Everett, ed. *William Plumer's Memorandum of Proceedings in the United States Senate, 1803–1807*. New York: Macmillan Co., 1923.

Calloway, Colin, ed. *Dawnland Encounters: Indians and Europeans in Northern New England*. Hanover, N.H.: University Press of New England, 1991.

————, ed. *North Country Captives: Selected Narratives of Indian Captivity from Vermont and New Hampshire*. Hanover, N.H.: University Press of New England, 1992.

Carter, Clarence, and John Porter Bloom, eds. *The Territorial Papers of the United States*. 26 vols. Washington, D.C: U.S. Government Printing Office, 1934–1973.

Corbitt, D. C., ed. "Papers Related to the Georgia-Florida Frontier, 1784–1800." *Georgia Historical Quarterly*, Vol. 24 (June 1940): 150–57.

Craig, Neville, ed. *The Olden Time*. 2 vols. Cincinnati: Robert Clarke & Co., 1876.

Cuming, Fortescue. *Sketches of a Tour to the Western Country*. In *Early Western Travels, 1748–1846*, edited by Reuben Gold Thwaites. Vol. 4. Cleveland, Ohio: A.H. Clark, 1904.

Denny, W. H., ed. *The Military Journal of Ebenezer Denny, An Officer in the Revolutionary and Indian Wars*. Philadelphia: J.B. Lippincott & Co., 1859.

Esarey, Logan, ed. *Governors Messages and Letters*. 2 vols. Indianapolis: Indiana Historical Commission, 1922.

Featherstonhaugh, George W. *A Canoe Voyage up the Minnay Sotor*. 2 vols. London: Richard Bentley, 1847.

Fitzpatrick, John C., ed. *The Writings of George Washington from the Original Manuscript Sources*. 39 vols. Washington, D.C: U.S. Government Printing Office, 1931–1944.

Ford, Paul L., ed. *The Works of Thomas Jefferson*. 12 vols. New York: G.P. Putnam's Sons, 1903.

Ford, Worthington, Gaillard Hunt, John Clement Fitzpatrick, Roscoe R. Hill, Kenneth E. Harris, and Steven D. Tilley, eds. *Journals of the Continental Congress, 1774–1789*. 34 vols. Washington, D.C.: U.S. Government Printing Office, 1907–1934.

Foster, H. Thomas, II, ed. *The Collected Works of Benjamin Hawkins, 1796–1810*. Tuscaloosa: University of Alabama Press, 2003.

Gambrel, Herbert Pickens, ed. *Memoirs of Mary Israel Ellet*. Doylestown, Pa.: Bucks County Historical Society, 1939.

Gales, Joseph, comp. and ed. *Annals of the Congress of the United States*. 42 vols. Washington, D.C.: Gales and Seaton, 1834–1856.

Gallatin, Albert. *The Writings of Albert Gallatin*. 3 vols. New York: Antiquarian Pres, 1960.

Garrett, Julia, ed. "Doctor John Sibley and the Louisiana–Texas Frontier, 1803–1814." *Southwestern Historical Quarterly* 45, No. 3 (Jan. 1942); 49, No. 4 (Apr. 1946).

Grant, C. L., ed. *Letters, Journals, and Writings of Benjamin Hawkins*. 2 vols. Savannah: Beehive Press, 1980.

Griswold, Bert. *Fort Wayne: Gateway of the West, 1802–1813*. Indianapolis: Indiana Library and History Dept., 1927.

Hazard, Samuel, ed. *Pennsylvania Archives*, First Series. 12 vols. Philadelphia: Joseph Severens & Co., 1852–1856.

Hening, William. *The Statutes at Large: Being a Collection of All the Laws of Virginia*. 13 vols. Richmond, Virginia: Franklin Press, 1819–1823.

Hume, David. *Essays, Moral, Political, and Literary*. Indianapolis, Ind.: Liberty Fund, 1987.

Jackson, Donald, ed. *Black Hawk: An Autobiography*. Urbana: University of Illinois Press, 1964.

Jackson, Donald, and Dorothy Twohig, eds. *The Diaries of George Washington*. 6 vols. Charlottesville: University Press of Virginia, 1976–79.

Jacobs, Wilbur, ed. *The Appalachian Indian Frontier: The Edmond Atkin Report and Plan of 1755*. Lincoln: University of Nebraska Press, 1967.

James, Edwin. *Account of an Expedition from Pittsburgh to the Rocky Mountains.* Reprint edition. 4 vols. Cleveland, Ohio: A.H. Clark, 1905.

Jennings, Jesse, ed. "Rush Nutt's Trip to the Chickasaw Country." *Journal of Mississippi History* 9 (Jan. 1947): 34–61.

Johnson, William, and the University of the State of New York. *The Papers of Sir William Johnson.* 14 vols. Albany: University of the State of New York, 1921–65.

Jordan, John, ed. "Journal of James Kenny, 1761–1763." *Pennsylvania Magazine of History and Biography* 37 (Jan. and Apr. 1913): 1–47, 152–201.

Journal of the Executive Proceedings of the Senate of the United States. Washington: U.S. Government Printing Office, 1828.

Kappler, Charles, ed. *Indian Affairs, Laws, and Treaties.* 7 vols. Washington: U.S. Government Printing Office, 1904.

Labaree, Leonard Woods, Ralph L. Ketcham, Whitfield J. Bell, Helen C. Boatfield, Helene H. Fineman, eds. *The Papers of Benjamin Franklin.* Vols. 4–5. New Haven, Conn.: Yale University Press, 1961–62.

Lawson, John. *A New Voyage to Carolina*, ed. by Hugh Talmage Lefler. Chapel Hill: University of North Carolina Press, 1967.

Lipscomb, Andrew, Albert Bergh and Richard Johnston, eds. *The Writings of Thomas Jefferson.* 20 vols. Washington, D.C.: Thomas Jefferson Memorial Association, 1904–1905.

Longworth's American Almanack, New York Register and City Directory for 1805. New York: David Longworth, 1805.

Louis-Philippe. *Diary of My Travels in America.* Translated by Stephen Becker. New York: Delacorte Press, 1977.

Lowrie, Walter, and Walter Franklin, eds. *American State Papers*, "Foreign Affairs." 6 vols. Washington, D.C.: Gales and Seaton, 1833–1859.

———, eds. *American State Papers*, "Indian Affairs." 2 vols. Washington, D.C.: Gales and Seaton, 1834.

———, eds. *American State Papers*, "Military Affairs." 7 vols. Washington, D.C.: Gales and Seaton, 1832–1861.

Marshall, Thomas Maitland, ed. *The Life and Papers of Frederick Bates.* 2 vols. Saint Louis: Missouri Historical Society, 1926.

McClinton, Rowena, ed. *The Moravian Springplace Mission to the Cherokees.* 2 vols. Lincoln: University of Nebraska Press, 2007.

McKenney, Thomas L. *Memoirs, Official and Personal, with Sketches of Travel among the Northern Indians.* Second Edition. New York: Paine & Burgess, 1846.

Memorial of Sundry Manufacturers of Hats, in the City of Philadelphia, Dec. 10, 1805. Washington, D.C.: A&G Way, 1806.

Meriwether, Robert Lee, William Edwin Hemphill, and Clyde Norman Wilson, eds., *The Papers of John Calhoun.* 28 vols. Columbia: University of South Carolina Press, 1959–2003.

Michigan Pioneer and Historical Society. *Historical Collections of the Pioneer and Historical Society of Michigan.* 40 vols. Lansing, Mich.: The Society, 1876–1912.

Miller, John. "The Military Occupation of Green Bay." *Mississippi Valley Historical Review*, 13 (March 1927): 549–53.

Montesquieu, Baron de (Charles Secondat). *The Spirit of the Laws*. Translated by Thomas Nugent. 2 volumes. New York: The Colonial Press, 1900.

Nelson, George. *My First Years in the Fur Trade: The Journals of 1802–1804*. Edited by Laura Peers and Theresa Schenck. Saint Paul: Minnesota Historical Society Press, 2002.

Nuttall, Thomas. *Travels into the Arkansa Territory, 1819*. In *Early Western Travels, 1748–1846*, edited by Reuben Gold Thwaites. Vol. 13. Cleveland, Ohio: The Arthur H. Clark Company, 1905.

Oddy, J. J. *European Commerce, Shewing New and Secure Channels of Trade with the Continent of Europe*. 2 vols. Philadelphia: James Humphreys, 1807.

Peters, Richard, ed. *The Public Statutes at Large of the United States of America*. 8 vols. Boston: Little, Brown, 1844–54.

Quaife, Milo Milton, comp. and ed. *The Development of Chicago, 1674–1914. Shown in a Series of Contemporary Original Narratives*. Chicago: Caxton Club, 1916.

———, ed. *The John Askin Papers*. 2 vols. Detroit: Detroit Library Commission, 1928.

Richardson, James D., ed. *A Compilation of the Messages and Papers of the Presidents, 1789–1897*. 10 vols. Washington, D.C.: U.S. Government Printing Office, 1896–99.

Rowland, Dunbar, ed. *Official Letter Books of W.C.C. Claiborne, 1801–1816*. 6 vols. Jackson, Mississippi, 1917.

Russell, Donna Valley. *Michigan Voyageurs*. Detroit: Detroit Society for Genealogical Research, 1982.

Ryan, Harold, ed. "Jacob Bright's Journal of a Trip to the Osage Indians." *Journal of Southern History* 15 (Nov. 1949): 509–23.

Seaver, James. *A Narrative of the Life of Mrs. Mary Jemison*. Syracuse: Syracuse University Press, 1990.

Smith, James Morton, ed. *The Republic of Letters: The Correspondence between Thomas Jefferson and James Madison, 1776–1826*. 3 vols. New York: W.W. Norton and Company, 1995.

Smith, Paul Hubert, and Ronald M. Gephart, eds. *Letters of Delegates to Congress, 1774–1789*. 26 vols. Washington, D.C.: Library of Congress, 1976–2000.

State Historical Society of Wisconsin. *Collections of the State Historical Society of Wisconsin*. 40 vols. Madison, Wisc.: The Society, 1888–1931.

Thornbrough, Gail, ed. *Letter Book of the Indian Agency at Fort Wayne, 1809–1815*. Indiana Historical Society Publications, Volume 21. Indianapolis: Indiana Historical Society, 1961.

Thwaites, Reuben Gold, ed. *Early Western Journals, 1748–1765*. Lewisburg, Pa.: Wennawoods Publishers, 1998.

Thwaites, Reuben Gold, and Louise Kellogg, eds. *Documentary History of Dunmore's War*. Madison: Wisconsin Historical Society, 1905.

Van Doren, Mark, ed. *The Travels of William Bartram*. New York: Dover Books, 1955.

Walker, Joseph, ed. "Plowshares and Pruning Hooks for the Miamis and Potawatomis: The Journal of Gerald T. Hopkins." *Ohio History* 66 (Autumn 1972): 361–407.

Weld, Isaac. *Travels through the States of North America and the Provinces of Upper and Lower Canada in the Years 1795, 1796, and 1797.* Fourth Edition. 2 volumes. London: J. Stockdale, 1807.

Williams, Roger. *The Complete Writings.* 7 vols. New York: Russell and Russell, 1963.

Secondary Sources

Books

Adams, Henry. *The Life of Albert Gallatin.* New York: Peter Smith, 1943.

Allen, Robert. *The British Indian Department and the Frontier in North America, 1755–1830.* Ottawa: Parks Canada, 1975.

Ammon, Harry. *James Monroe: The Quest for National Identity.* Charlottesville: University Press of Virginia, 1990.

Anderson, Fred. *Crucible of War: The Seven Years' War and the Fate of Empire in British North America, 1754–1766.* New York: Knopf, 2000.

Anderson, Fred, and Andrew Cayton. *The Dominion of War: Empire and Liberty in North America, 1500–2000.* New York: Viking Penguin, 2005.

Anderson, Gary. *Kinsmen of Another Kind: Dakota-White Relations in the Upper Mississippi Valley, 1650–1862.* Lincoln: University of Nebraska Press, 1984.

Andrew, John A., III. *Rebuilding the Christian Commonwealth: New England Congregationalists & Foreign Missions, 1800–1830.* Lexington: University Press of Kentucky, 1976.

Aron, Steve. *American Confluence: The Missouri Frontier from Borderland to Border State.* Bloomington: Indiana University Press, 2006.

Bailyn, Bernard. *Voyagers to the West: A Passage in the Peopling of America on the Eve of the Revolution.* New York: Knopf, 1986.

Banner, James. *To the Hartford Convention: The Federalists and the Origins of Party Politics in Massachusetts, 1789–1815.* New York: Knopf, 1970.

Banning, Lance. *The Jeffersonian Persuasion: Evolution of a Party Ideology.* Ithaca, N.Y.: Cornell University Press, 1978.

Barber, John Warner, and Henry Howe. *Our Whole Country, or, the Past and Present of the United States.* Cincinnati: Henry Howe, 1861.

Barr, Juliana. *Peace Came in the Form of a Woman: Indians and Spaniards in the Texas Borderlands.* Chapel Hill: University of North Carolina Press, 2007.

Bearss, Edwin C. *Montgomery's Tavern and Johnson and Armstrong's Store: Historic Structure Report.* Washington, D.C.: National Park Service, 1971.

Bell, David A. *The First Total War: Napoleonic Europe and the Birth of Warfare as We Know It.* Boston: Houghton Mifflin, 2007.

Berkhofer, Robert, Jr. *A Behavioral Approach to Historical Analysis.* New York: The Free Press, 1969.

———. *Salvation and the Savage: An Analysis of Protestant Missions and American Indian Response, 1787–1862.* Lexington: University of Kentucky Press, 1965.

———. *The White Man's Indian: Images of the American Indian from Columbus to the Present Day.* 1978. Reprint, New York: Vintage, 1979.

Blackhawk, Ned. *Violence over the Land: Indians and Empires in the Early American West.* Cambridge, Mass.: Harvard University Press, 2006.

Braudel, Fernand. *The Structures of Everyday Life.* Vol. 1 of *Civilization and Capitalism, 1500–1800.* Berkeley and Los Angeles: University Press of California, 1982.

Braund, Kathryn E. Holland. *Deerskins and Duffels: The Creek Indian Trade with Anglo-America.* Lincoln: University of Nebraska Press, 1993.

Broadwater, Jeff. *George Mason: Forgotten Founder.* Chapel Hill: University of North Carolina Press, 2006.

Brown, Jennifer. *Strangers in Blood: Fur Trade Company Families in Indian Country.* Vancouver: University of British Columbia Press, 1980.

Buel, Richard. *In Irons: Britain's Naval Supremacy and the American Revolutionary Economy.* New Haven, Conn.: Yale University Press, 1998.

Callahan, North. *Henry Knox: General Washington's General.* New York: Knopf, 1958.

Calloway, Colin. *The American Revolution in Indian Country.* Cambridge: Cambridge University Press, 1995.

———. *New Worlds for All: Indians, Europeans, and the Remaking of Early America.* Baltimore: Johns Hopkins University Press, 1997.

———. *One Vast Winter Count: The Native American West before Lewis and Clark.* Lincoln: University of Nebraska Press, 2003.

Cangany, Catherine. *Frontier Seaport: Detroit's Transformation into an Atlantic Entrepôt.* Chicago: University of Chicago Press, 2014.

Carlos, Ann M., and Frank D. Lewis. *Commerce by a Frozen Sea: Native Americans and the European Fur Trade.* Philadelphia: University of Pennsylvania Press, 2010.

Carp, E. Wayne. *To Starve the Army at Pleasure: Continental Army Administration and American Political Culture, 1775–1783.* Chapel Hill: University of North Carolina Press, 1985.

Carson, James Taylor. *Searching for the Bright Path: The Mississippi Choctaws from Prehistory through Removal.* Lincoln: University of Nebraska Press, 1999.

Cayton, Andrew. *Frontier Indiana.* Bloomington: Indiana University Press, 1996.

Child, Brenda J. *Holding Our World Together: Ojibwe Women and the Survival of Community.* New York: Viking Penguin, 2012.

Chittenden, Hiram. *History of the American Fur Trade of the Far West.* 3 vols. New York: Francis Harper, 1902.

Christian, Shirley. *Before Lewis and Clark: The Story of the Chouteaus, the French Dynasty That Ruled America's Frontier.* New York: Farrar, Straus, and Giroux, 2004.

Coker, William S., and Thomas D. Watson. *Indian Traders of the Southeastern Spanish Borderlands: Panton, Leslie & Company and John Forbes & Company, 1783–1847.* Pensacola: University Presses of Florida, 1986.

Corkran, David. *The Creek Frontier, 1540–1783.* Norman: University of Oklahoma Press, 1967.

Crane, Verner. *The Southern Frontier, 1670–1732.* Ann Arbor: University of Michigan Press, 1956.

Cronon, William. *Changes in the Land: Indians, Colonists, and the Ecology of New England.* New York: Hill and Wang, 1983.

Cunningham, Noble. *The Presidency of James Monroe.* Lawrence: University of Kansas Press, 1996.

Curtin, Philip. *Cross-Cultural Trade in World History.* Cambridge: Cambridge University Press, 1984.

Cushman, H. B. *History of the Choctaw, Chickasaw, and Natchez Indians.* Greenville, Tex.: Headlight Print House, 1899.

Dalton, George, ed. *Primitive, Archaic, and Modern Economies: Essays of Karl Polanyi.* Boston: Beacon Press, 1971.

Dangerfield, George. *The Awakening of American Nationalism, 1815–1828.* New York: Harper & Row, 1965.

Davidson, Victor. *History of Wilkinson County, Georgia.* Macon, Ga.: J. W. Burke Co., 1930.

Davis, James E. *Frontier Illinois.* Bloomington: Indiana University Press, 1998.

DeRosier, Arthur H., Jr. *The Removal of the Choctaw Indians.* Knoxville: University of Tennessee Press, 1970.

Dickerson, Oliver. *American Colonial Government, 1696–1765: A Study of the British Board of Trade in its Relation to the American Colonies.* Cleveland, Ohio: The Arthur Clark Company, 1912.

Diener, Alexander, and Joshua Hagen. *Borders: A Very Short Introduction.* New York: Oxford University Press, 2012.

Dolin, Eric Jay. *Fur, Fortune, and Empire: The Epic History of the Fur Trade in America.* New York: W.W. Norton, 2010.

Dowd, Gregory Evans. *A Spirited Resistance: The North American Indian Struggle for Unity, 1745–1815.* Baltimore: Johns Hopkins University Press, 1992.

———. *War under Heaven: Pontiac, the Indian Nations, & the British Empire.* Baltimore: Johns Hopkins University Press, 2002.

Downes, Randolph. *Council Fires on the Upper Ohio.* Pittsburgh, Pa.: University of Pittsburgh Press, 1968.

Dunbar, Seymour. *A History of Travel in America.* Indianapolis, Ind.: Bobbs-Merrill, 1915.

Dunbar, Willis, and George May. *Michigan: A History of the Wolverine State.* 3rd rev. ed. Grand Rapids, Mich.: Eerdmans Publishing Co., 1995.

DuVal, Kathleen. *The Native Ground: Indians and Colonists in the Heart of the Continent.* Philadelphia: University of Pennsylvania Press, 2006.

Eccles, W. J. *The Canadian Frontier, 1534–1760.* Albuquerque: University of New Mexico Press, 1983.

——. *France in America.* New York: Harper and Row, 1972.

Edling, Max. *A Revolution in Favor of Government: Origins of the U.S. Constitution and the Making of the American State.* New York: Oxford University Press, 2003.

Edmunds, R. David. *The Potawatomis: Keepers of the Fire.* Norman: University of Oklahoma Press, 1978.

Elkins, Stanley, and Eric McKitrick. *The Age of Federalism: The Early American Republic, 1788–1800.* New York: Oxford University Press, 1993.

Ethridge, Robbie. *Creek Country: The Creek Indians and Their World.* Chapel Hill: University of North Carolina Press, 2003.

Ethridge, Robbie, and Sheri Marie Shuck-Hall, eds. *Mapping the Mississippian Shatter Zone: The Colonial Indian Slave Trade and Regional Instability in the American South.* Lincoln: University of Nebraska Press, 2009.

Farmer, Silas. *History of Detroit and Wayne County and Early Michigan.* New York: Munsell & Co., 1890.

Fenn, Elizabeth. *Encounters at the Heart of the World: A History of the Mandan People.* New York: Hill and Wang, 2014.

——. *Pox Americana: The Great Smallpox Epidemic of 1775–1782.* New York: Hill and Wang, 2001.

Ferguson, Gillum. *Illinois in the War of 1812.* Urbana: University of Illinois Press, 2012.

Flexner, James. *Mohawk Baronet.* New York: Harper, 1939.

Foley, William. *Wilderness Journey: The Life of William Clark.* Columbia: University of Missouri Press, 2004.

Frazier, Patrick. *The Mohicans of Stockbridge.* Lincoln: University of Nebraska Press, 1992.

Gallay, Alan. *The Indian Slave Trade: The Rise of the English Empire in the American South, 1670–1717.* New Haven, Conn.: Yale University Press, 2002.

Gibson, Arrell Morgan. *The Chickasaws.* Norman: University of Oklahoma Press, 1971.

Gitlin, Jay. *The Bourgeois Frontier: French Towns, French Traders & American Expansion.* New Haven, Conn.: Yale University Press, 2010.

Goetzmann, William H. *Exploration and Empire: The Explorer and the Scientist in the Winning of the American West.* New York: Norton, 1978.

Green, Michael D. *The Politics of Indian Removal: Creek Government and Society in Crisis.* Lincoln: University of Nebraska Press, 1982.

Griffin, Patrick. *American Leviathan: Empire, Nation, and Revolutionary Frontier.* New York: Hill and Wang, 2007.

Haeger, John Denis. *John Jacob Astor: Business and Finance in the Early Republic.* Detroit, Mich.: Wayne State University Press, 1991.

Hagan, William. *The Sac and Fox Indians.* Norman: University of Oklahoma Press, 1980.

Hall, Joseph M. *Zamumo's Gifts: Indian-European Exchange in the Colonial Southeast.* Philadelphia: University of Pennsylvania Press, 2009.

Hämäläinen, Pekka. *The Comanche Empire*. New Haven, Conn.: Yale University Press, 2008.

Hammon, Neal O., and Richard Taylor. *Virginia's Western War, 1775–1786*. Mechanicsburg, Pa.: Stackpole Books, 2002.

Harmon, George Dewey. *Sixty Years of Indian Affairs: Political, Economic, and Diplomatic, 1789–1850*. 1941. Reprint, New York: Kraus Reprint Co., 1969.

Hatfield, Joseph T. *William Claiborne: Jeffersonian Centurion in the American Southwest*. Lafayette: University of Southwestern Louisiana History Series, 1976.

Havighurst, Walter. *Alexander Spotswood: Portrait of a Governor*. New York: Holt, Rinehart, and Winston, 1967.

Henri, Florette. *Benjamin Hawkins and the Southern Indians, 1796–1816*. Norman: University of Oklahoma Press, 1986.

Heyrman, Christine Leigh. *Commerce and Culture*. New York: Norton, 1984.

Hickey, Donald. *Don't Give Up the Ship! Myths of the War of 1812*. Urbana and Chicago: University of Illinois Press, 2006.

———. *The War of 1812: A Forgotten Conflict*. Urbana and Chicago: University of Illinois Press, 1989.

Higginbotham, Don. *The War of American Independence: Military Attitudes, Policies, and Practice, 1763–1789*. Bloomington: Indiana University Press, 1971.

Hill, Leonard U. *John Johnston and the Indians in the Land of the Three Miamis*. Columbus, Ohio: Stoneman Press, 1957.

Hinderaker, Eric. *Elusive Empires: Constructing Colonialism in the Ohio Valley, 1673–1800*. Cambridge: Cambridge University Press, 1997.

Holton, Woody. *Forced Founders: Indians, Debtors, Slaves, and the Making of the American Revolution in Virginia*. Chapel Hill: University of North Carolina Press, 1999.

Horsman, Reginald. *Expansion and American Indian Policy, 1783–1812*. 1967. Reprint, Norman: University of Oklahoma Press, 1992.

———. *Matthew Elliott, British Indian Agent*. Detroit, Mich.: Wayne State University Press, 1964.

———. *The New Republic: The United States, 1789–1815*. New York: Routledge, 2013.

———. *The War of 1812*. New York: Knopf, 1969.

Howe, Daniel Walker. *What Hath God Wrought: The Transformation of America, 1815–1848*. Oxford: Oxford University Press, 2007.

Hudson, Charles. *The Southeastern Indians*. Knoxville: University of Tennessee Press, 1976.

Hurt, R. Douglas. *The Ohio Frontier: Crucible of the Old Northwest, 1720–1830*. Bloomington: Indiana University Press, 1996.

Innis, Harold A. *The Fur Trade in Canada: An Introduction to Canadian Economic History*. New Haven, Conn.: Yale University Press, 1930.

Jennings, Francis. *Empire of Fortune: Crowns, Colonies, and Tribes in the Seven Years War in America*. New York: Norton, 1988.

———. *The Invasion of America: Indians, Colonialism, and the Cant of Conquest.* Chapel Hill: University of North Carolina Press, 1975.

Jones, David S. *Native North American Armor, Shields, and Fortifications.* Austin: University of Texas Press, 2004.

Jones, Dorothy. *License for Empire: Colonialism by Treaty in Early America.* Chicago: University of Chicago Press, 1982.

Kastor, Peter J. *The Nation's Crucible: The Louisiana Purchase and the Creation of America.* New Haven, Conn.: Yale University Press, 2004.

Kohn, Richard. *Eagle and Sword: The Federalists and the Creation of the Military Establishment in America, 1783–1802.* New York: The Free Press, 1975.

Kukla, Jon. *A Wilderness So Immense: The Louisiana Purchase and the Destiny of America.* New York: Knopf, 2003.

Larson, John Lauritz. *The Market Revolution in America: Liberty, Ambition, and the Eclipse of the Common Good.* Cambridge: Cambridge University Press, 2010.

Lavender, David. *The Fist in the Wilderness.* 1964. Reprint, Lincoln: University of Nebraska Press, 1998.

LaVere, David. *The Caddo Chiefdoms: Caddo Economics and Politics, 700–1835.* Lincoln: University of Nebraska Press, 1998.

———. *Contrary Neighbors: Southern Plains and Removed Indians in Indian Territory.* Norman: University of Oklahoma Press, 2000.

Lewis, James E., Jr. *The Louisiana Purchase: Jefferson's Noble Bargain?* Chapel Hill: University of North Carolina Press, 2003.

Liebersohn, Harry. *Aristocratic Encounters: European Travelers and North American Indians.* Cambridge: Cambridge University Press, 1998.

Lossing, Benson J. *Pictorial Field Book of the War of 1812.* New York: Harper and Brothers, 1868. Available online at http://freepages.history.rootsweb.ancestry.com/~wcarr1/Lossing2/Contents.html (8 June 2015).

Malone, Dumas. *Jefferson the President: Second Term, 1805–1809.* Boston: Little, Brown, 1974.

Mancall, Peter. *Deadly Medicine: Indians and Alcohol in Early America.* Ithaca, N.Y.: Cornell University Press, 1995.

Martin, Joel. *Sacred Revolt: The Muskogees' Struggle for a New World.* Boston: Beacon Press, 1991.

Matson, Cathy, and Peter Onuf. *A Union of Interests: Political and Economic Thought in Revolutionary America.* Lawrence: University Press of Kansas, 1990.

McConnell, Michael. *A Country Between: The Upper Ohio Valley and Its Peoples, 1724–1774.* Lincoln: University of Nebraska Press, 1992.

McCoy, Drew R. *The Elusive Republic: Political Economy in Jeffersonian America.* Chapel Hill: University of North Carolina Press, 1980.

McDonald, Forrest. *Novus Ordo Seclorum: The Intellectual Origins of the Constitution.* Lawrence: University Press of Kansas, 1985.

McLoughlin, William. *Cherokee Renascence in the New Republic.* Princeton, N.J.: Princeton University Press, 1986.

Meinig, D. W. *The Shaping of America*, Volume II, *Continental America, 1800–1867*. New Haven, Conn.: Yale University Press, 1993.

Merrell, James. *The Indians' New World: Catawbas and Their Neighbors from European Contact through the Era of Removal*. New York: Norton, 1991.

———. *Into the American Woods: Negotiators on the Pennsylvania Frontier*. New York: Norton, 1999.

Morgan, Edmund S. *Inventing the People: The Rise of Popular Sovereignty in England and America*. New York: Norton, 1988.

Mueller, Ken S. *Senator Benton: Master Race Democracy on the Early American Frontiers*. Dekalb: Northern Illinois University Press, 2014.

Murphy, Lucy Eldersveld. *Great Lakes Creoles: A French-Indian Community on the Northern Borderlands, Prairie du Chien, 1750–1860*. New York: Cambridge University Press, 2014.

Mustafa, Sam A. *Merchants and Migrations: Germans and Americans in Connection, 1776–1835*. Aldershot, UK: Ashgate, 2001.

Nelson, Larry. *A Man of Distinction among Them: Alexander McKee and the Ohio Country Frontier, 1754–1799*. Kent, Ohio: Kent State University Press, 1999.

Nichols, David Andrew. *Red Gentlemen & White Savages: Indians, Federalists, and the Search for Order on the American Frontier*. Charlottesville: University of Virginia Press, 2008.

Nichols, Roger. *Indians in the United States and Canada: A Comparative History*. Lincoln: University of Nebraska Press, 1999.

Nugent, Walter. *Habits of Empire: A History of American Expansion*. New York: Knopf, 2008.

O'Donnell, James H. *Southern Indians in the American Revolution*. Knoxville: University of Tennessee Press, 1973.

Oliphant, John. *Peace and War on the Anglo-Cherokee Frontier, 1756–1763*. Baton Rouge: Louisiana State University Press, 2001.

Onuf, Peter. *Jefferson's Empire: The Language of American Nationhood*. Charlottesville: University of Virginia Press, 2000.

Osterhammel, Jürgen. *The Transformation of the World: A Global History of the Nineteenth Century*. Princeton, N.J.: Princeton University Press, 2014.

Owens, Robert M. *Mr. Jefferson's Hammer: William Henry Harrison and the Origins of American Indian Policy*. Norman: University of Oklahoma Press, 2007.

Owsley, Frank Lawrence, Jr. *Struggle for the Gulf Borderlands: The Creek War and the Battle of New Orleans, 1812–1815*. Gainesville: University of Florida Press, 1981.

Palmer, Friend. *Early Days in Detroit*. Detroit, Mich.: Hunt and June, 1906.

Parry, J. H. *The Age of Reconnaissance: Discovery, Exploration, and Settlement, 1450 to 1650*. New York: Praeger Publishers, 1969.

Peake, Ora Brooks. *A History of the United States Indian Factory System*. Denver, Colo.: Sage Books, 1954.

Perdue, Theda. *Cherokee Women: Gender and Culture Change, 1700–1835.* Lincoln: University of Nebraska Press, 1998.

———. *"Mixed-Blood" Indians: Racial Construction in the Early South.* Athens: University of Georgia Press, 2003.

Phillips, Clifton J. *Protestant America and the Pagan World: The First Half-Century of the American Board of Commissioners for Foreign Missions, 1810–1860.* Cambridge, Mass.: Harvard University Press, 1969.

Piker, Joshua. *Okfuskee: A Creek Indian Town in Colonial America.* Cambridge, Mass.: Harvard University Press, 2004.

Polhemus, Richard. *Archaeological Investigation of the Tellico Blockhouse Site (40MR50): A Federal Military and Trade Complex.* Knoxville: University of Tennessee Dept. of Anthropology, 1977.

Porter, Kenneth. *John Jacob Astor.* 2 volumes. Cambridge, Mass.: Harvard University Press, 1931.

Prucha, Francis Paul. *American Indian Policy in the Formative Years: The Trade and Intercourse Acts, 1790–1834.* Cambridge, Mass.: Harvard University Press, 1962.

———. *American Indian Treaties: The History of a Political Anomaly.* Berkeley and Los Angeles: University of California Press, 1994.

———. *The Great Father: The United States Government and the American Indians.* Abridged edition. Lincoln: University of Nebraska Press, 1986.

———. *The Sword of the Republic: The United States Army on the Frontier, 1783–1846.* New York: Macmillan, 1969.

Quaife, Milo M. *Chicago and the Old Northwest: A Study of the Evolution of the Northwestern Frontier, Together with a History of Fort Dearborn.* Chicago: University of Chicago Press, 1913.

Quinn, David. *North America from Earliest Discovery to First Settlements.* New York: Harper and Row, 1977.

Ray, Arthur. *Indians in the Fur Trade: Their Role as Trappers, Hunters, and Middlemen in the Lands Southwest of Hudson Bay, 1660–1870.* Toronto: University of Toronto Press, 1998.

Reid, John Phillip. *A Better Kind of Hatchet: Law, Trade, and Diplomacy in the Cherokee Nations during the Early Years of European Contact.* University Park: Pennsylvania State University Press, 1976.

Remini, Robert V. *Andrew Jackson and His Indian Wars.* New York: Penguin, 2001.

———. *Henry Clay: Statesman for the Union.* New York: W.W. Norton, 1991.

Richter, Daniel. *Before the Revolution: America's Ancient Pasts.* Cambridge, Mass.: Harvard University Press, 2011.

———. *Facing East from Indian Country: A Native History of Early America.* Cambridge, Mass.: Harvard University Press, 2001.

———. *The Ordeal of the Longhouse: The Peoples of the Iroquois League in the Era of European Colonization.* Chapel Hill: University of North Carolina Press, 1992.

———. *Trade, Land, Power: The Struggle for Eastern North America.* Philadelphia: University of Pennsylvania Press, 2013.

Rohrbough, Malcolm. *The Land Office Business: The Settlement and Administration of American Public Lands, 1789–1837.* Belmont, Calif.: Wadsworth Publishing Company, 1990.

———. *The Trans-Appalachian Frontier: People, Societies, and Institutions, 1775–1850.* Belmont, Calif.: Wadsworth Publishing Company, 1990.

Ronda, James P. *Astoria and Empire.* Lincoln: University of Nebraska Press, 1990.

Rothman, Adam. *Slave Country: American Expansion and the Origins of the Deep South.* Cambridge, Mass.: Harvard University Press, 2005.

Rowland, Kate Mason. *The Life of George Mason, 1725–1792.* 2 vols. New York: G.P. Putnam's Sons, 1892.

Ryan, Mary. *Cradle of the Middle Class: The Family in Oneida County, New York, 1790–1865.* Cambridge: Cambridge University Press, 1981.

Sahlins, Marshall. *Stone Age Economics.* Chicago: University of Chicago Press, 1972.

Salisbury, Neal. *Manitou and Providence: Indians, Europeans, and the Making of New England, 1500–1643.* New York: Oxford University Press, 1982.

Saunt, Claudio. *A New Order of Things: Property, Power, and the Transformation of the Creek Indians.* Cambridge: Cambridge University Press, 1999.

Sellers, Charles. *The Market Revolution: Jacksonian America, 1815–1846.* New York: Oxford University Press, 1991.

Shannon, Timothy. *Indians and Colonists at the Crossroads of Empire: The Albany Congress of 1754.* Ithaca, N.Y.: Cornell University Press, 2000.

Sheehan, Bernard. *Seeds of Extinction: Jeffersonian Philanthropy and the American Indian.* Chapel Hill: University of North Carolina Press, 1973.

Shell, Marc. *Wampum and the Origins of American Money.* Urbana: University of Illinois Press, 2013.

Shoemaker, Nancy. *A Strange Likeness: Becoming Red and White in Eighteenth-Century North America.* New York: Oxford University Press, 2004.

Shuck-Hall, Sheri Marie. *Journey to the West: The Alabama & Coushatta Indians.* Norman: University of Oklahoma Press, 2008.

Silver, Peter. *Our Savage Neighbors: How Indian War Transformed Early America.* New York: W.W. Norton, 2008.

Silver, Timothy. *A New Face on the Countryside: Indians, Colonists and Slaves in South Atlantic Forests, 1500–1800.* Cambridge: Cambridge University Press, 1990.

Smelser, Marshall. *The Democratic Republic, 1801–1815.* New York: Harper & Row, 1968.

Snapp, J. Russell. *John Stuart and the Struggle for Empire on the Southern Frontier.* Baton Rouge: Louisiana State University Press, 1996.

Snyder, Christina. *Slavery in Indian Country: The Changing Face of Captivity in Early America.* Cambridge, Mass.: Harvard University Press, 2010.

Sosin, Jack. *The Revolutionary Frontier, 1763–1783.* New York: Holt, Rinehart, and Winston, 1967.

———. *Whitehall and the Wilderness: The Middle West in British Imperial Policy, 1760–1775.* Lincoln: University of Nebraska Press, 1961.

Sugden, John. *Blue Jacket: Warrior of the Shawnees.* Lincoln: University of Nebraska Press, 2000.

———. *Tecumseh: A Life.* New York: Henry Holt & Co., 1997.

Sunder, John E. *The Fur Trade on the Upper Missouri, 1840–1865.* Norman: University of Oklahoma Press, 1965.

Tanner, Helen Hornbeck. *The Atlas of Great Lakes Indian History.* Norman: University of Oklahoma Press, 1986.

Taylor, Alan. *American Colonies.* New York: Knopf, 2001.

———. *The Internal Enemy: Slavery and War in Virginia, 1772–1832.* New York: W.W. Norton, 2013.

Thompson, Neil, and Charles Anderson, eds. *A Tribute to John Insley Coddington.* New York: Association for Promotion of Scholarship in Genealogy, 1980.

Trelease, Allen. *Indian Affairs in Colonial New York: The Seventeenth Century.* Ithaca, N.Y.: Cornell University Press, 1960.

Trigger, Bruce. *The Children of Aataentsic: A History of the Huron People to 1660.* 2 vols. Montreal: McGill-Queens University Press, 1976.

Turner, Frederick Jackson. *The Character and Influence of the Indian Trade in Wisconsin.* Baltimore: Johns Hopkins University Studies in Historical and Political Science, 1891.

Unrau, William E. *The Kansa Indians: A History of the Wind People, 1673–1873.* Norman: University of Oklahoma Press, 1986.

Usner, Daniel H., Jr. *American Indians in the Lower Mississippi Valley: Social and Economic Histories.* Lincoln: University of Nebraska Press, 2003.

———. *Indians, Settlers and Slaves in a Frontier Exchange Economy.* Chapel Hill: University of North Carolina Press, 1992.

Vinkovetsky, Ilya. *Russian America: An Overseas Colony of a Continental Empire, 1805–1867.* New York: Oxford University Press, 2011.

Viola, Herman. *Thomas L. McKenney: Architect of America's Early Indian Policy, 1816–1830.* Chicago: Sage Books, 1974.

Wade, Richard. *The Urban Frontier: The Rise of Western Cities, 1790–1830.* Cambridge, Mass.: Harvard University Press, 1959.

Wallace, Anthony F. C. *Jefferson and the Indians: The Tragic Fate of the First Americans.* Cambridge, Mass.: Harvard University Press, 1999.

Ward, Henry. *The Department of War, 1781–1795.* Pittsburgh: University of Pittsburgh Press, 1960.

Ward, Matthew. *Breaking the Backcountry: The Seven Years' War in Pennsylvania and Virginia, 1754–1765.* Pittsburgh: University of Pittsburgh Press, 2003.

Waring, Alice. *The Fighting Elder: Andrew Pickens (1739–1817).* Columbia: University of South Carolina Press, 1962.

Watts, Stephen. *The Republic Reborn: War and the Making of Liberal America, 1790–1820.* Baltimore: Johns Hopkins University Press, 1987.

Weber, David. *The Mexican Frontier, 1821–1846: The American Southwest under Mexico.* Albuquerque: University of New Mexico Press, 1982.

———. *The Spanish Frontier in North America.* New Haven, Conn.: Yale University Press, 1992.

Weeks, William. *John Quincy Adams and American Global Empire*. Lexington: University of Kentucky Press, 2002.

Weisberger, Bernard. *America Afire: Jefferson, Adams, and the First Contested Election*. New York: William Morrow, 2000.

White, Richard. *The Middle Ground: Indians, Empires, and Republics in the Great Lakes Region, 1650–1815*. Cambridge: Cambridge University Press, 1991.

———. *Railroaded: The Transcontinentals and the Making of Modern America*. New York: Norton, 2011.

———. *The Roots of Dependency: Subsistence, Environment, and Social Change among the Choctaws, Pawnees and Navajos*. Lincoln: University of Nebraska Press, 1983.

Wilentz, Sean. *The Rise of American Democracy: Jefferson to Lincoln*. New York: Norton, 2005.

Wilkins, Thurman. *Cherokee Tragedy: The Ridge Family and the Decimation of a People*. Second Printing. Norman: University of Oklahoma Press, 1986.

Williams, Robert. *Linking Arms Together: American Indian Treaty Visions of Law and Peace, 1600–1800*. New York: Routledge, 1999.

Winslow, Stephen Noyes. *Biographies of Successful Philadelphia Merchants*. Philadelphia: James K. Simon, 1864.

Wishart, David J. *The Fur Trade of the American West, 1807–1840*. Lincoln: University of Nebraska Press, 1979.

Wolf, Eric. *Europe and the People without History*. Berkeley and Los Angeles: University Press of California, 1982.

Wolferman, Kristie. *The Indomitable Mary Easton Sibley: Pioneer of Women's Education in Missouri*. Columbia: University of Missouri Press, 2008.

Wyman, Mark. *The Wisconsin Frontier*. Bloomington: Indiana University Press, 1998.

Young, Mary. *Redskins, Ruffleshirts, and Rednecks: Indian Allotments in Alabama and Mississippi, 1830–1860*. Norman: University of Oklahoma Press, 1961.

Articles and Essays

Adelman, Jeremy, and Stephen Aron. "From Borderlands to Borders: Empires, Nation-States, and the Peoples in Between in North American History." *American Historical Review* 104 (June 1999): 814–41.

Baumann, Roland M. "John Swanwick: Spokesman for 'Merchant Republicanism' in Philadelphia, 1790–1798." *Pennsylvania Magazine of History and Biography* 97 (April 1973): 131–82.

Bennett, David C. "A New Perspective on the Last Days of Fort Madison: Part II, Defense Under Siege." *Journal of the War of 1812* 12 (Summer 2009): 7–15.

Binnema, Ted, and William A. Dobak. "'Like the Greedy Wolf': The Blackfeet, the St. Louis Fur Trade, and War Fever." *Journal of the Early Republic* 29 (Fall 2009): 411–440.

Bloch, Ruth. "The Gendered Meanings of Virtue in Revolutionary America." *Signs* 13 (Autumn 1987): 37–58.

Bradley, Jared. "William C.C. Claiborne, the Old Southwest, and the Development of American Indian Policy." *Tennessee Historical Quarterly* 33 (Fall 1974): 265–78.

Braund, Kathryn Holland. "Guardians of Tradition and Handmaidens to Change: Women's Roles in Creek Economic and Social Life during the Eighteenth Century." *American Indian Quarterly* 14 (Summer 1990): 239–58.

Bushnell, Amy Turner. "Gates, Centers, and Peripheries: The Field of Frontier Latin America." In *Negotiated Empires: Centers and Peripheries in the Americas, 1500–1820*, edited by Christine Daniels and Michael Kennedy, 15–28. New York: Routledge Press, 2002.

Calloway, Colin G. "The End of an Era: British-Indian Relations in the Great Lakes Region after the War of 1812." *Michigan Historical Review* 12 (Fall 1986): 1–20.

Cangany, Catherine. "Fashioning Moccasins: Detroit, the Manufacturing Frontier, and the Empire of Consumption." *William and Mary Quarterly*, Third Series, 69 (April 2012): 265–304.

Cayton, Andrew. "Radicals in the 'Western World': The Federalist Conquest of Trans-Appalachian North America." In *The Federalists Reconsidered*, edited by Doron Ben-Atar and Barbara Oberg, 77–96. Charlottesville: University of Virginia Press, 1998.

Chambers, Nella. "The Creek Indian Factory at Fort Mitchell." *Alabama Historical Quarterly* 21 (1959): 15–53.

Cheney, Paul. "A False Dawn for Enlightenment Cosmopolitanism? Franco-American Trade during the American War of Independence." *William and Mary Quarterly*, Third Series, 63 (July 2006): 463–88.

Choquette, Leslie. "Center and Periphery in French America." In *Negotiated Empires: Centers and Peripheries in the Americas, 1500–1820*, edited by Christine Daniels and Michael Kennedy, 193–206. New York: Routledge Press, 2002.

Clayton, James L. "The Growth and Economic Significance of the American Fur Trade, 1790–1890." In *Aspects of the Fur Trade: Selected Papers of the 1965 North American Fur Trade Conference*, edited by Dale Morgan et al., 64–72. Saint Paul: Minnesota Historical Society, 1967.

Cleves, Rachel Hope, Nicole Eustace, Paul Gilje, Matthew Rainbow Hale, Cecilia Morgan, Jason Opal, Lawrence A. Peskin, and Alan Taylor "Interchange: The War of 1812." *Journal of American History* 99 (Sept. 2012): 520–55.

Coman, Katherine. "Government Factories: An Attempt to Control Competition in the Fur Trade." *American Economic Review* 1 (April 1911): 368–88.

Countryman, Edward. "Indians, the Colonial Order, and the Social Significance of the American Revolution." *William and Mary Quarterly*, Third Series, 53 (April 1996): 342–62.

Crosby, Alfred. "Virgin Soil Epidemics as a Factor in the Aboriginal Depopulation in America." *William and Mary Quarterly*, Third Series, 33 (April 1976): 289–99.

Davis, Karl. "'Remember Fort Mims:' Reinterpreting the Origins of the Creek War." *Journal of the Early Republic* 22 (Winter 2002): 611–36.

Dorland, W. A. Newman. "The Second Troop Philadelphia Cavalry." *Pennsylvania Magazine of History and Biography* 49 (1925): 75–96, 163–91.

Downes, Randolph. "Creek-American Relations, 1790–1795." *Journal of Southern History* 8 (Aug. 1942): 350–73.

DuVal, Kathleen. "Debating Identity, Sovereignty, and Civilization: The Arkansas Valley after the Louisiana Purchase." *Journal of the Early Republic* 26 (Spring 2006): 25–58.

Eccles, W. J. "The Fur Trade and Eighteenth-Century Imperialism." *William and Mary Quarterly*, Third Series, 40 (July 1983): 341–62.

Edmunds, R. David. "The Loyal Shawnee and the War of 1812." In *The Sixty Years' War for the Great Lakes*, edited by David Skaggs and Larry Nelson, 337–52. East Lansing: Michigan State University Press, 2001.

Essington, Joseph. "The French Claims to the Ohio Valley." *West Virginia History* 8 (July 1947): 365–81.

Faragher, John Mack. "'More Motley Than Mackinaw': From Ethnic Mixing to Ethnic Cleansing on the Frontier of the Lower Missouri, 1783–1833." In *Contact Points: American Frontiers from the Mohawk Valley to the Mississippi, 1750–1830*, edited by Andrew Cayton and Fredrika Teute. 304–26. Chapel Hill: University of North Carolina Press, 1998.

Gillingham, Harold. "Calico and Linen Printing in Philadelphia." *Pennsylvania Magazine of History and Biography* 52 (1928): 97–110.

Gitlin, Jay. "Private Diplomacy to Private Property: States, Tribes, and Nations in the Early National Period." *Diplomatic History* 22 (Winter 1998): 85–99.

Gregg, Kate. "The History of Fort Osage." *Missouri Historical Review* 34 (July 1940): 439–88.

Haggard, J. Villasana. "The House of Barr and Davenport." *Southwestern Historical Quarterly* 49 (July 1945): 66–88.

———. "The Neutral Ground between Louisiana and Texas, 1806–1821." *Louisiana Historical Quarterly* 28 (October 1945): 1001–128.

Hämäläinen, Pekka, and Samuel Truett. "On Borderlands." *Journal of American History* 98 (Sept. 2011): 338–61.

Harmon, George. "Benjamin Hawkins and the Federal Factory System." *North Carolina Historical Review* 9 (April 1932): 138–52.

Heaton, Herbert. "Non-Importation, 1806–1812." *Journal of Economic History* 1 (November 1941): 178–98.

Humins, John. "Furs, Astor, and Indians: The American Fur Company in the Old Northwest Territory." *Michigan History* 69 (March/April 1985): 24–31.

Isenberg, Andrew. "The Market Revolution in the Borderlands: George Champlin Sibley in Missouri and New Mexico, 1808–1826." *Journal of the Early Republic* 21 (Fall 2001): 445–65.

Jaenen, Cornelius. "The Role of Presents in Amerindian Trade." In *Explorations in Canadian Economic History: Essays in Honor of Irene Spry*, edited by Duncan Cameron, 231–50. Ottawa, ON: University of Ottawa Press, 1985.

Jarvis, Michael, and Jeroen van Driel. "The Vingboons Chart of the James River, Virginia, circa 1617." *William and Mary Quarterly*, Third Series, 54 (April 1997): 377–94.

Jones, David. "Virgin Soils Revisited." *William and Mary Quarterly*, Third Series, 60 (Oct. 2003): 703–42.

Larson, John Lauritz. "'Wisdom Enough to Improve Them': Government, Liberty, and Inland Waterways in the Rising American Empire." In *Launching the "Extended Republic": The Federalist Era*, edited by Ronald Hoffman and Peter Albert, 223–48. Charlottesville: University Press of Virginia, 1996.

Lavender, David. "Some American Aspects of the American Fur Company." In *Aspects of the Fur Trade: Selected Papers of the 1965 North American Fur Trade Conference*, edited by Dale Morgan et al., 30–39. Saint Paul: Minnesota Historical Society, 1967.

LaVere, David. "Edward Murphy: Irish Entrepreneur in Spanish Natchitoches." *Louisiana History* 32 (Fall 1991): 371–91.

Lecompte, Janet. "Pierre Chouteau, Junior." In *Mountain Men & Fur Traders of the Far West*, edited by LeRoy Hafen, 24–56. Lincoln: University of Nebraska Press, 1982.

Leftwich, George. "Cotton Gin Port and Gaines' Trace." *Publications of The Mississippi Historical Society*, 7: 264–70. Oxford, Miss.: Mississippi Historical Society, 1903.

Lucas, Joseph. "Civilization or Extinction: Citizens and Indians in the Early United States." *Journal of the Historical Society* 6 (Jun 2006): 235–50.

MacFarlane, Ronald. "The Massachusetts Bay Truck-Houses in Diplomacy with the Indians." *New England Quarterly* 11 (March 1938): 48–65.

Magnaghi, Russell. "The Bellefontaine Indian Factory, 1805–1808." *Missouri Historical Review* 75 (July 1981): 396–416.

———. "Michigan's Indian Factory at Detroit, 1802–1805." *Inland Seas* 38 (Fall 1982): 172–78.

———. "Michigan's Indian Factory at Mackinac, 1808–1812." *Inland Seas* 39 (Spring 1983): 22–30.

———. "The Sandusky Indian Factory, 1806–1812." *Inland Seas* 39 (Fall 1983): 174–79.

———. "Sulphur Fork Factory, 1817–1822." *Arkansas Historical Quarterly*, 37 (Summer 1978): 168–83.

Mattison, Ray H. "The Creek Trading House—From Coleraine to Fort Hawkins." *Georgia Historical Quarterly* 30 (Sept. 1946): 169–84.

McCrocklin, Claude. "The Site of the Sulphur Fork Factory, Southwest Arkansas, 1817–1822." *Arkansas Archaeologist* 31 (1990): 53–63.

McLoughlin, William. "Thomas Jefferson and the Beginning of Cherokee Nationalism, 1806 to 1809." *William and Mary Quarterly*, Third Series, 32 (Fall 1975): 547–80.

Merrell, James. "'The Customes of Our Countrey': Indians and Colonists in Early America." In *Strangers Within the Realm: Cultural Margins of the First*

British Empire, edited by Bernard Bailyn and Philip D. Morgan, 117–56. Chapel Hill: University of North Carolina Press, 1991.

———. "Declarations of Independence: Indian-White Relations in the New Nation." In *The American Revolution: Its Character and Limits*, edited by Jack Greene, 197–223. New York: NYU Press, 1987.

———. "Shamokin, 'the Very Seat of the Prince of Darkness': Unsettling the Early American Frontier." In *Contact Points: American Frontiers from the Mohawk Valley to the Mississippi, 1750–1830*, edited by Andrew R. L. Cayton and Fredrika Teute, 16–59. Chapel Hill: University of North Carolina Press, 1998.

Miller, Christopher, and George Hamell. "A New Perspective on Indian-White Contact: Cultural Symbols and Colonial Trade." *Journal of American History* 73 (1986): 311–28.

Morris, Wayne. "Traders and Factories on the Arkansas Frontier, 1805–1822." *Arkansas Historical Quarterly* 28 (Spring 1969): 28–48.

Murphy, Lucy Eldersveld. "Autonomy and the Economic Roles of Indian Women of the Fox-Wisconsin River Region, 1763–1822." In *Negotiators of Change: Historical Perspectives on Native American Women*, edited by Nancy Shoemaker, 72–89. New York: Routledge, 1995.

———. "To Live Among Us: Accommodation, Gender, and Conflict in the Western Great Lakes Region, 1760–1832." In *Contact Points: American Frontiers from the Mohawk Valley to the Mississippi, 1750–1830*, edited by Andrew Cayton and Fredrika Teute, 270–303. Chapel Hill: University of North Carolina Press, 1998.

———. "Women, Networks, and Colonization in Nineteenth-Century Wisconsin." In *Contours of a People: Metis Family, Mobility, and History*, edited by Nicole St-Onge, Carolyn Podruchny, and Brenda Macdougall, 230–64. Norman: University of Oklahoma Press, 2012.

Murrin, John M. "The Great Inversion, or Court versus Country: A Comparison of the Revolution Settlements in Britain (1688–1721) and America (1776–1816)." In *Three British Revolutions, 1641, 1688, 1776*, edited by J. G. A. Pocock, 368–453. Princeton, N.J.: Princeton University Press, 1980.

Nichols, David A. "Land, Republicanism, and Indians: Power and Policy in Early National Georgia, 1780–1825." *Georgia Historical Quarterly* 85 (Summer 2001): 199–216.

O'Brien, Greg. "The Conqueror Meets the Unconquered: Negotiating Cultural Boundaries on the Post-Revolutionary Southern Frontier." *Journal of Southern History* 67 (Feb. 2001): 39–72.

Onuf, Peter. "Liberty, Development, and Union: Visions of the West in the 1780s." *William and Mary Quarterly*, Third Series, 43 (April 1986): 179–213.

Owens, Robert. "Jeffersonian Benevolence on the Ground: The Indian Land Cession Treaties of William Henry Harrison." *Journal of the Early Republic* 22 (Fall 2002): 405–35.

Plaisance, Aloysius. "The Arkansas Factory, 1805–1810." *Arkansas Historical Quarterly* 11 (Autumn 1952): 184–200.

———. "The Chickasaw Bluffs Factory and Its Removal to the Arkansas River, 1818–1822." *Tennessee Historical Quarterly* 11 (March 1952): 41–56.

———. "The Choctaw Trading House, 1803–1822." *Alabama Historical Quarterly* 16 (Fall-Winter 1954): 393–423.

Pressly, Paul. "Scottish Merchants and the Shaping of Colonial Georgia." *Georgia Historical Quarterly* 91 (Summer 2007): 135–68.

Quaife, Milo M. "An Experiment of the Fathers in State Socialism." *Wisconsin Magazine of History* 3 (March 1920): 277–90.

Rabruzzi, Daniel. "Cutting Out the Middleman? American Trade in Northern Europe, 1783–1815." In *Merchant Organization and Maritime Trade in the North Atlantic, 1660–1815*, edited by Olaf Uwe Janzen, 175–97. Saint John's, NL: International Maritime Economic History Association, 1998.

Richter, Daniel. "'Believing That Many of the Red People Suffer Much for the Want of Food': Hunters, Agriculture, and a Quaker Construction of Indianness in the Early Republic." *Journal of the Early Republic* 19 (Winter 1999): 601–29.

———. "War and Culture: The Iroquois Experience." *William and Mary Quarterly*, Third Series, 40 (July 1983): 528–59.

Risjord, Norman K. "1812: Conservatives, War Hawks, and the Nation's Honor." *William and Mary Quarterly*, Third Series, 18 (April 1961): 196–210.

Rountree, Helen. "The Powhatans and Other Woodland Indians as Travelers." In *Powhatan Foreign Relations, 1500–1700*, edited by Helen Rountree, 21–52. Charlottesville: University Press of Virginia, 1993.

Sadosky, Leonard. "Rethinking the Gnaddenhutten Massacre: The Contest for Power in the Public World of the Revolutionary Pennsylvania Frontier." In *The Sixty Years' War for the Great Lakes, 1754–1814*, edited by David Skaggs and Larry Nelson, 187–213. East Lansing: Michigan State University Press, 2001.

Salisbury, Neal. "The Indians' Old World." *William and Mary Quarterly*, Third Series, 53 (July 1996): 435–58.

Saunt, Claudio. "Taking Account of Property: Stratification among the Creek Indians in the Early Nineteenth Century." *William and Mary Quarterly*, Third Series, 57 (Oct. 2000): 733–60.

Shannon, Timothy. "The Native American Way of War in the Age of Revolution, 1754–1814." In *War in an Age of Revolution, 1775–1815*, edited by Roger Chickering and Stig Forster, 137–57. Cambridge: Cambridge University Press, 2010.

Sheldon, Craig T., Jr. "Archaeology, Geography, and the Creek War in Georgia." In *Tohopeka: Rethinking the Creek War and the War of 1812*, edited by Kathryn E. Holland Braund, 200–21. Tuscaloosa: University of Alabama Press, 2012.

Skeen, C. Edward. "Calhoun, Crawford, and the Politics of Retrenchment." *South Carolina Historical Magazine* 73 (July 1972): 141–55.

Smith, F. Todd. "Dehahuit: An Indian Diplomat on the Louisiana-Texas Frontier, 1804–1815." In *Nexus of Empire: Negotiating Loyalty and Identity in the*

Revolutionary Borderlands, 1760s-1820s, edited by Gene Allen Smith and Sylvia L. Hilton, 140–59. Gainesville: University Press of Florida, 2010.

Smith, Timothy. "Wampum as Primitive Valuables." *Research in Economic Anthropology* 5 (1983): 225–46.

Springer, James Warren. "An Ethnohistoric Study of the Smoking Complex in Eastern North America." *Ethnohistory* 28 (Summer 1981): 217–35.

Stagg, J. C. A. "The Madison Administration and Mexico: Reinterpreting the Gutierrez-Magee Raid of 1812–1813." *William and Mary Quarterly*, Third Series, 59 (April 2002): 449–80.

Symonds, Craig. "The Failure of America's Indian Policy on the Southwestern Frontier, 1785–1793." *Tennessee Historical Quarterly* 35 (Spring 1976): 29–45.

Trigger, Bruce. "Early Native North American Responses to European Contact: Romantic versus Rationalistic Interpretations." *Journal of American History*, 77 (March 1991): 1195–215.

Turgeon, Laurier. "French Fishers, Fur Traders, and Amerindians during the Sixteenth Century: History and Archaeology." *William and Mary Quarterly*, Third Series, 55 (Oct.1998): 585–610.

Van Der Zee, Jacob. "Fur Trade Operations in the Eastern Iowa Country from 1800 to 1833." *Iowa Journal of History and Politics* 12 (Oct. 1914), 479–567.

Way, Royal B. "The United States Factory System for Trading with the Indians, 1796–1822." *Mississippi Valley Historical Review* 6 (Sept. 1919): 220–35.

Weber, David. "Bourbons and *Bárbaros*: Center and Periphery in the Shaping of Spanish Indian Policy." In *Negotiated Empires: Centers & Peripheries in the Americas, 1500–1820*, edited by Christine Daniels and Michael Kennedy, 79–103. New York: Routledge, 2002.

Wesley, Edgar B. "The Government Factory System among the Indians, 1795–1822." *Journal of Economic and Business History* 4 (May 1932): 485–511.

White, Bruce. "Balancing the Books: Traders' Profits in the British Lake Superior Fur Trade." In *New Faces of the Fur Trade: Selected Papers of the Seventh North American Fur Trade Conference, Halifax, Nova Scotia, 1995*, edited by Jo-Anne Fiske, Susan Sleeper-Smith, and William Wicker, 175–92. East Lansing: Michigan State University Press, 1996.

———. "'Give Us a Little Milk': The Social and Cultural Significance of Gift-Giving in the Lake Superior Fur Trade." *Minnesota History* 48 (Summer 1982). 60–71.

Witger, Michael. "The Rituals of Possession: Native Identity and the Invention of Empire in Seventeenth-Century Western North America." *Ethnohistory* 54 (Fall 2007): 639–68.

Wright, J. Leitch. "Creek-American Treaty of 1790: Alexander McGillivray and the Diplomacy of the Old Southwest." *Georgia Historical Quarterly* 21 (Dec. 1967): 379–400.

Wright, Louis, and Julia Macleod. "William Eaton, Timothy Pickering, and Indian Policy." *Huntington Library Quarterly* 9 (August 1946): 387–400.

Dissertations and Theses

Plaisance, Aloysius. "The United States Government Factory System, 1796–1822." PhD diss., Saint Louis University, 1954.

Wade, Susan. "Indigenous Women and Maple Sugar in the Upper Midwest, 1760 to 1848." M.A. thesis, University of Wisconsin—Milwaukee, 2011.

Index

Note: Entries pertaining to U.S. territories, or to locations within the boundaries of future states, are given under the names of those future states (Orleans Territory excepted). Native American individuals' names are usually alphabetized by first name, unless the individual appears in the volume under their European name.

References to figures, illustrations, and tables include the page number and the lower-case letter f, i, or t, respectively.

Mississippi River, 3, 50, 62, 64, 89, 101, 102, 141, 165; Americans seek lands adjoining, 51, 53; as boundary, 56, 67; as transport route, 76, 95

Mississippi Valley, 6, 20, 53, 56, 81, 113, 160; upper valley, 46, 59, 64, 101, 102, 106, 143

Missouri, 1, 56, 57, 58, 59, 116, 118, 125, 139, 141, 152, 160

Missouri River, 1, 21, 60, 68, 76, 97, 100, 116, 117, 139, 165, 170

Missouri Valley, 59, 60, 97, 113, 141; Indians of, 170, 171

Mitchell, David, 148

Mobile, 54, 76, 77, 78, 95, 120, 130

Moccasins, 70, 81, 104, 142

Mohawk River, 76

Monroe, James, 11, 57, 126, 157, 158, 159, 162, 166

Montagnais, 16

Montreal, 27, 46, 49, 86, 159

Morales, Juan, 54

Morgan, Benjamin, 61

Morrison, James, 130

Mules, 121, 138

Munro, Robert, 45–47

Murdock, William, 73

Muscle Shoals, 28

Mushulatubbe, 119

Muskrat, 46, 80, 101, 104, 105, 132, 142, 144, 145, 146

Muslin, 50

Nacogdoches, 66, 121

Napoleonic Wars, 49, 73, 152

Nashville, 30, 50

Natchez, 50

Natchez Trace, 50, 51, 96

Natchitoches, 58, 64, 66, 74, 76, 118, 121, 122, 137. See also Factory: Natchitoches

National Intelligencer, 161, 166

Native Americans. See Indians

Nativists, 22, 109, 118. See also Prophets

Needles. See Sewing supplies

New England, 16, 25, 73, 123

New France, 19, 20

New Jersey, 74

New Netherland, 15, 19

New Orleans, 57, 61, 63, 80, 95, 130; and War of 1812, 121, 125; marketing and storage center, 76, 79, 97, 139, 142

New Spain, 64. *See also* Mexico

New York, 19, 28, 163

New York City, 69, 71, 73, 74, 79, 80, 83, 104, 130

Niagara, 76

Niles, Hezekiah, 153

Nonesopretties. See Ribbons

Non-Intercourse Act, 79, 112

North Carolina, 28

Northwest Company, 45, 49, 114

Northwest Indians. *See* Great Lakes region: Indians of

Northwest Indian War. *See* Great Lakes Indian War

Northwest Territory, 31

Nutt, Rush, 96

Ocmulgee Old Fields, 78, 90. *See also* Factory: Ocmulgee Old Fields

Ocmulgee River, 91

Oconee River, 38–39, 78, 91

O'Fallon, Benjamin, 163, 170

Office of Indian Trade, 7, 11, 72, 88, 113, 126, 129, 137, 163, 164, 169; auctions and sales, 69, 71, 72, 80, 83, 87t, 122, 124t, 130–31, 166; liquidated assets of, 166; shipments to factories, 123t, 129, 131t, 132, 142, 146, 204n37

Officials, 6, 18, 25, 34, 39; American, 8, 27–28, 29, 55, 56, 57, 63, 92, 103, 159; British, 22, 23

Ohio, 24, 30, 31, 106, 162, 163

Ohio River, 21, 24, 29, 31, 47, 76, 77

Ohio Valley, 12, 21, 24–25, 26, 28, 119; Indians of, 21, 22, 26, 28